MOVING THE CHAINS

MOVING THE CHAINS

THE CIVIL RIGHTS PROTEST THAT SAVED THE SAINTS AND TRANSFORMED NEW ORLEANS

ERIN GRAYSON SAPP

LOUISIANA STATE UNIVERSITY PRESS
BATON ROUGE

Published by Louisiana State University Press
lsupress.org

Copyright © 2023 by Erin Grayson Sapp

All rights reserved. Except in the case of brief quotations used in articles or reviews, no part of this publication may be reproduced or transmitted in any format or by any means without written permission of Louisiana State University Press.

LSU Press Paperback Original

DESIGNER: Mandy McDonald Scallan
TYPEFACE: Sentinel

COVER PHOTO: The University of Pittsburgh's Bobby Grier rushes past Georgia Tech defenders during the 1956 Sugar Bowl in Tulane Stadium. The Historic New Orleans Collection, Gift of the Sugar Bowl, Acc. No. 2007.0208.2.

Library of Congress Cataloging-in-Publication Data

Names: Sapp, Erin Grayson, author.
Title: Moving the chains : the civil rights protest that saved the Saints and transformed New Orleans / Erin Grayson Sapp.
Description: Baton Rouge : Louisiana State University Press, [2022] | Includes bibliographical references and index.
Identifiers: LCCN 2022017751 (print) | LCCN 2022017752 (ebook) | ISBN 978-0-8071-7792-1 (paperback) | ISBN 978-0-8071-7909-3 (pdf) | ISBN 978-0-8071-7908-6 (epub)
Subjects: LCSH: New Orleans Saints (Football team)—History. | National Football League—History—20th century. | American Football League—History. | Football—Social aspects—Louisiana—New Orleans—History—20th century. | African American football Players—History—20th century. | Race discrimination—Louisiana—New Orleans—History—20th century. | African Americans—Segregation—Louisiana—New Orleans—History—20th century. | New Orleans (La.)—Social conditions—20th century.
Classification: LCC GV956.N366 S27 2022 (print) | LCC GV956.N366 (ebook) | DDC 796.332/640976335—dc23/eng/20220630
LC record available at https://lccn.loc.gov/2022017751
LC ebook record available at https://lccn.loc.gov/2022017752

To Scott,

*for showing me that the most
important truths come through even when
the words aren't perfect.*

CONTENTS

ACKNOWLEDGMENTS ix

INTRODUCTION:
Motion Prior to the Snap 1

1. The Concession Stands 5

2. A Long Return 22

3. Three and Out 47

4. A Naked Bootleg 65

5. Crossing Routes 90

6. Check Downs 112

7. Stutter Step 129

8. Busted Coverage 142

9. Unbeaten and Untied 164

10. Running Out the Clock 191

11. Open Field 208

NOTES 229

BIBLIOGRAPHY 265

INDEX 273

ACKNOWLEDGMENTS

This book began as a term paper in one of Rachel Devlin's history courses at the end of my doctoral work. I couldn't make it my dissertation topic, but I also couldn't let it go. Her early input and encouragement, and that of my other beloved Tulane mentors, Molly Travis, Joel Dinerstein, and Michael Plante, got me buckled in for this journey.

The idea of book-length expansion, however, never would have gotten off the ground without the treasured resources, human and archival, of The Historic New Orleans Collection. As their Williams Scholar in Residence, I was supported for the bulk of my research, an opportunity graciously facilitated by Priscilla Lawrence, Daniel Hammer, and Jessica Dorman. I would list every member of the Collection if I could, because the support was overwhelming. At the very least, I must applaud Alfred Lemmon for the well-oiled machine that is the Williams Research Center, as well as two reference gurus, Bobby Ticknor and Matt Farah, for months of supplying me with VHS game tapes, rolls of microfilm, and savvy advice.

Likewise, Jon Kendle and Saleem Choudhry of the Pro Football Hall of Fame opened up more than the museum's archives to me, sharing their invaluable contacts and expert knowledge as well.

I don't even know where to begin praising and thanking Theresa Moore, the founder and president of T-Time Productions and the director and producer of the documentary *Third and Long*. Not knowing me or owing me anything, she spoke with me at length about my project and generously shared precious resources from the greater "Third and Long" educational project. I felt honored to join the conversation in which she has had such an important voice.

There were also kitchen-table conversations that meant the world to me and this book. First, Wade and Mary Lu Mitchell invited me into their home, fed me, and answered hours of questions. Moreover, they lured two other

Sugar Bowl vets, Allen Ecker and Carl Vereen, into my tentacles, and those chats were equally enjoyed and appreciated.

Similarly, the legendary Norman Francis made me feel right at home in his dining room, where he gave me an entire morning of his time and even a tour of the photographs that pepper his walls and document his extraordinary life.

Hall of Famer Bobby Bell was generous enough both to send me a note recounting his experience as a pro All-Star and to autograph my copy of his 1964 football card.

I subjected Jimmy Taylor and his wife, Helen, to what felt like a starstruck ambush during a chance encounter. Both were too kind to appear bothered and granted me a makeshift interview that was as cherished as it was impromptu.

I'm beholden to Greg Stewart for my affiliation with the Tulane Center for Sport, the priceless conversations and experiences I've had through this association, and their commitment to celebrate and safeguard the power of athletics.

To the exceptionally professional and helpful staff at the archives of Tulane, Georgia Tech, University of New Orleans, Amistad Research Center, New Orleans Public Library, New Orleans City Park, and the Library of Congress: you have my sincere appreciation for what you do and how well you do it.

A thank-you feels too small for the folks at LSU Press. This is especially true of my unfailingly enthusiastic and patient editor, Jenny Keegan, who somehow still maintains that there are no bad questions, even after walking *me* through the publication process.

One part of that process I had braced for, the peer review, turned out to be more rewarding than I could have imagined. My anonymous reader's critiques and suggestions were brilliant and generous, making my manuscript a stronger document and me a better writer.

I have long needed to formally thank my selfless mom, Nancy, for always sharpening her pencils (and then usually wearing them down) whenever I have needed a proofreader, for this project and so many others. And I am indebted to my dad, Larry, and brother, Adam, for welcoming the annoying little sister with all her questions into their game-day parties and backyard scrimmages, where I grew to learn and love football. I am also eternally grateful to this Sapp trio for all the times they literally and figuratively picked me up, dusted me off, and got me back on the field of play.

Above all, my husband, Scott Grayson, believed in the need to tell this story, seemingly as much as I did, from the moment I uncovered the first kernel. He went along with some strange travel requests, endured my consuming passion for the project, and even helped chase down leads. Without a doubt, what follows would still be untold without his incredible support.

MOVING THE CHAINS

INTRODUCTION
Motion Prior to the Snap

On Christmas Eve 1954, Santa Claus was waking everyone he visited, asking for a ticket to the Sugar Bowl, at least in a New Orleans newspaper cartoon. Members of the Mid-Winter Sports Association (MWSA), the wizards behind the city's annual New Year's Day football classic, were fielding twice as many orders as they could fill. They had a marquee matchup. The first postseason appearance of a service academy team in three decades (and only the second of all time) was slated for Tulane Stadium, where fifth-ranked Navy would face the sixth-ranked University of Mississippi, on January 1, 1955.[1]

The Big Easy desperately needed a big game. The previous year's classic had been dubbed the "Lemon Bowl" from the moment its two schools were signed. The closest thing to an endorsement was one columnist arguing that locals owed the MWSA support even "if they wanted to name two high school teams to the Sugar Bowl." Unfortunately, the pairing, which was "much discussed—and cussed," fulfilled its doomsday expectations. In a tilt chock-full of action and barren of suspense, Georgia Tech scored 42 points on West Virginia, which eked out 19, mostly against the Yellow Jackets' reserves. And the timing could not have been worse. This was the product sent across the country in only the bowl's second year of a nationwide television contract. Moreover, 1953's inaugural coast-to-coast broadcast had not even showcased an intersectional scrimmage, instead showing America two Southeastern Conference (SEC) squads—and the monotony of four unanswered scores to boot.[2]

By then, these were the best matchups the city could muster. The pool of schools willing to talk to Sugar scouts had been drying up for years. For starters, five of the nation's top teams were betrothed to other New Year's Day bowls through tie-ups that sent certain conference champs to the Rose, Orange, and Cotton games. The Sugar Bowl, on the other hand, stayed stubbornly independent, touting freedom to choose the most exciting teams regardless of geography or rankings. But gone were the days when the MWSA could truly view the whole country as its catalog and base bids on merit alone.

Even more damning than other bowls' automatic berths, though, were New Orleans's unyielding color lines. By midcentury, most integrated squads had abandoned the once common practice of leaving Black players behind on trips to the South, and this was true even for prestigious postseason play. American sports were changing, and the other big bowls were keeping pace. But as more and more schools fielded Black athletes, Sugar's dance card shrank and shrank.[3]

As the Navy–Ole Miss bowl approached, however, newsmen hailed the MWSA for snagging the "foremost" matchup in "an otherwise drab series." Sugar was the only 1955 bowl bringing in a pair of top ten teams, and the rejection of tie-ups seemed like a stroke of brilliance. Considering the previous year's snoozer of a blowout, even better press came from the oddsmakers favoring Mississippi by a mere point and a half.[4]

Then, a week out, Clarence Mitchell, director of the Washington, DC, branch of the National Association for the Advancement of Colored People (NAACP), approached Navy authorities about the academy's contract. Mitchell called it a "gross violation of the Navy policy of racial integration" for the school's allotment of thirteen thousand seats to go strictly to "the Caucasian race," as was printed on the tickets. "Unless you act," the NAACP argued, "the shadow of Jim Crow will loom larger than the American Eagle when the midshipmen march on the field."[5]

A spokesman initially responded that the academy was participating "at the invitation" of the MWSA, suggesting the school would play by the host's rules. It was also noted that spots were still available in the seven-hundred-seat end zone section designated for the bowl's Black patrons. Within two days, however, Secretary of the Navy Charles Thomas issued a retraction regarding the Middies' ration, guaranteeing that it had been distributed like any other academy tickets "and will be so honored regardless of any printing thereon." At that point, the only lingering uncertainty was how New Orleans would handle her new orders.[6]

In addition to the reactionary forces then blanketing the Deep South, the Big Easy had its own complicated relationship with change. On one hand, stagnation was part of the city's unique allure, and locals guarded what *Time* magazine called their "charming ruins." Preservation of the town's distinct heritage, traditions, and pleasures long justified shirking progress wholesale. On the other hand, this lazy, permissive culture painted "The City That Care Forgot" as the least likely of the southern sisters to make a fuss over much of anything, particularly racial mixing, as it teemed with blended neighborhoods and a mélange of Creole identities. At midcentury, it was anyone's guess which way the Big Easy would fall on integration.[7]

And there was yet another piece of locals' pride at play: their legacy as a football town. "Sugar Bowl fever" swept through the city during the winter holidays, becoming "the hub of everything that lives and breathes" for New Orleanians. Theirs was one of only four major bowls, and in many years of the not-too-distant past it had rivaled even granddaddy Rose Bowl in prestige. Likewise, the Tulane Green Wave, a force of the 1920s and 1930s and charter member of the SEC, had led the conference in attendance during its recent midcentury resurgence. Love of the gridiron had unmatched leverage in New Orleans as burgeoning civil rights struggles put football—and far more—at stake.[8]

Such was certainly the case in December 1954. No one wanted to rock the boat, much less the aircraft carrier that was in port to revive Sugar's reputation. When MWSA president Bernie Grenrood responded to the academy's notice, his press release was equally unequivocal: "I believe the Navy's statement speaks for itself." The countdown to kickoff resumed.[9]

On January 1, 1955, fans who paid fifty cents for a souvenir program could read Grenrood's celebration that, for the first time, all forty-eight states and multiple foreign nations were represented in the stands. He called New Orleans the "International City" and boasted the Sugar Bowl's ability to unite disparate populations "so that we might get to know each other better, develop an understanding, a bond of friendship that would help create a happier world." A few pages back, general manager (GM) Fred Digby likewise advertised his home turf as the "Sportsmen's Mecca," saying, "Here in New Orleans is a mingling of all the races of the world."[10]

Digby's claim was clearly debatable, but it was truer for that Sugar Bowl than for any before it. Like Navy's inaugural postseason win that afternoon, their integration of the east side of Tulane Stadium was a first, and yet no "mingling" visitors or disapproving locals reported any problems. Grenrood announced afterwards, in his typically pithy manner, that his group was "happy over the success of our program."[11]

The city's African American newspaper, the *Louisiana Weekly*, had a lot more to say. Headlines exclaimed, "Navy Mauls Ole Miss and 'Jim Crow,'" prefacing celebration and speculation in equal measure. After all, precedent had been set for more mixing in the bowl. Fully integrated stands were still a long shot, but as early as January the local Black press predicted that the 1956 Sugar Bowl would have African American athletes on the field. It would, the *Weekly* argued, be essential to "keeping sports alive in New Orleans."[12]

CHAPTER 1
The Concession Stands

When Sugar Bowl scouts were assigned to late-season games in 1955, West Virginia was again in consideration, despite its dreadful showing in the "Lemon Bowl" two years earlier. The Mountaineers were undefeated and untied on their way to face the 5–3 Pittsburgh Panthers. So MWSA vice president Paul DeBlanc and Claude "Monk" Simons, star of Sugar Bowl I, were dispatched to Pennsylvania with a clear agenda, which was about to change.[1]

West Virginia University's unbeaten stars were eclipsed, in more ways than one, by Pitt's two 225-pound ends, "Mean John" Paluck and Joe Walton. Walton was a junior who entered college the year the National Collegiate Athletic Association (NCAA) revoked unlimited substitution and restored one-platoon football. And he was excelling on both sides of the ball. On that November afternoon, he scored Pittsburgh's first touchdown, off a 6-yard pass. The next two Panther touchdowns came within a minute and twenty-six seconds of each other as Walton and Paluck caused a fumble each that set up a scoring drive.

Late in the game, Panther third-stringers not only kept West Virginia scoreless but also tallied 7 points of their own. The sellout crowd saw the scoreboard clock tick down to zero. Thousands rushed onto the field. Both goal posts were torn down. Scouts headed for the locker rooms. Then everyone went back to their seats. Pass interference was called on Pittsburgh in the last play, giving West Virginia one more down from Pitt's 6-yard line. The Mountaineers scored their only touchdown and got a "forfeit" extra point, since there were no standing uprights to split. Once the game ended, again, DeBlanc and Simons scrapped their map to the visitors' showers and instead shook hands with Panther head coach John Michelosen and athletic director Tom Hamilton.[2]

On that Friday, November 18, Sugar execs voted unanimously to invite the University of Pittsburgh if it won the last game of its season the next day.

Most schools, including several still in the running for a bid, had one more game the following week, but the MWSA jumped to sign Pitt even before the final records and rankings were known.

The Panthers' season finale did, however, showcase one particularly notable change to their lineup. After missing the West Virginia game with a leg injury, the team's one Black player, second-string fullback Bobby Grier, returned quite conspicuously to the active roster, scoring Pitt's second of three unanswered touchdowns at Penn State. Regardless, after Pittsburgh handed the Nittany Lions their first shutout of the year in a Saturday afternoon snowstorm, Vice President DeBlanc beckoned the entire Panther squad down South.[3]

On Monday, as the MWSA awaited an answer, bowl speculation swirled through New Orleans. GM Fred Digby fielded a barrage of questions at the Quarterback Club. He conceded that the upcoming Army–Navy game could influence the popular idea of inviting another service academy. He quashed intrigue over Duke by explaining the fine print in Orange's tie-up with the Atlantic Coast Conference. And he mentioned that Pittsburgh was being discussed. He added flatly that the integration issue would not sway selections, and this was tossed into the media's bowl gossip without comment. In fact, after Pittsburgh's wild victory over the Mountaineers, the team gained considerable favor with local sportswriters and football fans, who were impressed, if not also a little grateful, that the Panthers had removed West Virginia from consideration.[4]

Later that day, Tom Hamilton called to RSVP affirmatively. Before hanging up, however, the athletic director insisted that Bobby Grier would be in their lineup. DeBlanc carefully explained the regulations against boarding Blacks in white hotels and clarified that Grier's "entertainment" was Pitt's responsibility. Hamilton was confident that he could make proper arrangements and prevent any "embarrassment." With that, it was set. The University of Pittsburgh was bringing the first African American player to suit up for the Sugar Bowl.[5]

The next morning, the story was front-page news. "Pittsburgh's invitation was hailed with delight throughout the east and in New Orleans, too," according to the sports editor of the local *Times-Picayune*, Bill Keefe, who expected the game "to take rank among the best ever seen." Harry Martinez of the *New Orleans States* rejoiced that Pittsburgh gave the Sugar Bowl "a national flavor its committee has been seeking for some time." The *New Orleans Item*'s Hap Glaudi had polled over a hundred members of the Quarterback Club and reported that Pitt was in each of the top four preferred pairings. The *States* cover story mentioned Grier but focused less on his race than on his "standout" performance in Saturday's drubbing of Penn State. Otherwise, the focus was on Paluck and Walton, leaders of the powerful Pitt line, and not on Grier or any other backs.[6]

There were other new operating procedures the MWSA also made public at that time. Pittsburgh's ten thousand tickets were being printed without the old race labels. Black and white members of the Panther marching band had accepted their invitation to perform at the game. And it was even announced that the press box at Tulane Stadium would be integrated for the 1956 classic.[7]

The MWSA, the area's beloved "Sugar Bowlers," had sanctioned a radical break with several long-standing local customs. But there were no rallies or riots, no boycotts or petitions. Even the White Citizens' Council of New Orleans openly supported the game despite its very foundational doctrine of racial segregation. The city was backing the Sugar Bowlers, as long as they were offering first-rate football for 1956.[8]

Fans were still awaiting one pretty big detail, though. Pitt needed an opponent. Even without official ties, the Sugar men traditionally bid to their favorite—although not necessarily the conference-leading—Southeastern squad. It was even considered the "home" team, in this case facing an "Eastern invader."[9]

With Tulane and Louisiana State University (LSU) battling for "the Rag" on Saturday, the selection committee opted for a Friday lunch to chat about their top choices from the SEC. There was agreement over the final four: Mississippi, Auburn, Georgia Tech, and Vanderbilt. Ole Miss led the conference with only one loss, Auburn and Tech each carried a loss and a tie, and Vandy had tallied two defeats. At adjournment, there was an impasse. One more critique was required before another show of hands. Likewise, Pitt's coaching staff was splitting up and lugging binoculars and notebooks to all relevant games.[10]

Sugar's sacrificial few members not at LSU's Tiger Stadium reconvened on Saturday afternoon, November 26. With four traditional in-state rivalries being watched or heard simultaneously, deliberation lasted to final whistles. Vanderbilt dropped its last game, but Ole Miss and Auburn both walked away with 26–0 shutouts. They also held on to the top two spots in the SEC. But the Yellow Jackets quashed a late Bulldog rally to beat the University of Georgia 21–3 in an electrifying performance that head coach

Bobby Dodd believed was their most impressive in years. The Sugar Bowlers thought so too. Every vote went to the SEC's sensational (even if third-place) Georgia Tech.[11]

The Jackets rushed off their home turf, Grant Field, expecting calls from bowl sponsors any moment. As they huddled in the locker room, Dodd polled the players on their top pick for the postseason. Every last one of the Engineers voted for a New Year's date with the Pittsburgh Panthers in New Orleans. Minutes later, they looked on anxiously as Dodd answered the telephone. When he put his right thumb and forefinger together to flash the OK sign, a roar from the team rang out over the long-distance telephone wire into the Sugar Bowlers' office.[12]

| | | | |

Because New Year's Day fell on Sunday in 1956, the four big bowl games were scheduled for January 2, Bobby Grier's birthday. His coaches alone would determine whether or not he took the field that afternoon, a fact that was publicized from the moment Pitt was signed. So the Tech players expected an integrated game from the start, and theirs was not the only pulse Coach Dodd took before accepting the bid. Thinking Sugar was on the table, Dodd got approval from both the athletic association and school president Blake Van Leer ahead of the University of Georgia game. Dodd and Van Leer each contacted Georgia governor Marvin Griffin, who advised accepting the invitation. He added, however, that he could not condone it publicly.

On November 30, Dodd received a telegram from a member of the States' Rights Council (a new Georgia reactionary group), asking him to pull out of the postseason. Dodd ignored the wire, but it was published in the following day's press. Asked to comment, the chairman of the Georgia Board of Regents said simply that integrated out-of-state games were "no innovation" and no cause for action. With that, a big brouhaha began. So Griffin entered the fight—and not on the side of the Engineers. The governor, elected eleven months earlier, had campaigned on a commitment "to take whatever steps necessary to preserve segregation." In public, he kept his toe on the party line.[13]

On Friday, December 2, a telegram from the governor to the board of regents, demanding that Tech be scooped from the bowl, was publicized. Griffin called for the state to shield student athletes from integrated foes and integrated fans. "The South stands at Armageddon," the wire proclaimed.

"We cannot make the slightest concession to the enemy in this dark and lamentable hour of struggle."[14]

In that night's dark hours, the governor became the enemy of the Yellow Jacket faithful. Outside Grant Field, smoke swelled through the intersection of Fourth and Fowler, and Tech students crowded the street corners. Two stuffed figures wearing long sleeves, slacks, and neckties, fashioned to mirror Governor Griffin, were being accessorized with knotted ropes. One effigy was dangled from a pole and lowered into a roaring bonfire, and the other was hung from a noose off a nearby tree. Meanwhile, placards of protest were tacked on dormitories and planted in the quad. But this was not just a campus rally. Around midnight, the avid young football fans began their march into downtown Atlanta, leaving some charred wood and martyred clothes smoldering on the asphalt behind them.[15]

Wade Mitchell, the school's starting quarterback, looked out his window as the parade made a right turn some fifteen feet below, but he was sure being spotted in the ruckus would land him in hot water with his coaches. One had already surveyed the scene to ensure no players were involved, somehow overlooking the six-foot-six, 224-pound tackle Carl Vereen and the other dozen or so gridders in the mix.[16]

Along the two miles to Five Points, the heart of the city's business district, the throng racked up a couple thousand members. They carried signs reading "To hell with Griff," "Grow up, Marv," and "Griffin sits on his brains." Downtown, another dummy was hurled over a light pole and ignited in front of a band of city cops, who then simply shadowed the students to the Georgia State Capitol building a few blocks away. When they reached the hilltop, however, things escalated. A splinter group broke into the statehouse, shattered windows, stretched fire hoses down hallways, and overturned trash cans, cigarette urns, and spittoons. Outside, another faction pulled up shrubbery, historical markers, and parking meters and defaced two statues of Georgians with legacies of white supremacy.

Naturally not finding Griffin there in the wee hours of the morning, the untiring horde embarked on an hour-long hike to the governor's gray granite mansion. But by then police were wielding lockup and backup. Guys nabbed for damaging property were loaded into a paddy wagon, while more than twenty-five state patrol cars were dispatched from surrounding counties. Prepared to use tear gas and nightsticks, officers kept the crowd fifty feet from Griffin's home, where he paced the floor, chatted with aides, and watched the swarm buzzing on his lawn.

During a chorus of "We'll hang Old Marvin from a sour apple tree," State Representative Muggsy Smith emerged from his house across the street. A former Yellow Jacket football star himself, Smith was a magnet for attention. He was boosted onto a pair of brawny shoulders and carried to the center of the crowd, where he pleaded with the flock and haggled with the cops until finally some detainees were released in exchange for a mass retreat. By half past three on the morning of Saturday, December 3, 1955, the demonstration was over, but the media frenzy was just beginning.[17]

|||||

After the march in Atlanta, Tech hired two detective agencies to assign responsibility for the rioting. One fraternity member told investigators that students sparked it to bring national attention to Griffin's demands. They succeeded. When the Georgia Board of Regents assembled on Monday morning, December 5, it looked more like a media convention. Reporters and cameramen crammed into the hallway, awaiting a climax to the story gripping America's attention.[18]

Presiding at the head of a long conference table, the chairman opened with a prayer for the "courage to carry out our convictions." He also announced that the governor would accept whatever decision they reached. Sources close to Griffin had already leaked the likelihood of a compromise that would allow Tech to play Pitt but would regulate future university system athletics. Despite the apparent softening of the governor's stance, however, the board included two staunch segregationists, Roy Harris and Charles Bloch, who backed Griffin's original request throughout the tense three-hour meeting.[19]

President Van Leer and Coach Dodd attended the opening session, but newsmen were kept outside, where a police captain stood guard. Van Leer's weekend bout with the flu had limited him to one public appearance, in which he told reporters, "I'm 60 years old, and I have never broken a contract. And I'm not going to break one now." Speaking before the Regents he was even more direct. "Either we're going to the Sugar Bowl, or you can find yourself another damn president of Georgia Tech."[20]

The following session was just as heated. Dour-faced Roy Harris paused from puffing his cigar to attack Van Leer's defiance of the governor. Regent David Rice, already outspoken about Griffin's "asinine and ridiculous" request, countered that the governor was meddling beyond his authority.

Harris called Griffin's proposal "the finest thing that ever happened to this state," before Rice offered a resolution condemning the governor's interference and asserting the board's independence. Rice's motion got no second, but the Regents did finally vote on the game itself.²¹

It was approved. As expected, there was a caveat. It stipulated that all future games within state lines would be segregated from tickets to turf but that games outside Georgia would conform to hosts' customs. This newly formalized rule was identical to the unofficial policy followed for years. Nothing was any different for the state of Georgia than if the governor had never released his fiery telegram.²²

What the uproar in Atlanta *had* done was put Bobby Grier, New Orleans, and the Sugar Bowl in the spotlight. Journalists hounded Grier and reported on everything from his size and stats to his experience flying jet planes and the Bible he kept on his bedside table. As for New Orleans, it would soon be overrun by media outlets that had never before covered the Sugar Bowl and by reporters who knew nothing about football.²³

Despite all the attention, comparisons with Atlanta's politics actually softened New Orleans's image, making some trade-offs more tolerable. Black sportswriter Butch Curry of the *Pittsburgh Courier* originally urged a boycott of the bowl. Speaking of the bulk of Tulane Stadium remaining segregated, he protested, "The same old buzzard's roost way at the far end of the field and at the extreme top is what they shove down Negro fans' throats." However, when the dust settled in Georgia and the Big Easy stayed committed to Pitt, Curry applauded the city's openness. "With Outstretched Arms," he cheered, "Orleans to Welcome Grier."²⁴

Curry even divulged that the team would bunk at Tulane because racial restrictions ruled out the swank hotels otherwise offered. But instead of condemning the compromise, he praised the university's progressiveness. The same sports page also suggested that instead of boycotting, Black fans should skirt segregation: "New Orleans Negroes and others who want to attend the game should write Frank Carver, Director of Public Relations, University of Pittsburgh, Pittsburgh, Pa., enclosing $6.00 per ticket, plus fifty cents for registered return mail."²⁵

| | | | | |

The Panthers' field was frozen. Their gym was cramped. So they headed south a week early, arriving in New Orleans the day after Christmas. They surrendered a few minutes for photographs at the airport but then went straight to Tulane, dropped their bags at Phelps Hall, and rushed out for late afternoon drills.

The players were limbering up and testing equipment when first-string fullback Tom Jenkins put his shoulder against a two-man blocking sled. When he hunkered down and pushed off, his right knee buckled. Trainers whisked him off and concluded, "Time is the best medicine," and "Time is very short in this case." Suddenly, Grier was the projected starting fullback.[26]

The whole team's availability was in question when a virus struck the squad midweek, and the team physician prescribed prudence and prophylactics. Nevertheless, Coach Michelosen ran two-a-days, including full-scale scrimmages in the as-advertised weather, which was proving a little too warm. On the sideline with Jenkins sat tackle Jim McCusker, Pitt's biggest player, nursing a rib injury from Tuesday's contact.[27]

Conversely, Bobby Dodd brushed off inquiries about injuries. "We won't work that hard," he explained. "We haven't scrimmaged since Oct. 1." The Yellow Jackets came to the Big Easy with a very different mentality than that of the Pitt camp.[28]

Michelosen had only a one-year reputation as head coach: he was "stern." Dodd had long been known as a "player's coach," who *Sports Illustrated* ultimately gauged to be a "Low-Pressure Engineer" and *Time* called the "Happy Coach." Dodd thought football should be fun, especially for a team that earned a bowl trip. By the postseason, he ordered rest and avoided injuries, even at the cost of some physical conditioning. So while the Panthers were in full pads as late as Saturday afternoon, Tech was playing volleyball over the goalposts with the pigskin. But as an Atlanta newspaper explained, after six bowl wins, "sideliners have ceased to challenge the Dodd system of turning the event into a picnic."[29]

This pattern also applied to off-the-field activities. When one reporter noted Tech players' stamina during a morning practice, it was a comment on the previous night's revelry and not on the demands of the drills. Dodd's only real rule was curfew. Players dined, danced, sneaked Hurricanes, watched floor shows, and hit the strip clubs in the French Quarter. Pitt, on the other hand, was rarely seen off the practice field. They ate in the school cafeteria and only left campus on team buses.

The contrast served New Orleans well. Press on Tech's "nightclub training routine" made Pitt look focused rather than restricted. Plenty of other schools kept their guys off Bourbon Street, but no other team was known for Tech's "pregame frivolity." Fortunately, the Engineers' carousing made more colorful news than the Panthers' seclusion. Even Tech players joked that Pitt was boarded uptown to distance the team from French Quarter vices.[30]

Another striking difference was observed at the shared practice facilities. As the Panthers trotted off and the Yellow Jackets swarmed in behind them, reporters tugged at their eyeglasses. "Well, they must have a big man somewhere," one remarked. This was even after several guys packed on a few extra pounds during the extended holiday break Dodd gave them. Some fun was had in the sports pages about Tech's "gremlin brigade" looking like a prep squad next to Pittsburgh's massive roster, but the Jackets were fast. And with the weatherman sparing them the sluggishness of a muddy field, score forecasters favored speed over power—but, fortunately for the game's billing, only by a touchdown.[31]

This East versus South match had the feel of some early thrillers that launched the classic, such as Sugar Bowl I's Tulane–Temple pairing and the 1941 meeting of Tennessee and Boston College. Both were decided by only six points. The Sugar Bowlers themselves were hyping the parallels, but the link they left out was that Boston also brought a Black player, though Lou Montgomery did not even dress for the game.[32]

When the University of Pittsburgh kicked off to Georgia Tech on January 2, 1956, Bobby Grier was on the field. After a week of more crutching than running, Tom Jenkins was slated for spot duty, and this swapping of starters got a lot of folks talking. However, the fuss was about Pitt's pass defense, since Jenkins had been the strength of the secondary. As for breaking racial precedent, having Grier start rather than sub in was even less earth-shattering. As one sportswriter put it, "A man going out for the kickoff attracts little or no attention," although in Grier's case he made the tackle on the opening return.[33]

|||||

Pitt's fourth offensive play of the game was a fumble, which Tech's Allen Ecker seized on the Panther 32-yard line. Dodd dialed up a pass from Wade Mitchell, the Kingsport play, going for a quick payoff from the takeaway. Mitchell faked a handoff to his left halfback and bootlegged to the right, but Joe Walton was not baited. He barreled down on Mitchell, who got the ball off just as he was hit. The pass lofted up over the end zone, where Grier was guarding wideout Don Ellis. The pair made contact, Grier fell to the turf, and Ellis leaped in vain for the ball soaring overhead.

Out came the back judge's yellow flag: defensive pass interference. A clamor from the crowd erupted as Grier pleaded his case, to no avail. From the press box, Sugar Bowler Sam Corenswet looked down in dismay. "Oh, my goodness," he groaned. "Why did that have to happen?"

"It was definitely pass interference," said the man next to him. This was particularly comforting, coming from Jack Sell of the *Pittsburgh Post-Gazette*, but Corenswet could already hear the charges of discrimination coming.[34]

Nearby, Bill Keefe and his binoculars agreed with Sell. But Keefe, too, feared the almost certain implications of Alabama-native Frank Lowry calling a 31-yard game-opening penalty against Grier. "Everybody would have felt better," Keefe figured, "if it had been a 'Yankee' official who called it."[35]

The ball was placed on the 1-yard line, only to be moved a half yard closer when Pitt was flagged for encroachment on the next play. From there, Mitchell's sneak and his point-after kick put 7 on the scoreboard for the Yellow Jackets. Panthers and Sugar Bowlers alike were left hoping that would not be the game's deciding touchdown.

The controversial call, however, was not the only hiccup of the first quarter. Hopes for suspense and uncertainty had not included the stadium's game clock providing those elements. It flashed erratically for a while and then lost power completely, meaning the officiating crew kept time and everyone else was in the dark. Moreover, calling the right plays at the close of each half would require bugging a ref and mastering estimation.

Late in the second quarter, after a long defensive battle, Pittsburgh orchestrated their longest drive of the game, stringing together short-yardage rushes to the Jackets' 1-yard line. On fourth down, thinking there was little time, quarterback Corny Salvaterra hustled to break huddle and quickly took the snap into his own short grasp for the end zone. Tech not only defended their goal but also, adding insult to injury, even had a little spare time on offense before intermission.

It stayed a one-score contest well into the fourth quarter. As expected, Tech stuck to their ground game, eating a lot of the clock. They only ran one pass play in the second half. In it, despite Dodd's words of caution, substitute quarterback Toppy Vann was intercepted 3 yards from the end zone, keeping the Panthers' hopes alive.

On their last possession, Pittsburgh muscled downfield in an exhilarating drive that involved two more passing plays and 42 more passing yards than Georgia Tech tallied the whole game. At the 10-yard line, the Panther quarterback checked with officials and was confident there was ample time for a few more plays. They got halfway to the goal in one, power up the middle. They quickly lined up again for another shot at a tied game. Before the center snapped the ball, however, officials waved their arms. The game was over: Georgia Tech 7, Pittsburgh 0.[36]

|||||

In addition to notoriety as a player's coach, Bobby Dodd had another reputation: he was lucky. Every controversial call or unusual turn of events always seemed to go his way, and he left a trail of bitter and baffled opponents in his wake. "I guess we do win a lot of games when the other team does most of the moving," Dodd conceded, resting on an equipment trunk in the Tech locker room. But he also admitted, "I didn't relax the entire game."[37]

Pittsburgh dominated nearly all the bragworthy statistics—except points scored. Both coaches were clearly exhausted. As one sportswriter put it, "It had been a fingernail, cigarette destroyer for both of them." The Sugar Bowlers had achieved the down-to-the-last-play game they banked on when they bid. Ironically, they now feared better press might have come from a two-possession tilt. The one touchdown was on every reporter's lips.[38]

Grier sat by his locker, holding an apple in one hand and gesturing with the other, as he answered questions. He adamantly denied shoving Ellis. "He pushed me from behind," Grier told newsmen tearfully. "That's why I fell forward." Of course, next door, Don Ellis was claiming he missed the catch because Grier's shove knocked them both off balance.[39]

For better or worse, attempts to have the tape tell the true tale were thwarted. The cameraman followed the ball's high arc and only showed Grier and Ellis—and Lowry's line of sight—after contact was made. The story would remain one player's word against another's, and Sugar's officiating crew was off the hook.[40]

The classic appeared to be an overall success. Black media men had been welcomed into the press box cordially. Some grumbled about their seats, but this was an annual occurrence. Sugar Bowlers always had welcome difficulty gratifying all their crammed-together sources of publicity. There were complaints over views but not over what was seen. As one reporter commented, the teams "showed as fine a spirit of good sportsmanship as ever was," and "the crowd was just as gallant." Not one problem was reported to the increased security, advertised as a "'battalion' of police" with a "portable 'jail.'" Even the weather had been a perfectly sunny seventy-six degrees.⁴¹

After interviews, Pitt players got cleaned up, put on their dress clothes and matching school blazers, and headed downtown to the St. Charles Hotel. The MWSA had a good relationship with the manager, who appreciated the flood of business during an otherwise slow season. Against city policy, they arranged to have Grier attend the postgame banquet under no restrictions, although he was indeed singled out as soon as he stepped into the ballroom: he was given a booming applause as the leading rusher of the day.⁴²

Once all the awards, tokens, and toasts were delivered, players dispersed. Some stayed for a formal dance, but most opted for less-refined New Orleans nightlife. Grier, on the other hand, was taken to a party in his honor at Dillard University. President Albert Dent had extended the invitation in early December, and the school spared no effort or expense. Grier felt he was treated "like a celebrity" that night.⁴³

The national Black press, however, blasted Dent and Dillard. Privately entertaining Grier was labeled the "most wanton of all racial frauds." It was said to have given New Orleans, the Sugar Bowlers, and the University of Pittsburgh a free pass after promises were made that Grier would not be separated from his teammates.⁴⁴

Monday night's arrangement did bear an eerie resemblance to Pitt's other visits to the segregated South, like those to Virginia and North Carolina. Grier was staying on a Black college campus while his white teammates enjoyed a downtown hotel. The difference was that Bobby Grier *was* a celebrity in New Orleans. He had received stacks of letters and invitations from local groups (schoolkids and adults alike) that wanted to honor, interview, and host him. He was told he was "just as much of a trailblazer as Jackie Robinson" and invoked as much pride as Jesse Owens, Roy Campanella, and Bill Russell. In these letters, amid grandiose offers, there was also an awareness that he *should* be treated as "just another player," but the "tremendous morale boost for the Negro citizens of the city" justified an exception.⁴⁵

Arguably, New Orleans and the Sugar Bowlers were given several free passes as the classic came together. Maybe a little of Dodd's luck rubbed off on them. Some papers tried to find crises to make good stories, describing Grier as hounded by security, sneaked through back staircases, or abandoned on a street corner. But overall, reports on the city were favorable and accounts of the game were even better.⁴⁶

"As smooth as any year," GM Fred Digby rejoiced, as praises poured in and newspaper clippings were compiled. The January 2 Sugar Bowl was not the only game integrated during that 1955–1956 Mid-Winter Sports Carnival. Al Avant became the first African American in an MWSA event when Marquette's basketball team faced Utah at Loyola Field House, four days before the classic. Overshadowed by the bowl, Avant's debut met with little publicity but also no problems.[47]

In February, when Paul DeBlanc became president, he declared the MWSA's carnival the king of the postseason and vowed to preserve their reign. During one of the first meetings under his watch, DeBlanc seconded a motion by Irwin Poché, and the executive committee voted to again print race-free visitors' football tickets. The group then formalized another policy: "We do not refuse to invite universities into our games merely because they might have colored players on their teams." There was renewed optimism in the room. However, they had to be careful. The business, prestige, and excitement they provided did not grant them carte blanche, and public relations rivaled matchups in importance.[48]

In fact, at their June 7 huddle, DeBlanc described letters he received from prominent, longtime patrons fretful about further integration. Aware of the delicate balance keeping the bowl afloat, DeBlanc had personally visited each of these men and guaranteed the "home" stands would remain strictly segregated. Satisfied with the sanctity of their seats, they had repaid DeBlanc with ticket orders.

However, at that same June meeting, DeBlanc also reported on House Bill 1412, which was introduced into the Louisiana legislature four days earlier. If passed, it would outlaw all interracial sports and integrated spectators. At that moment, it was as if someone sucked all the optimism back out of the room. Everyone could feel the enormity of the dire implications for the Sugar Bowl. A long conversation ensued about lobbying to have the bill withdrawn or amended. One member thought he had useful contacts, so behind-the-scenes inquiries and influences were approved. Despite their desperation, there was a clear emphasis on staying under the radar.[49]

The Pelican State was like much of the South, with many whites keeping one eye on the Supreme Court and the other on the lookout for new ways to stave off integration. In recent years, the high court had ruled against racial segregation in public schools, parks, beaches, golf courses, and swimming pools, and southern legislators were invoking "states' rights" and devising new laws to counter the federal mandates. This trend was reaching dangerous levels in Louisiana by the summer of 1956. When the House and Senate met in June and July, their hoppers were flooded with segregation bills, and dissent was considered political suicide.[50]

Late in the evening on June 14, the Louisiana House prepared to adjourn. Then, just before leaving, with neither debate nor dissenting vote, representatives quickly passed all segregation bills on the docket. A total of five measures were adopted, including H.B. 1412.[51]

Two weeks later, when the Senate Judiciary Committee broached the bill, there were actually discussions. First up was Senator William Rainach, chairman of the Joint Legislative Committee on Segregation (JLCS) and leader in the White Citizens' Council. He did not challenge the text but wanted the effective date pushed back to October 15 so the Shreveport Double-A baseball team could finish its season in the integrated Texas League. While the bill's advocates envisioned the league shedding its Black players in the off-season, the team's owner foresaw the death of his franchise.

Next came two surprising voices questioning the bill's reach. Senator J. D. DeBlieux of East Baton Rouge Parish argued the law would handicap athletics at LSU. However, his claim was quickly dismissed on the basis that no Tigers board members had come forward in opposition. At that point, Senator Theodore M. Hickey of New Orleans announced that H.B. 1412 was the only segregation measure constituents had asked him to contest. "I have been tormented by this one," he divulged. He had one main argument against the bill: "It would hurt the Sugar Bowl."[52]

Still, no one voted nay, and the measure moved to the Senate floor. There, Senator Hickey chose not to revive his tepid opposition, but DeBlieux re-upped and streamlined his appeal. H.B. 1412 did not only apply to sporting events. It also outlawed interracial dancing, social functions, entertainment, and training. Only religious gatherings were exempted. DeBlieux proposed removing athletic competitions and practices from the scope but stressed that he supported the prohibition of all other social contact. He argued simply that schools could better handle their athletic programs themselves.[53]

It was already known that Tulane and LSU would have to revise their upcoming schedules if the bill passed. In February, both universities unveiled their football opponents for the next two years. Tulane was scheduled to play Navy and Army at home, without imposing full segregation of the stands. Louisiana State announced a home-and-home series with Wisconsin, whose freshman roster indicated they would soon be fielding Black upperclassmen. Although the LSU board had discussed imposing athletic segregation, it was repeatedly voted down. Plenty of voices were heard and votes cast behind closed doors in both New Orleans and Baton Rouge, but only J. D. DeBlieux was putting his face on the resistance.[54]

"It's kind of hard to get up here and run the gauntlet and take a position that you think may not be popular," DeBlieux admitted from his lonely stand before the Senate. As he spoke, a large group from the White Citizens' Council lined the railing of the chamber. Aware he was jeopardizing his political career, DeBlieux continued. "Nevertheless, even if I don't come back to this Senate, I hope to serve out these four years as an honorable and courageous senator." He concluded, "We should have enough courage to stand here and do what you know ought to be done." A vote was taken on his proposed amendment. It received only one additional vote of support, from Clifton Gaspard of Abbeville. The full bill was then put forth and passed unopposed, 33–0.[55]

|||||

"I don't know," replied Governor Earl K. Long, when asked if he would sign the sports bill. "I'll cross that bridge when I come to it." As soon as the House approved the new effective date, the measure would be on Long's desk. He had a week and a half to decide.[56]

Long had been inaugurated only two months earlier into his second (nonconsecutive) four-year term. A racial moderate, he solicited and received the lion's share of Black votes. Even as a flood of bias legislation flowed through the House and Senate, many African Americans expected the governor to dam up the surge.[57]

Ultimately, that summer, Long would approve several segregation bills, with little hesitation, but he was particularly torn on athletics. Before taking office, he disclosed that he was not "altogether" opposed to interracial prizefighting, which had come one vote shy of approval by the state's boxing commission. Even so, mixed bouts could be seen regularly in New Orleans, at Curley's Gym, for varying admission fees based on which fighters were "working out." These fights often drew packed houses that left white fans scurrying for seats in the Black stands. H.B. 1412, however, would outlaw such training as well, and Long was not "altogether" sure what he would do about it.[58]

The Sugar execs arrived at their next meeting astonished and distraught. DeBlanc recounted all the friends called on and favors called in to prevent the bill from passing, with no luck. Then, Sam Corenswet, head of the group's television interests, confirmed their worst fears. His contacts at both the National Broadcasting Company (NBC) and World Sports warned him that if the measure passed, the Sugar Bowl would in all likelihood not be on the air New Year's Day. Any matchup fitting the law was expected to garner only regional interest at best. Besides, sponsorship would reek of dangerous implications for national advertisers.

It was clear that underground efforts were insufficient and more overt action was needed to save the Mid-Winter Sports Carnival. Irwin Poché, a devotee of athletic integrity, disclosed that he had personally telegrammed the governor a veto request and leaned on the executive committee to make a like move as a united front. There was a long debate about a short drive, and the consensus was to rush a delegation to Baton Rouge for an audience with Long. Joseph David left the room to telephone a contact and make the arrangements, but he returned with bad news. Reportedly, the decision had been made and the sports bill was signed. At that point, instead of road-tripping, the group addressed the months-old basketball contracts that were on the verge of being illegal.[59]

Joe David tried again the next day to get the governor's ear. This time he succeeded, and he learned that Long was in fact still soliciting opinions, asking constituents to relay their views to the media. David hurriedly called together the necessary quorum for a special meeting at 9:00 p.m. on Friday, July 13. Again at the behest of Poché, the committee composed a formal petition and designed a full-page newspaper ad. "DON'T LET HYSTERIA REPLACE REASON" was printed in giant letters at the top. The text celebrated New Orleans's twenty-two years as the "Mid-Winter Sports Capital of the Nation" and explained that H.B. 1412 would relegate the Sugar Bowl to a dustup between neighboring schools. Readers were reminded that there had always been segregated "home" stands at the classic, even without the law. In bold, underlined letters was an appeal for fans to wire Long that day asking for his veto.[60]

The ad ignited a storm of response from segregationists, and considerable back-and-forth played out in news outlets over the weekend. Dr. Emmett Irwin, chairman of the New Orleans White Citizens' Council, questioned why no one from the MWSA appeared before the Senate, claiming the body twice postponed action to allow opponents to speak. Rather than admit to riding the fine line of cautious public relations, DeBlanc stated that the MWSA withheld protest because it had been "inconceivable" such legislation would pass.[61]

Another biting rebuttal came from Harry Gamble Sr., president of the Society for the Preservation of State Government and Racial Integrity. He was one of the men DeBlanc visited to discuss stadium segregation for locals, and Gamble had already put in another ticket order. Now, however, he called their piecemeal integration "taking rails off the fence one at a time," which "finally lowers it to where stock of every breed have access."[62]

DeBlanc released one final attempt to counter criticisms and sway the governor, arguing that the whole state benefited from the Sugar Bowl's "national significance." He noted an obligation to the eleven thousand bondholders who had made that possible, investing $1.25 million to enlarge Tulane Stadium from 25,000 to more than 80,000 seats. Finally, he appealed to "the ideals of American sportsmanship" and spoke of Louisiana's obligation to its student athletes, to allow them to compete at the highest levels.[63]

"It's a hard decision," Governor Long told reporters. "It's a lot of responsibility for one little old man." He even revealed that several senators had admitted that they had voted under pressure but then encouraged him to use his own judgment.[64]

On this issue, however, Long, too, sided with popular opinion rather than his own. Gauging the statewide pleas to be roughly 4 to 1 in favor of the ban, on July 16, 1956, he signed into law the prohibition of all integrated athletics. He said he had given folks what they asked for, and he reminded the public that no sports boosters had appeared before either legislative body when they had the chance. He also predicted that the law would easily be contested in court. But perhaps even more prophetic was his earlier comment, made as the measure was being greased through the legislature: "I wish the people would be calm and not too hasty about these things. They might learn too late how far-reaching the effects would be."[65]

CHAPTER 2
A Long Return

"I signed one of brother Garrett's bills which makes it a penitentiary offense for a Negro to stick his head in a place where a white man is sitting," Governor Earl Long scoffed. Bus and train stations were getting new partitions. "I don't know how much good these bills will do, but I don't want Garrett to think I'm courting the colored people," Long explained to reporters. He had just signed the first four of the summer's avalanche of new laws, in June of 1956. Representative John Garrett sponsored each, as vice-chairman of the JLCS. This "watchdog" group had their fellow lawmakers—and the governor—fearful of appearing soft on integration.[1]

Some measures, like the sports bill, would actually be deliberated. These first four, however, had so much momentum behind them that they flew across the House and Senate floors and the governor's desk. They safeguarded three forms of segregation that the Supreme Court had recently ruled against. Along with the bill policing public transportation, two others countered the threat of integrated schools. The fourth addressed the "most talked of thing" that summer: public parks.[2]

Swimming pools, playgrounds, and golf courses had been a hotbed of frenzy since a federal verdict the previous November called for such spaces to be integrated. Back in January, panic-stricken park officials from across Louisiana congregated in Baton Rouge's Heidelberg Hotel for a crisis prevention confab. After running through the consequences of compliance, they adopted a resolution of resistance: parks would stay divided up or be closed down.

They then called over members of the JLCS, who needed little stirring to cook up another biased bill for the summer session. The mold was set on H.B. 435, putting strict segregation of parks under "the state's sovereign police powers." There was no doubt it would pass. Still, a New Orleans group from the Heidelberg summit soon called on the JLCS for even more help.[3]

The City Park board was, at that time, negotiating a contract with Xavier University for use of the park's gridiron to host two tilts with other Black colleges that autumn. In early 1956, as in previous years, the school had sent a written request, and as before, general manager Ellis Laborde replied that the New Orleans prep school league would be given first choice of dates.

This was, of course, a contract with local *white* Catholic and public high schools. Although there were no comparable alternatives, Black preppers never scrimmaged at City Park. Their pivotal games overflowed even the biggest rec center grandstands, but at best they relied on the generosity of Xavier and Dillard, using their fields when available. Even then, as neither school's stadium had lights, juggling prep and collegiate schedules was taxing and quickly approaching a breaking point.[4]

After verifying that the reservations Xavier requested for 1956 were again in conflict with the prep calendar, Laborde had written back offering alternative dates. He attached familiar lease terms and said if Xavier still wished to use the stadium, he would happily make the arrangements. This year, however, the school's response changed. Chairman Asa H. Atkins wrote to Laborde and explained that Xavier could not accept sections (f) and (j) of the rental policy, which required segregation of ticket booths, seating, concessionaires, and all other facilities. According to federal decree, Atkins reasoned, the pair of Thursday night slots must yield a wide-open City Park Stadium. So the chairman requested an updated set of terms and conditions.

The board's legal committee quickly began working on revisions—but to pending legislation, not to their rental contract. H.B. 435 was virtually guaranteed, but park supervisors were eyeing a constitutional amendment working its way through House channels. It was a long shot preemptive move to ward off federal suits against some agents of the state. However, segregation was not specifically cited as grounds, and any coverage of parks was unclear. Board members pressed the JLCS for more explicit language and a wider reach. Again, this was not a tough sell.

When lawmakers adjourned that summer, park authorities had the security of H.B. 435, which extended the state's police power to split up their spaces, and H.B. 1412, segregating every stadium event. Likewise, the constitutional amendment, freshly stipulated to shield parks from integration suits, was approved for the November ballot. At the start of the 1956 football season, well-fortified City Park remained open—and segregated.[5]

Ironically, back in December, while all eyes on Atlanta were trained at Tech's bowl wrangle, the Georgia capital stealthily started integrating its parks. Governor Griffin vowed to "get out of the park business" before complying with a recent federal verdict on the city's golf courses, and yet on Christmas Eve all municipal links were opened to all citizens. Alfred and Oliver Holmes, plaintiffs in the decisive suit, became the first Black players to legally integrate an Atlanta green. They teed off at the North Fulton course alongside several white golfers, who complimented the Holmeses' swings, exchanged scores with them, and added, "We are glad to have you. It's been a long time."[6]

For Griffin, that day had come far too soon. He felt spurned by Mayor William Hartsfield's choice to "throw in the towel." However, this move was neither a surrender nor a surprise. The city's business bigwigs and mainstream media had long been sour on Griffin's extremism. Hartsfield's decision also was not the result of exhausting all legal trickery, despite Griffin's push to hawk the fairways. While the state attorney general prepped parks to be auctioned off or boarded up, city officials studied merged greens in places like Dallas and Miami. Hartsfield announced, "We endeavor to meet this new situation with the same calmness and levelheadedness which many of our sister cities of the South have already shown." He was not referring to New Orleans.[7]

After the 1956 Sugar Bowl, comparisons with Atlanta had bolstered the old image of New Orleans as ahead of the rest of the Southeast in racial matters. And the Big Easy's infamous reputation for carefree indulgence and tolerance was cast in a redeeming light. In February, the *Nation* proffered that "New Orleans, always the scarlet sister among Southern cities, might yet become nursemaid to a stripling regional virtue."[8]

But a lot changed in the first half of 1956. "For a while," one NAACP official commented in the spring, "I thought Louisiana would remain dormant and be on the wait and see side, but now it seems that we are pulling for first place in the segregation issue." The state's White Citizens' Councils multiplied from two to twenty-nine units by June, championing their mission to preserve "historical Southern social traditions in all their aspects." They were getting plentiful help from lawmakers, who one newspaper reported were "out to segregate everything from television to square dances."[9]

And unlike Atlanta, New Orleans was fully entangled in its state's reactionary forces—and even those of Georgia. Five months after Atlantans twice snubbed Griffin's "massive resistance," Mayor Chep Morrison of New Orleans gave him keys to the city and honorary citizenship. A parade toured Griffin through the streets, and around six thousand Louisianans gathered at Pelican Stadium to hear him speak. It was May 17, the anniversary of the *Brown v. Board of Education* decision. Marvin Griffin stood on a New Orleans baseball diamond and ruled out even one breech in racial barriers, claiming "close personal contact on terms of equality perils the institutions of the South." Lending their voices to the official business of their hosts, the Citizens' Council, the crowd then adopted three resolutions, one of which called for a ban on integrated sports. Two months later, Louisiana's H.B. 1412 passed. Back in Georgia, however, an identical bill had been killed in February and would be killed again in 1957 and in 1958.[10]

|||||

H.B. 1412 was not part of the massive segregation package sponsored by William Rainach, John Garrett, and the rest of the JLCS. It was introduced by another pair of North Louisiana representatives, Lawrence Gibbs and E. D. Gleason. Initially, even Rainach was hesitant to govern every sports scenario with one piece of blanket legislation. He told reporters, "I want to check on its effects, how far it reaches, what it touches." But by the time of the Senate tally, his vote had admittedly been forged in the heat of public pressure. The outlook for sports was grim under the Gibbs-Gleason law, and still this social strong-arming was ever-escalating.[11]

Newsmen scoured affected institutions for an impending fight, but one by one the biggest players indicated intent to comply. "That's the law, and we will try to live under it," Paul DeBlanc conceded, leaving sportswriters to assure locals that "other groups will undoubtedly give it a test." Reverend James Molloy, Loyola's athletic director, vaguely commented, "We will have to study it and see what we will have to do," prompting hopeful forecasts of a suit, which never materialized. LSU's board chairman announced all Tigers athletics would obey, and Tulane was silent. As local sports bodies signaled capitulation, reporters looked for legal action from national groups such as the NCAA and the Amateur Athletic Union.[12]

Even Governor Long searched for someone to contest the law. He deflected blame by describing the opposition as too little and too late, but he looked into a suit, anonymously. A colleague of the governor contacted Black

New Orleans attorney A. P. Tureaud of the NAACP and disclosed that Long was willing to fund a challenge from behind the scenes. Tureaud refused to take the case, saying influential whites should have the courage to oppose the ban publicly. He later told the press, "We are satisfied to let the law punish those who are responsible for its creation."[13]

Likewise, the *Weekly* noted that "token resistance from those directly harmed" gave Black activists no inclination to save white institutions from themselves. African Americans' only talk of action was a call to boycott segregated events. Otherwise, as several sports pages explained, Black locals would just sit back and watch "while the rest of the country moves along with sports" and the city's programs "hit rock bottom." Besides, several civil rights leaders expected the law to grow into quite a force for integration as its effects played out.[14]

Like politicians and administrators, the city's mainstream sports columnists approached the subject with kid gloves, although each had already given the nod to intersectional collegiate play and the Pitt–Tech bowl. An instance or two of snarky humor wore Hap Glaudi's byline, but otherwise his column's rare criticisms of the ban were in reader letters or in excerpts from out-of-state papers. Harry Martinez devoted a day's ink to a Pollyanna argument that seeing the same schools over and over could make SEC football "more interesting." Bill Keefe, however, developed a more complicated outlook.[15]

Keefe was a huge cheerleader for the Pitt–Tech contest, calling it "one of the most thrilling and maybe the hardest-fought of all the great Sugar Bowl games." He had also long argued that intersectional matchups benefited the area and its athletes. So in February, when the debate on mixed sports was heating up, Keefe suggested a compromise on accommodations might forestall a blanket ban.[16]

By the summer, though, Keefe's columns were the concessions of a worn-out sportsman. Critics repeatedly dug for trouble with the Pitt–Tech bowl and used it as ammunition. After what Keefe saw as "so much uncalled for, false, vicious and damaging hog-wash," he traded his pennant for a white flag and concluded that "the experiment was unsatisfactory." He was happy to close the SEC in on itself, create a "full rotating schedule," and shut out the noise. Keefe also made the strained argument that all-SEC Sugar Bowls could be a "national attraction." He had only one example, and the best he could say of Georgia Tech's four unanswered scores on Ole Miss in 1953 was that the game was "a whole lot closer" than the stats suggested.[17]

When the law passed, Keefe did not question the legislators' or the public's motivation to enforce it. Rather, he pointed at the individual he claimed had driven them to such extreme measures: Jackie Robinson. Keefe's column provoked national attention and a written response from Robinson when it claimed the star had been "the most harmful influence" on sports integration. Keefe called Robinson "insolent," "antagonistic," and "troublemaking" and cited a years-old incident when the player flung a bat into the stands after striking out. According to Keefe, Robinson's behavior—and the league's failure to "muzzle" him—made the star an "enemy of his race" and forced the retreat from interracial sports.[18]

Across the rest of the country, on the other hand, folks expressed far less complicated views. As expected, the University of Wisconsin announced "there's not a chance" it would fulfill its football contract with LSU. Loyola, which integrated its basketball program in 1954, hemorrhaged games: Marquette, American University, Iowa, and Cincinnati. It was simply taken for granted that the service academies would yank their grid agreements from Tulane. And talk of Major League Baseball's spring tour showcasing nine clubs in New Orleans turned to hopes that one team might still play in Pelican Stadium.[19]

Three of the four basketball teams signed by the MWSA pulled out. St. Louis University and Notre Dame refused to leave behind their Black cagers, and Dayton chose not to "condone" the law despite the team's all-white roster. Likewise, Pitt protested by withdrawing its name from any future Sugar Bowl, even though Grier had graduated and no other Black players had joined the team. It was still only July. Long's signature was barely dry. *The Pittsburgh Courier* summarized the early "squeeze" and noted that "the situation is expected to get worse."[20]

The darkest doom-and-gloom forecast came from Shirley Povich of the *Washington Post and Times-Herald:* "It is clear now that the Louisiana legislature has legislated the Sugar Bowl right out of importance." More years than not, Povich ranked New Orleans's attraction above even the Rose Bowl, but he predicted, "It won't be like that anymore." As he saw it, with the stroke of a pen, the Big Easy's classic had become "a provincial thing without impact." The disintegration of MWSA basketball proved to him how outside schools would respond to the Sugar Bowl. So, he declared, "It will be known henceforth merely as a sectional contest to settle some kind of a Dixie championship only." The other New Year's Day games, Povich added, could benefit, "while the Sugar Bowl withers on its vine of bigotry."[21]

||||

Every August, when the college All-Stars played the National Football League (NFL) champions at Soldier Field in Chicago, the Sugar Bowlers threw a cocktail party for the country's top sports authorities. It was considered "always one of the highlights of All-Star week" and provided an annual public relations boon for the MWSA. In 1956, the Sugar Bowlers needed all the goodwill they could muster, and DeBlanc and Digby had far greater obligations than their normal hosting duties. They had a lot of explaining to do.[22]

Representative Gibbs, still not doing the bowl group any favors, had just provided a hot sound bite that got nationwide attention, including a spotlight in the "Famous Last Words Department" of a Dallas newspaper. Unfortunately, he also seemed to speak for the MWSA. Arguing that he had not killed the Sugar Bowl, Gibbs declared that northern and integrated schools would still accept bids from New Orleans because "teams would put first things first." He reasoned, "They get about $120,000 for appearing in the Sugar Bowl, and don't think they overlook the prestige either." He then concluded crudely, "This will be a strong inducement for leaving their colored players at home." On the heels of that, DeBlanc and Digby spent much of the three-hour affair clearing the air.[23]

However, the questioning continued back home as well, even within their own ranks. A *consensus* of the executive committee had elected "that we not attack the law, because of the effect it would have on our public relations." But dissent could be found among junior and senior bowlers alike.[24]

Most notable of the dissidents, not surprisingly, was Irwin Poché. At one of the group's midsummer meetings, he sat quietly through a mad scramble to salvage basketball. Only one school had been found to replace the three that withdrew, and the committee considered pairing the college squads with two Industrial League teams. Someone suggested recovering lost schools by holding the event out of state. Others argued that it was best to protect the sports carnival's standards and cancel the tournament outright. At that point, Poché unleashed a furious argument for dropping their guarded public relations plan and attacking their root problem head-on. Still, the logic in the room did not outweigh the furor outside, and he asked to at least be "placed on record as favoring such a move."[25]

Two weeks later, he had even more arrows in his quiver. The basketball committee was still missing one team, and the deadline of a week was set to either finalize or scrap the two-night tourney. More importantly, American

Broadcasting Company (ABC) and NBC reps confirmed that neither station would carry the football classic. It was also made clear that not being on the air in 1957 would almost certainly be a forever forfeiture of Sugar's spot on the elite New Year's Day lineup.[26]

The consequences of not being broadcast coast to coast would snowball, validating Long's theory of the law's effects being graver than expected. When the bill passed, sportswriters everywhere saw the same crystal ball: the Sugar Bowl would pair the top Southeastern team with the second-best team from either the SEC or the Southwestern Conference (SWC), whose champ was promised to Cotton. Predictions differed on the quality of the competition but not on its makeup. However, even with a sold-out stadium, losing $125,000 from television and radio would reduce schools' payouts to the point that even Deep South squads would turn down bids. Any up-and-coming bowl would happily pick up Sugar's slack, its team selections, and its television slot.[27]

This threat of imminent collapse still did not offset the backlash expected if the MWSA had the courts wipe out the whole sports law, now Act 579. The Sugar men did, however, start looking for some middle ground. Long would soon be calling lawmakers back together in a special session, and they would vote on whatever topics the governor tagged. Aside from several sticky tax issues, the list was unknown and unfinished. If anything could be done to soften the blow of the sports bill, it would happen in the special session.[28]

DeBlanc contacted a longtime associate of Long, former New Orleans mayor Robert Maestri. Out of that chat came the idea of suspending the law for the date of the classic. When DeBlanc mentioned this at the next MWSA meeting, Poché piped up about his own discussion with a "prominent politician," who suggested postponing the law's enactment until after New Year's Day. With expert opinions and a glimmer of hope, the Sugar Bowlers lined up for a Hail Mary.[29]

They approached the governor with their appeals. It was a short conversation. Long refused to put his name behind any revision to the sports law. What he *would* do for the MWSA was get them in the door. After that, they were on their own. Long's mulishness was not just about dodging heat. He resented interested parties idly watching the measure roll through the House and Senate. The bill picked up massive public sentiment and landed on his desk before any group laced up their gloves. By then, a veto would have been a huge expenditure of political capital. The same was true for the special session, so the Sugar men would have to find someone else to stick his neck out.[30]

They did. They found an ally in Representative George Tessier, a former Tulane guard and veteran of Sugar Bowl I. MWSA execs were meeting twice a day, searching for some Sugar-saving action that could get the necessary votes. When word got out that the bowlers might seek suspension or postponement, Gibbs and the gang announced that they would fight any such move with their full arsenal. So the ally called an audible. Tessier and DeBlanc began drafting a replacement bill. Instead of lifting or delaying the statute, they would offer a nearly identical but more Sugar-friendly substitute.[31]

They also solicited the help of attorney Clem Sehrt, Long's top political contact in New Orleans. Sehrt could advise them professionally on legislation and personally on dealing with Earl, "the most bull-headed man" he knew. Sehrt also said he would try to swing some votes but thought asking anyone to cosponsor would be going too far.[32]

Tessier did not stop there. After a closed-door luncheon at City Hall, he hung around the mayor's office with several city officials and tossed the new sports bill on the table. There was no shortage of sympathy or suggestions, but confidence was hard to come by. Even the very idea of a substitute bill was deemed dangerous because it required repeal of the original law. There was also consensus that any revisions should only affect large cities. A population minimum of 100,000 got several nods, and Mayor Morrison concurred that it would make Tessier's request "more acceptable to the country delegation."[33]

When Tessier finalized the new measure, it was reduced to the smallest possible change to Act 579 that would allow the Sugar Bowl to continue its current operations. He even raised the population figure. The suggested minimum of 100,000 would have included Baton Rouge and Shreveport, and there were rumblings that Lafayette wanted a number that would squeeze their beloved baseball into the exemption. But the MWSA was looking out for number one. If their measure had any shot at passing, it had to make as small a ripple as possible. The new number, 300,000, would affect only New Orleans. Tessier also carefully talked around notions of replacement or repeal. "The primary purpose," he explained to the press, "is to re-enact the present segregation bill"—with a tiny new provision. The only integration stipulated was for out-of-state athletes and blocked-off seats for their fans.[34]

Meanwhile, segregationists anticipated calls for small concessions and got a head start. Dr. Emmett Irwin, who invited Georgia's governor to town in May, borrowed Griffin's rhetorical style for a flamboyant press release. Irwin asserted that any alterations to Act 579 would "nullify and destroy all other segregation measures" and ultimately lead to a "mongrelized race." No compromise could be considered, he declared, because "there is no middle ground." And as Irwin urged folks to contact their representatives, Rainach applied his pressure straight to the other lawmakers. "If a legislator voted to change the measure," he announced, "it would leave a stigma that would mark him for the rest of his life."[35]

Despite extensive lobbying, only Representatives Nicholas J. Lapara and Lucien T. Vivien Jr., both of New Orleans, backed Tessier. Even then, presenting the bill "by request" of the Sugar Bowlers was seen as deflection of ownership. And despite one last appeal from Poché, Long indeed stayed out of it.[36]

Still, Tessier stood bravely before his fellow lawmakers on Friday, August 31, and stated, "Without this additional provision, the Sugar Bowl as it exists today is doomed to death." He stressed that the original law would be untouched for every city but his. "We ask only to add a section permitting the Sugar Bowl to continue," he pleaded. "We ask only for permission to live."[37]

Representative Wellborn Jack of Shreveport jumped from his seat. "We passed this segregation bill one hundred percent," he shouted in his raspy voice. He wanted the issue tabled entirely. "That is my motion, and I ask the people to vote on it," he barked, before adding ominously that "it will be recorded in history how they voted."[38]

Speaker of the House Robert Angelle ruled the motion to table was out of order and the measure would roll over to the Saturday session. Jack did not flinch. He moved to have the rules suspended. Tessier objected, but the motion passed in a count of 57 to 24. Jack then put forth his original request, which was not open to debate, according to whatever rules were still being followed.

After a 67 to 15 vote to table, the measure was killed. So too, it seemed, were the Sugar Bowl and New Orleans's future in national sports. As DeBlanc tried to slip away, reporters snagged him for a hint at the group's next move, but the Sugar Bowlers had put themselves as far out as they were willing to go. He remarked simply, "There isn't anything to be done at the present time."[39]

If her football was dying, New Orleans was prepared to throw it one of her time-honored jazz funerals. After the Gibbs-Gleason law passed, Tulane's game with Navy was assumed to be scratched. However, when Rainach pushed the bill's effective date to October 15, 1956, he unknowingly created a two-day buffer for the Greenies to host the Midshipmen on Saturday, October 13, under the racial policies used for the past two Sugar Bowls.[40]

With the matchup falling on the 181st anniversary of the U.S. Naval Department, a spectacular fete was planned for the preceding week. An aircraft carrier, the *Saipan,* and a destroyer, the *Vogelgesang,* docked at the Bienville Street Wharf and opened to visitors. The launching and christening of the USS *Grant County* took place at Avondale Shipyard. There were speeches by admirals and banquets for various Navy VIPs. And roughly a dozen prominent New Orleans families invited groups of midshipmen to their homes for dinner parties, where the city's lovely young debutantes entertained the guests of honor.[41]

Still, the football game was by far the highlight. The previous year's Green Wave squad belied all predictions. After two years with only one victory each, they had pulled off a winning record. It was their first since 1950, just before Tulane administrators "swung a heavy ax" at the once powerhouse of the SEC, officially deemphasizing football. In a complicated and controversial decision that risked undermining long-standing community support, the university had raised academic standards for student athletes while scaling back player scholarships, coaching salaries, and scouting practices. Also declining, as a result, were the size and success of the next four squads. In 1956, however, excitement over Tulane was back, for now, and ticket sales were rebounding.[42]

With the Midshipmen en route, the Greenies were riding high off an intersectional win over the Big Ten's Northwestern. Local papers bragged that the Navy and Northwestern games made Tulane the only SEC squad playing "big-time" teams that season. And although the Wave suffered a host of injuries in Illinois, coach Andy Pilney's biggest fear was not about having hurt players on the bench but about having them on the field. He worried that excitement over Navy would have guys disguising injuries. Unbeaten and boasting the number one offense in the country, the Middies were favored, but as banged-up Greenies recovered, the margin shrank to a point and a half.[43]

On game day, twenty booths opened outside Tulane Stadium to handle the long ticket lines, to which the Wave had grown unaccustomed. As fans found their seats, the show was already under way. Always a crowd favorite, Navy goat Billy XIV was paraded across the field, cloaked in his silken banner. He was soon challenged for popularity by television's comedic chimpanzee, J. Fred Muggs, who appeared in a full football uniform. Then a motorcade escorted Miss New Orleans onto the field before the Midshipmen's drum and bugle corps conducted a rousing fifteen minutes of music and marching. Finally, the nearly three hundred members of the schools' color companies coordinated for the raising of the American flag. Fans stood, the Pensacola Naval Aviation Cadet band played the national anthem, and Old Glory was lifted above the stadium.[44]

The Green Wave got off to a fast start. On their first possession, Tulane went 74 yards on thirteen rushing plays and scored a touchdown and an extra point. Although the Middies blocked a later field goal attempt to keep the lead at 7, the most impressive defending of the first two periods came from Tulane's pass coverage. Navy got into the red zone twice, but their "pet plays" for short yardage were not fooling the well-studied Greenies. Navy's flare and screen passes into the flat proved useless; even when completed, they lost yards. Both visits inside Tulane's 20 were turned over on downs, and the Midshipmen were scoreless at intermission.[45]

The halftime show further fanned excitement over Navy Week. The Tulane marching band honored their team, the visiting service academy, and the nation with "Roll On, Tulane," "Anchors Away," and "God Bless America." Navy's mallet-twirling drummers and banner-waving bugle corps strutted displays of bright blue and gold across the field during another impressive precision routine. Then the Pensacola aviation ensemble resumed its dominance of the airspace above the east stands.

Likewise, Tulane resumed its dominance of the game. The Greenie defense kept the scoreboard unsoiled well into the fourth quarter. Meanwhile, the Wave's Gene Newton threw a 9-yard touchdown pass in the third quarter, and another from 8 yards out in the fourth. With tackle Emmett Zelenka's flawless extra-point attempts, the Greenies were up 21–0.

Even with more and more reserves subbing for injured stars, Tulane was promising fans a shutout with less than three minutes remaining. Then their third-string left halfback fumbled on the Tulane 11. It set up the Middies' only touchdown, but the point-after kick went wide right, leaving Tulane a 21–6 win over the mighty Midshipmen.[46]

Tulane Stadium quieted down as ticket holders journeyed on to the next of the weekend's seemingly endless festivities. In many ways, however, the party was over for New Orleans. In two days, Act 579 would take effect, making that service academy game, with all its pomp and national significance, the last intersectional show for the city's foreseeable future.

|||||

"I sometimes wonder if you New Orleans people really appreciate the tremendous contribution the Sugar Bowlers have made to American football, competitive sports, to the nation and to this city," sports dynamo Arch Ward said in 1953. At an appreciation dinner for the MWSA's twentieth anniversary, Ward declared, "Theirs is the spirit that makes America great." He concluded, "The Sugar Bowl belongs to the nation, not to New Orleans alone."[47]

In 1956, Hap Glaudi used a similar phrase to explain why the Naval Academy could never return: "The Navy, Army, and Air Force cannot permit their athletic teams to perform where there are racial bans. They belong to all the people." The Sugar Bowl, on the other hand, was being given back to New Orleans.[48]

ABC declined the 1957 classic without even surveying advertisers. Previously, the company had issued a formal sponsorship proposal arguing that New Orleans consistently brought in the best game. It gave one reason: "Unrestricted choice of the best teams." "Each year different teams qualify as the best in the land," the old ads boasted. "The Sugar Bowl alone is free to select the best teams each year." But in 1956, ABC's praise no longer applied. In fact, it better fit Cotton's annual search for the Southwestern champ's opponent. As Bill Rives of the *Dallas Morning News* put it, "The Cotton Bowl now is riding high; it's the King of the Bowls and is free to roam the nation in selecting a visiting team."[49]

The best any network could offer was a willingness to talk again if the Sugar Bowlers themselves secured backers. So in the fall they were in a mad scramble, using every contact they had. Mayor Morrison reached out to the steel industries, while Poché met with petroleum entities. The help of Les Arries of World Sports was solicited, and he pitched to tobacco companies. After months of shopping the game around, by December only one quarter was sold, to L&M cigarettes. It was time to issue bids, and Sugar did not have a spot on the January 1 TV lineup.[50]

The signing of bowl teams that year took several odd turns. The Orange Bowl, with its Big Seven tie-up, had dibs on the nation's number one team, Oklahoma, but a conference rule blocked the school from back-to-back appearances. As a result, Miami's event ended up with twentieth-ranked Colorado, and the Buffaloes were contractually paired with the Atlantic Coast Conference's nineteenth-ranked Clemson. The perennial Rose Bowl was automatically hosting third-ranked Iowa and tenth-ranked Oregon State. However, for the first time in the game's forty-three-year history, this was a repeat of a regular-season matchup, and the event was billed as "warmed-over stuff."[51]

"King" Cotton should have received the top SWC team, but fifth-ranked Texas A&M was on NCAA probation. Texas Christian University (TCU) had the second-best conference record and got the berth instead. Then Cotton's first bid for an opponent was rejected. Navy officials thought tied games with Duke and Army—on top of their defeat by Tulane—did not justify the reward of postseason play. So Syracuse accepted a secondhand offer.[52]

Even without a TV contract, MWSA funds existed, for the moment, to make proper bids, meaning the top SEC choice was not yet a flight risk. By mid-November, a good-faith deal had unofficially reserved Tennessee for New Orleans, thanks in no small part to decades of tradition and Fred Digby's friendship with athletic director Robert Neyland. Tennessee not only led the SEC but also was ranked second nationally. Oklahoma's ineligibility made the undefeated Volunteers America's most attractive bowl prospect.

Turning their eyes westward, the Sugar Bowlers, in another year, might have been fulfilling predictions of the SEC's top team facing the second-best SWC squad. However, although TCU received the Cotton berth via the best (eligible) conference record, the Baylor Bears had a better overall win/loss ratio at the season's end. And they were ranked three notches above the Horned Frogs in the national polls. Baylor's record-marring midseason losses to TCU and Texas A&M came during a spate of injuries and were decided by a total of only 7 points. After walloping Rice in their final game, Baylor happily accepted a well-earned but nearly missed invitation to the postseason. As a result, New Orleans clinched the highest-ranked team in any bowl and the highest-ranked bowl team from *both* the Southeastern and Southwestern Conferences.[53]

While the selection committee was celebrating their coup, the broadcasting bunch was staring off a cliff. In the first week of December, they were ready to make big compromises in a last-ditch effort to stay on the air. They discussed offering around a 50 percent discount for their game and having it carried on a cooperative basis, given their failure to find a major national sponsor.

Les Arries, however, believed they had just renewed their bargaining power, and he asked them to wait one more day. On December 7, it was announced that the American Broadcasting Company would again air the Sugar Bowl Classic coast to coast. When the postseason pairings fell together the way they did, implications for TV ratings were clear, and the Oldsmobile Division of General Motors put up top dollar. Against all odds, the Sugar Bowl would be on the air New Year's Day 1957.[54]

|||||

"Gay old perpetual-carnival New Orleans," one Dallas sportswriter observed, "has the smug air of a guy who expected the worst and wound up making a million." All the major hotels in New Orleans were booked solid, and overflow was filling motor courts across the Gulf Coast. Giant "Pullman cities" popped up as five railroad companies parked more than a hundred overnight cars to house the record-breaking number of out-of-state ticket holders.[55]

The contest was even more intriguing for true fans than indicated by the rankings or point spread (Vols by seven and a half). Tennessee's revival of the single-wing offense, which confounded their weekly opponents all season, would be tested against the more common T formation—and a defense with a full month of film study.

Even before lining up in the T, however, the underdog Bears stunned Tennessee, returning the opening kickoff for 52 yards to the Vols 44. Still, as Baylor chipped through Tennessee territory, the Volunteer band played "Hound Dog" and an Elvis Presley impersonator gestured at the Bears offense. That is, until the ball was placed on the 4-yard line. The stands were pretty still during Baylor's long fourth-down huddle. But when delay-of-game yardage forced a field goal attempt and halfback Donnell Berry's boot went wide left, the rock-'n'-roll music cranked up again.

Soon, though, it was Baylor's secondary that cut the party short. All-American tailback Johnny Majors's first pass was intercepted by Art Beall, and the remainder of the first quarter was a deadlock. Both teams protected their end zones, but Baylor barely let Tennessee into Bear territory. The Vols shifted their single wing from left to right but it rarely moved forward. In fact, early in the second period, a first down quick kick from their 34 seemed like a surer ticket to good field position. Even then, however, what started as a healthy Tennessee bounce dribbled just inside the goal line for a touchback.

On the next play, Bears halfback Del Shofner broke loose along the sideline, gaining 54 yards, getting well past Tennessee's last line of scrimmage, and setting up the game's first touchdown. Berry overcorrected from his first kick and sailed the extra-point attempt wide right, but Baylor led by 6.

Tennessee did make it 20 yards into Baylor real estate before intermission, but tailback Bobby Gordon's pass for Buddy Cruze in the back of the end zone was intercepted off the fingertips of the airborne Del Shofner, killing the Vols' closest shot at scoring before the break. Fittingly, an ominous sky set in, bringing a slight chill and drizzly rain, as shock swept over Tennessee rooters. It also did not go unnoticed that the Baylor mascot, a large, live North American black bear, stalked the east sidelines.

When the second half opened, however, a lot looked different. Even the dark clouds dispersed. Moreover, the Bears handed the Vols their first possession inside Baylor territory by capping Majors's punt return with 15 yards for piling on. The Volunteers now ripped apart the Baylor line on both sides, muscling their way to the end zone in ten rushing plays, and the fullback's true point after touchdown (PAT) put his team on top by one.

The Bears, on the other hand, punted on every drive of the third quarter, and they opened the fourth from midfield in the same fashion. Shofner aimed for the coffin corner, but Majors fielded the ball on the 7. When he reached the 15, however, he was mauled by a sloth of Bears, emerged empty-handed, and threw the momentum back to the other bench.

Baylor nibbled the clock and the red zone for five plays before bulldozing through the orange line for the score. With Berry's try centered this time, the Bears reclaimed a 6-point lead. And when Majors turned the ball over again on the next drive, throwing his second interception, the final minutes were looking good for the guys in green.

Then, in front of a favorable scoreboard and 82,000 bewildered fans, Baylor chose not to punt on fourth-and-1 from midfield. When their reserve quarterback missed the conversion by inches, they again gifted Tennessee some of their best starting field position of the day.

At the drive's outset, the single wing was swift, averaging 6 yards per carry. But the Bears defense soon snapped back into first-half form and ultimately forced Tennessee to punt from behind where it had taken possession.

After three conservative plays, Baylor punted deep into Volunteer territory. Pressured by the clock, Tennessee went to their emergency stash of passes. Tailback Al Carter started the air attack with a 20-yarder to the team's most reliable receiver. But with Cruze overthrown and Baylor in soft coverage, the ball sailed straight into Beall's hands and sealed the game for the Bears.[56]

The next day, sportscasters were debating whether it was the most or the second-most exciting Sugar Bowl of all time. Tulane's *Hullabaloo* commented, "This year the Sugar Bowl Committee fell in... and came out smelling sweetly as never before." DeBlanc worded it less colorfully, but he reveled in their success, acknowledging that the outlook had been "anything but bright." He also felt his promise was fulfilled and their bowl still held the top spot.[57]

NBC executives agreed, or at least considered Sugar second best, behind Pasadena's Rose Bowl. In early September 1957, months before team selections and without any sponsors lined up, the MWSA finalized a five-year contract with the National Broadcasting Company. The Sugar contest would be immediately followed by Rose Bowl coverage to round out a nonstop New Year's Day football package. A year earlier, the director of NBC Sports cited Act 579 as a damning problem and went with Cotton as an opening act. Now he was committed to a five-year diet of Sugar, with the law still on the books.

The game had been carried on the younger and more limited ABC since beginning coast-to-coast coverage, but on January 1, 1958, it would be sent to as many as two hundred stations nationwide. After facing the likelihood their bowl would never again be on the air—and would fold altogether—the MWSA expanded its market and sewed up half a decade of security.[58]

|||||

While the MWSA was signing its five-year deal, a three-year-old football contract was being challenged. Tulane was scheduled to host Army on November 16, 1957, and the Black Knights had no official policy on playing in the segregated South. So when the NAACP protested a year in advance, Army coach Earl Blaik stated he had no Black players and that seating was beyond his purview. The game stayed as scheduled. Two months out, plans began for an elaborate "Army Day" at Tulane Stadium, to rival the previous year's Navy celebration, and arrangements were being coordinated with West Point.

However, Congressman James Fulton of Pennsylvania sent a telegram to President Eisenhower, requesting that "as commander in chief" and "as a matter of fairness" Eisenhower use his station to scratch the game. Fulton informed the president that otherwise "West Point will be the first Northern college to break the unofficial boycott against playing in Louisiana." The congressman also wired the secretary of defense as well as Coach Blaik and Lieutenant General Garrison Davidson, West Point superintendent and former Army football coach.[59]

Davidson responded that after review, Army had decided to proceed to New Orleans, but without the original plans to bring the academy band and the Corps of Cadets, which included seven African Americans. According to Davidson, this was not a concession but purely "a matter of economy." Thinking everything was squared away, Davidson concluded, "Our responsibility is to play the game" and "We are going to honor our contract."[60]

Letters and telegrams poured into Army offices. Among them was a renewal of the NAACP's year-old request that the whole event be canceled. Likewise, the nation's newspapers weighed in on a military academy bowing to segregation. Sports pages called it "another step backwards" and "shameful." One even questioned whether the Cadets' football uniforms would be "white sheets and hoods."[61]

Army's tactic protected the official academy party, but they misjudged the exposure of their extended family. "Further study" revealed that Army's tickets (unlike those issued to Navy the year before) would be racially marked. Army officials certainly could not comply. There was no way either institution could compromise on terms at Tulane, so they reached an agreement that moved the game to West Point's Michie Stadium.[62]

The settlement brought little peace. Both sides were scathed. Integrationists argued that Army was still sanctioning segregation and the game should be canceled. Tulane took heat for shifting a home game out of state rather than insisting that its contract be fulfilled. In fact, the announcement came three days before the first Greenie game and gave some folks time to return their full season ticket books in protest.[63]

The loudest southern yelp came from Louisiana congressman F. Edward Hebert, who called it "a sad day in our history when the defense establishment of this country, for political reasons, is to pass judgment on the laws of a sovereign state." Oddly, although a staunch segregationist, Hebert stated, "For the record, I do not personally subscribe to the law in question, but I defend the right of a state to pass its own laws." He made bold proposals, such as aborting the appointment of candidates from New Orleans to West Point and refusing to provide Louisianans for the draft. Still, despite all the hoopla, the decision was final, and the Greenies boarded a northeast-bound plane.[64]

To the delight of Bill Keefe, who advocated the exposure of intersectional travel, the students enjoyed the bus ride along the Hudson from New York to West Point, viewing the mountains, hills, winding roads, autumn leaves, and massive standing fleet of ships. But their experience on base would be heartbreaking—and in one case, leg-breaking.

The hit Tulane took on the move was far more than stadium revenue. The reversal of home field advantage was both palpable and audible. No one showed up to greet the squad, so a meandering search for practice facilities cut training time. The visitors' space was lacking expected amenities, and some procedures used at Michie Stadium got under Pilney's skin on game day. Most problematic, however, was the crowd noise. Army rooters were so disruptive to the Greenie offense that officials repeatedly intervened, with little result.

Despite all that, the scoring tandem of Claude Mason and Richie Petitbon had the underdog Wave ahead by 1 over the tenth-ranked Black Knights in the final minutes. By then, though, injuries were adding up. Tulane's quarterback was hobbling, their starting left halfback was on a stretcher, and the reserves were tapped. Their reduced manpower was outgunned by a late Army offensive strike, and the Green Wave limped away with a loss to the cheers of the Cadet crowd.[65]

According to Keefe, Tulane was given a "cold reception" in general. The lack of a welcome wagon was followed by an equally inhospitable dinner engagement. Although the teams ate side by side in the mess hall, none of the Cadets spoke to the guys in green jackets, even "to say howdy or ask about the trip." Tulane's gridders were essentially segregated and unacknowledged. Without even a hint of intended irony, Keefe wrote that he "would hate to think any Southern school would be so chilly to any visiting group of athletes or officials as West Point was."[66]

New Orleanians would, however, get used to being cut off from national sports teams. Air Force's agreement to visit Tulane in 1958 included a stipulation against segregation, so the Falcons easily dropped the Wave shortly after the West Point uproar. With that, the last of the city's intersectional tilts was snuffed out, and New Orleans settled into a sports domain of segregated southerners.[67]

| | | | |

In 1957, local Black high schools were dropping entire sports programs. There just were not enough fields and gymnasiums. Dillard and Xavier had curtailed third-party use of their facilities, and privately owned Pelican Stadium, used some in recent years, was facing demolition. Unrest in the African American community over separate and unequal youth sports was coming to a head, and city administrators knew they had to make a move. Even Bill Keefe argued that New Orleans owed its Black athletes either new play spaces or use of City Park.[68]

Consequently, a city construction crew took the path of least resistance along the Industrial Canal to the lakefront and erected a new multisport stadium at Black-designated Pontchartrain Park. A floodlighting system more than doubled the cost, and the mayor's office hoped the "grade A" field would meet the needs of African American youth.[69]

Any expectation that it would take City Park off the table, however, was quashed within the week. Five days after the mayor's ribbon-cutting ceremony, district court judge J. Skelly Wright declared unconstitutional the segregation of New Orleans's largest municipal park. The suit being resolved was filed in 1949 and had led to an agreement opening the park's golf and tennis spaces to Blacks on Tuesdays and Fridays. Since then, the case was held in abeyance as Wright monitored Supreme Court decisions. With his ruling of May 15, 1957, came a lot of conjecture about officials' next move. After all, newspapers noted, Atlanta, Miami, and Houston had chosen to "gracefully abide by the law."[70]

New Orleans, on the other hand, dragged the case out for another year and a half. Even when legal counsel advised that further struggle was in vain, the park board agreed, with one dissenting vote, that "we owe it to ourselves and to the public to offer every possible resistance." They continued their fruitless filing spree until just before Christmas 1958, when it was announced that interracial recreation had reached the Crescent City. The implications seemed monumental.[71]

Two weeks later, a pair of white men carried their clubs to the golf course nearest their homes, but their cash was refused. "You can't play here," the Pontchartrain Park aide explained. "This golf course is for Negroes." City officials confirmed it. New Orleans was adhering to the ruling as narrowly as possible. The forced desegregation did not extend beyond the borders of City Park, the only party named in the suit. Until a new trial determined otherwise, no whites could use Pontchartrain's links and Audubon was closed to Blacks.[72]

Although extremely limited, this desegregation was dicey. In the first two months, there were verbal harassments, fistfights, broken windshields, and an attack on a mixed group of young boys riding bicycles. The scare tactics worked, and the number of Black patrons waned. Moreover, petitions were calling for the park to be sold or shuttered. But police superintendent Joseph Giarrusso assigned five cops to the park during the week and ten on weekends, and City Park remained open—and open to all.[73]

|||||

Five months later, in the spring of 1959, City Park officials were still sorting out the details of desegregation. They considered applications for Black high schools to use the stadium and debated whether the pools could be reopened that summer. Just then, another Supreme Court decision came down that would dictate park operations. The verdict was in: Louisiana's integrated sports ban was out.[74]

The suit resolved in May 1959 was also an older case. It originated in 1955, when African American light-heavyweight boxer Joe Dorsey challenged the state's regulation against mixed matches. He claimed that if popular Black and white fighters could appear on the same card, his annual income would be more than $10,000, rather than his average $600. By mid-1957, the case had not been heard, and Dorsey amended his complaint to attack Act 579.[75]

Coincidentally, at that time, another Big Easy boxer was fighting to secure an estimated $50,000 the law threatened. In April 1957, the light-skinned lightweight pugilist Ralph Dupas was scheduled for what Bill Keefe described as "one of the most important matches that could be arranged right now among white boxers." Then someone claimed Dupas was Black. Seventy-four-year-old Lucretia Gravolet informed Senator Rainach that New Orleans's favorite son, the world's fourth-ranking lightweight, was really a Black man named Ralph Duplessis from Plaquemines Parish. Rainach, of course, dutifully reported this to the state athletic commission. It resulted in a stormy hearing clouded with suspect documents and conflicting testimonies. In the end, the evidence was ruled insufficient, and Dupas decisioned Vince Martinez in ten rounds at Pelican Stadium.[76]

Within three weeks, however, the state boxing commission ordered Dupas to produce a birth certificate. He had attended white public schools and had fought on the city's white cards for more than seven years, but he had no documentation of his birth in Orleans Parish to white parents. So he took his in-state action from the ring to the courtroom, vowing to spend "every nickel" necessary to prove his Caucasian heritage. Although a lower court sided with him early, the ruling was overturned, and Dupas would spend more than three years fighting for what he and his attorney called "the rights of thousands yet unborn." Critics, many of whom believed he was indeed "passing," argued that Dupas would have truly championed the rights of others—and better spent his legal fees—by simply kayoing the ban on mixed bouts.[77]

The financial benefits of that route, at least, were undeniable. A year into his legal marathon, Dupas challenged lightweight champion Joe Brown for his title, and the two Louisiana prodigies were projected to draw the largest gate ever made in New Orleans. However, Brown was Black, Act 579 was untouched, and Dupas's claims were unchanged. Ultimately, the match was moved to Houston, where it netted significantly lower profits. One Black Los Angeles sportswriter announced a quarter of a million dollars had been guaranteed Dupas and Brown for a bout in the Big Easy. The columnist considered that the price Dupas was willing to pay to have "'bought' his way into the white race."[78]

So it was with boxing just as it was with other sports: those with the most to lose or gain worked around Act 579 instead of attacking it directly. Joe Dorsey's suit, on the other hand, required a fundraising drive. His attorneys cited precedent, appealed to the Fourteenth Amendment, and then said of the law what everyone already knew: it was "obviously unconstitutional." The Louisiana attorney general argued that white boxers also could make more money in mixed bouts and were equally injured, indicating there was no discrimination. This alone was the meat of the defense, and as expected, there was no need for a ten count. On Friday, November 28, 1958, a three-judge federal court struck down Louisiana's law against integrated athletics.[79]

It also happened to be the last week of the college football season. The MWSA was wading through a tiny puddle of desirables to face top-ranked, undefeated LSU in the classic's silver anniversary game. Immediately, conjecture churned over Sugar landing an exciting intersectional team that only days earlier had been off-limits. Newsmen even contacted the Department of Defense asking if a service team could be green-lighted.

After Saturday's tilts, however, it was announced that the bowl's technically "intersectional" team would come from South Carolina. The Atlantic Coast Conference's twelfth-ranked Clemson, with its two losses in a notoriously weak schedule, was signed to face the national champion Tigers. A lot of hope had built up in one weekend, and bitter disappointment stirred up Lemon Bowl flashbacks. Still, sportscasters reasoned that the ruling had come too last-minute but that big changes were in store once the state's appeals were exhausted.

That point was reached on Monday, May 25, 1959. Governor Long's prediction of the law's easy demise was affirmed. Unfortunately, he was not available for comment. When the news hit the press, Long was fighting in the Louisiana House to protect Black voting rights. Two days later, he was confined to a Galveston, Texas, mental asylum.[80]

|||||

William Rainach choreographed the lawmakers' summer meeting as a personal duel with Earl Long. The senator was eyeing the next governorship and looking to thwart Long's rumored run for reelection. The governor was scheming to resign just before the end of his term in order to sidestep the state's law against back-to-back tenures, and Rainach was getting a head start in using Long's racial moderation against him. First, Rainach doubled the appropriations for the JLCS, knowing that Long could strike down the $10,000 increase, and probably wanting him to. The senator saw public pressure on the issue as "tremendous." "He can veto it," Rainach told reporters, "and take the consequences." Long replied without hesitation, "I'll veto the hell out of it."[81]

Likewise, the senator's comrades in the White Citizens' Councils had their own devious conspiracy. They launched widespread voter purges, using tiny registration errors to remove thousands of African Americans from the rolls. This strategy was two-pronged. It deprived Long of a large bloc of Black votes *and* coerced him to fight for Black rights, costing him additional ballots from reactionaries. Again, Long fought. He pushed forward bills to ease voter registration, only to have Rainach crush them in the Senate.[82]

Long did not back down, though. He dusted off his voting measures and walked them over to the House, where they were tacked to another bill as amendments. This required some clever and risky maneuvering by Long's allies, particularly Representative Ben Holt of Alexandria. In fact, the bill was eliminated from the session by a one-vote margin before Holt moved for reconsideration. He boldly tried to pry lawmakers from the grip of the JLCS.

"You don't have to shake your knees and hide under a desk just because Garrett and Rainach say a bill is a bad bill," Holt blasted. "Stand up and be a man."[83]

A suspiciously long recess ensued, after which one representative announced that he had misunderstood and had voted opposite his intentions. Another claimed that someone else pushed his button. Holt again asked for another vote. Speaker Angelle approved the motion, based on the "confusion" surrounding the initial tally. Wellborn Jack, who had rules suspended to kill Tessier's proposal in 1956, waved his little red rule book at Angelle, insisting the issue remain tabled.

"I am not going to be one of your admirers," Jack told the Speaker.

"Thank you," Angelle replied. "The same goes for you, Mr. Jack."

Garrett, too, raised frenzied objections, which Angelle informed him were out of order.

"It is you who are out of order, sir," Garrett replied.

The Speaker fired back, "Well, try to put me in order if you can."

As Earl Long stood quietly in the rear doorway, a new vote was taken, and the decision was reversed. The amended bill would go before Judiciary Committee B in two days.[84]

The following night, the governor held a party at his home, and the Senate adjourned early so lawmakers could attend. Long admittedly "danced, and jigged, and cut-up at the mansion party" but did not sleep. His appearance at the next morning's hearing was haggard, but it reflected more than one night of hard living. For months, the governor had been pushing his limits and alternating between alcohol, cigarettes, sleeping pills, and stimulant drugs. His image was shocking. His legendary humor and idiosyncrasies had turned to violent outbursts and incoherent ramblings. Rumors were stirring that the governor was ill.[85]

The judiciary hearing was advertised like a prizefight, pitting Rainach and Long head-to-head, and spectators filled the gallery. Holt made another eloquent appeal. "I'm tired," he said, "of sitting here and watching bills go through this House which deprive people of their rights," and he warned his fellow legislators against being "too meek or too weak to represent their people." After arguing that the state should uphold the rights of all its citizens, he prodded, "Don't you think so, Mr. Garrett?"[86]

Garrett said nothing, but Holt further singled out Rainach's cronies, saying, "I am not going to swallow every pill that two or three men try to hand me." He endured some hoots as he made his case, but he had the committee's vote, at 9 to 6 in his favor. Then he encountered an unexpected threat.

The governor, who had been pacing the room and changing seats, started interrupting his loyal supporter. Occasionally swigging from a spiked soda bottle, Long repeatedly took the microphone to tell strange and inappropriate stories with little if any relevance to the bills. Despite the tape recorders, schoolchildren, and nuns in the room, Long spoke obscenely and only became more offensive the longer he talked.

He even solicited questions. "I hope Rainach asks me something," he announced. "I'm loaded for Willie."

"You're loaded, period," barked the attorney for the JLCS.

Another onlooker suggested that the governor's rumored illness was "constipation of the brain and diarrhea of the mouth." Undeterred, Long discounted the "slander" and continued his erratic performance. Finally, three hours into the meeting, the governor staggered out, and the committee promptly voted down his amendments.[87]

Once he regained a clearer head, Long realized the damage he had done. He called his advisers to the mansion and it was decided the governor could make amends by issuing a sincere, statesmanlike apology before the legislature. A carefully worded speech was prepared, and the next evening Long again stood in the House.

The instant he started speaking, it was clear all was lost. He took off his glasses, set the speech on the podium, and talked off the cuff. He bellowed with wrath and shelled out indiscriminate insults. Adversaries were singled out as hypocrites and hustlers. Even supporters were debased as "flunkies." At least two legislators were bullied to tears, and others were flushed with rage. Sweat poured from Long's forehead as he shouted and banged on the lectern. He occasionally touched on the bills, but everything was punctuated with garbled mumblings and disjointed anecdotes. This went on for ninety minutes. Then, after several refused attempts, the governor's aides finally convinced him he had said enough and escorted him from the chamber.[88]

The next morning, Long's family had him committed to a mental health facility, leaving many Black supporters believing that segregationists had "broken" their governor. Meanwhile, the legislature carried on, and Rainach told reporters the racial fight was consuming all his time. Still, he found a moment to comment on Act 579. He called the decision "reckless" but said he believed "the custom still remains with or without the law." Likewise, Garrett announced with cast-iron certainty, "We will continue to have segregated athletics in the state of Louisiana."[89]

CHAPTER 3
Three and Out

When City Park administrators filed into their boardroom on Sunday, March 20, 1960, the chairman announced a lineup change. The leadoff would now be Jack DeFee, former president of the New Orleans Pelicans farm team. DeFee wanted the stadium for a two-game exhibition series between the Cleveland Indians and the Boston Red Sox. Given his long-standing relationship with City Park, the application seemed largely a formality. Contracts with the two Major League Baseball clubs were signed, and the dates requested were only three weeks away.

Still, DeFee gave a customary presentation and accepted questions. One member asked whether any Black players would be fielded on the local diamond, and DeFee casually affirmed that Boston and Cleveland were integrated, as were all the big league teams by then. Believing all legal roadblocks had been dismantled, he was surprised the issue raised concerns. But when asked directly, he realized he was not entirely sure about the status of the interracial sports ban.

When the chairman excused DeFee, assuring him of a quick decision, the deliberation that followed was less about the spring exhibitions than the state legislation. DeFee was not alone in his uncertainty over Act 579. Out of two dozen park execs, not one could guarantee whether it was still in effect. Some thought it had been overturned, but the majority believed it remained on the books. So they prepared a statement explaining that Louisiana law stood between the Big Easy and big league baseball.

As the group calculated its wording, one leery member pushed for a watered-down alternative. He suggested rejecting the request outright, without reference to the racial issue. The substitute motion received no second, however, and the board's full response was released: "Inasmuch as the state law prohibits mixing of races as participants in athletic games, until the law is declared unconstitutional, this board is not in a position to consider such athletic events."[1]

It had been ten months since the Supreme Court confirmed the demise of Louisiana's law against integrated play, and yet the ruling had not made enough of a ripple for even these sports administrators to notice. Not much fuss was made, because the statute's undoing seemed inconsequential. As Rainach and Garrett predicted, the custom of segregated sports could continue independently of any law. Politicians and sportswriters alike pointed out that racial mixing was not demanded, merely decriminalized. Even Irwin Poché, who thought the ruling "should help sports in Louisiana," also acknowledged the more popular outlook. "However, it doesn't mean we have to compete against Negroes," he conceded. "It just gives us the privilege to invite them."[2]

Moreover, when the decision was announced, there were doubts that any athletics beyond boxing would integrate. If, as with New Orleans's narrow adherence to the City Park verdict, the litigation freed only the sport mentioned in it, not even the Mid-Winter Sports Association would be affected. The group had just voted to drop boxing from its calendar, sensing growing public distaste for organized fights.[3]

The Sugar Bowlers were hesitant to make early predictions, although several members, like Poché and newly elected president Monk Simons, were optimistic that a revolution was in store. Before announcing any policy change, they consulted their attorneys, who determined that all sports were included in the sweeping decree. The Supreme Court declared "unconstitutional on its face 'Louisiana's Act 579 of 1956,' so far as it deals with athletic contests."[4]

That statement, however, actually indicated that the MWSA would *not* soon be scouting outside the Deep South. The second half of Act 579—dealing with crowds rather than contests—was untouched. Even where athletes might be integrated, segregation of spectators was still state law. It would have benefited Sugar Bowlers more in reverse. On their wish list, universities with policies against segregation far outnumbered those with Black athletes. The list of off-limit schools was no shorter.[5]

Not even boxing had integrated in town. Despite some early optimism about interracial cards bringing in a torrent of cash, public pressure and long-held customs prevailed. The only integrated local contest since the May 1959 decision was a February basketball game at Loyola's private Field House. The local Jesuit school brought in Loyola of Chicago's squad, with its two Black players, on a Wednesday night. With a small, niche crowd, the tilt received neither opposition nor much attention. As it was, by March, even gatekeepers of the city's largest municipal stadium were unaware they could host integrated athletics.[6]

Aware or not, City Park was in a unique position to bring national sports back to New Orleans. Unlike the Sugar Bowl's Tulane Stadium, City Park Stadium had been unchained from *both* aspects of Act 579. The stands were desegregated along with the other park facilities when the Supreme Court affirmed Judge Wright's ruling in December 1958. Still, not surprisingly, few African Americans had ventured into newly accessible stadium spaces in the previous fifteen months. For example, only two of thirty-eight prep football games played there that year were between Black high schools.[7]

The stadium had actually been integrated for all of the city's 1959 Double-A baseball games, which were held at City Park after the leveling of Pelican Stadium. But this hardly resulted in enough racial mixing to cause any community buzz. Black New Orleanians had boycotted the hometown team (in the all-white Southern Association) for the previous four seasons, following the club's refusal to hire African American players. Around a half dozen Black baseball fans "tested" the stadium's integration in 1959, but they went largely unnoticed by white ticket holders. So few people of any race attended the lackluster Pels games that year that no fans had to "mix" at all in the mostly empty stadium. In fact, the club folded before the 1960 season, and DeFee's proposed big league series was intended to recoup losses and pay down debts.[8]

The City Park board's statement on the games hit the press on Monday morning and was quickly criticized for citing a defunct statute and canceling the city's first taste of pro baseball in years. Embarrassed and on the spot, the board consulted the city attorney, who confirmed that the ban's erasure had been finalized nearly a year earlier. The group hurriedly repolled its members. Although they had very little precedent preparing them for a large-scale, completely integrated event, they also had no reason to forbid it. DeFee was given the green light.

Teams were rushing to finalize their tours, and the integration issue raised red flags about New Orleans anyway. By Monday night the Red Sox were arranging to park the two tilts in Houston instead. Mayor Morrison, however, was always willing to go to bat for baseball. He immediately telephoned Boston's traveling secretary with a personal guarantee. Afterwards, it was announced that big league baseball was coming back to New Orleans.[9]

Morrison's repeated efforts to rescue baseball previously had sparked outrage in the Black community. He had been the principle force in securing City Park Stadium for the homeless Pelicans, and for years he organized fundraisers to keep the sinking club in town. This quest to save a segregated private business stood in stark contrast to the little attention Morrison gave to Black school sports or to minimally equipped Black-designated parks. Now the mayor's zeal for the Major League series provoked the wrath of the White Citizens' Council, which orchestrated its own boycott. And Black baseball fans relinquished to white segregationists the long-used slogan of putting "principles before pleasures."[10]

Morrison had not given up on reviving the Pelicans and was using every opportunity to drum up local interest in the national pastime. He attacked the Citizens' Councils for "trying to deprive their communities of major league sports" and pointed out that "practically every major Southern city today is begging for these big league games." Lamenting that New Orleans was missing out on the "name and fame" and "dollars and cents" sports generate, Morrison stated that all big-time sports were integrated and that New Orleans needed to be a part of them.[11]

The Citizens' Council's call for a boycott had little impact. No Major League team had played in town since 1957. After Act 579 passed, only the then all-white Boston club stopped in New Orleans, scrimmaging one game with the Pels. Following that, the only big league action in town was Joe DiMaggio's four swings at Pelicans training camp in 1959. When Morrison invited the Yankee Clipper, fans packed Kirsch–Rooney Stadium and erupted in deafening applause when Joltin' Joe knocked his fourth pitch over the left field fence. Columnist Bob Roesler wrote, "You would have thought the blow had just won the World Series." Locals were hungry for big-time sports.[12]

Advance ticket sales relieved any fears about draggy turnstiles. On the other hand, there were concerns over the expected crowds packing together in the unpartitioned stadium. Between City Park's blunder and the Citizens' Council's boycott, the racial situation was getting national attention, and the teams were questioned about needing to relocate. Boston's GM told reporters that the mayor and city council sanctioned the event. "We're only acting under contract," he said. "What happens is their baby."[13]

Between the two games, more than 21,000 tickets were sold, and over a quarter of the fans were Black. The only confrontation was in the stadium's front office, when the teams' brass squabbled with DeFee over complimentary tickets he issued. The biggest takeaway on integrated baseball was that Cleveland's new 6-foot-7, 223-pound rookie, African American Walter Bond, was the most entertaining of all the powerhouse hitters to show off in the small playing area that night.

The turnout looked good for a city begging back into national sports. The general feeling was that locals would buy into the changing world of athletics if the quality of play was high enough. There was optimism in the city's papers that "New Orleans is a 'sports town' that could grow by leaps and bounds."[14]

Some locals were particularly optimistic. Within a month, Bob Roesler leaked a teaser about the "ambitious plans" of an "energetic new organization," which had Jack DeFee as vice president. Without spoiling the "big sports story to break on the local front," Roesler merely assured fans that "some of the city's top sportsmen, who think big, are in on the operation."[15]

|||||

At the April meeting of City Park execs, a happy recap of the baseball experiment led to quick approval of another pro exhibition. This request came from Jack Ciolino, an eager young attorney at the head of nine civic leaders and businessmen who fronted $50,000 to stage the city's next professional tilt. Several members, like DeFee, were previously involved with the city's farm team, but his new cohort was not merely focused on bringing in more Major League exhibitions or retrieving the cast-off Pelicans.

A banquet was held a week later at the Regal Brewery to consummate freshly minted New Orleans Professional Sports Inc. and to announce their first event: an August 1960 preseason clash between the Green Bay Packers and the Pittsburgh Steelers of the National Football League. It had been eleven years since NFL action was staged in New Orleans. It was big news for local fans, and yet that was not the juiciest information released that evening. "Our ultimate aim is to purchase a National Football League franchise," Ciolino revealed. "I think this city is ripe for a pro grid team." The young lawyer checked his enthusiasm by conceding, "Of course, it's a long-range proposal, but that's the final goal, which we're working up to."[16]

The NFL's popularity skyrocketed in the 1950s, and more than half a dozen cities had expressed interest in franchises, though the league made no moves until January 1960. Dallas and Minneapolis were approved, and the long-awaited decision to expand gave countless others hope.[17]

New Orleans got some individualized encouragement when Packers business manager Jack Vainisi sat down with Ed Devenport of the *Times-Picayune*. Vainisi stated, "The game in New Orleans is primarily one of 'feeling out' the prospects of a potential new entrant into the league." Considering the small population and harsh winters in Green Bay, he reasoned, "A city the size of New Orleans has tremendous potential, and the climate down here would be perfect." Vainisi expected the league to award three new franchises "in the not too distant future" and disclosed, "When we think of expansion we immediately look toward the South."[18]

Ciolino's group put out ads telling folks the exhibition was a tryout for New Orleans as a pro football town—and why they should care. The Big Easy was not yet sold on the play-for-pay brand of the sport. Its most recent sampling, a 1949 Detroit–Philadelphia contest, did not make much of an impression. Despite the Eagles showcasing New Orleans's own Steve Van Buren, only a mediocre crowd braved the threat of rain, and the Lions were dominated 45–14. As Devenport explained, "They came; they saw ... and then they went home ... and forgot."[19]

College football was still king in the Deep South, but promoters and sportswriters used that fact strategically. Locals might have forgotten the 1949 NFL exhibition, but they were expected to remember the 1948 Sugar Bowl and to want to see Texas's Bobby Layne lead the Steelers into New Orleans. They also were reminded that Green Bay had former Tulane wideout Max McGee, to receive "wizardly" passes from Alabama alum Bart Starr. And Packer fullback Jimmy Taylor needed no introduction after his glory days at LSU. Bill Keefe devoted a third of a column to listing all twenty-seven incoming players from southern colleges, including African American Willie Davis of Grambling.[20]

There were ample pro-specific story lines to entice fans as well. Layne was just 22 yards shy of breaking Sammy Baugh's total-yards-passing record, and Starr had come off the bench his fourth year with the Pack to close out the 1959 season with four straight wins. Even more intriguing was Vince Lombardi's Cinderella story, coaching a formerly one-win team to a 7–5 record the previous year, his first with Green Bay. Curious locals were encouraged to watch team workouts on Friday, free of charge.[21]

On Saturday night at 7:30, in typically humid mid-August air, two bantam teams further warmed up the field for the pros, who kicked off at eight o'clock. Although it was not the blowout of 1949, the first half was just as forgettable. After newspapers had hyped the league's thrilling aerial attacks and bulldozer running backs, both offenses bogged down. At halftime the squads had just a pair of field goals each. There was an expected lack of gusto in preseason play, but it was also clear that the stadium's sauna effect was further slowing the two northerly teams.

Fortunately for underwhelmed ticket holders and invested sponsors, the second half opened with a spark. Lombardi subbed Lamar McHan in place of Starr, and the veteran started the quarter with an 80-yard drive, capped by a touchdown pass to ex-Greenie Max McGee. On the next drive, Hank Gremminger intercepted Bobby Layne on Green Bay's 5-yard line and returned the ball deep into Steeler territory. Two plays later, Paul Hornung took a lateral from McHan and passed to the 1959 NFL Rookie of the Year, Boyd Dowler, for another score.

The Steelers then orchestrated their own 80-yard series, climaxed by a 4-yard touchdown run through right guard by John Henry Johnson, one of a dozen Black players on the field that night. Taylor even gave his "hometown" fans one more closeout thrill, zigzagging through a porous Steelers defense for 54 yards before the teams dragged their soggy bodies off the muggy field.

For Ciolino and colleagues, the goal had been twofold: to get New Orleans interested in the NFL and vice versa. The results were mixed. Much of the game was undeniably dull. Even Steelers coach Buddy Parker complained his team "just stood still." It was, however, only an exhibition, and the second half provided more than a few highlights. Local sportswriters assured fans that during the regular season—the fall—higher stakes and lower temps brought more fast-paced action. At the very least, many New Orleanians got their first taste of the professional ranks, seeing big names and familiar faces in a close game.

Expecting to match the 10,000 advance sales on game day, Ciolino and DeFee were admittedly disappointed that only around 17,000 (of 26,000) seats were filled. Still, it was a good-looking turnout for a glorified practice, and investors came out in the black. Moreover, Vainisi was not the only Packer looking favorably toward the Big Easy. Three days after scrimmaging the Steelers—and after an eleven-year pro football drought in New Orleans—Green Bay announced plans to revisit in 1961.[22]

|||||

Ciolino and DeFee were not the only New Orleanians with feelers in pro football. Another local businessman, David Dixon, had made quiet contacts a year earlier, but his plans did not involve auditioning through exhibitions and waiting for the NFL to expand again. In the summer of 1959, his goal had been to field a team in 1960.

The upstart American Football League (AFL) was taking shape then, led by a group of potential owners tired of brushoffs from the NFL, and Dixon sat down with the circuit's architects, Lamar Hunt and Bud Adams. The league was soon to be christened as an even number of teams, presently six, but Dixon believed New Orleans had a shot at getting in (perhaps along with Miami) for the inaugural season. He left the talks hopeful—and schooled on the importance of a proper stadium.[23]

Dixon's next stop was the office of attorney Joseph Merrick Jones, president of the Tulane University Board of Administrators. The 26,000-seat City Park Stadium was not equipped for housing pros and would be difficult to expand. Dixon needed Tulane Stadium, and he took his request straight to the top. Jones agreed to a brief chat on short notice but asked for a written proposal. Once Jones reviewed Dixon's outline, the two gentlemen met for a lengthier conversation at Pascal's Manale Restaurant.[24]

Dixon sounded much like Mayor Morrison, with whom he also spitballed his ideas that summer, arguing that both Houston and Dallas were laboring to go "major league" in baseball and/or football, making New Orleans seem "bush league." Unlike Morrison, however, Dixon preached, "Baseball here is dead." "Football, on the other hand," he argued to Jones, "could be a smashing success." It would also, he added, spare New Orleans "the embarrassment of being 'out in the cold.'" Dixon dismissed a catalog of potential concerns, from interference with Tulane football to complaints from nearby residents. He flipped the script on every issue, claiming that attendance for the Greenies would increase with the pros in town and that the school's neighbors would "gladly cooperate" because of the "importance of major league football to the community."[25]

Jones's response reined in his companion's enthusiasm, just a little. This would not be a quick sell to the board of administrators. Dixon's own laundry list of sticking points was proof. Tulane would need much more than a rough sketch and an energetic salesman before agreeing to house a team. Jones did, however, give Dixon personal encouragement to push on.

That was even more reinforcement than Dixon needed. Still, he paused on the project for a couple of years. Not long after his meeting with Jones, Dixon's plywood company received a shoddy shipment from abroad and his priority became disposing of inventory and saving his business. And there was one other reason Dixon chose to sit back before again inviting a national sports league into New Orleans: in late 1959 he felt "a more prudent course would be to observe carefully the results of racial legislation then imminent."[26]

|||||

After three successful big league events in four months and promises of more on the way, in August 1960, New Orleans was trending upward in national sports. When Ciolino announced the town's spot on the NFL's next tour, however, it took less than twenty-four hours for the area's racial problems to again make national news. On August 17, Louisiana governor Jimmie Davis seized control of Orleans Parish schools in an attempt to prevent federally mandated integration.[27]

In the summer of 1959, the local board of education was given seven months to create a desegregation plan. When the group failed, Judge Wright issued his own plan, ordering integration of the entire first grade when classes resumed in September 1960. Three weeks out, Davis usurped authority over the city's schools and vowed to be jailed before allowing racial mixing in a Louisiana classroom.[28]

James H. Davis, a professional country music singer, had just beaten Chep Morrison for the governorship. Rainach stayed in the race long enough to keep segregation the hottest topic and then threw his support to Davis. Morrison forfeited his reputation as a racial moderate for the sake of the election, but Davis still rode his promises of racial separation into the governor's mansion.[29]

Widespread reports of Davis's takeover also detailed two suits filed to stop it, giving the governor ample warning of federal marshals' plans to serve him with a subpoena. Consequently, Davis evaded the summons for two days. Nevertheless, marshals issued a copy to his secretary and ordered workmen to secure it to a coffee table under a sheet of clear plastic. When Davis's receptionist shrank back from a duplicate and it fluttered to the floor, it too was affixed under a plastic cover. A third document was left on the steps of the governor's mansion, weighted down by concrete blocks.

Once the marshals left, Davis strode back into town. Blushing and laughing with reporters, the governor claimed he would never hide from anyone. He explained that he had gone fishing, had caught a catfish and a turtle, but incidentally never saw a subpoena. Davis was adamant he had no reason to appear in court.

National media had a field day with the unfolding circus. Newspapers printed photos of workmen bolting Plexiglas to office furniture and of a cinder block paperweight labeled "Do not touch." Davis's antics invited comparisons to Orval Faubus. New Orleans was shaping up to be another Little Rock. And the whole country was watching.[30]

There was not an empty seat for the federal hearing on August 26. Counsel for both the NAACP and a group of thirty-one white parents asked the court to keep schools open. Davis indeed did not show, but State Attorney Jack Gremillion was present, briefly. After having all his motions for dismissal or continuance denied, Gremillion snapped at the judges, "You are not playing the game according to the rules." He then slammed a law book on his table and stormed out, screaming as he barreled down the aisle, "I'm not going to stay in this den of iniquity." Absent any state representation, the judges ordered schools returned to local authority and forbade the governor from interfering.[31]

Days later, four of the five members of the Orleans Parish School Board went to Judge Wright's chambers with white flags in hand. They presented what he had asked for in March, a workable strategy for initiating integration. The board requested additional time to implement a gradual pupil placement plan. Such blueprints, already used in the South, were essentially federally sanctioned ways to comply at a bare minimum.

Wright granted an extension, trusting that the board was acting in good faith and that *some* first-grade classes would integrate when the second quarter opened in mid-November. After 137 applications were reviewed under the vague and subjective criteria of the plan, four African American six-year-old girls were burdened with desegregating New Orleans public schools.[32]

As the new academic term approached, the Louisiana legislature established a committee to again usurp control of Orleans Parish schools, and on November 14, 1960, plainclothes troopers were sent to every New Orleans grade school to enforce a freshly minted statewide holiday. Mayor Morrison, however, invoked the tenet of "home rule," which he pointed out was a favorite of Garrett and his cronies in their fight for states' rights. In an election six days earlier, a singular vacant school board slot had been filled by the only candidate calling for open schools, and the mayor equated the vote to a local referendum on the matter. Morrison promised to maintain order, told principals to open classes, and instructed city police to preserve the peace.[33]

Just before nine o'clock on that Monday morning, federal deputy marshals did one final sweep of the Ninth Ward and drove unmarked cars to the homes of four first-grade girls. The names of the students and schools had been withheld, but as police presence increased near the McDonogh 19 and William Frantz elementary schools, locals caught wind, and crowds formed around the campuses.

On St. Claude Avenue, before several hundred onlookers, U.S. marshals stepped from their vehicles, wearing dark suits with gold armbands and lapel badges. They walked three students and their parents into McDonogh 19 Elementary. When an uproar erupted from some white spectators, police quickly ushered the gathering from the sidewalk and onto the median, which, ironically, locals call the "neutral ground." Jeering and chanting continued, but that was it. The most dramatic action was white parents withdrawing their children from class and being cheered as they reemerged with their young, confused symbols of opposition.[34]

Similarly, at 9:25 a.m., on North Galvez Street, when little Ruby Bridges approached the doors of her yellow brick schoolhouse, clutching her mother's hand, she was met by throngs of adults and teenagers shouting and singing. However, this was nothing altogether unusual for a New Orleanian child to see. As she walked along the noisy, heavily lined streets in her stiffly starched dress with a big white bow in her hair, she thought she was in a Mardi Gras parade.[35]

School board president Lloyd Rittiner told reporters on Monday afternoon that the lack of an "appreciable amount of demonstration" signaled that "the people of New Orleans are going to accept the inevitable." National media depicted New Orleans favorably, emphasizing the defiance of the Louisiana legislature and the overall lack of violence. Tuesday's coverage brought new stories of decreasing attendance at McDonogh and Frantz, along with increasing "rowdiness" of protesters. But even these reports looked good for New Orleans. Police arrested a dozen white demonstrators for disturbing the peace or breaking barricades. In addition, the school board announced it would begin truancy procedures against students who were being held out of class. National newspapers reported Rittiner's other comment as if it were fact: "The worst is over."[36]

Then, on Tuesday night, there was a three-hour Citizens' Council rally in the city's Municipal Auditorium. In April, when the NAACP had asked to use those facilities, Morrison denied the request, saying he did not want to endanger racial harmony. NAACP reps countered that segregationist groups often staged events there in which speakers "urge discord and violation of the law." These were certainly the themes of the rally on November 15.[37]

A crowd of well over five thousand packed the auditorium, singing songs, stamping feet, waving signs, and passing petitions, but Rainach and Garrett stole the show. Garrett announced that the fight for segregation was "no longer a legal battle." "We are now ready for action," he exclaimed. Rainach called on the crowd to "use the 'scorched earth' policy," proposing that the city "empty the classes where they are integrated." He argued, "A day lost can be made up; a week, a year lost is not fatal." Garrett reinforced the call by announcing the legislature had revoked the state's truancy laws. But the pair did not stop there. Rainach urged the audience to use "every sort of pressure available." He declared, "If we extend this civil disobedience far enough, we'll bring the courts to their knees in this battle." The auditorium boomed with applause when it was announced that this renewed backlash would begin with a march on the school board offices the next morning at ten o'clock.[38]

As instructed, a crowd amassed near City Hall early Wednesday. With the number of protesters growing into the thousands, New Orleans police redoubled their presence. A bus of reinforcements unloaded on the lawn of the supreme court building, and many officers patrolling around the two integrated schools were reassigned downtown. Raising crudely lettered signs and angry voices, the swelling group set out to besiege the school board a few blocks away. Cops maneuvered three-wheeled motorcycles to hold back the mob, but crazed demonstrators broke through and wrestled with club-yielding patrolmen in the street. As one officer seized a pair of offenders, he shouted, "They've gone berserk. There's at least five thousand of them."

Unable to contain the rioters, police turned to the fire department. A warning sounded that the crowd would either "break up or be hosed down." "Turn on the water. Turn on the water," screamed ringleaders. The firemen obliged. When hoses were on, the group retreated slightly, but each time the spraying stopped, the crowd rushed forward again. When the drenched insurgents tired of this back-and-forth, the mob splintered and dispersed, leaving sopping Citizens' Council pamphlets littering the streets. That was when the real trouble began.[39]

What started as one giant mass of loud demonstrators with signs quickly turned into countless small bands of thugs with weapons, and any African American was a potential target. Cars, trucks, and buses carrying Blacks were hit with rocks and full glass soda bottles. Several Black men who crossed paths with these roving groups were stoned, jumped, and beaten. One African American teen was stabbed on his walk back to work from lunch. The city's cops, two of whom were injured, stayed busy through the rainy afternoon.

By nightfall, many Blacks were retaliating, reversing the daytime trend when almost all arrests were of whites. In the worst violence, a group of African Americans shot a Caucasian man, but many other confrontations occurred on dimly lit downtown streets. By sunrise on Thursday, more than two hundred arrests had been made, and dozens of citizens, Black and white, had been hurt.[40]

Downtown New Orleans was relatively quiet on Thursday, as the focus of segregationists—and salivating journalists—returned to the integrated campuses. The call for emptying those schools was almost a total success. No more than five white students attended Frantz or McDonogh 19 after the riots. However, a group of white women made it their mission to render the boycott complete. Every school day, around forty of them, most dressed in toreador pants, tattered coats, and colorful head scarves, clustered to block the entrance to William Frantz Elementary.[41]

In response, a group of white, liberal, upper-class female activists created a "ferry service" to escort Black and white parents and children to and from school, but even they were bombarded with eggs, spit, insults, threats, and curses. Some were shoved and pummeled before police intervened. The protesters, so-called cheerleaders, banged on car roofs and threw stones. The Citizens' Council obtained the identities and addresses of white boycott breakers and their protective allies, leading to vandalized property, slashed tires, rocks thrown through windows, and the pouring of red paint on porches. Angry, obscene, and threatening phone calls continued day and night.[42]

These cheerleaders relished seeing themselves in newspapers, on television, and in *Time* and *Life* magazines, even when they were photographed screaming at a wide-eyed, confused six-year-old girl. They put on a spectacle, not in spite of the media but for it. And yet television stations had to obscure their soundtracks and newspapers could not print the utterances of these women, which writer John Steinbeck described as "bestial and filthy and degenerate." This was what the world knew of New Orleans, which from all accounts was only one misstep away from another bloody race riot.[43]

| | | | |

On October 24, 1960, three weeks before the schools integrated, the MWSA announced the earliest sellout of tickets in the classic's history—and teams were not even selected yet. The Sugar Bowl was still riding the wave of good fortune that had carried it through the previous four years not only intact but thriving. The January 1, 1960, pairing of Ole Miss and LSU had been a deliberate rematch of a regular season Halloween meeting sportswriters deemed the "Game of the Century." That bowl brought in many thousands of ticket requests beyond capacity and left executive secretary Edna Engert returning roughly $35,000 to disappointed fans. Consequently, for 1961, folks were getting their orders in early.[44]

Just before New Year's Day, however, the two incoming squads, Ole Miss and Rice, returned more than a third of their tickets. Sugar Bowlers were stunned. In years past, Ole Miss had used its full allotments and would have eagerly sold the opposition's leftovers as well. The announcement of a sellout was based on seats sold through Sugar's local office. Now they were facing an eleventh-hour, 10 percent vacancy. Never wanting TV viewers to see empty seats, they went into damage-control mode. Although the weather forecast helped sell some of the surplus, the bulk was donated to the armed forces.[45]

The classic had seemed bulletproof, but images of the still-raging integration crisis were splattered across the nation's news, and memories of the bloody riots were only a month and a half old. Now even other southerners were skipping the Sugar Bowl, and the MWSA could come up with just one explanation: the "school situation." In that year's program, the president's welcome message no longer called New Orleans the International City but rather referred to it more realistically—and ambiguously—as America's Most Interesting City. During bowl week, hotels advertised vacancies and restaurants had open tables.[46]

The same was true for Mardi Gras in February. The tourism and hospitality industries were wrecked. Some French Quarter merchants saw business fall off worse than it had during the Depression. New Orleans was no longer the destination for revelry and leisure but a place of violence and indifference.[47]

The indifference hurt the city more than the violence. As the school crisis wore on, reporters noted that a very small minority had sparked the chaos publicized around the world. Journalists from Los Angeles to Wall Street to London also pointed out that the bigger problem was the disengagement of the majority. One British newsman observed that "the general public did little to help," and the *New York Times* noted that most citizens "were reluctant to make any public attempt to resolve the problem."[48]

Although the mayor and police department took a tough stand during the first two days, after the rioting they put up the least possible resistance.

Two months earlier, six African Americans were arrested while peacefully picketing for fair employment, outside a South Claiborne shopping center. Morrison said he had ordered the arrests based on state laws against public disturbances and blocked sidewalks. He vowed that "henceforth" the police would disallow such demonstrations and preserve "peace and order." Yet none of the cheerleaders were arrested. One cop even told the women it was OK to throw eggs but just not to hurt anyone by throwing a rock.[49]

A white boycott breaker disclosed, "The worst thing is that no one seems to care about us. They think they can close their eyes and all this will pass away." One of two families bullied out of town was given political asylum in the Northeast. The parents were honored by the governor of Massachusetts and the mayor of Providence, Rhode Island. The mother was named "Woman of the Year" by a Brooklyn high school. Yet Mayor Morrison dismissed their plight, referring to them as "floaters," who had "no real roots in New Orleans" and suffered no hardship in leaving.[50]

Morrison said little and did even less to curb the crisis. He was safeguarding his political ambitions, but his reticence was also born of resentment. Much like Earl Long's stubborn stance on the sports ban, Morrison's hands-off position reflected his frustration with the city's complacent elite. Any criticism from local business leaders was directed at the media's "unfair misrepresentation" of New Orleans. On the rare occasions that businessmen spoke of being "ashamed" or "disturbed" by the chaos, they always did so anonymously.[51]

It was not only public pressure, however, that silenced the Establishment, which had long been happy to preserve its power in the status quo. As activist Betty Wisdom said at the time, there was nothing new about "the deadly apathy toward progress in New Orleans." "This is one of the few American cities I know of," she lamented, "in which the populace is still content with bread and circuses once a year and the aristocracy, having provided the free show, feels no obligation to provide anything further."[52]

|||||

Once thought of as the "Paris of the South," New Orleans had become one of the South's cautionary tales. Atlanta and Dallas were on deck for school desegregation in autumn 1961. Officials there looked at the successes of Houston and Miami but learned far more from New Orleans's template of what *not* to do.[53]

In Dallas, city police studied "mob control" and adopted the catchphrase of "law and order." However, the driving force for peaceful integration in that city was an all-white group of local business leaders. In addition to producing pamphlets and films to foster a favorable climate, the group organized a stepped program for integrating thirty-six white downtown restaurants and cafeterias in July. A spokesman explained, "We thought this should be an adult experience before it is a child experience."[54]

Similarly, a truce was reached in Atlanta, stopping lunch counter sit-ins to ensure a peaceful atmosphere when schools reopened, and merchants agreed to desegregate immediately thereafter. The feisty Mayor Hartsfield announced as early as April that any segregationists wanting to cause trouble in his town should know they were "going to get their heads knocked together." "We're going to ride herd on these damned rabble rousers," said the mayor. His force of seven hundred cops were specially trained in riot control and equipped with K9 units.[55]

In these last months of Hartsfield's tenure, changes were occurring that would invite more industry and visitors to the Georgia capital, which he declared was "a city too busy to hate." When the new international airport opened with no racial designations in late May, the city's taxicabs also removed their NEGRO and WHITE passenger signs. The mayor talked excitedly about "living through this changing south," in which he believed "Atlanta is the leader."[56]

When Atlanta's four integrated high schools opened peacefully in late August, the nation's media—and its president—agreed with Hartsfield. President Kennedy urged all cities facing desegregation to "look closely at what Atlanta has done." Documentaries were aired showing white and Black civic groups working together the previous year to achieve "quiet integration." Newspapers exclaimed, "The whole nation is deeply indebted to Atlanta for its fine example."[57]

A week later, eighteen Black first-grade students walked through the doors of eight formerly all-white Dallas schools, and the police taskforce was not even called to escort them. The closest thing to a crowd of spectators was a few curious residents peeking from behind window curtains or over fences. The most arduous charge law enforcement undertook was traffic control. Describing both Atlanta and Dallas, the media noted "public indifference," but this meant something very different than it had in New Orleans. In Georgia and Texas, the integration of schools unfolded "as though it was an everyday occurrence."[58]

As New Orleans made its own preparations for the reopening of schools in 1961, civic leaders conceded that they could not afford to remain "indifferent." In addition to the vital tourism industry, also hanging in the balance was a colossal NASA contract for the city's Michoud plant to build rocket boosters in the nation's race to the moon. There were no efforts to prepare adults for integration or to motivate locals to buy into racial progress, but there was a last-minute drive to exert pressure against protesters. A week before school started, a full-page "Declaration of Principles" ran through local papers, asserting that *"lawlessness, intimidation,* and *coercion* are not tolerated in our city" and listing the names of hundreds of prominent New Orleanians who supported the campaign.[59]

The day before on-campus registration, three television channels and eight radio stations aired a program in which civic leaders and public officials called on locals to prevent another embarrassment that would jeopardize the city's industries. Mayor Victor Schiro, newly in office, emphasized repairing the city's image, but he did so without calling for any deeper change. He reminded citizens that the "whole world is looking at New Orleans," and pushed, "This must be the public's concern." Then, to preempt knee-jerk grasping at the old ways of doing things, Schiro assured listeners the city could be *both* "the traditional city and the city of progress."[60]

Likewise, the city's chamber of commerce announced that it had "no position to make" beyond requesting an orderly school year. The Central Labor Council put it more bluntly, stating that it was "not asking citizens to change their opinions but only to respect the law," explaining that "the growth and prosperity of the city" depended on it. Finally, the police superintendent announced that his men would avert even the slightest incident. Giarrusso made it clear that this time cops would "draw no lines," saying, "They must act against anyone who violates the law."[61]

When classes resumed, twelve African American first- and second-graders integrated six New Orleans schools without any "cheerleading," rioting, or violence. Police dispersed one small group of white female picketers near Frantz within minutes, something not done in three full quarters of the past academic year. At recess, a tiny shoving match started between a little Black girl and an older white girl over a jump rope, and the sight of a teacher ended it. That was the most sensational story reported. The next day, NASA granted Michoud a multimillion-dollar manufacturing contract for the *Saturn* space vehicle project.[62]

Federal and local law enforcement reduced their spot checks, as did journalists. Reporters were bored out of town and industry was lured in, but nothing more had been achieved beyond a citywide agreement to keep local problems in-house. White attendance was still disturbingly low at all the integrated schools, particularly at McDonogh 19 and Frantz, where less than twenty of the roughly one thousand expected white students were present the first week. Moreover, a few days without hurling eggs would not undo the damage to New Orleans's reputation. As the moderator of the preregistration broadcast put it, the image of the Big Easy had gone from "The City That Care Forgot" to "The City That Forgot to Care."[63]

Despite the promising three-game showcase of 1960, in 1961 there was no big league diamond or gridiron action in the city. DeFee tried to get New Orleans on Major League Baseball's training schedule and Ciolino pushed for a September NFL stop-off, but no pro teams signed with the troubled city. Even plans for the smitten Packers to revisit were canceled. Both professional football leagues were still flirting with the South, just no longer with New Orleans.[64]

Nearly three decades earlier, in 1933, the *New Orleans Item* had editorialized about why the city was lagging in national sports: "Dallas and Atlanta usually do the things that New Orleans ought to do, and get the things that New Orleans ought to get... We sweat at carnival preparations, and fuss with each other over local politics, while the Texans and Georgians go and get what they want, which very often is what we ought to have."[65]

CHAPTER 4
A Naked Bootleg

"I assume that you think that this French wine has made me flip my lid," David Dixon wrote from a rented suite at 34 Rue du Docteur Blanche in Paris. Two years had passed since Dixon shelved his pro football ambitions, and in November 1961 he was making up for lost time. His two arresting concerns had climaxed. As he saw it, the surge and ebb of the school crisis, as well as the profitable sale of his business, "proved the wisdom of postponing further plans." Now he found the project "almost consuming" and spent that week of his European sabbatical drafting letters about it. After all, his wife, Mary, was in Rome visiting her college roommate, there were a few "jeunes filles" to look after his three sons, and failures at ice skating had already immobilized him. So he wrote.[1]

To make the match between New Orleans and pro football, Dixon knew, both parties needed convincing that integration was not a deal breaker. He was also decidedly not timid about his gift for salesmanship. As he penned each letter, he found a new way to spin the issue.

"Integrated seating is no problem if carefully planned," Dixon told a collaborator, Robert Monsted. "Actually, the threat of it would be of tremendous assistance in ticket drives." Envisioning outrage over racial mixing might have tightened most investors' purse strings, but Dixon saw it as a marketing tool. He figured that if sales were opened to bulk orders first, groups would rush to reserve seats as a form of self-zoning. "We can make a great showing of having 'open' seating, yet from a practical standpoint there would not be enough to cause trouble," he reasoned. He also added, with his usual optimism, "I don't think there would be any problem anyway. Did you see the Red Sox–Indian game at City Park last year? Completely integrated seating, and everybody seemed happy."[2]

Still, as this was all moot without a stadium, Dixon got back in contact with Tulane's Joseph Merrick Jones. He even tossed out a new pitch. A mutual friend, Charles Rosen, divulged over a Parisian dinner that the city's tarnished image tormented Jones. So Dixon now pushed that a pro club in Tulane Stadium could generate "counter-propaganda before a national television audience."[3]

Dixon also reached out to another member of the Tulane board, Lester Lautenschlaeger, known to some as "Mr. Tulane," especially when it came to football. "My life is built around Tulane," Lautenschlaeger once said, "or Tulane is built around me." The undefeated 1925 team he quarterbacked sparked the drive to erect Tulane Stadium, and Dixon knew housing a pro squad there would mean going through Lautenschlaeger. Dixon started by plugging the symbiosis between the Ivy League's Pennsylvania and the NFL's Eagles, but he knew he had to address the requisite racial mixing. What he did not know was Lautenschlaeger's take on it. Thus, Dixon simply declared the "racial situation" history. He talked of the "final efforts of the die-hards" and offered the now peaceful schools as proof, dismissing any hesitations as outdated.[4]

There was one more person Dixon needed to persuade, NFL commissioner Pete Rozelle. In 1959, when the AFL was forming, Dixon saw his best shot as being with the tenderfeet. However, their circuit crystalized without him. He also feared they took a "death-blow" with the National Football League elbowing into Dallas and Minneapolis ahead of the AFL's plans to set up shop in both. Consequently, he now made his moves on the NFL.[5]

During a two-year tenure, Rozelle had built a reputation for handling league affairs with integrity. This included a no-nonsense approach to segregation, whether in the Redskins roster or in exhibition stadia. It was clear he would have no patience for the New Orleans on the news the previous year.

Dixon opened his letter to Rozelle with the city's undeniable strengths: its history as a football town, ideal winter weather, popular tourist attractions, and colossal (and *likely* available) Tulane Stadium. But he soon broached "the one question" Rozelle might have about New Orleans's "suitability." Dixon called it "ridiculous" to claim the area had no racial problems but argued that it was "equally ridiculous" to claim that about any American cities, including those housing NFL teams. He referenced the town's history as a port and its "Old World background" to argue that New Orleans was "undeniably one of the very few truly cosmopolitan cities in America." Therefore, Dixon said, it was also "completely unlike any other city in the geographical South." He gave his assurance that "public racism is out of date in New Orleans and probably never has been 'in style.'"⁶

After that week of thinking about little more than an NFL franchise, Dixon became convinced he could make it happen. He also became impatient with trying to set it in motion from an ocean away. Waiting was not his strong suit. He shot off a follow-up to Jones before receiving any reply, and he peppered letters to Monsted with prods like "Incidentally, did you break your typewriter?"⁷

Dixon stayed in touch with American football. He made fake bets and complained that he never picked so well when money was at stake. He followed the Sugar Bowlers' bidding saga, predicted Coach Pilney's dismissal from his two-win Tulane team, and regretted that the LSU clippings his mother sent left him "cold," lacking the excitement of a live gridiron.⁸

Dixon determined that if he received "even a faint ray of encouragement" from Joseph Merrick Jones or Pete Rozelle, he would fly stateside immediately. On the last day of November, Dixon got a tiny flicker from the commissioner. It was a note saying simply, "I sincerely appreciated your letter indicating an interest on the part of New Orleans for a National Football League franchise. I would be pleased to meet with you to discuss New Orleans on your next visit to New York City."⁹

Dixon just needed to decide what business to claim was bringing him to the Big Apple straightaway. He sent sidekick requests to Monsted and other influential friends, including former mayor Chep Morrison and local oil tycoon William Helis. Of course, Dixon also checked the NFL schedule to try to squeeze in a Giants game at Yankee Stadium.

Anxious as he was, he had an uncharacteristic bout of hesitation. He still had no word from Jones, or from Lautenschlaeger, who was undoubtedly preoccupied with Tulane's search for Coach Pilney's replacement. Dixon also suspected that Rozelle might be more receptive after the league's season ended. Besides, the winter holidays were approaching, when families made plans to be together, not splinter apart.¹⁰

This mattered a great deal. Dixon's love for Mary topped even his football obsession. But when she returned to find him manic over the venture, she gave him and his go-bag the go-ahead. He was lucky to have it in advance. A week before Christmas, Dixon received the faintest reassurance regarding Tulane. Charles Rosen, having chatted with Jones, sent a note suggesting there was more reason for optimism than pessimism about the stadium.

Dixon took that as a vicarious reply from Jones, and all hesitation vanished. "Consequently, I'm going to New York," he declared. He arrived at the Waldorf around 5:30 on Tuesday evening, December 19, had Wednesday to shake off jet lag, and appeared at Rozelle's office Thursday morning.[11]

Robert Monsted could not clear his calendar, William Helis was himself in Paris at the time, and Chep Morrison's plans to attend were ruined when Dixon's cable giving the date and time was wrongly transmitted. Thinking, "I would also like a little moral support in my bed," Dixon walked up to 1 Rockefeller Plaza at ten o'clock armed instead with only excitement, charisma, and a lot of civic pride.[12]

Rozelle looked impressed, particularly with the warm climate and beautiful, football-specific stadium. On the subject of race, however, the commissioner seemed far less dazzled. Dixon not only insisted that the problems broadcast around the world were securely in the past but also guaranteed integration across the board, including in hotel accommodations and stadium seating. To Dixon's delight, Rozelle seemed relieved by the pledge and recommended preparing a brochure for the league's spring meeting, which was the earliest time when expansion would be discussed.

On his way out, Dixon asked a fanciful question: whether an existing franchise might be up for sale or transfer. Rozelle said no but asked Dixon to send his addresses along as he toured through Europe, so the league could get in touch if necessary. The request knocked Dixon off his game a bit, and he left with a swelling list of questions.

He made it back to Mary and the boys by Christmas Eve but spent much of that day with his mind still in the commissioner's office. As he connected Rozelle's comments with some sports reports, Dixon wondered whether the St. Louis Cardinals were itching to get out of Busch Stadium, without waiting for a new facility to be retrieved from the bog of politics. He imagined the Cardinals in New Orleans in 1962. He even tossed around some new names, maybe the Cajuns, Buccaneers, or Rebels. "They might take it all next year, you know, assuming no injuries like this year," he thought. "A pennant winner in our first try!"[13]

Unable to wait until after Christmas, Dixon began another letter to Rozelle. Having neither a mastery of the French typewriter nor a secretary to call on that holiday weekend, he prepared a handwritten description of a Cardinals move to the Big Easy benefiting everyone. He spoke boldly. As usual, he wittingly "stepped on toes and then apologized as carefully and diplomatically as possible." Sitting in Paris on Christmas Eve, as visions of pigskins danced in his head, he wrote the commissioner, "Our group can act promptly; in fact, I could be in New York, Miami, or any place within twenty-four hours after receiving your cable."[14]

|||||

On the following Saturday, a Tulane skipper negotiated gusty winds on Lake Pontchartrain, trying to hold the lead in the final race of the MWSA's December 1961 regatta, but a sail of another color nipped ahead at the finish, putting the Green Wave one point behind Rensselaer Polytechnic Institute in the eighteen-race series. It was the first Mid-Winter Sports regatta since 1958, when the event was cut to preserve the carnival's standards. The Tulane hosts now had ten pricey new vessels to offer, and the down-to-the-final-moments scoring signaled a triumph of the reinstated sport. However, for the Sugar Bowlers, success was measured not by the points separating the schools but rather by the miles between them.

Back at their March meeting, each topic made it clearer how greatly segregation handicapped them. The defining feature of their carnival, "the intersectional appeal," was long gone. Paul DeBlanc conceded that the group had "been exceedingly fortunate in the last five years," but he was unsure how long the luck would last. "We still cannot go into another area for our teams," he lamented. "We are the only bowl contained by this thing."[15]

Then they realized that a regatta presented a loophole. First, they learned no Black student had ever sailed in an American collegiate race. Sailing was also a club sport, handled by a dean of students, exempting it from policies of university athletics. Furthermore, MWSA regattas were "open to the public." No tickets were sold.[16]

Sailing offered the MWSA its first step outside the South in five years. DeBlanc sounded hopeful again arguing, "If we can produce good public relations by bringing crews from integrated sections to New Orleans, then it would be a good investment." They ultimately enticed four schools from the East (Coast Guard Academy, Yale, Cornell, and Rensselaer) and four from the Midwest (Michigan State, Ohio State, Ohio Wesleyan, and Purdue).[17]

The football classic, on the other hand, had fielded strictly southern schools for the past five years, and four of those featured LSU or Ole Miss—or both. Consistent with the group's good fortune, these locally popular and Sugar-friendly programs regularly fielded powerhouses. The trend also worked well for both schools, which would have to break precedent, if not policy, to enter an integrated bowl. (This left them eligible for Sugar and for

Cotton, which accepted integrated "visitors" but always fielded an all-white SWC "home" team.) Again in late 1961, LSU and Ole Miss were in the top five and led Sugar's bid talks.[18]

Still, bowl plans were full of headaches. There was no way to know how much ticket sales would rebound so soon after the school crisis. The MWSA considered lowering team allotments and focusing on local sales, but this would only worsen a years-old shriveling of Sugar's expected tourism spike. Recently, even when caravans of fans came in from these neighboring locales, they considered trips to New Orleans old hat and stopped vacationing beforehand. One sportswriter called them "lunch basket carriers," who took off without contributing even a meal's worth of cash to the city's economy.[19]

In addition, the game's five-year contract with NBC was expiring, and the network was hesitant to sign a big, long-term renewal with the rather repetitive Sugar Bowl. The 1961 ratings did not give the MWSA much leverage, and they had nowhere else to go. It was a "delicate situation," in which pushing for a bigger take risked being taken off the air.[20]

Monotony aside, the reliability of LSU and Ole Miss had been a vital crutch for the geographically limited Sugar group. Then it was knocked out from under them in 1961. When bowl speculation began, another all-SEC classic seemed likely, but appealing. It was assumed that fourth-ranked LSU, with rushing sensation Jerry Stovall, would take on number two University of Alabama, which was reasserting its dominance in Bear Bryant's fourth year as head coach. Although the SEC prohibited midseason signings, the MWSA extended a pilot invitation to LSU in early November. The conversation did not go as expected.[21]

The sentiment was growing in, and leaking out of, the Tigers locker room that the squad preferred an out-of-state bowl. An eighty-mile bus trip had never been much of a bonus and by now had lost all novelty. At the November 9 Sugar session, Corenswet reported that LSU's athletic director, Jim Corbett, had stated that his team had no interest in another rematch against Mississippi. Corenswet was told to call Corbett immediately and guarantee him that "under no circumstances" would he have to play Ole Miss again. Mississippi was already (unofficially) committed to Cotton anyway, and the MWSA had its eyes on the Tide.[22]

They feared, however, that the matter might already be meaningless. Corbett had not even asked about other scenarios, suggesting that Sugar was getting little discussion at all in Baton Rouge. Monk Simons wondered whether coach Paul Dietzel would be the "agent" himself or let the players vote. "If he is going to let the squad pick, we would be on thin ice," Simons predicted.[23]

Indeed, on November 15, Corbett announced that LSU would reject any bid to play in New Orleans on January 1. The Tigers had no Rose or Orange invitation, nor any certainty the LSU board would even approve a bid for an integrated bowl. But if it turned out that Sugar was their only option, the team would ring in 1962 from home. This put the MWSA in a tough spot, with little control over their fate. There were extremely few top-quality southern teams left on the board. The committee did what it could, much of which was just wait and hope.

By the end of the week, however, Sugar scooped up Arkansas, which sneaked just inside the top ten with a season-ending blowout of Texas Tech. An upset University of Texas loss to Texas Christian University actually made the Longhorns and Razorbacks SWC cochampions. Cotton's algorithm put Texas in their host seat, but signing Arkansas still gave New Orleans a conference-leading team.[24]

However, that TCU upset also knocked Texas off the top of the national rankings and moved Alabama to number one, which made the Crimson Tide even more attractive to the already flirtatious Rose Bowl, whose Big Ten contract had not been renewed. So when the faculty council of second-ranked, undefeated Ohio State declined the school's invitation to Pasadena, all eyes turned from the Big Ten champ to poll-leading, still-uncommitted Alabama.

The deck was stacked heavily against the Sugar Bowl. The University of Alabama had no policy against playing on an integrated gridiron, and Bear Bryant made no secret of his preference to play in Pasadena. The school had far more history with the California game, and Bryant himself had played for the Tide in the Rose Bowl when Sugar was in its inaugural year. Playing UCLA on the biggest national stage would also be a much more dramatic means of confirming Alabama's resurgence as a football powerhouse. If Alabama went to the West Coast, the MWSA would be left empty-handed. There were no other available southern schools in the top ten, and even thirteenth-ranked Georgia Tech already made a handshake deal with the young Gator Bowl.[25]

This time, a locker room vote swung in Sugar's favor. Bryant's Red Elephants elected, contrary to his preference, to go to New Orleans. Enough of the city's old reputation lingered to lure this band of white, southern, college-age males, and the university kept its word that the squad's choice would hold sway. With the SEC champion, also the number one team in the nation, matched against the SWC cochamp, the MWSA again landed a monumental attraction. They also acquired much-needed fresh blood. It was only Alabama's third appearance in the New Orleans classic, and the first for Arkansas.

This year, the schools matched the local sellout, and both requested extra tickets rather than returning any. Well ahead of the Monday game, downtown sidewalks, shops, and hotels were flooded with out-of-towners munching pralines and talking football. As one newsman commented, "New Orleans was beginning to look like the Sugar Bowl city it is Thursday as early sports fans poured into town for a few days of sightseeing, dining and merrymaking before the New Year's Day football classic."[26]

At their final 1961 meeting, the Sugar men noted the complete sellout, the gratitude of local businesses, and a congratulatory letter from Mayor Schiro. There was also news on their pending television deal. Corenswet announced NBC's offer of a multiyear extension with a 25 percent increase in the bowl's revenue. NBC even agreed to remove some "undesirable clauses" from the new contract. Summing up the latest TV deal for the last all-white classic, Sam added, "Ours will be the only bowl in full color."[27]

|||||

The holidays were anything but restful for David Dixon. By New Year's Day he had polished a complete draft of his brochure for the NFL and sent two copies to the commissioner, one intended for written feedback and the other for Rozelle to have at the league's winter meeting in Miami, just in case.[28]

In the document, Dixon repeated his claims about New Orleans's exceptionalism within the region, which had, regardless, seen its racial troubles "run their course." The brochure read, "Today, our North Louisiana politicians have long since finished making their speeches." A space was left for a letter requested from former mayor Chep Morrison to explain that the school crisis had been both exaggerated by the media and ultimately resolved. Dixon again promised complete integration, from stadium facilities to the city's hotels. He touted that "integrated athletic contests have been conducted," leaving "no precedent to overcome."[29]

He also guaranteed the support of the local press and wanted to include a welcoming note from Cro Duplantier of the *New Orleans States-Item*. However, this was not the first request sent from Europe to the sportswriter. At Dixon's urging, Duplantier had begun in his column a series pushing for professional football in the Big Easy. "My purpose?" Dixon asked. "I do not think that Tulane can be pressured into anything, but I damn sure am not going to make it easy for them to turn us down." He saw no harm in "making pro ball an item of community discussion." Administrators might "think twice when even their grandchildren are talking of it," he reasoned.[30]

Despite confessing to friends that he worried about being "a pest" on the Tulane front, Dixon maintained, "I feel it necessary to continue to hit Mr. Jones every couple of weeks, so that he can't possibly think that I have dropped the matter." The thought itself was comical. "Rozelle will have to have me bumped off before that will happen," Dixon mused.[31]

He also learned from Monsted that a golfing buddy, Edward Poitevent, wanted to join their "pro football conspiracy." Knowing Poitevent to be a skillful attorney with a stellar reputation, Dixon considered him "a most welcome addition." The fact that he was a law partner of Joseph Merrick Jones did not hurt either. Dixon immediately fired off a long epistle to Poitevent, being careful to word things just as he wanted Jones to hear them.[32]

Dixon knew Poitevent worried about the logistics of integration and saw "no use in mincing words." "Our stand in this regard will have to be honest and above board and subject to public scrutiny," he declared. "If any or all of our group want to back off because of personal feelings or misgivings I invite them to do so." Of course, Dixon still saw value in "sensible season ticket planning" and reiterated his idea about group sales making segregation "to a large extent a fact without being official policy." But he left no question about what their "official policy" would be.[33]

"Would New Orleans have turned down the Saturn rocket project because of integrated restrooms at Michoud?" he asked Poitevent. "If our city allows the racial question to keep us out of the NFL we might as well secede from effective participation in national affairs." Before he moved on to solving parking problems at Tulane he added, "I also wish that you would express these views to Mr. Jones."[34]

By mid-January, Dixon still had no word from Tulane's head man, but he again picked up secondhand encouragement from an engagement in Paris, this time with potential investor William Helis, who also believed that Tulane was on board. Furthermore, Dixon thought Helis himself seemed ready to front the funds for the franchise.[35]

Believing the facilities and capital were in the bag, Dixon decided to "withdraw from the situation at home and to concentrate on the problem at hand." He launched a "full-scale campaign" toward the NFL. His strategies became both more inventive and more intrusive. First, Dixon supplemented his many letters with transatlantic phone calls, including one that was patched through from Rozelle's New York office to his Miami hotel, interrupting his post-conference vacation with his wife.[36]

Not long after, Dixon stayed up until 3:00 a.m. counterfeiting correspondence to show Rozelle. In one letter, an unnamed investor was portrayed as doubting the NFL's interest and urging Dixon to woo the AFL instead. The anonymous partner talked of a backyard barbeque where other potential shareholders discussed similar concerns, which were laid out in a bulleted list. There were blank spaces in place of names, and Dixon claimed to have deleted identifying information to protect his friends. He could insist he was not trying to play the leagues off of one another. But his colleagues, he claimed, were getting antsy. In one last letter, Dixon "replied" to this nameless pal, reiterating New Orleans's strengths and guaranteeing "the NFL is not going to drive a city with these qualifications into the other league."[37]

During all this convolution, a (real) letter from Monsted interrupted Dixon's willful neglect of the home front. Dave had sent copies of the brochure to his associates but received no feedback until that late January day. Dumbfounded by the commentary, he immediately fired off a response, which he copied to Poitevent for his legal opinion.

"I did not know that segregated seating was still the law," Dixon wrote in disbelief. "Are you sure?" He had no idea the fully integrated games at City Park rested on a narrowly administered court decision nor that desegregating elsewhere would break more than precedent. As usual, however, Dixon's unfailing optimism kicked in, and he reasoned there was surely a solution devoid of public uproar. "Regardless," he told Monsted, "with the amount of time there is no reason that we cannot get somebody else quietly to file a little suit."[38]

Any fears Monsted's note induced were eclipsed within days as a personal letter from Jones finally arrived. Brief and noncommittal, it was still firsthand affirmation that the board would entertain Dixon upon his return.[39]

"I'm sitting here in Zell am See about to go nuts," he wrote to Monsted. "The skiing is magnifique, but I'm beginning to smell success on this whole deal." The Dixons were only days into a month's reservation at an Austrian resort, and there were four months remaining on their European itinerary. But Dixon could not stand the waiting. "At lunch today I did not hear a word that was said," he lamented. "I had Dior designing uniforms, I had JFK at our opener, I was arranging a trade for Mason and Petitbon."[40]

Mary Dixon was fully aware that even if her husband stayed on their vacation, he was, as he put it, "much too restless to enjoy it fully." "Bless her," he told Monsted. "It is her suggestion that I come home now." Dixon and his luggage would pile onto the *Queen Mary* ocean liner, and if he could survive four idle days at sea, he would disembark in New York on Valentine's Day.[41]

One last letter arrived before Dixon set off for the docks at Liverpool. Poitevent had reviewed the brochure and sent a lengthy reply. He opened with an apologetic warning: "I am in no way attempting to throw cold water on any phase of the matter but am only trying to set out in the cold light of reality the various problems with which we must contend." He confirmed the remaining reach of Act 579. Poitevent agreed it could see a quick defeat but cautioned, "Here, however, the problem presents itself of who will take this step."

But this was not even the greatest hurdle the attorney saw in fulfilling Dixon's promises. "There is a Louisiana law prohibiting the housing of whites and Negroes in the same hotel or tourist court," Poitevent explained. "This is a criminal act, and I do not have any ready solution to this problem as of now." On top of that, he explained another state law allowing restaurants to refuse either race. As he understood it, owners could serve both, but he knew of no white restaurateurs who did.

Poitevent also pointed out that separating teammates would no longer stay under the radar as it might have even a few years earlier. Loyola of Chicago's basketball tilt in New Orleans provided a prime example. Although locals mostly overlooked the game, accommodating the squad in dual hotels and a "colored" restaurant received "very unfavorable publicity" elsewhere. League attorneys could access Louisiana laws, which did not match Dixon's claims. "We would have to have some ready answer," Poitevent concluded.[42]

With weighty information to digest and plenty of cruising time, Dixon headed to America. His first full day on land, he dropped in on Rozelle, catching him just as he left for Baltimore, where the AFL's antitrust suit against his league was being heard. The younger circuit charged that the NFL had moved into Minneapolis and Dallas in 1960 to exclude the competition of its then-budding rival, which initially planned to install franchises in both cities. With the gears of pro football on showcase at the trial, Dixon decided to stop in Maryland himself, to gain a little insight—and to do a lot of schmoozing.[43]

Dixon savored being in the Sheraton-Belvedere Hotel, the leagues' headquarters, less for politicking than for experiencing a spy movie. "Everyone here is suspect," he thought. All the whispering in restrooms and peeking over newspapers amused him. He relished being a momentary subject of intrigue when Rozelle shook his hand in the lobby before a dozen suspicious observers.[44]

The commissioner introduced Dixon to several owners, including George Halas, Art Rooney, and John Mara. Dixon talked up New Orleans, mentioned his franchise interests, and played to the NFL's side in the trial. He quickly learned that even dropping a name from the AFL "is like waving a red flag."[45]

When Dixon returned to New Orleans, his home was still closed up for his intended yearlong sabbatical, so he checked in to a furnished apartment at the Orleanian on St. Charles Avenue. Although his suite sat on the parade route for Carnival's most celebrated krewes, he spent Mardi Gras day, March 6, 1962, making long-distance phone calls and writing follow-up letters to league execs. He also updated the commissioner on an upcoming meeting with Tulane. After that, he did the last thing Pete Rozelle could have expected. He backed off.[46]

|||||

David Dixon was inherently hopeful, but he was also extremely savvy. He crossed an ocean under the belief NFL entry was imminent, but he had a pair of backup plans in his pocket the whole time.

He pondered the antitrust immunities American professional sports enjoyed. "I am confident that Congress's intent was not to set up a special privilege for a select little group," he told Poitevent. "I am also certain that abuse of this legislation would be looked upon most unfavorably." Consequently, he contacted his congressman.[47]

Nine days after Hale Boggs was sworn in as House majority whip, in January 1962, Dixon sent a "premature" request. The two were acquainted well enough that Dixon could expect a response from his fellow Tulane alum. Dixon was selling a racially liberal plan and banking on Boggs's penchant for bridging disparate groups. "The world is moving too fast these days, and we in the South are going to be left in the lurch if we do not move a little faster, too," Dixon asserted. He argued that integrated pro football would give New Orleans and Louisiana a chance "to recover our good name nationally." He claimed "the entire South could benefit." He then explained the reason for his letter.[48]

Dixon conveyed his fear of a perpetual NFL runaround and his thoughts on the antitrust laws. "Would it be completely improper," he asked Boggs, "for me to suggest that a kind word from the very top might even be in order someday in view of the most unusual opportunity for helping a whole section of our country?" He was merely planting a seed, and he assured Boggs,

"I want to follow only perfectly normal channels for the time being." Still, Dixon brooded over the NFL. "I feel it in my bones that at the decisive moment they are going to have to be prodded."[49]

This was not Dixon's only insurance policy. He had also renewed contact with the *AFL,* phoning Houston Oilers owner Bud Adams and Commissioner Joe Foss from the Grand Hotel in Zell am See. With the trial ongoing, the future of pro football was up in the air, and Dixon did not want to look like a nonbeliever if the junior loop prevailed. He imagined Adams saying, "I remember that joker . . . Where was he while we were sweating so hard? Let's let him sweat now." Keeping his options open, Dixon had submitted a formal letter of interest to the AFL from Austria.[50]

Dixon soon was standing before a Tulane committee, which, as expected, was headed by Lautenschlaeger, who alone had more than a few questions and concerns. And for some, Dixon did not yet have an answer. Still, he was satisfied with the outcome. The proposal lived on, and he could smoothen any rough spots at future meetings. There was certainly no rush. Dixon understood the best expansion scenario to be an April promise of a 1964 NFL team. That left plenty of time to hammer out lease details and racial legalities.[51]

The NFL was putting off all business through the trial, but in early 1962 the AFL was on the offensive, working aggressively to assert its staying power and to shore up its strength—win, lose, or draw in the courts. Beating the NFL into the untapped Southeast could potentially gain the younger league an edge, and execs were feeling out virgin territories of Georgia, Florida, Alabama, and Louisiana. Four preseason games were assigned to Atlanta, one each was planned for Miami and Mobile, and Bud Adams was negotiating with New Orleans's City Park for an Oilers exhibition in August. He was on the hunt for local promoters.[52]

Dixon, however, sent a note explaining that his group could not finalize an agreement with Tulane in time and was not interested in promoting anything anywhere else. "Incidentally," he confided to Adams, "City Park has been a graveyard in the past for many hopes."[53]

Jack DeFee, on the other hand, was also still hunting a franchise, and City Park had been good to his group. Especially after their 1961 NFL plans collapsed, they were eager to sponsor the 1962 AFL tilt. Besides, while Dixon was focusing on the NFL from afar, DeFee witnessed firsthand the AFL "courting" the Big Easy. Adams not only cold-called City Park to stage a game but also gushed to local media about the town's franchise potential, and he even worked on warming diehard college fans to the idea.[54]

Dixon had kept the AFL in reserve all along, but he was home less than two weeks before he picked up on the shifting terrain and shuffled his priorities. Ten days after meeting with Lautenschlaeger, Dixon flew to the Dallas Texans' headquarters to talk face-to-face with team owner (and league pioneer) Lamar Hunt. Dixon was not merely recycling the sales pitch on his city. He was prepared to revolutionize pro football, and the founder of the AFL was primed for a gutsy idea to put his league on top.

Over the previous three years, Dixon had schemed a lot about how to present the South as indispensable to the pros, and in the process he developed the idea of a two-season football calendar. The plan was elaborate and involved years of future planning, reorganization of the circuit, and even rental of stadia in nonleague cities. But the heart of the proposal was simple: admit New Orleans and Atlanta immediately, before the NFL could swoop in and wreck everything.

Adding these key southern cities would make half the AFL stadia warm-weather sites. Expanding to both fall and winter meant home games timed for ideal temperatures. Furthermore, during the winter, the AFL would have competition from neither the NFL nor college ball, meaning a monopoly on TV revenue. This shift in power could also drive the older league to seek a compromise. "The NFL has already demonstrated that they will move only under pressure. Perhaps this would be the sledgehammer needed," Dixon told Hunt. "Regardless," Dixon emphasized, "the important point is that the AFL would be the league dealing from a position of strength."[55]

Hunt immediately contacted Adams, and days later Dixon repeated the proposal in Houston. He admitted he had also floated the idea past Rozelle, whose knee-jerk reaction was that their season was already too long. But the conversation had happened and was yet another reason for the AFL to move quickly. Dixon was convincing; it would be wise to tie up Atlanta and New Orleans for 1963. Within the week, Hunt, Adams, and Dixon were brainstorming how a player pool from existing clubs could kick-start the two new franchises.[56]

| | | | | |

Dixon returned to the Tulane board for a follow-up that week. He disclosed, in confidence, that franchise talks had accelerated and now involved a much shorter timeline. Questions seemed endless, and satisfying them impossible. Dixon knew there would be no agreement by the time of the AFL's summer meeting. So he asked instead for a one-year "exclusive option" to ensure no other promoter could scoop up his pending contract, and he left with that small consolation.[57]

Dixon's next task was even more daunting. He had to convince his associates that despite his previous statements, City Park would not be a "graveyard" for their hopes and that they should hang their hat in the AFL. "Seemingly, the ideal investment situation would be a National League franchise at Tulane Stadium," Dixon confessed to would-be shareholders. "Why then are we considering what seems to be a less attractive combination?" he asked, queuing up his pitch.[58]

"For various reasons Tulane Stadium seems unavailable at the present time," Dixon conceded, but then he detailed how an expanded City Park Stadium "might be much more attractive than Tulane in the long run." He proposed an increase to 46,300 seats, which was in the range favored for pro football. "Large enough for a good payday," Dixon explained, "and, unlike Tulane, small enough so that fans cannot wait until the last minute to buy tickets." Furthermore, there was plenty of parking at the municipal stadium and no fear of bugging Tulane's neighbors, a team there would not have to play "second fiddle" to a collegiate program, and the team would have access to practice facilities, which was one concession already made to the university. But the biggest plus for City Park, of course, was its full and already executed racial integration. Avoiding legal battles was invaluable, given both the short timetable and the need for public approval. And there was one more precedent already broken at City Park that could be big in garnering local support: the permissible sale of beer.[59]

As for the league switch, Dixon went beyond the claim that a franchise "in hand" was "worth a dozen on paper." He cited the stunning progress the AFL had made in just two years, closing the gap with the NFL and outsigning it for college players. However, he was not just downplaying the risk in banking on upstarts. He argued that the AFL's surge made waiting on the older league the bigger gamble. There was already speculation about a pro football merger, and Dixon believed that any interleague compromise would likely nix expansion.[60]

Perhaps his salesmanship was too good the first time, but his colleagues were not easily sold on the new path to the pros. So, throughout April and May, when he was not negotiating with Hunt and Adams or polishing his brochure, Dixon hammered away at the holdouts.[61]

Meanwhile, the lawsuit concluded in Baltimore. Judge Roszel C. Thomsen dismissed the AFL's claim. The league would get none of the $10 million it sought, and the Cowboys would remain in Dallas. Still, AFL officials handled the verdict like sportsmen and faced the future with optimism. Lamar Hunt commented with a sigh, "Well, as I said when we lost Don Meredith, I'm sure this isn't the last thing we'll ever lose." Commissioner Foss called the decision "very disappointing" but remarked calmly, "This case was just one of the steps forward in the progress of the AFL." The next was expansion, and according to various owners, adding at least two franchises was the top priority for their summer conference.[62]

The NFL's owners meeting, on the other hand, had come and gone with no talk of expanding. The prolonged suit pushed the April assembly to late May, and then the hottest news was Commissioner Rozelle's pay raise. Otherwise, they celebrated their legal victory and sizable new single-network TV contract. The New Orleans group received no invitation to present its case.[63]

Dixon spent much of his wedding anniversary, June 11, leaning on Poitevent about their group's "timidity and doubt." "There is none on my part," Dixon declared. "I definitely want to take two shares instead of one," he added, hoping his enthusiasm would trickle down to the other eight investors.[64]

A week later, Dixon stood before the City Park board, and his stadium proposal indeed carried the names of all nine partners. He gave a thirty-minute, well-rehearsed presentation, thanked the committee, and left the room so objectors could be heard. He had judged City Park's neighborhood situation as wholly different from Tulane's. However, a small grid of exclusive residential blocks jutted in near the stadium, and representatives of the Park Place Association appeared that night with a petition against a pro team. Before the special session adjourned, however, the board reached a consensus. One member voted nay, another went on record as supporting the Park Place group, and Ernest A. Carrere Jr. recused himself because a law partner, Edward Poitevent, was invested in the venture. All other ballots went to give Dixon a "vote of confidence."[65]

It was no secret that the group was close to landing an AFL team. The stadium was secured, $25,000 in "earnest money" was sent to the league, and Dixon's name was on the owners' June 26 Boston itinerary. Furthermore, the founder of the league himself trumpeted that he would lobby for New Orleans's entry. Locals were getting excited. The idea of following college stars after graduation still felt like a fad to many fans, but there was a new football fever spreading. And DeFee's upcoming exhibition was expected to feed the epidemic.[66]

Around that time, a fresh but familiar-sounding voice echoed Edward Poitevent's words of caution. This skepticism, however, was shared with the entire city. One of the younger columnists for the *Times-Picayune,* Buddy Diliberto, agreed with Dixon's passion. "That New Orleans needs big-time sports promotion is undeniable," he wrote. However, the journalist not only questioned rushing into a "vastly inferior" league rather than earning a spot in the NFL but also pointed out the bigger problem with the current plan: even if promoters got the stadium ready, met the season ticket minimum, and secured a companion city in Atlanta, "they'll still have the toughest hurdle of 'em all to clear," he announced. "The integration–segregation problem." Diliberto believed that this glaring weakness would be exposed the moment Dixon stepped before the AFL owners.[67]

"Will the visiting teams be allowed to be housed together and eat together? Doesn't Louisiana law prohibit this?" Diliberto asked his readers. Sounding even more like Poitevent, he wondered, "Who will take that problem by the horns and wrestle it?" He likewise assured his audience, "By no means is this an attempt to discourage pro football in New Orleans. But it is an attempt to face the situation as it exists." He also stated unequivocally, "Until someone comes forward with the answers there's no use fooling ourselves." He had opened his column questioning how close the city was to a pro team and concluded, "We're closer to the moon."[68]

|||||

After Judge Thomsen's decision, AFL owners approached expansion brazenly, viewing new franchises as both proof and insurance of their resilience. As the Boston meeting approached, however, talk of swelling dwindled. Although it was long understood that teams would be added in pairs—and one owner called for four—reports emerged that only one franchise would be awarded for 1963. This turned Atlanta from companion to competitor overnight.[69]

There was also a third applicant in Boston, a relative newcomer in the race: Kansas City. KC's representative, Warren Lockwood, was the first to present. After flaunting the attendance numbers for the city's baseball Athletics, Lockwood explained that there was no college or pro gridiron team within a forty-mile radius to satisfy the more than 1.2 million residents who were "starved for football." He boasted that an incoming team would monopolize this market and be housed at the ideally sized, forty thousand–seat home of the A's. It was an impressive pitch, but there had been no time for any study of the area or games to gauge the fan base. Furthermore, taking a Midwestern town would not plant a flag in the Southeast.[70]

Atlanta's agent was next. Bill McCane, president of the Greater Atlanta Athletic Association (GAAA), produced blueprints of a venue already under construction expressly for the four upcoming AFL exhibitions. At ribbon cutting it would hold around 28,000 fully integrated seats. McCane also reported nearly two thousand "season" tickets for the August series were already sold. Although McCane envisioned breaking ground on a larger structure as soon as he got an AFL nod, the committee doubted that plans would materialize quickly in Atlanta, where stadia were repeatedly but fruitlessly discussed.[71]

Dixon gave the final presentation before owners adjourned for a golf and yachting party held by a Boston Patriots exec. Dixon was asked early about the facilities at City Park. He noted the small capacity but tried to hype his plans for enlargement. Fearing that this underwhelmed owners, he could not help mentioning his optimism that Tulane Stadium would soon be available, but this invited an onslaught of interrogatories on integration.

Dixon downplayed the city's biases, emphasizing that Tulane's seating issue was based on state law, which he claimed New Orleanians did not endorse. This distinction only led to questions about local hotels. That ban, Dixon boldly declared, would be off the books by the end of the year, well before football resumed. All this left Dixon just a brief moment to go through his familiar selling points, like climate, tourism, and size. He also snuck in a plug that in his town, unlike in Kansas City, there would be no conflicts with baseball in September and October.[72]

When the three presenters reentered the lobby of the Hotel Kenmore, they all appeared nervous but sounded confident when reporters approached. Lockwood was happy to have described his investors, explaining that "every one is a millionaire." McCane said the owners "seemed to be very interested" and "asked questions galore." Dixon's comments were the most humble. "This is a darned difficult decision for them to make," he said. "I'd hate to be in their spot."[73]

The issue was about to get more complicated. Comments in the press had painted New Orleans as the sweetheart of the expansion committee. So when deliberations began on June 27, the *Afro-American* newspaper sent telegrams to numerous league officials and warned that adding New Orleans "will be interpreted as an affront to 17 million American citizens." The wire read, "Attention is respectfully called to the fact that the city of New Orleans and its environs practice racial discrimination in brazen defiance of law and reason, with no evidence of desire to do otherwise." With that, the *Afro-American* ensured the AFL at least could not "plead ignorance."[74]

Hunt sent an acknowledgment of receipt, and according to sports columnist Sam Lacy, "He expressed understanding of the *AFRO* position and noted that the league planned no immediate action." Indeed, no city was voted in. There were too many lingering concerns across the board. Expansion was deferred, and the owners decided to wait and see what happened at the preseason games in Atlanta and New Orleans.[75]

|||||

In Atlanta, Bill McCane made masterful preparations. Promotions were plentiful, and by mid-July, sales of "season" booklets approached ten thousand. This looked particularly good for a fan base that notoriously preferred the game-day queue.[76]

McCane actively ensured racial integration in all operations. Atlanta businesses wanted neither to tarnish the city's progressive new image nor to get out of favor with the recently installed, Hartsfield-esque mayor, Ivan Allen Jr. Still, the integration of hotels, motels, and their dining spaces remained incomplete. Consequently, McCane made painstaking arrangements for all teammates to be housed together and accommodated completely. He also held integrated news conferences in downtown restaurants and called for complete equality in the stadium's press box. The unquestioned integration of the stadium itself was a first for DeKalb County, where the new facility was located, southeast of downtown Atlanta.[77]

When the games were signed, America Field did not exist, but everything was in place for opening night. On August 4, 1962, McCane and crew arrived at their shiny new stadium, anticipating a crowd that would seal their entry into the AFL. But as the Dallas Texans' halfback-fullback combo of Abner Haynes and Jack Spikes ran all over the Oakland Raiders defense, only around eight thousand seats were occupied. The GAAA expected gate sales to match if not exceed advance purchases. Instead, there were several thousand unused tickets in locals' pockets elsewhere in the city.

Multiple factors worked against McCane's group that night. The previous day, Atlanta had hosted the Georgia high school all-star game, tapping some folks' allotments of gridiron time. Besides, it was easy to skip the Dallas–Oakland scrimmage. Not only were there three more AFL exhibitions coming but also the opener could certainly have been more appealing. As one Atlanta sportswriter put it, "Oakland fans don't even want to see Oakland." Moreover, the *NFL* had also booked two preseason dates in Atlanta through local promoter Jim Clay, meaning half a dozen pro games were happening in four weeks.[78]

On the following Friday, the GAAA slashed prices for Houston–Denver, but that weekend their competition was Saturday's pairing of the NFL's Steelers and Bears at a high school in Midtown. The Oilers–Broncos booking brought in just 3,500 more bodies than the first game. AFL owners were unimpressed, and McCane's bottom line was nowhere near his heavy guarantees.

"As of now we have one problem and one problem only," McCane told the press. "There are too many pro football games too close together in Atlanta." The GAAA canceled the upcoming clash of the New York Titans and Buffalo Bills, allowing promoters to focus solely on their final game, Titans–Patriots, on August 25. It was their last hope. They announced, "We wish to give the football fans of Metro Atlanta an opportunity to prove their desire for pro football by purchasing sufficient tickets for game number four by Friday, August 17." Otherwise, that match would be scrapped as well. The onus was on the community to make the game and the franchise happen.[79]

They failed. By the deadline, it was clear that the final tilt would be another huge loss, and the clubs voided the contract as a courtesy. Ultimately, half of the GAAA's preseason games were canceled. The turnstiles at America Field clicked less than twenty thousand times for the exhibitions. McCane was left hoping he could salvage the "white elephant stadium" through rodeos and wrestling.[80]

|||||

After club owners Harry Wismer and Ralph Wilson Jr. agreed to release McCane from his Titans–Bills contract for August 18, the pair contemplated relocating it, and New York's Wismer impulsively told reporters a switch to New Orleans was favored. "We would like to have it as the opener of a doubleheader," he said, given that DeFee's Houston–Boston show was scheduled for the same day. "After all, the National Football League plays exhibition doubleheaders," he argued, "so there is no reason why we can't." Retracting his earlier support of the Georgia capital, he claimed no surprise at Atlanta's flop. "But I do think it would go over well in New Orleans," he cooed.[81]

Local media telephoned DeFee. "This is all news to us," he revealed. "Mr. Wismer has not contacted us." Regardless, DeFee dismissed the idea of hurriedly pasting another game onto the event his group planned for months. "We have a contract with Houston and Boston and feel we should do nothing that would detract from that promotion," he stated.

Building up the Oilers–Patriots clash, however, did not take much effort. Coach Pop Ivy's promise that Houston would field LSU legend Billy Cannon was assumed to be enough to keep black ink on DeFee's ledger, but the draw of college fans reached beyond Tiger town. Three-quarters of the Oilers backfield alone were Louisiana boys. Among them, Charlie Hennigan and Charlie Tolar, star alumni of Northwestern State, were bringing in a sizable crowd from Natchitoches.[82]

Meanwhile, Dixon worried that many locals felt strung along by the AFL and were losing confidence in the league after "the Boston disappointment." However, behind-the-scenes work was advancing considerably. Bargaining continued, and by late July it resulted in a generous "player stocking plan." A month before DeFee's game, Hunt even wired Dixon with instructions for the season ticket drive that needed to begin as soon as the franchise was official.[83]

Dixon got a head start. With DeFee's consent, he printed season ticket pledge cards to be distributed at the upcoming game. He even had little pencils inscribed "New Orleans Saints 1963." Dixon became sold on the team name before he left Europe. He was not a lifelong Catholic, and the connection to the city's dominant religion was accidental. While abroad, he heard "When the Saints Go Marching In" played on a long alpine horn at a Zurich music club, and again performed for the pope by a chorus of French nuns. He simply thought it would play well at a football game.[84]

As advance ticket sales increased, promoters repeatedly revised their estimates. The day before the game, they erected temporary bleachers, allowing for an extra three thousand spectators. When DeFee looked out the main office an hour before kickoff, City Park Stadium was already half filled. By the time "Miss Pro Football" was named, long lines snaked down the street behind the ticket windows. When the coin was tossed, the permanent seats were all assigned and the temporary tiers were teeming. Standing-room-only passes were issued until mobs of latecomers obstructed the view for the early birds. At that point, around seven thousand fans were turned away.

The crowd settled in, packed together in the motionless, humid air, hoping the quality of the show would top the oppressiveness of the heat. For the first quarter, unfortunately, it did not even come close. The most gripping play was George Blanda's 32-yard field goal attempt that sailed wide left.

The second period, however, opened with an 8-play, 82-yard Oiler drive. An 11-yard screen pass to crowd darling Billy Cannon brought some noise, but the real hero of the night was Charlie Hennigan, who gobbled up over half the field on that series alone. After Hennigan's sideline catch put the Oilers on the 2 and validated the drive for the upstate throng, their other favorite, Tolar, powered up the middle for 6 points. Proud Louisianans were getting excited.

Then the Patriots showcased offensive prowess of their own, and the crowd proved to be, at heart, nonpartisan. Cannon and his backfield mates were said to have filled the stadium, but as the pace of the game picked up, spectators simply became fans of action and skill by players of both teams and both races. An Oilers touchdown off a surprising pass from Cannon to a sandwiched Charlie Hennigan brought no higher decibels than the Pats' Babe Parilli connecting with African American fullback Larry Garron for a one-handed snatch in the end zone.

After this third-quarter Boston score, there was another momentum change. It did not jump back to the Oilers; it just slowed to a crawl. The only thing moving was the scoreboard clock, and even that seemed to drag. A few ticket holders took off, but the majority just leaned in closer.

After a rare 55-yard field goal attempt by Blanda fell well short of the uprights at final whistle, reporters swarmed both the teams' stars and their executives, whose reactions to the turnout were candid. Billy Sullivan, part owner of the Patriots, stated, "My first act on returning to Boston will be to get telegrams off to the other clubs telling them that New Orleans must have a franchise in 1963." He explained, "It is the only thing an intelligent man could do after seeing the response of New Orleans football fans here tonight." He concluded simply, "We need New Orleans." Likewise, Bud Adams remarked, "After this record turnout, I would have to say New Orleans is No. 1 territory for AFL expansion."[85]

The truncated figure, 31,000, was in fact a record gate for an AFL exhibition. Throughout the next week, there were more sound bites from owners about the overflow crowd and the need to lock down the fan base. Hunt commented that all the application requirements were in order and that Dixon's twelve thousand pledges signaled success for a forthcoming season ticket drive. The three-man expansion committee of Hunt, Adams, and Wismer was set to convene in Miami on September 1, and a league-wide telephone polling would follow. Adams announced on his way to South Florida, "Unless something startling happens here to change my mind, I'm going to ask Lamar Hunt and Harry Wismer to vote for New Orleans."[86]

|||||

When the first postgame issue of the *Louisiana Weekly* came out, there was none of the celebration that blanketed the city's mainstream papers all week. In the smaller crowd watching the Packers and Steelers two years earlier, many Black fans suspected block seating. Before this year's match, sports columnist Jim Hall attempted to squeeze out of promoters how "open" the seating would be. He got no answer until early fans arrived on game day.

"It was no mere coincidence that Negroes purchasing $4 seats were in Section 7 on the east side of the stadium," the *Weekly* declared. "The same pattern followed in the $2 seats," the article continued, pointing out that even Black patrons with last-minute bleacher passes were directed to the structure's southeast section. The plot fell apart as mobs of latecomers invaded any spaces available, but there was no doubt about the segregation scheme.[87]

It was assumed that sponsors remained mum beforehand because confirmation or denial of block seating would have provoked either the White Citizens' Council or local civil rights groups. The silence itself kept many Black fans away from the box office or sent them back to return tickets purchased early. Other than that, however, the African American community took no action.

Had there been a picket line at the game, Boston's Black players would not have crossed it. They made that decision at the newly opened Mason's Motel, while their white teammates checked in to the Fontainebleau two miles away. "There is nothing wrong with Mason's; it is great, but it is wrong in principle," an African American Patriot told the *Weekly*. Another commented, "Our team should not play here or any place where there is a racial question." At least one Black gridder vowed it would be the last time, declaring, "I, for one, will not return next year if I have to subject myself to separation of players."[88]

For two weeks, the city at large patted itself on the back and these issues stayed under the AFL's radar. Then, on September 1, when the expansion committee was scheduled to meet, the next *Louisiana Weekly* hit newsstands. By this time, the paper's office was flooded with reactions to the block seating and separate accommodations—and to the idea the Black community would support a franchise under those conditions. Fifteen of these letters were in that Saturday's edition. Regardless, this was nothing Hunt, Adams, and Wismer would see from their Miami hotel, and New Orleans was expected to be voted into the pros that day.[89]

At the last minute, however, Harry Wismer was admitted to a New York hospital, and expansion talks were postponed until the trio could regroup. Still, mainstream sportswriters announced that a telephone ballot would be administered soon. What those reporters overlooked was that Sam Lacy and the *Afro-American* had again adopted the cause. The syndicate had already reached out to Commissioner Foss for word on whether he had received commitments from New Orleans on racial matters.

"Please rest assured," Foss wired the *Afro-American* in response, "that any AFL move to New Orleans will involve assurances that integrated seating will be effected" and "that there shall be no discrimination against colored athletes."[90]

Soliciting such guarantees from New Orleans was not so easy. Lacy's paper went after the man thought to be receiving the franchise, rather than the sponsors of the game in question. Dave Dixon, however, was unreachable. His telegram was returned with the notation "Undeliverable because addressee has left the city." Long-distance telephone attempts also struck out. Lacy's group even contacted Representative Eddie Hebert but received little assistance in their manhunt, which validated suspicions that Dixon was riding a well-worn, fine line of public support.

In a series of three articles, Lacy aired his assessment of the AFL's courtship of the Big Easy, and he had done his homework. His sources in Louisiana, including Jim Hall, were convinced that sponsors wanted to "do the right thing" but were lassoed by "a 'messy political situation' and fear of the White Citizens' Council." He described local promoters' attempts to "sneak integration in" via block seats and "separate but equal" accommodations and announced matter-of-factly, "Once upon a time that would have been acceptable in lieu of nothing better, but that isn't the case today."

Among owners, Hunt and Adams understandably had more patience and confidence in the process, having experienced the growing pains of civil rights in Dallas and Houston. So Lacy addressed the non-Texan majority, writing with hope, "They recognize the risks involved in playing footsie with discrimination."[91]

Lacy sealed his assessment by pitting the two leagues head to head on the issue. "The National Football League has waged a determined fight against the jim-crow bugaboo, and just about has it licked," he declared, and he listed the preseason sites the older league abandoned over discrimination. The NFL, Lacy reasoned, "prefers to sacrifice the few extra dollars" to preserve "nationwide goodwill."[92]

Sam Lacy's articles were matter-of-fact, as if to politely inform the upstart league and the southern city about changes of which they seemed unaware. "Young colored America is refusing, point-blank, any bootleg issuance of civil rights," he explained. There was even compassion for progressive whites in a difficult position. "Colored fans, however," he elaborated, "are in no mood to let the AFL ease in to a middle-of-the-road policy."[93]

"Then came the long silence," wrote Bob Roesler. After a month passed with no updates, the *Times-Picayune* called the AFL. Assistant commissioner Milt Woodard said there was "nothing new" to report and merely offered that Foss was "conducting a poll of the owners."

"How is he polling 'em?" Roesler quipped. "By pony express?"[94]

The newsman then called Lamar Hunt, who also gave the party line: "There is nothing new." When pressed further, however, the typically reserved Hunt unsealed. "We have more problems than we can handle right now. This whole expansion has been out of line. Everyone is riled up," he steamed. "The way it has been handled wasn't the way to do it." He then regained his composure and gave a vague dismissal. "We are working on the project. If left alone we can accomplish something."[95]

There was another month of silence. Then, in early November, Bud Adams gave a statement, ruling out establishment of any new franchises "in the near future." The previous spring, both Atlanta and New Orleans had seemed like shoo-ins for the expanded 1963 American Football League. The cities' failures were polar opposites. Criteria that one city aced, the other failed to meet. It was one of those times when a tie really was a loss for both sides.[96]

CHAPTER 5
Crossing Routes

Joe Foss gnawed wearily on the stub of his cigar as he fielded questions from Dallas sportswriters. He had vowed to stay in New York until Harry Wismer locked down a deal and sold the bankrupt Titans. After several fruitless weeks, however, the commissioner decamped to Cotton Bowl Stadium. For six months, Foss had been asked which cities would be in the 1963 American Football League, and Thanksgiving weekend was no different.

When the AFL-NFL trial ended, all the chatter was about expansion, with AFL executives speaking frequently (and inconsistently) about which and how many cities would be added. Now the commissioner was instead drilled about rumored sales of struggling clubs in New York, San Diego, and Oakland. Although Foss stuck to his "wait and see" line, media outlets again had no trouble getting predictions from teams' personnel. Even Billy Cannon piped up on an alleged move: "I feel sure that Oakland will be playing in New Orleans next year. The sale has already been approved."[1]

"Isn't that something," F. Wayne Valley replied to the *Times-Picayune*, "that Cannon, a player, knows more about it than league officials?" Valley, the Raiders' majority owner, was losing patience. In an earlier denial of the deal, he used full stops between his words to ensure that reporters could understand. But Valley had indeed entertained an offer from, among other cities, New Orleans. Only weeks after expansion was ruled out, the unflappable David Dixon was on the West Coast, making more pitches and promises for pro football, and AFL officials were listening. In fact, Adams said he expected the move, and Hunt openly favored it. "We could get a good triangular rivalry between Dallas, Houston and New Orleans," he predicted.[2]

Newspapers were reporting that Dixon was in Oakland "wrapping up" the move, and Foss could hardly expect his quiz on the winless Raiders to end as he watched the Texans sub in backups to seal a four-touchdown rout of orphaned Oakland. Dallas itself was only momentarily off the team transfer rumor mill because three other cities went center stage. Even while winning the Western Division that afternoon, the Texans only drew around thirteen thousand fans. So the "future of the league" interrogation continued, but it was apparent that both Foss and his cigar were burned out.[3]

Three days later, every owner and general manager in the AFL received a memo from the commissioner's desk announcing, "I will deem it an act detrimental to the American Football League if further announcements concerning franchise moves are made by AFL owners, coaches, players, or others connected with the League, without first clearing same with the Commissioner." None of autumn's rumors materialized. Wismer finally unloaded the New York Titans, but for half the publicized price and to none of the speculated shoppers. Barron Hilton retained the Chargers in San Diego. As for Oakland, by Thanksgiving, fear of losing its only pro sports team had launched a drive to sell twelve thousand season tickets and expedite a $25 million coliseum complex.[4]

Consequently, Dixon boarded an eastbound plane out of the Bay Area empty-handed, but his destination was Dallas. And the afternoon he spent with his buddy Lamar Hunt rekindled rumbles about a Texans shift to the Big Easy. Hunt, trying desperately to keep his team out of the tabloids, gave frank feedback: "We will stay in Dallas under our present plans. We are not moving to New Orleans, and I wish they'd quit rumoring it. I am tired of denying it."[5]

No one could have been happier that the commissioner had clamped down on transfer talk than Hunt, arguably the most private individual in professional football. Hunt did, however, need to replant his franchise outside Dallas. Both the Texans and the NFL's Cowboys were struggling, averaging only around ten thousand fans per game, even during the Texans' 1962 AFL championship run. It was also clear that the NFL would leave its contender in the fight until the final bell. In Hunt's case, it was important not only for his team but also for his whole league that he find his squad a one-team town. Still, it made him heartsick to think of alienating his few but faithful fans. This sentiment, on top of his innate secrecy, made discretion the most important factor in the fate of his franchise.[6]

| | | | |

Even in the chaotic summer of 1962, Lamar Hunt had been quietly on the lookout for relocation prospects, and New Orleans was on his radar. With the league abuzz about expansion at the time, he and Dixon spoke only in hypotheticals, but Dixon looped in his associates. He warned them in a memo marked "EXTREMELY CONFIDENTIAL" that secrecy was key. "This matter must be held in the STRICTEST of confidence," he stressed in late July. "A leak would hurt Lamar badly in Dallas this fall. I would suggest that you discuss this with NO ONE."[7]

Before Dixon's cohorts convened at the New Orleans Country Club a week later, however, lips had loosened. National newsmen cited big talk out of the Big Easy on Hunt's franchise moving east. Reporters called it a "strong possibility" but said no announcement was expected, "since the club is currently conducting a 1962 ticket drive." Still, the story was out there, and the damage was done.[8]

Around that time, another interested party appeared in the Texans office, and this man's mastery of discretion was rivaled only by Hunt's. Mayor H. Roe "The Chief" Bartle of Kansas City caught wind of the house hunting and threw his hat in the ring. Hunt explained the need to avoid another public relations nightmare for a team still peddling tickets, and Bartle said he would hold off until a more appropriate time.[9]

Dixon, on the other hand, was, as Hunt put it, "a very persistent fellow" that fall, even presenting a contract to be signed. But Hunt was hesitant to finalize anything midseason, and his closest advisers scorned such a move. The Texans GM, Jack Steadman, was wary of Dixon and of Hunt's fondness for the New Orleanian. With Dixon at every home game and traveling with the Texans to several others, the pair developed quite a friendship. As one sportswriter observed, "Hunt, the multimillionaire Texan who founded the league, thinks Dixon is the greatest thing to come along since oil." So Steadman hovered over his boss's dealings, counseling caution. Moreover, a colleague in Louisiana oil advised that a move to New Orleans would mean greasing palms every step of the way. "Everything down there is a payoff," he warned.[10]

Regardless, when the season ended the numbers were even more in favor of relocation. Then, Christmas Eve morning 1962, hours after the Texans' championship performance, an urgent message came to Hunt's desk from Mayor Bartle, knowingly marked as confidential. Over the next month, Hunt took several trips to Kansas City, doing business under the thickest cloak of secrecy and relishing every bit of it. First, his hotel reservations were made under a fake name. Later, he met with the head of the chamber of commerce over speakerphone, without identifying the team being moved. Likewise, when Bartle took Hunt and Steadman to the Kansas City Club, they were introduced as "Mr. Lamar" and "Jack X."[11]

From the shadows, they put together a generous lease for Municipal Stadium that included additional seats, new offices, and an adjacent practice facility. Hunt did not put pen to paper with Bartle either, but in Kansas City he settled on terms—and did business within terms—with which he was comfortable.[12]

Hunt and Steadman also flew to Louisiana to see the best that Dixon's city could offer. They knew his sales pitch on City Park, but by then they would settle for nothing less than Tulane Stadium. So at another meeting with Lautenschlaeger's committee, Hunt appeared as a league representative and requested Tulane's facilities to house an existing AFL team. To Dixon's delight, the proposal was advanced to the full board for final approval.

Lautenschlaeger asked Hunt for the name of the team being transferred, "so that we can take it to the board."

"I want that to be a secret," Lamar replied. Dixon was floored. He had no idea Hunt would demand anonymity at that late stage.

Dixon pulled his friend aside, pleading, "Lamar, these people, these are good businessmen. Your name won't get out or anything. I guarantee you it won't." No matter how much Hunt liked Dixon, there were plenty of reasons to doubt that promise, and the Texan would not budge. Likewise, the board refused to turn their stadium over to a faceless owner and nameless club. There was a stalemate.[13]

Haunted by how close he had come, again, Dixon ruminated constantly. Then, one night, a solution popped into his head. "My God," he thought, wishing he could reconvene the board from his bed. As soon as possible, he approached Tulane with a compromise and they signed off on a provisional agreement with the AFL, subject to later approval of the owner and franchise. Dixon hoped it was enough.

He called the Texans office immediately and got the secretary, whom he knew well from his many visits. "Oh, Mr. Dixon, you better get ahold of him right away," she said. "He's in Kansas City." She told Dixon how to most quickly reach her boss, which he did—less than an hour after a clandestine deal was finalized to move the AFL's Texans to Missouri.[14]

|||||

Dixon's timing was not always so bad. Actually, early 1963 was the perfect time to be negotiating pro football with Tulane.

Back in May 1954, just days before the *Brown* decision was delivered, Tulane's administration had been poised to implement gradual admission of Black applicants. Then, amid the general fear sweeping the state after the landmark case, the board retreated into deferment and an equivocal public stance. By 1960, however, segregation was jeopardizing Tulane's status as a leading research institution, not only scarring its reputation but also threatening its eligibility for federal and philanthropic grants.

The previous decade, Tulane had received sizable awards from the Ford Foundation, and in late 1960 the campus was humming with rumors about millions of dollars that were accessible through a special Ford education program. Soon, however, rejections from both the Rockefeller and Ford Foundations cited the school's segregation. And in December, the Ford program advised Tulane that it need not submit any applications unless the issue of integration was addressed.

In addition to any personal fears or biases, within the administration there was also a primary legal concern. Because of restrictive clauses in the original Tulane endowments, there was the haunting possibility of heirs suing to reclaim donations if racial policies changed. Nonetheless, something had to be done.

On April 12, 1961, the board released a statement explaining that the school was bound by its endowments' stipulations but vowing that it "would admit qualified students regardless of race or color if it were legally possible." "Times have changed since the University was founded," the statement continued, asserting that Tulane "must move ahead and assume its rightful place of leadership." As the Ford Foundation requested, this was a clear issuance of the school's liberal standpoint on integration. However, the most predictive part was the claim that the administrators' hands were tied.[15]

Aware that action required force, wealthy white integrationist Rosa Keller commissioned the necessary litigation. Professor John Furey of Dillard recruited two highly qualified Black female students, Barbara Marie Guillory and Pearlie Hardin Elloie, to apply for Tulane's graduate program in sociology. Their applications were rejected, and white attorney John P. Nelson filed suit on September 1, 1961. The board likely expected a "friendly" hearing for a simple *cy pres* judicial retrofitting of the original charter terms to the new legal climate. Nelson, however, was hesitant to invoke such a doctrine in the state courts, where judges likely had Tulane affiliations and the case could be drawn out for half a decade or more.

Nelson thought he had a better shot citing the Fourteenth Amendment before Judge J. Skelly Wright. And in late February 1962 Nelson asked the federal district court for a summary judgment declaring Tulane had adequate state involvement to render it a public institution, which would require it to integrate. Nelson got just that.[16]

Judge Wright's decision put the school in a very tough spot. Loss of their private status had monumental consequences, not least of which was legislative interest in all Tulane affairs. The board had to fight, but this seemed wholly inconsistent with promises to integrate as soon as legally permissible. Not only were faculty grumbling allegations of bad faith but also the Ford Foundation was regretting its decision to readmit Tulane. The request for a new trial smelled of hallmark delaying tactics and made the board look like "bitter enders."[17]

As fate would have it, just then Judge Wright was appointed to the federal court of appeals in Washington, DC, and Tulane's new "trial on the merits" was heard by his successor, Frank Burton Ellis, who was not shy about undoing Wright's work. On December 5, 1962, Ellis restored the university's private status but also nullified the endowments' racial clauses. A week later, the board voted unanimously to begin admitting Black students for the spring semester.[18]

In late January 1963, the first ten Black students in the school's 129-year history enrolled at Tulane. The following week, Lamar Hunt announced the Texans' move to Kansas City. David Dixon reversed field and again knocked on the door of the NFL. His new scheme also required the Tulane board's endorsement, and he had at his disposal two very valuable tools: the school's reaffirmed private status and its renewed need to please the Ford Foundation.[19]

Rebounding from their latest AFL heartbreak, Dixon's group went big in their next courtship with the NFL. They proposed a rare preseason doubleheader for the coming September. Although they had to woo four teams onto their program, the first contact was obvious: the Detroit Lions, run by William Clay Ford. When the Lions GM said they would be honored to play in famed Tulane Stadium, Dixon inquired whether it was too bold to ask Bill Ford himself to request the facilities. "Absolutely not," the GM replied, advising Dixon to simply send such a letter to Detroit.[20]

When the Tulane board received its version, on Ford Motor Company letterhead and with William Clay Ford's signature, the text was exactly as Dixon had written it, including his strategic reference to the Ford Foundation. Although Edward Poitevent thought Dave's flamboyant writing style was easily recognizable, the board was simply thrilled to have a glowing letter from the philanthropic family.[21]

Dixon did not have to look far for the Lions' opponent. During his many trips to Dallas, he had hedged his Texans bets by also schmoozing with Cowboys GM Tex Schramm, who had the commissioner's ear after a long tenure with Rozelle in Los Angeles. Dixon was always looking at the big picture.

Likewise, his choice for the second game was based on his understanding that despite the commissioner's authority, "Mr. Halas ran the NFL in those days." Dixon booked a flight to Chicago for himself and his wife, who he believed could charm anyone into anything. As he saw it, "Mary Dixon had somehow woven her magic spell again," and Bears owner George Halas not only agreed but also phoned Baltimore and encouraged the glamorous Colts to bring legendary quarterback Johnny Unitas to the Big Easy. There was just one piece of unfinished business between New Orleans and a flashy NFL doubleheader: the state ban on integrated seating was still on the books.[22]

Although Earl Long had been dead for more than two years, his advice would provide the solution. Back in 1959, when Dixon was just scratching the surface of his football campaign, he had spotted Long walking along Camp Street at Lafayette Square. Never one to let an opportunity pass by, Dixon jogged up, introduced himself, and bounced his franchise ambitions off the governor. Seeing Act 579 as a stumbling block, Long lamented that if the Sugar Bowlers had just sent some backup from the start, he would have blocked the bill somehow.[23]

"If you get far along, come to me and I'll help you," Long offered. "But," he added before they parted ways, "one thing to remember is private property." He confirmed a thought Dixon had already entertained about Tulane Stadium, stating bluntly, "You can do whatever the hell you want, Dave."[24]

Many legal minds sat on Tulane's board of administrators, and they concurred with the late Earl Long. Particularly in the wake of Judge Ellis's ruling, they were free to voluntarily desegregate their stadium. Blowback was inevitable, but the move would allow the university to take a courageous step forward without fighting a strongly supported state law. The vote was far from unanimous, but afterwards Joseph Merrick Jones gave Dixon his word on an integrated Tulane Stadium. After all, the NFL family, which included the Fords, would have it no other way.[25]

|||||

When the doubleheader was announced in late March, Dixon's public relations guy, David Kleck, noted that the early September kickoff would coincide with the massive American Legion convention. "It will be a tremendous weekend for our great city," Kleck predicted.[26]

A month later, a three-judge federal court heard a case with big implications for both events. The NAACP and the Congress of Racial Equality (CORE) filed suit against the state's ban on integrated hotels. On May 18, 1963, the lingering 1956 law was deemed unconstitutional and a preliminary injunction was granted.

The majority opinion, signed by Judges John Minor Wisdom and Herbert W. Christenberry, claimed, "Doors closed to Negroes in Louisiana since Reconstruction days will be opened." Yet the same document also stated that "the narrow question before the Court relates only to the constitutionality of R.S. 14:317." Although all three judges agreed that the Fourteenth Amendment invalidated the law, they did not all arrive at this decision by the same path, nor did they all foresee doors opening. The third judge, E. Gordon West of Baton Rouge, gave a different interpretation.[27]

Wisdom and Christenberry pointed to the law's discrimination against African Americans. West's "concurring opinion" held that "the statute is unconstitutional because it is an unreasonable interference by the state in a private business." Forced integration, he reasoned, would be equally invasive. West argued that the court's decision merely gave hoteliers the right to integrate. "It does not," he emphasized, "involve the right of the Negro to obtain accommodations at any particular hotel." During the readings, the Fourteenth Amendment was described as "both a sword and a shield." The "concurring opinion," respectfully described by Christenberry and Wisdom as one that "sharpens the issues," only muddied the outcome. The law was overturned, but integration was left to owners.[28]

Even with the law in place, local hoteliers had discussed the economic impact of segregation, realizing that it was costing the city conventions. The head of the Roosevelt Hotel, Seymour Weiss, lamented to colleagues that they were falling behind even sister cities in Texas and Georgia, saying, "For a long time we were not unlike our competitors in the South, with each city carrying on its business based on long tradition." By then, however, he saw his group "fighting for our lives." Still, Weiss concluded, "I am not advocating any change. I'm merely stating the facts as a realist." The prevailing position was to draw more (white) tourists to pick up the slack.[29]

Now, however, the American Legion convention was on the line. Three years of preparations were complete and the event was predicted to break all records, with sixty thousand delegates. Millions of dollars were earmarked for local coffers. Moreover, there had already been months of rumblings about the Legion pulling out unless it received assurance of integrated accommodations. Other cities, including Atlanta, Dallas, Houston, and Kansas City, were already applying as substitutes. The court decision came just in time to let local hoteliers make the necessary promises. But none did. In a decision one local Legion official termed "catastrophic" for New Orleans, the meeting was moved to Miami Beach.[30]

Still, the city's white elite expressed little remorse. Mayor Schiro termed the relocation "quite a surprise" and defended the rights of business owners, saying, "I am not disposed to interfere in any way with the policy of local hotel management." The *Times-Picayune* elaborated on the enormous forfeiture of revenue but reasoned that "it wasn't a total loss" to tourism, since the May issue of *American Legion Magazine* featured a spread depicting New Orleans as the "Paris of the New World."[31]

|||||

One spring evening, David Dixon walked into the meeting hall of the Knights of Peter Claver. He was nervous. He had arranged to meet with several Black civil rights leaders but really had no idea what to expect. He believed that plans to desegregate Tulane Stadium were sound, but he wanted to do everything possible to protect the university and his doubleheader. He was looking for someone willing to both challenge the seating law and keep his name out of it.

NAACP reps were sympathetic but told Dixon they had a stack of more pressing cases and few attorneys with federal court experience. He asked what, if anything, would float his agenda to the top. The gentleman in front of him chuckled a little and said, "Money."

Dixon stepped aside as the group deliberated an asking price. When they came back with the figure of $2,000, he remarked that it seemed "pretty high" and split off again for financial planning of his own. Once out of sight, he pulled $8,000 from his pocket and divided out a mere quarter of what he came prepared to pay. He rejoined the others, accepted their terms, and reached for the cash. He felt panicky again as he tried to remember which pocket was richer, but to his relief he guessed correctly and handed over the fee. He walked onto Orleans Avenue thinking he scored the deal of a lifetime.[32]

The guys back at the hall must have felt the same way. There was very little work left to do on the case. In fact, NAACP attorneys had filed the necessary suit months earlier.

Even after the rally that sparked an academic year of furor, the White Citizens' Council was permitted use of Municipal Auditorium for speakers preaching segregation as "the law of God." Meanwhile, Black civil rights groups like the NAACP and the Consumers' League were repeatedly refused the space to present Martin Luther King Jr. and Thurgood Marshall, on the grounds that such meetings would incite violence.[33]

Hence, back in July 1962, general counsel for the NAACP had airmailed a complaint from New York City to the president of the NAACP's New Orleans chapter, attorney Ernest "Dutch" Morial, and it was filed immediately in U.S. district court. By suing for nondiscriminatory use of Municipal Auditorium, they were challenging the constitutionality of Louisiana's law against integrated seating.[34]

The case was heard in June 1963 and was extremely straightforward. The verdict seemed almost foregone when, during the assistant city attorney's arguments, Judge Wisdom commented, "It makes one ashamed of this city."[35]

The opinion was delivered on July 1. The three-judge panel announced, "New Orleans here and now must adjust to the reality of having to operate desegregated public facilities." "Time has run out," they continued. "There is no defense left. There is no excuse left."[36]

Jim Hall reported with optimism, "The last roadblock in eliminating segregation from sports in Louisiana was removed." The city attorney planned a futile appeal, but the ruling would take effect once the preliminary injunction was filed. That did not happen for four weeks, however, and when cash-carrying fight fans lined up at the auditorium box office on July 22, tickets were being sold with racial tags. Inside was the live, closed-circuit telecast of the world championship heavyweight bout between Sonny Liston and Floyd Patterson in Las Vegas. Some eager Black fans bought their passes anyway and climbed up to the balcony, only to be chastised by Hall in the *Weekly* because they "sacrificed principles for pleasure."[37]

One pair of African American patrons, on the other hand, bought "white" tickets and went to the main floor. They received an initial, discrete offer of a refund and Black-designated tickets. When the offer was refused, arrests were threatened. Believing the law was finally on their side, the fans said calmly that officials should "go ahead and call the wagon." With the statute lingering in legal purgatory, there was sufficient confusion to allow the couple to stay seated in seats 1 and 2 of row M and be the first to integrate Municipal Auditorium. It was a short-lived victory, however, as Liston knocked Patterson out just two minutes and ten seconds into the first round.[38]

On August 5, 1963, the injunction was filed, and the last remnants of the Gibbs-Gleason statute were terminated—after seven years on the books and with one month to spare before the doubleheader. Dixon had indeed found "somebody else quietly to file a little suit," without any blowback on Tulane or on Dixon's investment group, the New Orleans Pro Football Club.[39]

That was not the only sports-centered case this "somebody else" took on in June. Dutch Morial, along with A. P. Tureaud, also presented a suit to desegregate the city's public parks, golf courses, and playgrounds. The week before the trial, both Atlanta and Houston opened fully integrated pools, but the New Orleans Recreation Department (NORD) announced that its swimming spots would stay closed for 1963 because of a "limited budget." City Park's pools had already been boarded up for its four desegregated summers, and this latest park suit had officials taking precautionary measures for all the others.[40]

Even with the outcome inevitable, the hearing was lengthy. City attorneys lobbed up every last-ditch argument imaginable. And Morial and Tureaud filed through witnesses testifying about segregation's impact on everything from children's races to adult pickup basketball. Before closing arguments, Judge Wisdom reminded the city's legal team that they carried a "heavy burden of persuasion." An order for integration was imminent.

However, between that time and the reading of the court's opinion, the event most symbolic of the inequities on trial was held on the Wisner Boulevard overpass. African American parents resented their sons' ineligibility for baseball, football, and basketball loops that could qualify for national competitions. But of all the activities open only to white boys, the most coveted was the annual soapbox derby.[41]

For years, there had been attempts to integrate the derby. Each year, despite the futility, Jim Hall had encouraged Black parents to register. United Clubs and the local NAACP repeatedly sponsored eager African American applicants and issued the thirty-five-dollar entry fee. Each time, instead of the rulebook and brochure, they had received their returned checks via certified mail.[42]

One hundred and forty white, teenage boys flew down the 975-foot course in that summer's championship round, which featured a prerace parade, a derby queen, majorettes, and several bands. The winner received a savings bond, trophy, and free trip to Akron, Ohio, to compete nationally for thousands of dollars in scholarship money—and perhaps to rub elbows with celebrities like Rock Hudson, Paul Anka, John Russell, and Paul Lynde. The Black community was instead offered a yearly skatemobile competition, but even NORD officials told the federal judges the substitute promotion could not compare.[43]

A few weeks after the 1963 soapbox race, Judges Wisdom, Christenberry, and Ainsworth announced that it was not prudent for them to hand down a verdict in the parks trial. They asserted there was "so little substance to the constitutional questions the city raises that a three-judge court should not decide the case." For the sake of "expediting justice," however, all three signed the order to desegregate recreation.[44]

|||||

With plans for the NFL doubleheader chugging along, WDSU TV and Radio ran a series of editorials titled "A Pro Football Franchise Needs Everyone's Help." One installment stated bluntly, "Kansas City picked up an American Football League franchise from under our noses by the concerted civic effort of its mayor, city council, chamber of commerce, and leading businessmen." "Isn't it about time," the segment argued, "that New Orleans started thinking 'big-time,' too?"[45]

Mayor Schiro not only saw the editorials but also saved two of the transcripts. They ended up in a file with letters to more than three dozen citizens he invited to serve on his sports advisory committee. He told members that "a well-organized sports program is vital to the progress of the modern American city." He foresaw an all-sports stadium, the Olympic Games, the PGA Golf Tournament, and professional sports franchises, as well as events in track, boxing, and bowling. "New Orleans has been and can again be a world sports center," he declared. The thirty-seven-man, all-white committee would have Dave Dixon as its chairman.[46]

Still, New Orleans was far from having collaborative buy-in from the local elite. Even after the American Legion pulled out, and while folks were again getting excited about pro football, no downtown hotels agreed to house the incoming NFL teams. By late summer, two national hotel chains ordered their New Orleans locations, the Sheraton–Charles and the Royal Orleans, to desegregate. Likewise, the owner of the Jung Hotel capped off his $3.75 million renovations by defecting from his hotelier cohorts and opening doors.

However, this tripartite integration was scheduled for September 10, 1963, three days after the glitzy twin billing. Dixon knew it was far more important for teammates to be in the same location than to be in the best location. So the four squads lodged at the Hilton Inn Motel near the airport, in Kenner.[47]

Finding housing was trivial compared to masterminding the first integrated ticket sales at Tulane Stadium. At first, Dixon's group made no announcement and let speculation run wild on whether the stands would resemble the checkerboard chalking of a Sugar Bowl end zone or be fully desegregated. This alone incited harassing calls from segregationists shouting racial slurs and obscenities. Dave and Mary Dixon decided to have a little fun with it, though. Mary picked up at each ring and explained that her husband was out but an uncle was available. Dave then intercepted the call with a feeble voice. He let the screaming continue a bit before feigning confusion and saying, "Thank you very, very much for calling. I'll tell Davie you called."[48]

Regardless, Dixon still believed that fear over integration could fuel the ticket drive and stuck to opening with group reservations. Fans marked whether they wanted eight-dollar box seats, seven-dollar east or west seats, or five-dollar north or south seats and gave the name of their group. This was open to cliques of friends as well as clubs and businesses. Individual tickets would go on sale only after preorders were mailed.[49]

This initial drive lasted for more than two months. Black fans were getting impatient with the "silent treatment," and Jim Hall pushed another "stay-at-home" policy until there was a public guarantee. Writing with a fool-me-once attitude, Hall described the Black community as "hipped" to promoters' "discriminatory tactics." Hall conceded that early bulk sales were fine as long as sellers of single seats had no "tricks up their sleeve." He also prepared to contact all four clubs at the first hint of segregation.[50]

When the box office finally opened for direct purchase, Dixon and Kleck went to the head of the *Louisiana Weekly*, C. C. Dejoie. They wanted to inform readers of full integration but did not want immoderate publicity to invite trouble. So the group's policy was released as "Tickets are being sold on a first-come, first-served basis."[51]

Even after the announcement, well-founded skepticism lingered, and African Americans did not rush to ticket counters. Dixon worried about the lack of Black support, but when he witnessed a trial run at the sales window, he understood. A couple of weeks into the drive, Dixon was uplifted by an African American man walking toward the Willow Street booths. The clerk conducted the sale just as she was coached, pulling out a large stadium chart and asking the fellow to select from the unsold seats. The gentleman saw unmarked spots scattered throughout every section of the stadium, glanced up, and asked, "You mean I can sit wherever I want?" Offered a nod, he uttered, "Hallelujah!" By the end of August, Jim Hall aborted the boycott and reported on the "large number of tan fans" securing seats.[52]

Sales in general looked good. The timing, the end of preseason, was ideal, showcasing polished starters rather than easy roster cuts. Locals were paying to see Johnny Unitas pinpoint Raymond Berry from 40 yards out, Mike Ditka rampage through the secondary off a Billy Wade pass, or Dick "Night Train" Lane top off an interception with a long return. There also were twenty-five former SEC stars on the incoming squads. It was even a homecoming for two Chicago defensive backs who were New Orleans natives: former Greenie Richie Petitbon and Grambling alum Roosevelt Taylor.[53]

Dixon envisioned a sellout and had two thousand bleacher seats ready, should the stadium's capacity be surpassed. On game day, though, weather conditions did not encourage last-minute decisions in his favor. Temperatures were in the nineties, and thunderstorms were forecast through the evening.[54]

Still, a crowd of more than 51,000 filed through the stadium's grand brick facade for the 6:30 kickoff. Dixon was clearly disappointed, but team execs were plenty impressed, unable to remember a bigger turnout in a non-league city. Besides, with four teams to compensate, admission fees were higher than many regular season prices, and league officials were thrilled that so many locals would pay big bucks for pro ball. What did not impress the teams' brass were the heat and humidity. "It must be like playing on the equator down there for those guys," one Colts official commented from the press box. If he did not like the weather, however, he truly just needed to wait a few quarters.[55]

At the start of game one's fourth period, even with quarterback Don Meredith and his bruised hip on the bench, the Cowboys were up by 10. With as many minutes remaining, the elusive Earl Morrall evaded enough linemen to find the end zone and get his Lions within a field goal's reach. Dallas then began chipping downfield, mostly through power plays behind masterful Cowboy blockers. They went 80 yards in twelve snaps and consumed most of the clock.

Then the weatherman made good on his promise and a heavy rain started. The Cowboys kept moving, and the fans stayed still. With fifty-eight seconds left, Dallas faced fourth-and-12 and lined up in field goal formation. Three points would keep it a one-score game and give the Lions' Morrall time to show off more scrambling skills. But the Cowboys faked the attempt, and backup quarterback Eddie LeBaron flung a swing pass to Amos Marsh, who slipped past a defensive back for his last three steps into the end zone. Dallas sealed a 10-point victory and gave the first contest a thrilling finish.[56]

As players left the field, the rain picked up, falling in thick white sheets. Fans ran for cover underneath the stands. Even with the nearby pumping station working as hard as it could, the area quickly began flooding. And as the crowd found shelter, folks also found themselves packed tightly together and ankle-deep in rainwater.[57]

Dixon looked out at the empty seats and started panicking. He pictured the thousands of people suddenly jammed together below the stadium. "Oh, my God," he thought. "There's going to be a race riot underneath there." He rushed down the ramps, envisioning the atrocious violence, vivid media reports, and death of his pro football dreams. When he got to ground level, fans were indeed attacking each other—with makeshift water balloons and playful splashing. Between furious claps of thunder, Dixon heard laughter. His civic pride swelled again, and he thought, "Man, that's New Orleans."[58]

He then went to the Chicago locker room for a heart-to-heart with Papa Bear. The storm was not letting up, and even if it did, Dixon had no idea how long the drainage system would need to clear the field. The scheduled nine o'clock starting time for game two had come and gone, and what was already planned as a long night was getting unpredictably longer. So he offered the Bears coach a way out.

"Mr. Halas, if you want to load up your plane and go back to Chicago—" he began.

"Oh, no," Halas interrupted. He promised they would play the full game, even if that meant staying "'til four o'clock Sunday morning."[59]

Fortunately, the delay did not get quite that bad, and the Colts and Bears kicked off at 9:50. The field looked very different. The sidelines were flowing rivers, there was barely a trace of chalk markings on the turf, and a gray mist shrouded the whole arena.

There was one aspect of the stadium, though, that looked almost exactly as it had during game one: the number of fans. Despite all the waiting and wading, nearly every ticket holder stuck around for another taste of NFL play. Attendance figures went from arguably low to astoundingly high by hardly changing at all.[60]

Unfortunately, some of the anticipated reward was revoked from the drenched but dedicated crowd. In that day's column, Buddy Diliberto had built up anticipation for hearing the stadium announcer exclaim, "And at quarterback for the Baltimore Colts—Johnny Unitas!" Buddy painted a scene of locals giving the "living legend" a welcome worthy of "the greatest quarterback alive." However, when the Colts starter under center was introduced over the loudspeakers, his name was Lamar McHan.[61]

Coach Don Shula had assured reporters that despite a week-old injury, Unitas would be in the starting lineup. Unitas was even expected to be calling the plays. On Saturday, though, the soreness in the legend's arm had not subsided, and so on jogged McHan. Although New Orleanians did not "holler and cheer and whistle and stomp their feet" as Diliberto had envisioned, they did stay glued to the game.[62]

In fact, even as Saturday turned into Sunday, starters were replaced with subs, and the sky intermittently sprinkled, most fans stayed to the final snap. NFL officials were already impressed with the big numbers paying high prices. After intermission's deluge, the size of the crowd willing not only to pay but also to prune for a wee-hour end to a preseason scrimmage was newsworthy. As executives gushed about the turnout, one *Times-Picayune* reporter asked Tex Schramm whether Rozelle and the owners would take notice. Schramm replied without hesitation, "Positively." That same reporter then hurriedly typed up his notes on the game. Describing the delayed, damp finish of the long night, Ed Devenport wrote, "In the end, the same 50,000 fans still sat there, defying nature's elements, absorbed in football." He was proud of how his city had made its mark, "as if to prove to the grid world that New Orleans was ready... rains or no rains."[63]

Jim Hall had a full six days to complete his write-up. He experienced "the peak of bliss" while overlooking a truly unsegregated crowd from the comforts of the Tulane press box. But he collected other accounts of the night, before typesetting his next column. Taking into consideration "all reliable reports," he concluded, "Saturday night proved again that integration can work in this town at sports events if only given a chance." He relayed stories of interracial groups trading player stats and sharing umbrellas and declared, "The average fan present didn't give a darn about rain or who was sitting next to him; he wanted to see pro football."[64]

|||||

Later that week, the MWSA grilled Sugar Bowler Joe David about how his colleagues in the New Orleans Pro Football Club had pulled off integration.

By the time of that September meeting, more than eight months of planning was completed for the 1963–1964 events, under the old segregation policies, and most events other than football were set. The injunction on the seating law was only a month old, and the MWSA was taking a crash course in its implications. Their attorney advised them that the decision on integration was theirs to make. However, it quickly became clear that was not entirely accurate.

When Irwin Poché invited the Eighth Naval District's color bearers for the Sugar Bowl pageantry, he received an eager response. Soon after, though, his attention was called to a notice from Washington, DC, which addressed Navy personnel's "public exhibitions." It required that, in addition to seating, "all other accommodations and facilities connected with the event or activity" must be "available to all without regard to race, creed, color, or national origin." Likewise, the track committee reported on the Orange Bowl's plans to initiate its own thinclad races, raising concerns over losing talent to the South Florida course. The MWSA knew that athletes were under pressure not to perform anywhere with "the least tint of segregation." Clearly, Miami could make promises the Sugar men could not, and four of their track teams ultimately ran to the Sunshine State.[65]

Then, when early feelers went out to the University of Pittsburgh about a football invitation, the Panthers pointed to the policy they had set in 1956 and refused to play without a guarantee of full access throughout the city for everyone in their party. So, as *Sports Illustrated* explained, "Rather than embarrass any member of its team, Pitt turned its back on the offer." The magazine also commented, "Good for Pitt."[66]

The long-awaited full repeal of the Gibbs-Gleason law had come and gone, but that was no longer enough to reopen the Sugar Bowl. A lot had changed in America over the previous seven years, and New Orleans matched very little. Invitees made demands that clearly were beyond the Sugar Bowlers' purview. Their reach went no further than the stadium facilities and the rooms they reserved. They could not even guarantee service at restaurants inside the few integrated downtown hotels. Although another all-white bowl would be another big black eye, the city was not yet ready for truly *national* sports.

As America changed, then, so did the Sugar Bowl's long-standing good luck. In late November 1963, the MWSA again had very few options. The unbeaten SEC leader, Ole Miss, was a sure thing based on tradition and on the school's own segregation policies ruling them out of most other bowls.

Beyond that, though, the southern pool was not deep. There were no strong runners-up in the SWC behind the Cotton Bowl's poll-leading Longhorns. This made the SEC's Alabama and Auburn, with one loss each, the extent of the MWSA's list.[67]

It also put Bama coach Bear Bryant in a position to make demands. With two games left, one of which was against Auburn, Coach Bryant gave the MWSA an ultimatum: either the Tide would receive a no-strings-attached bid or he would sign with Houston's young Bluebonnet Bowl instead. The Orange Bowl was also still courting both Alabama and Auburn, but Miami had the luxury of waiting, with backups like Pitt, Penn State, and Syracuse available to them. The New Orleans group needed to play it safe. So they gambled.[68]

They lost. Underdog Auburn had not even scored on Alabama in four years, until that windy afternoon when the Tigers pulled off an upset road win. The victory vaulted Auburn into fifth place, putting them above not only number nine Alabama but also the Sugar Bowl's SEC champs, seventh-ranked Ole Miss, who themselves pulled off only a tie against Mississippi State that day.[69]

The deal with Bryant forfeited Auburn to Orange, which paired the Tigers with the Big Eight champion, sixth-ranked Nebraska. Although this move got Miami two schools ranked higher than those going to New Orleans, it strangely left fourth-ranked University of Pittsburgh on the board.

As the events of late 1963 played out, Pitt's postseason was arguably martyred to the civil rights cause. The Panthers were having one of their best seasons in school history, their only loss coming at the hands of Heisman Trophy winner Roger Staubach and the second-place Midshipmen. Pittsburgh was consistently ranked in the top five that year and deserved a bid from a major bowl. Having removed themselves from Sugar's consideration, and with the Rose Bowl then operating a Big Six–Big Ten pairing, Pitt held out for a call from either Dallas or Miami.

In response to President Kennedy's assassination on November 22, several games scheduled for November 23 were postponed. One of these was Pitt's hosting of tough traditional rival Penn State. The Orange Bowl was not willing to wait until the December 7 makeup game, nor to risk a Pitt loss after an early contract, so they ran with Auburn off of Sugar's desperate fumble. Navy was the front-runner to meet Texas for a number one versus number two battle in the Cotton Bowl, but Pitt could still get the bid. It hinged on the outcome of the also delayed service classic and on the Pentagon's decision about whether academies would be withheld from the postseason out of reverence for the late commander in chief. However, Navy defeated Army and the bowl decision was deferred to the Middies locker room, leaving the 9–1 Panthers out in the cold.

When contracts were signed for New Year's Day 1964, the absence of Pitt had sportswriters scratching their heads and lineups looking "slightly absurd." Still, the MWSA at least had two ranked teams, the top dog in the SEC against an offense built around slinging sensation Joe Namath.[70]

But in early December, with three weeks of ticket sales still pending, things continued to get worse for Sugar. Namath's notoriety became a liability. When some Bama teammates had a few drinks and made a little noise at a restaurant near campus, the owner called the coaches. The singular unmistakable face that management could identify was that of the star quarterback. With no-nonsense Bryant having a rule against alcohol and players knowing better than to lie about it, Namath was suspended. It was broadcast that Joe Namath would not quarterback Alabama in the Sugar Bowl because of "an infraction of training rules." Sophomore Steve Sloan, who had thrown two passes in his college career—both incomplete—would get the nod at the start of the thirtieth anniversary of the New Orleans classic.[71]

|||||

Cliff Kern knew what time each of the other Sugar Bowlers got out of bed on New Year's Eve 1963. As soon as they looked out a window and saw snow falling, they immediately called the stadium committee chairman. Years of debates and $10,000 of MWSA funds had gone into the purchase of a new field cover. When the superintendent of Tulane Stadium, Nolan Chaix, said on Friday afternoon that his workers would not come out on the weekend to put it down, Kern made the one-man decision to lay it out for five full days, but he had feared it would land him in the MWSA doghouse. They could pull it up in sections to put down paint and chalk, but he was afraid it would create a greenhouse effect and make the grass shoot up through the markings. The morning before the game, however, he was a hero. "Don't worry! The field cover is down," he assured each caller.[72]

Kern then headed off to day two of the basketball tournament. Loyola Field House had been filled beyond capacity for the first set of matches, and with the championship pairing Kentucky and Duke, basketball passes were far harder to come by than football tickets. Kern and colleagues were settling in for the consolation game when the power suddenly went out. Heavy ice and snow had taken down a nearby electrical line, leaving the gym without lights for nearly an hour. As they sat in the dark, the Sugar Bowlers worried about the most popular basketball tourney in recent memory and also about the vulnerability of their football classic to a similar misfortune. But when the lights came back on, hoopsters took the court and bowlers relaxed.[73]

Then, as sneakers squeaked across the floor, someone tapped Kern on the shoulder. "We need you fellows over at the stadium," he said. "We've got a problem." When they got to the field, they found the tarpaulin buried in more than three inches of snow, and more was still coming down. They needed to get the field cleared and the cover up before kickoff. To Chaix, it looked "pretty hopeless." His staff would try, but they demanded at least proper shoes. So a couple of bowl execs ran out for two dozen pairs of rubber boots, and the snow relocation project began.[74]

Reinforcements arrived under heavy security when the sheriff sent over inmates from the parish prison. Volunteers from various city agencies also came and went throughout the night, passing off brooms and shovels. In the early morning, as Kern drove home from the group's New Year's Eve party at Antoine's, the lights were still on at Tulane Stadium.

Hours before gates were to open, things were no less chaotic. A patrol car ran lights and sirens to escort truckloads of nonskid grit from a local warehouse. The florist delivering poinsettias nearly carved ruts into the turf as he maneuvered his van past snowbanks surrounding the field. Admission was postponed thirty minutes while Boy Scout troops cleared the stands with sweeping, shoveling, and snowball fights. When NBC's cameras were turned on, less than half the seats were filled.[75]

Except for the playing field and benches, nearly every inch of the stadium floor was piled high with mounds of snow. While the Sugar Bowlers joked nervously about it looking like an actual bowl of sugar, the stadium was conspicuously all-white in other ways, too. All the deliberation on open seating had been meaningless. When another two segregated SEC squads were signed, the Black community resumed its long-standing boycott.[76]

More white fans did trickle in. Scalpers never did any business, but not long after kickoff few empty seats were noticeable. Moreover, the stadium looked beautiful. The grass kept its green tint, the markings were clear, and the turf was intact.[77]

Actually, it seemed the field condition was too good, as it left no excuse for the sloppy play that ensued. The classic had only survived seven years in a geographic cocoon because the Southeastern Conference had been a powerhouse of college football. There were already misgivings about Alabama's record and the absence of Joe Namath, but for the first three quarters of the 1964 Sugar Bowl, Ole Miss did not look like the champion of any section of the country, much less of the midcentury SEC.[78]

From their second possession, Johnny Vaught's Rebels were on pace for a record-setting performance—for the most fumbles in a single bowl. They ultimately coughed up eleven balls, nearly half of which were noncontact drops, and lost six of them to Alabama defenders. Mississippi did not get into Alabama territory or convert a single first down during the entire first half. An onside kick to their own 44 handed them their best field position of the opening two periods. Even then, a long pass was intercepted on the Alabama 18 to close the second quarter.

As the Rebels ran through a carved-out channel in the snow toward the locker room, they were trailing 9–0 to the underdog Elephants. Namath's backup, Sloan, was leading a relatively conservative offense for Bryant. He completed three passes for 29 yards but otherwise marshaled the ground game to keep putting the placekicker at a good angle to the uprights. Tim Davis's second of three field goals in the first half, a 46-yarder, broke his 1962 record for the longest in Sugar Bowl history. He was more than reliable, and with Bama's success on defense, they were happy to put up points three at a time.[79]

Spectators, sportswriters, and sponsors were getting antsy for some action in the second half. Diliberto was ready to type up that classic as "the dullest of all." After a good return of the opening kickoff, Ole Miss got one first down and 1 yard into Alabama territory before losing another fumble. Mississippi governor Ross Barnett looked down from his box and asked, "Why is it the boys can't hold on to the football?" Just as he concluded, "It looks damp out there," Bama fumbled it right back to the Rebs.[80]

After a punt and two more turnovers, Davis came back for an even longer field goal, this time from 48. While this meant another Sugar Bowl record, it also meant neither team was getting anywhere near its opponent's end zone. Late in the third period, the Tide had four field goals, the Rebels had one first down, and the Sugar Bowlers had an embarrassment on their hands.

Then, on the second play of the fourth quarter, Ole Miss's Perry Lee Dunn hit halfback Dave Wells with a 42-yard pass into the Alabama red zone, and after a shoestring tackle, the receiver even held on to the ball. Mississippi converted on fourth-and-2 and capped the drive with a soft completion from the 5 into the end zone. A true point after touchdown put 7 on the board for Ole Miss.

Next, it was Bama that lost a fumble on its ensuing possession, but Ole Miss promptly gave the ball back on downs. From there, every possession ended in either a punt or a fumble—or both, as when Ole Miss botched a return at midfield. The Rebels started their last drive from their own 20, down by 5. Three long Jim Weatherly passes got them to the Alabama 34 in time for one more play. However, a 15-yard penalty pushed them back to midfield. Weatherly dropped back and took a 21-yard shot, only to have the second half end just like the first—with an interception and a long return on an expired clock.[81]

Most sportswriters focused on the record-setting day of Tim Davis, who tied the classic's record for the most points scored by a single player. He also earned sole ownership of both the most field goals and the longest field goal in Sugar Bowl history. Even in celebrating this feat, though, Pie Dufour pointed at the (red) elephant in the room. He questioned the quality of a football game whose Most Valuable Player was a "kicking specialist." "Davis didn't make a tackle," Dufour commented. "He didn't throw a block. He didn't gain a yard." He added, with slight exaggeration, "In fact, he didn't even wear pads of any kind."[82]

Under the stadium, while Bryant's players serenaded him with the school fight song, Vaught answered reporters about why his guys looked so out of championship form. "I have no idea—or will I even suggest one," he conceded.

"I have one," Diliberto thought. "The Rebels simply looked like a team that had grown weary of New Year's visits to New Orleans. Mississippi played here four of the past five years."[83]

Even before the MWSA had its first meeting of 1964, a junior member gave an anonymous interview to the *Pittsburgh Courier*, describing the "utter disillusionment" surrounding the classic. Afterwards, Butch Curry reported, "A new breed's angling to get firmer control of the Sugar Bowl." It was said to be a group that would no longer "pussyfoot along with the whims of segregation."[84]

CHAPTER 6
Check Downs

Like the MWSA, local civil rights groups also had a younger generation "angling to get firmer control." In late 1963, the New Orleans chapter of the Congress of Racial Equality and the Youth Council of the city's NAACP branch were questioning their elders' quiet negotiations. Racial strife had been minimal since schools reopened peacefully in 1961, and for years deference had been given to secret meetings and interracial compromises. However, this route had become ineffective.

Back in 1960, the city's first major civil rights demonstration was staged in the shopping corridor of Dryades Street. Just before Easter, when the predominantly African American patrons would be buying new church clothes and spring fashions, the Consumers' League organized picketers and a "Don't Buy Where You Can't Work" boycott. Within a month, all but one store acquiesced, and dozens of Black cashiers, clerks, and sales personnel were hired.[1]

Late that summer, the Consumers' League planned another march for fair employment, and Reverend Avery Alexander distributed signs at South Claiborne and Washington Avenues. That was when Mayor Morrison began his selective enforcement of the state's demonstration bans, though this would not be applied to the "cheerleaders" springing into action two months later. After the reverend and five other activists were jailed, Alexander's group instead pushed a "selective buying" campaign through the press and began litigation to have the newly levied laws on picketing annulled.[2]

However, another clique of former Dryades picketers had a different response. They viewed police interference as a tool in their fight. The young Rudy Lombard, Jerome Smith, and Oretha Castle were drawn together at the initial Easter demonstration. Joined by other student activists, both Black and white, they soon formed the local chapter of CORE to initiate nonviolent direct action. They saw their likely arrests and the inevitable publicity as a way "to sting consciences a little." They were prepared to win hearts and change minds through "redemptive suffering."[3]

They also started with more aggressive goals than asking stores in Black neighborhoods to hire Black employees. On September 9, 1960, they held their first lunch counter sit-in at the Woolworths at Canal and Rampart Streets, which led to the arrests of five Black and two white students. The next day, members of the NAACP's Youth Council showed their support by picketing the area and putting themselves at risk. Another sit-in and more arrests occurred a week later, and direct action was picking up steam in New Orleans.[4]

Demonstrations, boycotts, and picketing lightened cash registers, but the threat of racists' reprisals indicated a no-win situation for many merchants. They still were not risking a public stance on integration, but they knew something had to be done. Consequently, fifteen businessmen formed a private alliance, asking influential whites, including attorney Harry Kelleher and the Tulane board's Darwin Fenner, to represent them in closed-door dialogue. In turn, Black lawyers Lolis Elie and Revius Ortique Jr. became spokesmen for a federation of local civil rights groups, known collectively as the Citizens' Committee. Together, these two parties worked behind the scenes for years to advance integration in downtown New Orleans, without publicity.[5]

During that time, the younger members of the Citizens' Committee, such as Oretha Castle, obliged the NAACP and Consumers' League, and CORE tabled plans for additional sit-ins. However, direct action remained influential, as Elie and Ortique always had at their disposal the threat of further demonstrations. By the summer of 1962, an agreement was reached with business managers and news outlets to integrate downtown lunch counters without media coverage. By the time most locals learned of it, it was old news. These tactics slowly led to more Black employment and fewer racial designations in various pockets of the city.[6]

Likewise, in early 1963 pacts with Canal Street merchants seemed promising. When they gave commitments for new hiring practices, a publicized mass action was postponed. But in late spring, employment numbers remained far below the established quota. The Citizens' Committee's response was again a patient one. A joint press release by Dutch Morial, Avery Alexander, and Oretha Castle reported that although it was "not as rapid as our groups would like to see it," there had been "some progress." Black citizens were asked to wait for future updates.[7]

The younger activists were restless. Clearly, the threat of mass demonstrations, which were always canceled when talks resumed, was no longer effective. Not only had negotiations slowed to a crawl but also white leaders repeatedly reneged on promises altogether. So in August, the NAACP Youth Council began daily picketing and leafleting in front of Canal Street stores. The Citizens' Committee distanced itself from the action, which it said would derail mediations. Marches continued anyway, and soon the full NAACP backed its junior members.[8]

Still, even as its coalition unraveled, the greater Citizens' Committee held its ground. Later that month, Reverend A. L. Davis called off another planned march on City Hall, this one pushing for desegregation of municipal buildings and employment. Davis told an eager overflow assembly at the St. John Institutional Missionary Baptist Church that Mayor Schiro had agreed to a six-point proposal and firm deadline. When the deadline passed, though, racial signs still hung in some city buildings and promised jobs were unassigned. The mayor gave excuses and pleaded that New Orleans must "work things out at the conference table" to avoid becoming "another Birmingham." But that was a breaking point in the city's civil rights movement.[9]

On the last day of September 1963, more than ten thousand Black New Orleanians and hundreds of white supporters marched from Shakespeare Park to City Hall, led by Morial, Alexander, Davis, and Castle. "Freedom! Freedom! Freedom!" rang out, as they trekked four miles to the municipal plaza, where they sang "The Star-Spangled Banner."

"This is a big beginning," Reverend Davis proclaimed from the steps of City Hall. "We are marching on until victory is ours in New Orleans."[10]

He also read a petition, which was presented to the city council. When it went unanswered for many weeks, City Hall became the focus of the first mass direct action of the new era of New Orleans civil rights. In early November, groups repeatedly assembled in the mayor's parlor and the city council chamber, and several demonstrators were arrested when they ignored orders to leave.

The biggest uproar occurred when Black activists integrated the building's cafeteria. Policemen carried out two women still sitting in the chairs they refused to vacate. Then, when Reverend Alexander announced he would stay until served, two officers seized him by his ankles and dragged him up the basement stairway, through the lobby, and back down the front cement steps of City Hall. As images of his abuse were splashed across the nation's media, the fifty-three-year-old reverend became the face of the local movement's new ethos of "redemptive suffering."

The next time Reverend Davis stood before a church rally, he declared, "We thought we had city officials we could talk to. But now it is obvious that talking is out! We must have action!" From the same pulpit where he had recently canceled a demonstration in favor of discussion, he laid out a colossal agenda, including stepped-up Canal Street picketing, boycotts of various businesses, stand-ins at local theaters, and daily sit-ins at the City Hall cafeteria. Instead of asking citizens to idly trust mediators, he now insisted, "Everyone who believes in this cause must assist." He repeated his own willingness to face violence or incarceration and concluded, "We have gone too far to turn back now."[11]

|||||

By early 1964, theater stand-ins were key in New Orleans. Activists would await their turns at a box office window, inquire about seating, refuse to patronize a segregated venue, and return to the back of the queue, forming a revolving thread, which would slow if not suspend sales.

In late February, a like demonstration was staged at Loew's Theatre to oppose segregation at the upcoming telecast of Sonny Liston and Cassius Clay's championship fight. Three female CORE members were arrested. When released on a twenty-five-dollar bond, one of them dispatched a game-changing telegram to both fighters. The local CORE vice-chairman, twenty-two-year-old Ruthie Wells, informed the pair that their bout would be shown in segregated venues across the South and that individuals were being jailed in protest. She asked each boxer to deny the broadcasts and become "an all-time champion in the eyes of twenty million Negroes."[12]

Within three days, both Loew's and the Saenger Theatre announced cancellations. Liston had released a statement reading, "I feel that the color of my people's money is the same as anyone else's. They should get the same seats. If not, I don't want those places to have the fight." While several other southern cities, such as Jackson and Montgomery, also canceled the showing, others, including Atlanta and Miami, agreed to Liston's terms.[13]

Those terms left Municipal Auditorium as the only place in the Big Easy to see the championship fight, but during the week of the match, even this venue's right to show the bout was challenged. The New Orleans Philharmonic Society asked a civil court judge to stop the telecast from being shown as contracted—on the opposite side of the auditorium from their concert. "It is well known," their spokesman eloquently stated, "that persons viewing boxing exhibitions engage in shouts of encouragement and disparagement and are in general enthusiastic in their vocal expressions." Schiro apologized for the "conflict in booking," but having just promised the city big-time sports, he said the fight must go on. A judge agreed that the space's partition was legal, even if not sufficiently soundproof. In the end, the schedule was shifted and only the final minutes of Ravel's *Shéhérazade* cycle received the vocal accompaniment of every fight fan in the city with eyes on Liston and Clay.[14]

CORE was also fighting continued segregation in most downtown hotels. In the spring, the group alerted Washington, DC, officials to policies of the Roosevelt, where a World Trade Conference was scheduled for May. DC agreed that the attendance of Undersecretary of Commerce Franklin D. Roosevelt Jr., among others, in a segregated venue would "compromise the dignity" of the nation's officers, and the convention was moved to the Jung Hotel.[15]

Aside from operating one of only three integrated downtown hotels, Arthur Jung also found a way around a crippling city ordinance that required racial separation by a solid, floor-to-ceiling partition anywhere alcohol was sold. In early 1964, African American Frank Pania, proprietor of the famed Dew Drop Inn, was fighting the law in federal court. He had been arrested repeatedly for serving both races in his club. Repeal of the ordinance would allow Pania to maintain the white clientele who flocked to his shows and would also remove the last barrier to Black guests having full hotel accommodations. In the meantime, Jung indulged integrated conventions, including the Roosevelt's defectors, by establishing a private space for parties to enjoy their meals with an open bar.[16]

Even as activism evolved and tactics changed, the Citizens' Committee neither dissolved nor stopped petitioning political leaders. In early May, Oretha Castle and Reverends Davis and Alexander spent an hour in Baton Rouge with newly elected governor John McKeithen. He listened courteously to their thirteen demands, which included fair access to employment, housing, education, public accommodations, and the vote. They also stated that "unrest cannot be lulled into complacency by mere tokens of equality and opportunity." Afterwards, McKeithen's takeaway message was that he feared further demonstrations would spawn violence, hurt Louisiana's image, and "do their cause no good." Despite his sincerity, the governor's caution merely sounded like more political stalling, which activists would no longer accept. They were prepared to continue direct action.[17]

Then, two months later, on July 2, President Lyndon Johnson signed into law the Civil Rights Act of 1964, prohibiting racial discrimination and addressing every topic in the local group's petition to the governor. This landmark legislation indicated vast new freedoms, but it also brought rumblings of reactionary violence. Within a day, New Orleans papers featured a half-page ad that resembled the "Declaration of Principles" regarding schools. This "Message to All Responsible Citizens" acknowledged varying degrees of disagreement with Johnson but declared, "We are in accord on this: PEACE and ORDER must be maintained." It was signed by 230 prominent citizens, including Seymour Weiss of the Roosevelt Hotel.[18]

Likewise, Mayor Schiro immediately held a press conference, asserting that "we can't pick and choose the laws we like and don't like" and directing everyone to adhere to the Civil Rights Act. "And I mean everyone," he stressed. He argued that the city could prevent violence and disorder "if cool heads and intelligent leadership among all our groups prevail." When asked about other southern leaders calling for defiance, he answered with no uncertainty, "We are going to comply with the law." The mayor also expressed confidence in the police and promised, "Anybody that has a legal right in this community will be protected in his legal rights."[19]

The next topic on the mayor's agenda, however, thoroughly muddied just what these rights were. Schiro called on City Attorney Alvin Liska to explain the effect of the Civil Rights Act on New Orleans and, supposedly, to clear up any confusion that might lead to trouble. Liska's description included a lot of maybes and loopholes.

He stated directly that hotels, motels, inns, and gas stations were officially desegregated. But he added that for other businesses to be affected, "the operation must affect interstate commerce." He explained that a restaurant, bar, or club was impacted when a "substantial portion" of its product came from outside Louisiana. "How the federal court will interpret 'substantial' is another thing," he added. Under the banner of clarifying what businesses might be exempt, he said, "The way the law is enforced will be by the individual himself." On top of that, it was announced that the city's police would keep the peace but not answer complaints of noncompliance. Those had to be taken to federal court.[20]

In essence, Schiro's firm warning against resistance was capped off with a winking acknowledgment that few establishments were without argument for exemption and that enforcement would not come from the city. Still, his zero-tolerance stance on violence and disorder was delivered without such qualifiers. And in this regard, the city's efforts were largely effective. There were a few instances of reactionary vandalism and aggression over the Independence Day weekend, such as a cross burned at Xavier Prep and a pair of assaults on Black men by white teenagers at uptown bus stops. But overall, civic leaders were proud of the immediate response.

Early news reports focused on order being maintained. They described African Americans visiting formerly off-limits theaters, coffee shops, and cafeterias, emphasizing that few met problems or pushback. By the end of the week, both the *Times-Picayune* and the *Louisiana Weekly* praised the community for taking the bill "in stride."[21]

While the city congratulated itself on staying out of international headlines, compliance was far from complete. Many spaces were not even "tested" that summer. African Americans did not make a mad dash to Bourbon Street nightclubs or French Quarter eateries. In fact, early probes of such touristy spots went no further than calls for reservations. Places like Brennan's restaurant and the Roosevelt's Blue Room received table requests from Black customers, who would later cancel, and Black patronage in such spots remained to be seen.[22]

Dutch Morial announced that the NAACP was not dispatching testers. The group stressed caution, especially as race riots raged in Harlem. They focused instead on litigation against clearly noncompliant establishments, such as a pair of hamburger joints maintaining "colored only" windows. Then, as more businesses opened up, Black citizens were urged to use these spaces and exercise their rights.[23]

CORE's regional director sent local activists a blueprint. It recommended small numbers of "cool and non-argumentative" agents to seek fair service and to merely report noncompliance. While failed attempts were to be revisited daily, the goal was "to achieve desegregation quietly." Safety was key. Local police were to be alerted before each endeavor, and the "least resistant" establishments were "first on the list."[24]

Other approaches were far riskier. When Reverend Alexander and five other activists integrated the Tango Lounge on St. Claude Avenue, they had pots of hot water and bottles of soda poured on them before gunshots were fired into the walls. Unaffiliated individuals were even more vulnerable, like the twenty-four-year-old Black man wounded by both a fist and a bullet while ordering two early morning sandwiches at the Royal Castle hamburger stand on North Broad Street.[25]

During the first six months, compliance was spotty and slow. It would take time before many establishments, particularly French Quarter tourist hangouts, were even tested. There was no headline-making violence, but the city had not achieved the overarching overnight acceptance that was suggested in national news. One syndicated columnist made the sweeping statement, in July, that the "only discrimination" on Bourbon Street "was against the man who lacked the price of a drink." But this grand claim was based on a few bartenders predicting there might not be much trouble *if* Black customers ever appeared.[26]

|||||

That year, both Black and white children were deprived of summer activities as the city's adults dug in their heels. For starters, New Orleans kept her pools closed again in 1964. Two weeks after President Johnson signed the Civil Rights Act, the number of local children dying in unsupervised waters rose to eight, as two African American boys drowned in Bayou St. John under the Wisner Boulevard overpass. Four days later, when the city's soapbox derby should have been held on that bridge, regular traffic flowed and no New Orleanian kids got the chance to qualify homemade race cars for national competition.[27]

|||||

Meanwhile, Dixon was still trying to play ball with the rest of America and prodded both pro grid loops from every angle. He not only had another pair of NFL exhibitions booked but also proposed to each circuit a remodeled championship series culminating in neutral, warm-weather New Orleans. Both leagues were even invited to move their All-Star games to the Big Easy.

The NFL's Pro Bowl was happily settled in a long-term contract with the Los Angeles Coliseum, but the AFL game's three years in San Diego had never filled the roughly thirty thousand–seat stadium. Some owners were already contemplating a move, and Dixon was welcomed to give his pitch at their May meeting, on the condition that he would not slip in plugs about expansion. Afterwards, only Barron Hilton objected, and the owners voted to give the offer more thorough investigation. Commissioner Foss appointed a committee of none other than Dixon's good buddies Lamar Hunt and Bud Adams to complete the study.[28]

On July 1, the day before President Johnson signed the Civil Rights Act, a joint statement was released from Mayor Schiro's office and AFL headquarters. The league's fourth All-Star game was set for the Big Easy in six months. Schiro proclaimed it a clear sign that New Orleans was moving ahead in "that ever vital aspect of sports." But he also rightfully said that Dixon deserved credit. Schiro had given his sports advisory committee "unlimited scope" and his full support but announced at their first meeting, "Your hands, however, are free." So the group remained a nominal collaboration of members nursing pet projects, just as Dixon continued working with his colleagues on the franchise hunt.[29]

Dixon believed that big attendance figures were the city's ticket to the pros and advertised the three upcoming games by telling locals as much. He even established a priority system, giving All-Star seat preferences to fans holding preseason stubs. He also addressed some of the downfalls of the doubleheader. When he stated his group thought "the fans, the ladies in particular, would prefer a shorter evening of football," Ed Devenport called it, "a masterpiece in the art of understatement." Although locals en masse stubbornly hung on through the end of game two, Devenport remembered that "the time factor . . . ran a close race with the weather in matters of misery." Single billings addressed one problem, but Dixon still fretted about the forecast.[30]

Consequently, he took his friend Al Wester to lunch on a July afternoon. Dixon was buying ad space on WWL radio for the day of the first exhibition, and the popular sports announcer had a voice guaranteed to get folks' attention. Dixon wanted Wester to read an encouraging report that would get fans off the fence and into the stadium. To accommodate Wester's travel plans, an "up-to-the-minute weather forecast" was recorded weeks in advance: "Clearing and cooler by game time."[31]

On the day of the Green Bay–St. Louis exhibition, Dixon drove through relentless rainfall toward the airport. The squads were again staying at the trusty Hilton Inn Motel, and Dixon stopped by as a one-man welcoming committee. As he made small talk with Vince Lombardi, the coach could tell Dixon was troubled about the downpour outside. "Oh, don't worry about the weather," Lombardi counseled. "Just before you came I heard a forecast for perfect weather for tonight." Dixon perked up, only to quickly realize that the "forecast" must have been the ad taped in July. He then needed to confess to, of all people, Vince Lombardi that he had doctored up a phony forecast to boost ticket sales. After doubling over in laughter, Lombardi gave the consolation that his guys always brought rain cleats, "just in case."[32]

Fortunately, Dixon's "up-to-the-minute forecast" not only endeared him to Lombardi but also proved pretty accurate. With the skies and temps improving just before gates opened, even fair-weather fans turned out. It was estimated that the full day of rain cost about ten thousand out-of-towners, particularly from Jimmy Taylor and Jerry Stovall's residual Baton Rouge base. But between the leagues' swelling popularity among TV audiences and the seasonal samplings of live action, the Big Easy had undergone a mass conversion to pro football fandom.[33]

That night, New Orleans broke her own record for the largest pro football crowd in a nonleague city, bringing in nearly 56,000. Again, NFL officials raved over the numbers but were also adamant that expansion was out until the young Minnesota Vikings and Dallas Cowboys achieved stable roster depth. Still, even Coach Lombardi, who himself never wanted for a packed house, predicted, "If New Orleans keeps getting crowds like this, it's bound to attract somebody who owns a football team."[34]

|||||

Actually, owners of one football team had recently been drawn toward the Southeast, but they eyed Atlanta. For most of July, relocation of the St. Louis Cardinals to the Georgia capital was considered a sure thing. League approval was granted, and local leaders had even redesigned their already-under-construction stadium. It was understood that Charles "Stormy" and Bill Bidwill would soon announce the move. Then, at the end of the month, the pair phoned Arthur Montgomery, chairman of the Atlanta Stadium Authority, to say that the Cardinals would stay in Missouri. "St. Louis has given us everything we wanted," they explained.[35]

Reporters described Georgians as scorned, used as pawns to squeeze new lease terms and lower taxes from St. Louis, but Atlanta officials were adamant that they remained on excellent terms with the NFL. In fact, within the week, Mayor Allen and Arthur Montgomery met with Rozelle to advertise their new facilities and reaffirm their franchise interests.[36]

There was, however, someone spurned by how the deal went down: Buddy Diliberto. Even after negotiations went sour, he was miffed that New Orleans had not been considered as a landing spot for the flighty Cardinals. After all, local ticket sales consistently outpaced those at Atlanta's exhibitions. So he cornered Stormy Bidwill on the subject, in the Tulane press box after the Cardinals–Packers game. The explanation was simple. "More of the official family in Atlanta was behind the pro football move," Bidwill offered plainly. "We saw more of 'em from the start."[37]

Dixon was about to see this for himself. Unlike Diliberto, Dixon was excited by the activity in Georgia. Right after the August 8 exhibition, he jumped on an eastbound plane. To him, Atlanta's near entrance but lingering eligibility "inevitably" meant "one of the leagues is going to expand into both New Orleans and Atlanta." Only one team had been on the move, but expansion ideally happened in pairs. For Dixon, Atlanta switched back from competitor to companion.[38]

As soon as he deplaned, he understood Bidwill's description. Dixon marveled at how Atlanta's whole sports project was orchestrated from the top. Mayor Allen personally spearheaded the drive for an $18 million multipurpose stadium with parking for ten thousand cars, seating for fifty thousand baseball fans, and another seven thousand sets of armrests for football. Architects even accommodated a future domed roof. Allen also authorized nearly an extra million dollars for around-the-clock labor for completion within one year. Despite the last-minute loss of the Cardinals, Allen anticipated welcoming Milwaukee's Braves by April 1965, and he wanted Atlanta's first Major League Baseball game to open the new arena.[39]

Allen was pressing his aldermen not only for stadium funds but also for their support in equalizing public accommodations. Since his annual State of the City message in January, Allen had challenged Atlantans to desegregate voluntarily but also vowed both to support the federal civil rights bill and to seek similar ordinances from his aldermanic board. "No longer can any business that seeks the public's patronage justify a position that it can refuse service to any portion of the public on the basis of race," he pronounced in early 1964.[40]

It was clear that equal access in Atlanta still was spotty. Some of the first test cases of the Civil Rights Act came out of the city, like those involving the Heart of Atlanta Motel and Lester Maddox's Pickrick Restaurant. It was also clear, however, that the city's leadership was not afraid to tell owners how to conduct their business. Allen was committed to advancement, and big league sports were a big part of his plan.

Dixon learned about it all through a series of meetings with invested Atlantans, who appreciated the value of a two-city expansion option. Dixon even conferred directly with Governor Carl Sanders, a former University of Georgia gridder, who passionately supported the push for pro ball. Before that weekend's Viking–Cardinal exhibition, Sanders hosted a party for NFL officials and surrounded them with city and state leaders versed in Atlanta's ambitions. Although only around twelve thousand locals drove through nonstop rain and a sketchy neighborhood for Saturday's scrimmage at a prep field, local leadership had shown big league status to the NFL—and to Dave Dixon.

When he returned home, Dixon described it to the cynical Buddy Diliberto. "I left with the impression that we're ahead of Atlanta in some respects, and behind her in others," Dixon confessed. He agreed with Diliberto that there was not as much demand for football in Atlanta. "The feeling just doesn't seem as intense," Dixon explained. "I can't help but feel that in New Orleans, we'd pack a 16,000-seat stadium no matter where it was located and no matter how bad the weather." However, he also conceded, "Atlanta seems to have a high personal regard for itself. Probably more so than New Orleans has for itself."[41]

|||||

Dixon returned from Atlanta inspired to attend to the finer details of hosting football. It proved wise, too. Within days, Pete Rozelle announced he would attend New Orleans's upcoming Cowboys–Bears exhibition. Dixon had two weeks.

Meanwhile, games in other cities were still going on, and those two weeks developed into, as Diliberto put it, "a midsummer nightmare." The writer assumed that during this time, Dixon had experienced "the realization that somebody up there doesn't like him." And by "up there," Diliberto could easily have meant Wisconsin.[42]

Local fans already bellyached about the Packers' lackluster performance at Tulane. The biggest disappointment was the biggest draw of the night, newly reinstated Paul Hornung, who logged only five carries, missed a chip shot field goal, and lost a fumble that set up the second Cardinal touchdown. Even Lombardi cracked, after his team's loss, that at least no one had played hard enough to get hurt.[43]

Next they faced Chicago. Apparently still fresh after their lackadaisical night in New Orleans, the Pack completely outshined the defending champs. And Hornung ignited the high-scoring offense, putting up 21 points on his own. The green and gold defense was equally punishing, holding the Bears to only a fourth-quarter consolation touchdown and injuring four Chicago offensive players, including Ronnie Bull and Mike Ditka.[44]

Going into the next week's game with so many starters out, the Bears naturally struggled on offense. But now, even George Allen's defense was unsteady, looking little like the unit that had earned him the last championship game ball. That night, Halas introduced a pair of televisions on the bench and reran tapes of previous series for players to study as they came off the field. Their performance was so bad, however, that Papa found it hard to judge whether the innovation was worth repeating. The Bears' next stop was Tulane Stadium, but between the defeats and the injuries, even a New Orleans sportswriter admitted, "The 'Monsters of the Midway' have not scared anyone but their own fans at this point."[45]

Green Bay was not done with the Big Easy, though. After souring New Orleanians a bit on preseason play and then ensuring that, as Dixon saw it, "the glitter has now been removed" from the league champs, the Packers went after the other half of the Crescent City's closeout billing. On the floor of Cotton Bowl Stadium, Lombardi's eleven outscored the home team five touchdowns to one field goal. Some of the overpowering came off of sloppy Cowboy play, like Green Bay returning a blocked field goal attempt for a touchdown when Dallas had only ten men on the field. Other highlights were simply of the type that New Orleanians had expected but missed, such as Zeke Bratkowski's 78-yard touchdown pass to Boyd Dowler or Hornung reversing on an option play to connect with Max McGee 61 yards downfield.[46]

The most painful moment for both Dixon and Diliberto, who watched from the press box with Rozelle, was a third-quarter Don Meredith pass. The quarterback leaped in the air, fired to his receiver, and was blindsided by Ray Nitschke before leaving the field with a busted knee.

After the game, Dallas sportswriter Gary Cartwright offered a small, sarcastic consolation. "Certainly the Cowboys looked more able than they had in any previous preseason game," he argued. "After all this is the first game all year in which they haven't had an extra-point attempt blocked." Likewise, Diliberto reasoned bitterly, "Despite the one-sidedness of the game, it was better played than the Green Bay–St. Louis contest." Neither sentiment was much comfort for Dixon, who knew he would have trouble drumming up excitement for the Bears and 'Boys.[47]

"I'm curious to see how New Orleans draws at the coming game," Rozelle commented, before taking off. Diliberto was quick to ask for a number that would impress the commissioner under the circumstances. "About thirty thousand," Rozelle replied.

The figure offended Dixon. "Nonsense," he said. "We'll put around fifty thousand in the stands."

"Around fifty thousand?" repeated Tex Schramm with disbelief. "That would be nothing short of fantastic considering what has happened leading up to the game." But then the group reminisced about team fortunes shifting from week to week, and Schramm summed up what they all understood: "Football is a funny game." Dixon left hoping that New Orleanians would understand that too.[48]

As Diliberto prepared his next columns, he collected sound bites from Dixon on the matchup's plummeting projections. Naturally, the promoter attempted to spin the hitches as "an unexpected test." Over the past several years, whenever sponsors advertised an event as a "test" of the public's interest, Diliberto repeatedly railed on the idea that it was the community rather than the performance that was being judged. "'Challenges' and 'tests' are things promoters and politicians talk about," he maintained, saying they "fall upon deaf ears among the ordinary folks."[49]

Diliberto had also long been convinced that no gates of any size would bring New Orleans closer to a franchise. "There are other factors governing that," he believed, not the least of which was the city's racial climate. In 1962, Diliberto had predicted DeFee's trouble with accommodations. And before Dixon's 1963 doubleheader, the reporter had argued that a sellout crowd and as many turned away would not be more important than "what that march on Washington Wednesday was all about."[50]

A lot seemed to have changed since then, however. Now Diliberto thought the size of the crowd just might matter. So he issued a "challenge" of his own. "I'm curious to see how our football public reacts," he admitted in Monday's paper. He told readers, "Any town will support the 'naturals.' Most cities won't support anything but the 'naturals.'" Changing his tune from previous years, he announced, "New Orleans, whether she knows it or not, is going to be very much on the NFL stage . . . The product is NFL football. That should be enough."[51]

While Dixon's cohort worried about a potentially embarrassing turnout, their companion city was recovering from a very real embarrassment of her own, in which Atlanta's August 29 AFL exhibition only narrowly missed disaster. On the eve of Georgia's San Diego–New York game, several Chargers visited a billiard room near their hotel. Several Black and white players had the balls racked when someone informed them that the African Americans were not welcome. Keith Lincoln, one of the white Chargers, confronted the manager, who made it clear that Ernie Ladd, Paul Lowe, Earl Faison, and Ernie Wright would have to leave. The whole group walked out of the pool hall—and debated walking out on the game.

"I was shocked," Faison told a local judge and NAACP leader, who interceded early on behalf of his hometown. "I thought Atlanta was a progressive city," he added. When news spread among city officials, Mayor Allen was outraged. He immediately called the team to apologize for what was, to him, completely unacceptable for any business operating in Atlanta. The next morning, Allen and the state attorney general met the Chargers players for breakfast to further express embarrassment and apologies. Governor Sanders expressed a similar sentiment by telephone later in the day.[52]

Head coach Sid Gillman said he supported whatever decision the team reached, and just before the scheduled start, the gridders announced they would play. Once they took the field, however, they realized they "weren't ready mentally for the game." "We just couldn't get started," one Charger explained, feeling that the team "stumbled around all night." Sonny Werblin's Jets (formerly Wismer's Titans) handed the reigning league champs their second preseason loss in team history. With a walkout averted, the story received minimal publicity, but Brad Pye wrote in the *Los Angeles Sentinel* that Jim Crow, not New York, had beaten San Diego that weekend.[53]

|||||

On Friday night, September 4, Commissioner Pete Rozelle, coaches George Halas and Tom Landry, and Cowboys owner Clint Murchison Jr. were seated in a grand banquet hall at the Jung Hotel. The dinner was sponsored by the Knights of the Charley Horse, a brand-new sports booster group comprising two dozen influential New Orleanians. Among their "honored guests" were all the white sports editors and directors from the city's mainstream media. Mayor Schiro was also there, as was a newcomer to the scene. Governor McKeithen, only about four months in office, made a quick impression on Dixon, introducing himself as "a tremendous football fan."[54]

The Knights presented several speakers who reaffirmed the city's commitment to advancing local sports. Head coach Tommy O'Boyle of the Green Wave gridiron talked about his resolve, despite the administration's continued deemphasis of the sport, to restore Tulane's football legacy and revamp the team's image. He even took issue with the "cute little Greenie a certain artist uses to depict a Tulane football player." He got fired up. "Look," he growled, "we don't want to be depicted as some nice little thing you'd want to cuddle. Why not something like the jolly green GIANTS?" He gave the impression that there might be a little something extra in the tank that fall.[55]

The crowd really came alive, however, when Pete Rozelle took the podium and told the locals that theirs was "one of the country's two leading cities in expansion plans." It was no secret that some owners were pushing the idea of two four-team divisions, requiring two new clubs, and Rozelle was adamant that "certainly Atlanta and New Orleans deserve the strongest consideration." Still, being the public relations pundit he was, Rozelle was careful to add that "no definite steps in that direction have been taken."[56]

The next morning, promoters read another miserable forecast, and as predicted, when gate sales were set to begin, storms did instead. After merciless rain, player injuries, team losses, and fan frustrations, there were only 38,000 warm seats in Tulane Stadium. Dixon was crushed, especially given his "guarantee" to Rozelle, not to mention his lost wager with sportswriter Pete Finney for an oyster lunch. And the idea of a domed stadium, which had sprouted in Dixon's mind during the doubleheader, was thriving.[57]

As for being tested, though, the city passed. The numbers were well over what the commissioner expected, even before the 5:30 showers, which he thought would normally be "a fatal blow." "Everything considered," Rozelle told reporters, "I believe the turnout was impressive." Likewise, Halas and Schramm, both advocates for a sixteen-team league, carried on about New Orleans's future in the pros.[58]

Dixon's group had heard it all before, though. As one of his buddies put it, "We won another 'medal' but still didn't pry anything that resembles a promise out of the NFL." Yet there was something different about where New Orleans stood in the summer of 1964.[59]

At that point, neither league was shy about the attractiveness of New Orleans and Atlanta. Moreover, New Orleans was getting an even bigger opportunity to impress the pros in the postseason. Given that the Big Easy could draw record-setting turnouts for exhibitions, there were realistic hopes for an overflow crowd to see a complete cast of All-Stars.[60]

The January AFL owners meeting also was bound for the Big Easy. Although the league heard no franchise bids at its May conference, the expansion committee's plan to add two teams for 1966 was known to be top priority for their winter assembly in New Orleans.[61]

The nation's sports pages questioned whether the older league would really let its upstart rivals beat it into New Orleans and Atlanta. What had long been a battle between cities for a franchise was morphing into a war between the leagues for the top two towns, even if it was, as one writer put it, a "snail's race." And while many locals still hoped the NFL would win the slow saunter over the finish line, the AFL had proven itself a dynamic, exciting brand that was not going anywhere, short of merging into the National Football League.[62]

Even longtime skeptic Buddy Diliberto saw an AFL franchise as "something the city could attach its shirttail to without fear of extinction." After all, in terms of big-time sports, he argued, "New Orleans is 'out' and it's time to get back 'in.'" He lamented that as soon as the Braves' move to Georgia was complete, the Big Easy would "suffer another indignity" as a spinster southern sister.[63]

CHAPTER 7
Stutter Step

"What's behind that Sugar Bowl door?" Buddy Diliberto asked in a late October column. "Progress," he reported, declaring that "the Sugar Bowl has gone modern." A day earlier the Mid-Winter Sports Association had hosted an off-the-cuff exchange with reporters from the city's mainstream media. Football scouting was in full swing, and MWSA president Theo Maumus announced that reps would be in Durham that weekend, sizing up Georgia Tech and Duke, while others watched Nebraska host Missouri.

"Does the Sugar's interest in Nebraska indicate that there will be no racial barriers?" one reporter asked.

"All eligible teams are being considered whether or not they have Negro players," Maumus answered. "Our interest is national in scope."

Relieved, the crowd took that opportunity to express its dread of yet another all-SEC event. "The chances of that happening again are slim," Maumus assured them. The sportswriters were quick to stipulate that pairing the SEC champ with an SWC runner-up was equally unattractive, and a Sugar exec tested that sentiment. He gave the scribes a hypothetical choice for the game's "visiting" squad: a third-ranked southern team or a ninth-ranked Big Eight champ. "Which would be more desirable?" he asked. It was an easy pick for the reporters: "We'd like to see some new faces."[1]

There was relief on both sides. The MWSA had already labored ten months to open up every event. That spring, the basketball committee worked feverishly to reunite with intersectional schools, focusing heavily on the Big Eight and Big Ten. Their contacts were cordial, but it was clear that these colleges feared putting students in "embarrassing situations." When the Sugar men settled on their final four, minus the Eight and Ten, one member said with hope, "They will probably change their opinions after we have had some games under actual conditions." The tourney could still technically be considered intersectional, with the Missouri Valley Conference's Louisville joining three southern schools. Moreover, the Cardinals were expected to showcase the school's first three African American cagers, Wade Houston, Sam Smith, and Eddie Whitehead.[2]

Prevention of "embarrassment" and "agitation" colored the entire 1964–1965 MWSA calendar, right down to the football halftime show. With the city planning a grand observance of the sesquicentennial anniversary of the Battle of New Orleans, Irwin Poché wanted to incorporate the occasion into his always elaborate pageantry. He invited both Miss America and Miss Great Britain, wanting the latter to be accompanied by an English nobleman. However, his plans to have a Washington dignitary escort his country's beauty queen caused quite a stir in Sugar's meeting room.

Charles Zatarain begged Poché to reconsider. He feared that if someone like the attorney general was chosen and Ole Miss wound up playing, chaos would erupt. Poché vowed not to bait the Rebels by putting Bobby Kennedy on the 50-yard line, but the thought of scandalous headlines had everyone on edge. A consensus endorsed Zatarain's caution, and Poché promised to find someone to "lend dignity" rather than political debate. In the end, Andrew Jackson Donelson and Edward Michael Pakenham, descendants of the generals, would meet on a different local battlefield on New Year's Day.[3]

A war of another kind threatened what Tulane track coach Johnny Oelkers thought would be "the greatest meet ever for the Sugar people." Oelkers sent invitations to Olympic stars from the top tier of the 1964 Tokyo podium, including Bob Hayes, Mike Larrabee, and Bob Schul. The meet was also moved from the West Bank's Behrman Stadium to Tulane's oval, where the bleachers would be integrated.[4]

Then, in mid-November, the ongoing battle between the Amateur Athletic Union and the NCAA forced the MWSA to settle for an all-collegiate show. With nearly all the Olympians disqualified, Oelkers scrambled to stretch the roster beyond white southerners. Although most of the salvaged races remained rematches from recent years, Oelkers ultimately secured two superstar Black sprinters with Olympic credentials. One was Richard Stebbins of Grambling, who ran a leg in America's gold medal 4-by-100-meter relay. The other was a local prodigy, Carver High alum Theron Lewis. The Southern University star had qualified in the 400-meter dash and made the trip to Tokyo with Team USA. Stebbins and Lewis signed on as the first African Americans to compete in Sugar spikes.[5]

As for filling football cleats, locals had two favorites to be the intersectional invitee: Notre Dame and Nebraska. But as the November 14 games approached, after which bids were expected, Notre Dame reaffirmed its no-bowl policy and undefeated Nebraska was clearly counting on Cotton. In Dallas, they could challenge the also unbeaten SWC champion Arkansas Razorbacks, ranked just one notch above them at number three.

Unfortunately, in the 1964 bidding war, Sugar did not have a flashy SEC lure. Second-ranked, SEC-leading Alabama ruled out back-to-back New Orleans appearances, opting to face the fifth-ranked Longhorns in Miami. With that, number nine LSU, having one loss and one tie, became the best Southeastern option. So Sugar scouts followed the Tigers to Mississippi State, prepared to discuss "unofficial" invitations.[6]

MWSA reps went to several games that weekend, including Tulsa at North Texas State and Virginia Tech at Syracuse. The Syracuse possibility had percolated in local papers for a while, even before Nebraska and Notre Dame were nixed. Despite Syracuse's two defeats and absence from the top ten, Buddy Diliberto and Pete Finney steadily plugged the Eastern entry. They surely did not want the bowl to default to tenth-ranked Georgia Tech, which despite recently going independent would not satisfy the veto of an all-SEC tilt. Likewise, for Diliberto and Finney, even scoring sensation Jerry Rhome did not justify bringing in not-so-distant neighbors from Tulsa.[7]

Diliberto and Finney hyped the "box office appeal" of Syracuse's two biggest stars. Sophomore halfback Floyd Little and senior fullback Jim Nance, both African American, were considered the most exciting backfield duo since Doc Blanchard and Glenn Davis at Army two decades earlier. Little, a former sprint champion, scored five rushing touchdowns against Kansas that season, which Diliberto pointed out was three more than Nebraska's whole squad managed. And Nance was fifth in the nation that year in rushing yards, inching into third place in school history, behind only legends Ernie Davis and Jim Brown. Diliberto and Finney argued that this one-two punch "would be a dramatic way to end the segregation thing" and recover the bowl's "national 'image.'"[8]

In their penultimate game, Syracuse answered Virginia Tech's 9 first-quarter points with a goal-line run each by Little and Nance, but they again trailed the upset-hungry Hokies by 2 late in the fourth. Then, with less than a minute and a half remaining, quarterback Rich King took his offense 54 yards in five plays and launched an 18-yard pass to Harris Elliott in the end zone with only seconds to spare. It gave Syracuse a 20–15 win and a spot in the top ten. It also gave Monk Simons the go-ahead to bid.

The next day, an "unofficially official" Sugar Bowl was announced: eighth-ranked LSU versus ninth-ranked Syracuse. The Tigers were required to wait, and the Orangemen coach opted not to give their next opponent added fuel. So both squads deferred for another week.[9]

|||||

On the following Saturday, sports reporters and Sugar Bowlers packed into the Tulane Stadium press box to watch the Greenies take on traditional rival—and MWSA selection—Louisiana State. The game was slated to be a now standard overpowering of the deemphasized Wave by their perennially ranked neighbors.

The Syracuse affair was about two periods ahead, and everyone hushed as updates arrived. Reports out of West Virginia had Syracuse up by 14 over the Mountaineers at halftime. Next, the third-quarter Orangemen lead was announced at 6 points, but their offense was marching aggressively downfield. Then, just before intermission at Tulane, the final score from Morgantown arrived. Two late Mountaineer drives upset Syracuse by a single point. Sugar scouts faced a tough chore, considering it "a sad duty to extend the invitation to a losing team."[10]

Likewise, the Sugar Bowlers in the Greenie press box were heartsick, and the glares they cast had Diliberto and Finney huddled together with their heads down for the rest of the game. Meanwhile, the local underdogs were holding on to their lead against the other half of Sugar's lineup. Tulane had put the first points on the board with a first-quarter field goal, and the Wave's "posse" defended its end zone flawlessly.

"We couldn't be that unlucky to lose 'em both," said one of the Sugar Bowlers, as they looked down at three ticks left before halftime and as many points in Tulane's favor. "But anything can happen in this game," was the only answer.[11]

The Wave were still pumped after their victory at Vanderbilt and were not giving Pete Fountain the credit, although he seemingly cursed his sixth team by playing at Vandy's homecoming. As Coach O'Boyle put it, his Greenies had the "victory taste in their mouths." LSU did match Tulane's field goal to close the half, but no Sugar Bowlers were relaxing.[12]

When game action resumed, the Bengal band roused the east stands with "Tiger Rag," and the LSU offense was cheered to the Tulane 1-yard line. However, the Greenies guarded three feet for three downs and forced a field goal attempt that went wide.

"I'll bet the Sugar Bowl people are squirming," Governor McKeithen commented to Tulane president Herbert Longenecker from the latter's field box. The Syracuse loss had been announced, fostering any-given-Saturday suspense.

The Tigers' next stab at a 3-pointer was true, however, and they entered the final quarter with their first lead of the afternoon. And after more of a scoreless stalemate, LSU got new life on a Tulane punt. Greenie quarterback Dave East, who executed a booming punt with tremendous hang time in the first half, had this one blocked, setting up stellar field position and 7 follow-up points for LSU. Soon after, Tigers students swarmed the field, flaunting the rivalry's victory symbol, known as "the Rag."[13]

The win secured LSU's spot in the top ten, but Syracuse fell off the list. Diliberto and Finney had argued that a New York team would garner big publicity from the Northeast's heavy media concentration. They just had not envisioned the headline being "Syracuse Loses but Still Gets Sugar Bowl Bid."[14]

Mail coming into the *Times-Picayune* for Diliberto picked up substantially. Seeing the desk of his *States-Item* counterpart, he noticed a mound of letters for Finney too. "Must be early Christmas cards," he quipped.[15]

Fans were not holding back. The 1965 classic looked like, as one fan put it, "the mismatch of the year," and its biggest advocates were taking the heat. The gentler readers called it "a dull affair." More fiery locals revived the "Lemon Bowl" moniker and dubbed Diliberto "Lemon Bowl King." One note informed the columnist, "The next bus for Syracuse leaves at 10 a.m.," and instructed him, "Be under it!" Another asked "Do you feel like a Little man now?"[16]

All the crowing about the bowl's one-sidedness only lasted two weeks, however. Hurricane Hilda had postponed LSU's October date with Florida, which was rescheduled for December 5. As it turned out, the bullet Sugar dodged at Tulane ricocheted.

The Tigers were walloped by the Gators, whose opening possession was an 80-yard, 14-play touchdown drive. In the second quarter, a hobbling Steve Spurrier connected with Jack Harper for a 35-yard touchdown. In the second half, Florida scored its third touchdown off a faked field goal attempt. LSU mustered only 6 points and had five turnovers. The game was touted as breaking whatever jinx had kept the Gators scoreless against Louisiana State since 1960. Now it was the Sugar Bowl that seemed jinxed. Instead of having a perceived SEC powerhouse and a weak Eastern foe, the game was considered simply a "losers' bowl."[17]

|||||

When the holidays arrived, the Sugar Bowl was undersold by roughly twenty thousand seats. The MWSA had been in panic mode throughout December, discussing a blackout area that would include Baton Rouge and hiring a public relations firm to improve the game's image. However, ticket sales lagged even before schools were signed, and more factors were at play than just disappointing team records or any backlash against integration.[18]

This year, the classic had new competition for postholiday, cash-strapped fans: the incoming AFL All-Stars. The MWSA was also vying with NBC's nine hours of full-color New Year's Day football. The Woolco department store urged locals to watch three back-to-back bowl games "without leaving your home" and guaranteed game-time delivery on "true-to-life" color televisions. On top of all that, Syracuse's ticket sales were the smallest of any Sugar Bowl team in history.[19]

With so much beyond their control, bowl reps focused instead on ensuring smooth operations and happy teams. An early task was to greet the Orange squad at the airport, and four bowlers made a two hundred–mile drive to be waiting when the team touched down in Pensacola. Syracuse had several similarities to the 1956 Pittsburgh Panthers, beyond integration. They, too, were escaping winter weather for workouts, arriving a week and a half early. And coach Ben Schwartzwalder, much like Michelosen, expected two-a-days until they departed for the Crescent City. December 25 was a scheduled holiday, but the team's publicist thought any midweek hiccups could have Schwartzie's group practicing "after they open their Christmas presents."[20]

"We have come here strictly for business," Coach emphasized. "This is no pleasure excursion."[21]

Team staff originally planned to use Tulane facilities but were warned that "the people" might not be "quite ready" for such a long stay by such a large integrated group. And it was Syracuse's policy not to protest host cities' segregation but rather to advance race relations through sportsmanship wherever they were scheduled to play. So school officials accepted cautious locals' advice and moved prebowl training to the naval air station in the Florida panhandle.[22]

On December 30, Schwartzie's "drill weary" gang lumbered onto two Southern Airways planes for their very brief stay in the Big Easy. Another practice, which their coach intended to stretch as late as possible, was set for the next afternoon, and the MWSA's many events could completely consume any residual off-the-field time. Little chance remained for Orangemen to tour New Orleans on their own. And again, when they deplaned, Sugar Bowlers were on the spot to shake hands and direct transportation.[23]

Team hotels were also prudently selected. Schools' headquarters had long been split between the famed St. Charles and Roosevelt Hotels. Since the former became the Sheraton-Charles in 1959, that had been the base for the SEC team, and the team from the outside conference (in the years there was one) stayed at 130 Roosevelt Way. This year, the setup was reversed, putting Syracuse at the Sheraton-Charles, which now had more than a year of experience with voluntary integration. Although Seymour Weiss put his name below the petition for order after the Civil Rights Act, that did not mean that the doors of the Roosevelt had suddenly and fully swung open.

An appeal of another kind was printed in the *Times-Picayune* on New Year's Eve, an editorial addressing integration and urging attendance. It stated that Supreme Court decisions enabled the MWSA to again compete for the nation's top talent. Having the best bowl in their own backyard was argued as something "all of us down here would favor." Moreover, Sugar Bowlers were said to "lose more perspiration than is ever shed on the gridiron," and to deserve the public's support.[24]

Still, on New Year's Day only around 65,000 seats were filled, and only about 60,000 of these were paid attendance. It was the lowest turnout since 1939. One segment of the community, however, bought far more tickets than ever before. Thousands of African Americans had patronized the box office. Since 1956, there had been a Black boycott, during which only seventy-five seats at the northeast end were designated "Negro." The eight-year embargo's biggest proponent, Jim Hall, now pushed support for Sugar, arguing that it "will be sweeter because some brown coloring has been added to the mixture in the bowl."[25]

When Hall entered the press box that Friday, he was overwhelmed. He marveled at how "the black mark of racial denial has been erased without any fanfare," seeing more than half a dozen Black journalists scattered among the sportswriters in the box and the photographers on the sidelines. As he looked over the enormous steel structure, every section was integrated. Flipping through his program, he saw eight African American gridders in the Syracuse lineup and a swath of Black musicians in their band. Even one of the always plentiful sugar ads introduced "a new member of the team." That year, Domino featured its Brownulated brand of patented, crystalized brown sugar.[26]

Pregame reports lamented the teams' "mediocre records," but in the same breath sportswriters had to admit it was, on paper at least, a pretty exciting matchup. Syracuse was bringing in the nation's top rushing offense and two backs, Little and Nance, who each outscored the entire Tigers squad in 1964. Still, LSU was a five-and-a-half-point favorite, as its flanker offense was expected to best Syracuse's more vulnerable pass defense.[27]

As usual, ticket holders arrived uptown well ahead of the pregame pageantry, paying anywhere from seventy-five cents to two dollars to park in residents' driveways. After a pleasant stroll in sunny, seventy-degree weather, however, fans encountered picketers marching before the iconic brick face of Tulane Stadium. Banners announced, "Integration has ruined the Sugar Bowl." But if the group expected to cause a stir, they were disappointed. Thousands of Black and white ticket holders filed past protesters, taking little notice, and demonstrations did not breach the turnstiles.[28]

Inside, the bowl started as predicted. The Orange ground game got inside the Tigers 10-yard line, with help from an 18-yard run by Little, and the series netted 3 points off a field goal from linebacker Roger Smith.

The game's next points also followed a handoff to Little, though not as expected. Actually, after Syracuse's opening drive, not much of the first half went as billed. After Buster Brown's punt masterfully came to rest on the Orange 3-yard line, Syracuse was operating out of their end zone, and their first play was a quick pitch out to Little in the backfield. But Tigers lineman George Rice caught his man leaning to the outside and shot the gap, nailing Little for a safety and leaving him thinking, "That guy must've come out of the ground."[29]

Although the Orangemen soon added to their 1-point lead, their record-setting offense was not involved. Rather, a high snap forced a delayed LSU punt, which Syracuse blocked, recovered, and returned for an 8-point underdog lead at halftime. With little of the advertised offensive prowess on display and the small crowd favoring LSU, Tulane Stadium was rather quiet until the third period.

However, the first drive of the second half, like that of the first, matched some of the pregame hype. Tigers quarterback Billy Ezell called "I-26 wide and go." At the snap, flanker Doug Moreau took off downfield, faked a cut to the sideline, and turned back just as Ezell delivered the ball. The play went for 57 yards and a touchdown, making the score 10–8.

LSU then did something no Sugar Bowl team had done. With a short toss from Ezell to Joe Labruzzo snatched from the fingertips of a defender at the goal line, the Bayou Bengals scored the classic's first 2-point conversion. It was a tied ballgame. Fans searched for their idle gold-and-purple pennants.

Although Syracuse's answer was a signature long drive with four conversions and a 20-yard run by Nance, the surprises picked up again. On third down in the red zone—with Little and Nance in their arsenal—they gambled with their short suit and went to the air. With no pass rush, quarterback Wally Mahle had time to both find an open receiver and overthink his mechanics. Releasing the ball, he knew immediately it needed "a little more zing," and LSU's White Graves intercepted it on the 5-yard line.[30]

From there, LSU's offense also disproved predictions. Although Syracuse's secondary left receivers open all afternoon, Tigers passes were repeatedly off target and incomplete. Likewise, Syracuse's offense was constantly pinned deep by LSU's punts. And although the Orangemen did stay out of their own end zone now, they got nowhere near LSU's, either.

Then LSU introduced a curiosity of a different type. Pat Screen subbed in at quarterback, despite the ligament and cartilage damage in his knee—and his surgery scheduled for three days later. He told coaches he felt fine, and had even danced the Monkey at a pregame party, so there he was, taking the snap, rolling out to his right, and seeing daylight. He took off for a 23-yard gain, setting up a would-be game-winning field goal attempt. After a time out to catch his breath from running routes, Moreau split the uprights from 28 yards and broke the 10–10 tie.[31]

"Frankly, Syracuse disappointed me," Diliberto admitted after the game. Their explosive rushing attack never materialized. The team bringing in the "Touchdown Twins" never entered the LSU end zone on offense. With just a couple breakout runs, Nance tallied 70 yards, while Little netted only 40. In fact, the Tigers' Don Schwab was the leading rusher, with 81. Likewise, LSU's deep passing game was its own worst enemy. The two Tigers quarterbacks rarely connected with open receivers, and in the end, Syracuse completed more passes than the reputedly high-flying Bengals.[32]

Postgame write-ups did not indicate much improvement in entertainment value over the previous Sugar Bowl. Kicking was again the biggest highlight, and another novel "kicking specialist" stole the show. Moreau was elected Most Valuable Player for his game-winning field goal and 57-yard touchdown, but the Tigers punter arguably had more of an impact. Despite the blocked kick giving Syracuse its only touchdown, Brown's pinpointed punts repeatedly kept the ball out of Little's hands and the Orangemen just outside their end zone. And Coach Schwartzwalder, at least, believed the game's MVP was yet another guy who never even threw a block or made a tackle.[33]

|||||

After their press box poll on the Miller-Digby Award for Most Outstanding Player, Black and white media men alike were given the red carpet treatment at the Jung Hotel. For four years, Sugar's awards dinner had been held in a Roosevelt ballroom, but in 1965, sponsors opted for Mr. Jung's years of experience hosting integrated affairs.[34]

As players milled about, rehashing the game and joking around, Jim Hall questioned Syracuse's Black co-captain, Billy Hunter, about playing in the first fully integrated Sugar Bowl. The interruptions told him more than the answers. After explaining that the shifty Tigers line was even tougher than Penn State's, and admitting that he fell for Moreau's fake on the offensive touchdown, Hunter was asked about his treatment in New Orleans. "The sponsors of the game have been very nice to us," he answered, looking at his commemorative watch. "They have treated us swell."

Just then, an LSU lineman sneaked up and ambushed Hunter with a big bear hug. "Nice going today, Billy," the Tiger said. He released the halfback and asked, "Where's Nance?" Hunter pointed toward the food tables, gathered himself, and looked at Hall. "Did you see that?" he asked. "Heck, that guy was doing that all afternoon with our backs," Hunter joshed. "Oh well, he's a darn nice guy off the field."

As Hall began his next question, Hunter stopped him. "Jim, I'll see you later." He explained that he needed to find Moreau before it got too late. "I want to catch him tonight," Hunter said, smiling. "I couldn't do it today."[35]

Like Hunter, other Black players and various Black sportswriters praised the MWSA's hospitality. The Syracuse chancellor expressed his entire party's gratitude, saying, "Never have we been treated with such exceptional thoughtfulness and kindness."[36]

Although the Sugar Bowlers planned more than enough events, they also tactfully advised Orangemen about which areas were *best* to visit, and they suggested that the guys always wear school blazers outside their hotel. Still, of course, the students found an opportunity to sightsee on their own terms.

As Hunter, Little, and Nance tried to hail taxis out front of the Sheraton-Charles Hotel, they watched one and then another pass without stopping.

When they spotted a third cab at the curb, they walked over and started climbing into the backseat. "Get away from that car, n——s! Get away from that car, n——s!" the driver yelled from the hotel entrance.[37]

The players were stunned and offended. The cabbie was irate and unrelenting. Just when it seemed a physical confrontation might arise, a white couple offered to drive the players wherever they wanted to go. Although what Hunter considered nearly a "headline-making incident" was averted, those were not the only racial slurs the group endured that night, and door after door was slammed in their faces as they wandered along St. Charles Avenue and Bourbon Street.[38]

All this was overshadowed by good press on the game's reintegration and the MWSA's etiquette. Less flattering accounts got little attention. However, Al Baxter of the *Louisiana Weekly* did a piece that included both story lines. He praised the Sugar Bowl committee, as well as the LSU team and coaches, for advancing racial progress. Then came a disturbing "but" and a summary of the trouble the Black Orangemen had encountered.

"This isn't the type of publicity true Orleanians like to hear," Baxter conceded, "but it is a fact and will continue until something constructive is done." He knew just who could do it. "The New Orleans Mid-Winter Sports Association, which has taken a step in the right direction, should take a bigger step," he argued, saying that the MWSA had the clout to bring sports groups, businesses, and political leaders together in the common goal of "eliminating further embarrassments." While most locals celebrated the city's success, Baxter warned, "It will not be until these organizations put forth an honest effort towards creating a true American atmosphere that New Orleans will become a member of the main stream of this Great United States of America."[39]

|||||

In early January, New Orleans newspapers were filled with year-end reviews and predictions for 1965. Day after day, headlines reported that 1964 had been the city's best economic year, particularly for tourism, and that the future looked even better. A new convention hall was scheduled to open in 1966, and some of the nation's largest groups were already booked. The head of the tourist commission rejoiced that the six-month-old Civil Rights Act had opened the city to many conferences that would not have considered the Big Easy before.

The chamber of commerce was ramping up "Operation Red Carpet" to showcase the city and state to new industries. According to the head of the New Orleans Board of Trade, "good guys" had taken over the region's political scene, which previously had "frightened outside investors away." Out of the State Department of Commerce were coming both praise for the new "aura of good government" and a bold prediction from director Al Terrebonne. He had long been critical of the area's "negative attitude" toward progress, but he now told the *States-Item*, "I believe we are going to see the end of provincial complacency."[40]

Professional football, with its citywide fiscal dusting, was certainly one of the new industries on civic leaders' radar. The local chamber of commerce awarded Dixon with a "resolution of appreciation" for coordinating exhibitions and landing the upcoming All-Star week. The chamber was also sponsoring several red carpet events for players, owners, and their wives, including parties, banquets, sightseeing tours, and a golf tournament.[41]

Moreover, fifteen of the city's leading businessmen had joined forces with the ten members of the New Orleans Pro Football Club to form a new nonprofit group, the New Orleans Sports and Cultural Activities Foundation. They were underwriting all the expenses of the All-Star game and pledging proceeds to the New Orleans Police Foundation, which provided college education for officers. The game was billed as "A Great Game for a Great Cause," and the New Orleans Police Department was assisting in ticket drives.[42]

A week out, sales reached around twenty thousand, which was the previous year's total gate in San Diego, and Dixon's group felt that sixty thousand in paid attendance was likely. With plans to distribute twenty thousand free passes to schoolchildren, sponsors were anticipating a capacity crowd. Extra insurance came from the announcement that Billy Cannon was a late addition to the West squad, as long as it did not interfere with his dental school classes.[43]

Locals believed that warming eighty thousand seats in Tulane Stadium on January 16, 1965, would make New Orleans a front-runner for a franchise. And although the AFL was slated for expansion in 1966, Dixon's group would not let time pass idly. First, they pitched making their city the permanent All-Star address. Second, Dixon's proposal for a reconfigured playoff system would be deliberated during the owners' conference. Mayor Schiro wired Commissioner Foss with last-minute encouragement on the subject and told citizens he was "going all out" to sway the vote. Newspapers even ran a "notice" that fans should save their All-Star stubs to redeem for priority tickets to the 1965 AFL Championship Game.[44]

This was New Orleans's big audition, a full week of hosting the American Football League's finest players and top brass. Visitors would get a look at every aspect of the Big Easy, which Dixon truly believed was "the greatest city in the world." He had no doubt that the AFL's experience would spark a franchise offer from *that* league *and* also "light a fire under the NFL." Likewise, Pete Finney hyped up New Orleans, saying, "It's a better football town than Houston, Atlanta, or Miami—but hasn't had a legitimate chance to prove it in a long time."[45]

CHAPTER 8
Busted Coverage

On Saturday, January 9, 1965, when Delta flight 837 arrived at New Orleans International Airport, AFL All-Stars Cookie Gilchrist, Jack Kemp, and Ernie Warlick stopped at the carrier's counter to make a claim. Gilchrist's $150 suit had been snagged on the flight. Given his hothead reputation, he was immediately asked, "You're not going to give us any trouble, are you, Cookie?" He did bristle a bit at offers to patch his pants but was appeased by referral of his case to Delta's downtown office. At that point, the trio made their way outside.[1]

No cars had been sent. No travel tips were provided. So it was time to flag a cab. Kemp, the white Buffalo Bills quarterback, waved first. When a taxi stopped, he climbed in with his African American fullback and tight end and the group was dropped off at the East squad's headquarters, the modern Fontainebleau Motor Hotel. They were handed three keys, and Gilchrist went straight to room 236 for an afternoon nap.[2]

Back at the airport, Clem Daniels and Earl Faison deplaned and followed signs to ground transportation. Before even breathing fresh air, Faison heard someone say, "Is that Ernie Ladd?" "No," another man replied blatantly. "Ernie Ladd is a big n——." He added, "He's a much bigger n—— than that guy."[3]

Faison processed the insult as the pair parked their bags on the curb outside. Daniels raised his arm and yelled, "Taxi!," but an empty cab breezed by. As another approached, he repeated the drill, only to watch it also pass. As this went on, he thought, "What is it about the taxis in this town?" Bobby Bell soon joined his marooned colleagues, but even with the extra arms waving, no taxis stopped. Finally, a Black porter approached. "Hey, you guys have to call a colored cab," he said. "They have to come from the city to get you."

Caught off guard, Bell at first wondered why he should care about the paint on a taxi as long as it got him downtown. Daniels, on the other hand, immediately felt the sting of a second affront and was tempted to turn around and fly home. He had ample time to deliberate during the long wait for a Black driver, but Daniels ultimately accompanied the other players to the famed Roosevelt Hotel.[4]

By then, Bell was ready to eat. When he scouted an empty table in the hotel restaurant, a lady walked over from the kitchen—but not to serve him. "You can order your food," she said, "but you can't eat here." Bell was dazed. Her comment alone was more than he could digest, so he walked empty-handed back to his room.[5]

Meanwhile, Abner Haynes was having similar luck outside the airport, waiting for two hours before a Black cabbie finally stopped for him. It had taken Haynes a while to catch on, but his driver confirmed the practice, muttering, "Oh, they ain't going to pick you guys up."[6]

Eventually, the last two West stars made it to the Roosevelt. Willie Brown and Buck Buchanan, two old Grambling buddies, had driven over from Lincoln Parish. Along the way, when they started picking up New Orleans radio stations, they heard DJs carrying on about all the incoming big-name players. When they checked in to the Roosevelt, however, any expectations of celebrity treatment were quashed. The reservations Dixon had made were honored, but Brown and Buchanan were told not to use the main elevator and were directed to a side lift outside the lobby, instead.[7]

At the Fontainebleau, the East squad was still incomplete. By the time Larry Garron and Houston Antwine's late flight touched down, they were unable to get a cab at all and were stranded until Bills guard Billy Shaw rescued them in his station wagon. During all of this, Gilchrist had been cloistered, resting up for a night out, which got under way with a call from the Roosevelt.

"Meet you at the Dew Drop Inn," Art Powell said, before heading out. Powell had not been given the same instructions as Brown and Buchanan, so he pressed the button for the main elevator and waited. When it stopped, he joined three white guests inside. As the descent commenced, one of them said, with no attempt to whisper, "N——s are the worst trash in the world." When the elevator doors reopened, Powell's thoughts were swirling, but he quickly found friendlier faces.[8]

His arrival completed the group of African American players bound for the LaSalle Street club. They exited the lobby and solicited white cabbies until they found one eager for the fare. When they got to Central City, however, the driver said he would not get within a dozen blocks of the nightspot.

He stopped the car, collected his cash, and left them to walk nearly a mile to their destination.⁹

Gilchrist, on the other hand, jumped in the first taxi he saw and chatted with his friendly white cabbie for the quick jaunt over to Frank Pania's famous club. As the fullback got out, however, the driver gave him a curious word of caution: "Be careful in this town."¹⁰

While Gilchrist and the gang were living it up at the Dew Drop Inn, most of the other All-Stars opted for an evening on Bourbon Street. "C'mon. Let's go down to the French Quarter," urged Jack Kemp and Mike Stratton.

"No, you guys go ahead," Ernie Warlick replied.

"No, c'mon, let's go," the pair continued, until their prodding proved stronger than his skepticism. Al Hirt's nightclub was their first stop, and there the celebrity treatment was thick. All-Stars drank for free, and every player present was introduced over loudspeakers and met with resounding applause. Warlick's group was "having a ball" but soon moseyed onward to see more of the Quarter.¹¹

They strolled up to another club, and the white players walked past the doorman. But as Warlick crossed the threshold, the bouncer stopped him. "Naw, we don't serve your kind," he drawled. When Kemp and Stratton saw Warlick was missing, they stepped back out on the street. "That guy won't let me in," Warlick explained.

Rather than make a scene, his buddies said simply, "We'll go some other place." The threesome meandered over to another interesting-looking spot and stepped inside. They were still sizing it up when a manager pulled the white players aside. "C'mon, we'll find another place," Kemp and Stratton said again, as they ushered Warlick back on Bourbon.

"Look," he said, "you guys go on ahead. I'm going back to the hotel." What he did not realize was he would have trouble getting back without them, something a group from the West was learning around the same time.¹²

Half a dozen taxis sat outside the Roosevelt, but as Clem Daniels, Dick Westmoreland, Ernie Ladd, and Dave Grayson approached, drivers walked away. When a player tried to get in one cab, the driver announced he could only carry Black passengers who were with a "white associate."¹³

The group walked down the sidewalk away from the hotel to flag someone not under peer surveillance. After several more vacant taxis passed, Clem Daniels lost his patience and stepped in front of the next oncoming cabbie, who stopped short of the halfback and agreed to haul them the short distance to the French Quarter. There, the group splintered and milled about, looking through windows and gauging music. Westmoreland, Ladd, and Grayson liked a tune coming from one little joint and decided to check it out. They were stopped instantly by a bouncer who stated that no African Americans were allowed inside. Turning away, Westmoreland wondered why a club opposed to Black presence was playing James Brown.[14]

Daniels strolled past a different venue, one with three rooms and a band in each. As he stepped inside the first space, the music stopped immediately, and walking into the other two got the same result. In the third, however, when the band broke, he sat down at the bar and had one drink, in nearly complete silence. Likewise, nearby, Earl Faison felt like a magician: when he entered the crowded foyer of the Playboy Club, he made everyone else disappear.[15]

Westmoreland was most shocked when walking around with Ernie Ladd, who was six-foot-nine and 320 pounds. Westmoreland could not believe how many scrawny white guys dared to speak slurs right to the players' faces. He also worried about Ladd's temper and lobbied for an early curfew. But the party tried one last club. This time, the bouncer pulled out a gun and barked, "You n——s are not coming in here." Everyone jumped back but Ladd, who took another step forward. The doorman put the gun to Ladd's nose and announced, "I will pull the trigger!"[16]

"Hey man, we better start thinking about getting out of here," Westmoreland said, looking around. "We kind of got a mob out here now." Ladd did not flinch. He stood his ground a moment more and then calmly stepped back to join the other All-Stars' tactical retreat. Again, however, cabbies claimed they could be arrested for driving a car of only African Americans. So the players got directions and started back to the Roosevelt on foot.[17]

The walk did nothing to temper their ire. "I don't need to take this crap," Ladd asserted.

"I'm taking my Black a' home," Westmoreland concurred, "I'm not playing."

"If you're not playing, I'm not playing," Faison declared in solidarity.[18]

When they reached the hotel, Westmoreland woke his roommate, Frank Buncom. "Hey, Frank, we're leaving here, man," Westmoreland disclosed. Buncom, a quiet guy who had stayed in all night, assumed the players had gotten into trouble, so he asked, "Oh, what'd you guys do, man?"[19]

While Westmoreland briefed Buncom, Ladd and Faison went to their room to spread the word on walking out. "I'm going to make sure that Sherman goes," Faison said, phoning Jets tackle Sherman Plunkett at the Fontainebleau. And so it began. Throughout the night, the phone tree grew, as did the list of abuses the players collected from just their first twelve hours in New Orleans. By morning, they were ready to take action.[20]

|||||

Around 10:30 a.m., Gilchrist woke up to the phone. He had been out until 2:30 before being dropped off at the doors of the Fontainebleau by a white cabbie who was a big pro football fan. Unlike many of his teammates, he was not left to walk the last six blocks by a driver wanting to duck the taxi stand while hauling Black passengers. Gilchrist had no idea anything like that even happened.[21]

"You better come right over here," Art Powell reported from the Roosevelt, explaining that a lot of guys were about to bolt. Gilchrist was shocked. He dialed Warlick's room, thinking he had breaking news.

"I know," Warlick told him. "I got my bags packed. I'm ready to go home."

"Stop kidding," Gilchrist said. "This is too serious."[22]

Warlick made it clear he was not staying even one more day. If his night out with Kemp and Stratton were not reason enough, his visit to the downstairs café for breakfast had sealed it. He had already been forced to remove his jacket from the coatrack to prevent it from touching a white woman's shawl when another angry white patron announced, for all to hear, "I don't want to eat in the same room with monkeys." At that point, Warlick was far more interested in an exit than an omelet. He simply went back up—to pack up.[23]

Practice was set for eleven o'clock at Tulane, but the Black players were instead heading for Ladd and Faison's room at the Roosevelt. At the Fontainebleau, East fellows looked for taxis. A white driver pulled up, got out, and headed over to a phone, saying, "I'll call two colored cabs." This was the first such instance Gilchrist encountered.

As the guy behind him shouted, "The hell with that!," Gilchrist sprinted to Lou Saban. "You see that?" he asked the coach. Saban nodded but quickly tried to bring down the heat. He offered to drive several players himself and arranged for another group to follow in Shaw's wagon. Soon, all twenty-one African American All-Stars were huddled in a two-room suite at the Roosevelt Hotel.[24]

Out front, the West squad's white players were on a bus. "Bobby Bell," coach Sid Gillman called, to no answer. "Earl Faison," he shouted, to more silence. As roll call continued to fail, someone yelled, "Hey, all the Black guys are missing!" Another voice responded, "They're all meeting back at the hotel."

"What about?" the coach asked, before hearing his first accounts of why a dozen of his players might not show for Saturday's game.[25]

Ron Mix walked to the front of the bus. "Sid, let me skip practice and talk to them," he said. The coach was still stunned. "Well, I don't see how . . ." he began, but then he paused and conceded. "OK, go ahead."[26]

After rehearsing some points in the elevator, Mix entered the suite where the Black athletes were gathered, many of them watching the NFL Pro Bowl on TV. He walked over to Faison and Daniels, who stood and shook his hand.

"Say, Clem, Earl, I'd like to talk to all you fellows," Mix requested.

"Sure," Faison replied. "Call the others in."

Everyone squeezed into the front room, finding seats where they could or leaning against the walls. Faison turned off the television and Mix had the floor. He tried to read the faces before him, thinking some were curious but most seemed impatient, even distrustful.

"Men, I want to talk to you because I feel that what you're doing is wrong," he began. "Some action is necessary, but your method will not do our cause any good. And that cause is to try to rectify all the injustices, to restore dignity to all men." Mix asked them to consider the effects of a walkout. "Will it serve any good to New Orleans? Hell no," he said forcefully. "The whole city isn't guilty." He argued that the game's promoters could not be blamed for any citizens' prejudices. "Do you think that those ignorant individuals who wrong you give a damn whether or not they see a football game?" Mix asked. "They'll be glad to see you go. And so what's been done? Those lowlifes have their way. You're gone."

"Look," Powell interjected. "We know we aren't going to change these people. But neither are they going to change us," he continued. "We must act as our conscience dictates."

"OK, Art," Mix began again. "What about the thousands of Negroes that cannot leave this place?" he asked. "I think that is a bad example for men in your position to set. The place stinks—so you leave."

Powell challenged Mix's logic. "You suppose it would be better to stay here, and by doing so, imply that we accept such treatment for ourselves and our people?" he asked. "Do you want us to condone it?"

Mix could see he only added to the anger. "Men, I think you're all acting in good faith. This whole mess is rotten," he granted. But then he argued that the city was clearly making progress. "That we have the game here indicates this," he claimed. Everyone had been aware of New Orleans's reputation for racial strife, and some arrived more skeptical than others. But Dixon's group had convinced the league of drastic improvements.[27]

"That's another point," Daniels said. "The promoters for this game assured us that there would be no problems. 'Bring your wives and children,' they said. 'We're also having a golf tournament,'" he continued mockingly. "It sounded like a big picnic."

Mix scanned the room again and realized that there was little interest in what he had to say. He wondered if some felt guilty about being spared the treatment many African Americans faced every day, if maybe they felt this could be their contribution. "Was this their freedom ride?" he asked himself.

"Ron," Earl Faison piped up, "I wonder if you are really aware of all that has happened here. It has been quite a bit more than that pool-hall incident in Atlanta." Once Faison finished relaying his experiences, another player recounted his. One after the other, each player explained what Mix then understood as "varying degrees of indignity." He saw their emotion and knew he had little chance of swaying them.

Abner Haynes then predicted that they would hear Mix's arguments again, along with plenty of promises, once the promoters appeared. "We realize the incidents aren't their fault," Haynes allowed. "They aren't ours either. We've got to do what we believe is right."

Mix went back to his room and lay across the bed, feeling drained. He had immense sympathy for his teammates, but he was still unconvinced that their decision was not made too hastily. He hoped league officials or local organizers could do something to change the players' minds.[28]

Back in Ladd and Faison's room, the Black All-Stars voted 21–0 to leave immediately. The East guys returned to the Fontainebleau and began (or resumed) packing around one o'clock. Gilchrist wasted no time booking a 2:35 flight to New York. As the exodus accelerated, however, a message came asking everyone to return to the Roosevelt. Game sponsors were on site. Gilchrist asked the obvious next question, "What about cabs?" This time, shuttles were run in the cars of Coach Saban and a Black Fontainebleau bellhop.[29]

Meanwhile, Coach Gillman had taken a busload of players to Tulane. Just before workouts were scheduled to open to the press and the public, Diliberto walked up to find fans turned away.

"The practices have been canceled," a security officer informed the reporter, who flashed his press pass. Opening the gate, the guard added, "I don't know what's wrong. One team is out there now, but they said they'd be leaving soon. The other team didn't come."

Diliberto was just in time to see the heavily depleted West squad running off the field in their clean white All-Star jerseys, and a staffer shouted, "All of the uniforms haven't arrived so the first practice has been put off until tomorrow." Detecting a "false ring," Diliberto followed them into the locker room.

Gillman sat slumped on a bench as Diliberto entered. "We're having trouble," the coach confessed. "The Negro players have threatened to quit." By then word had reached the stadium about a second Roosevelt conference. "They're down there meeting now," Gillman disclosed.[30]

Naturally, Diliberto drove straight to the hotel and rushed for a report from the first player he recognized. "We're not wanted here," Clem Daniels said bluntly, "so we are leaving." He gave Diliberto the skinny on the previous night's problems, but the writer said he felt sure Dixon's group could iron things out. "What could possibly be done now that wouldn't already have been done before we came here?" Daniels retorted.[31]

Meanwhile, Dixon was asking himself the same question. Attempts were made to have Mayor Schiro intercede, but an undisclosed illness was said to rule that out. So the closest thing sponsors had to a city representative was Harry Kelleher, the tireless attorney who had negotiated for years between the mayor's office and civil rights groups. Dixon was searching desperately for reinforcements as the athletes assembled in the room of Chuck Burr, the Bills' publicity director. The previous meeting space was empty; Ladd and Faison had already checked out.[32]

Diliberto intercepted Dixon in the ninth-floor hallway. "It looks bad," the promoter said with a pained expression. Just then, Gilchrist strolled past and flashed a smile. "I have nothing to say yet," he commented. "We're meeting. We've agreed to listen to them."[33]

Dixon followed Gilchrist into room 990 and the door was closed. Reporters gathered together outside and could hear nearly every word. "We're asking you men to cooperate with us," a voice argued. "This would be a deadly blow to our community, and it would undo all of the good that has been done in this area." The players were promised cars, access to the finest restaurants and clubs, and anything else they wanted that Dixon had not thought to prearrange.

"You're asking us to sacrifice our principles and play when the conditions that surround us outside are deplorable," another voice interjected. "This is an unfair request."[34]

The negotiators were not gaining much ground, but around 4:30 Dutch Morial arrived. David Kleck had telephoned the local NAACP leader at his home, and Morial agreed to buy some time for public officials to set things right. His presence, however, did not impress the players.

As the light-skinned Creole attorney spoke, the Black All-Stars became either dismissive or infuriated. Winston Hill whispered, "Who's this honky?" Ernie Ladd's take was little more than, "Sure enough, they brought in a Black guy." But Abner Haynes absorbed every argument and became more resentful the more he heard. Finally, Haynes told Morial outright that if he had fought as hard to clean up his hometown as he was fighting to keep the All-Star game, the abuse would never have happened.[35]

Dixon walked out of the room, rubbing his forehead. He looked at Diliberto and said wearily, "We'll blow pro football if they walk out."[36]

It was back up for a vote. Before deciding on the game, however, the players agreed to act in unison. The final tally was not unanimous, but it did not matter. All twenty-one Black AFL All-Stars were boycotting New Orleans.[37]

They had one last decision to make. They needed a spokesman. Eliminating Gilchrist, a renowned instigator, was a simple first step. Instead, they went with the mild-mannered Buffalo tight end, Ernie Warlick. Perhaps their statement would be even more powerful coming from him. As Gilchrist explained with his nomination, "Get a cat in the corner, and he'll scratch."[38]

Daniels slapped Ladd on the leg and said, "I'm outta here." When he opened the room door, he got all the newsmen's attention.[39]

"We're leaving," he announced. "Ask Ernie Warlick for a statement. He'll talk for us."

Gilchrist's sound bite was even terser: "See Warlick."

The others filed out, speaking only to one another, although reporters overheard one player say, "I'm flying out tonight. Most of the others are, too."[40]

Soon, room 990 was empty, except for Warlick, and the door was left open. Media reps entered just as the tight end finished booking his 10:00 p.m. flight. "The others said you had a statement," one reporter announced.

"They did, huh?" Warlick chimed. "Well, I've scribbled something down here. I'll read it to you." He looked at his paper and delivered the All-Stars' official announcement: "The American Football League is progressing in great strides and the Negro football players feel they are playing a vital role in the league's progression and have been treated fairly in all cities throughout the league. However, because of adverse conditions and discriminatory practices experienced by the Negro players while here in New Orleans, the players feel they cannot perform 100 percent as expected in the All-Star game and be treated differently outside."

Diliberto thought Dixon "had the look of a man who was watching a lifetime dream crumble before his eyes." Still, the columnist asked him for a comment as they headed out. "I'll have a statement tomorrow," Dixon muttered softly, "All I can say now is—I'm sorry."[41]

|||||

"The false sense of full integration is what disturbed us the most," Larry Garron told reporters, giving perhaps the most insightful summary of what went down. As he and Houston Antwine left the Fontainebleau in their coats and ties, carrying Boston Patriots duffel bags, newsmen swarmed them. The story was hot but incomplete. Early reports announced that the twenty-one Black All-Stars were boycotting the game but speculated that the show might go on with the nearly forty white gridders. Dixon was said to be awaiting word from Joe Foss.[42]

Meanwhile, the Black All-Stars were not exiting so swiftly that they neglected discussion with their white teammates. Ron Mix still believed it was wrong to pull out, but he vowed he would join the walkout. He wanted there to be at least one white guy saying, "We're with you." Just days earlier, Mix had described to a reporter the experience of playing pro football, saying, "The big attraction is the association with other players," even in "misery."[43]

Mix was not, however, the only white player to back the boycott. Jack Kemp told his Black counterparts that if they were leaving, he was leaving too. Next it was Jerry Mays, then Keith Lincoln, Bob Dee, and Babe Parilli. One by one, the white All-Stars concurred. There would be no AFL All-Star game in New Orleans in 1965.[44]

Commissioner Foss spent Sunday night and Monday morning on the telephone with owners, and it was agreed that the AFL could not afford the event going down as a strike. Besides, several suitors were lining up to play host. One tempting offer came from Miami, which successfully took in the American Legion after New Orleans blew its last big opportunity. With little time to investigate new options, however, officials opted for a league city. In the interest of time and proximity, Houston was given the game.[45]

Thus began the rushed preparations to move the contest to 37,000-seat

Jeppesen Stadium. Many players had just gotten home when they received orders to report to Texas. Brown and Buchanan were still driving toward Grambling when they heard over the radio that they would be suiting up after all. So they got back on Interstate 10 and continued west toward a southern city that had made a lot more progress over the previous five years.[46]

|||||

A *Times-Picayune* editorial on the walkout stated, "We regret, of course, that the incidents that caused the offense occurred here," and it called them "no doubt irksome." However, it simultaneously rebuked the players for appearing "to balk whenever they experience some unpleasantness." The piece concluded, "It seems... some people were wearing their pride on their sleeves."[47]

Even the more openly sympathetic Pete Finney was guilty of similar logic. He caught himself, though, and added the qualifier "I'm not saying a little discrimination is all right." Yet he still suggested that the warm welcome at Al Hirt's should have made up for other nightclubs turning players away. Bob Roesler also belittled the All-Stars' complaints by comparing their experience to his own trouble getting a taxi in New York when his destination was across a congested highway. He boasted that he stayed "to do a job," as if it were the inconvenience of spotty transportation and not the indignity of discrimination that had sparked the athletes' revolt.[48]

White fans and newsmen alike put typewriters to work arguing that racial progress could be hastened through an advance of a franchise but not through the act of withholding it. One local wrote, "A pro football team in New Orleans would be a great step forward for the acceptance of the Negro in the South," but "you can't convince people that they should be tolerant of you if you refuse to go even halfway with them." Likewise, Finney stated, "The reason this story is being read today in Moscow as well as New York is because athletes—well-known athletes—were involved." He claimed, "These athletes had the opportunity to strike a blow for nobility—and muffed it."[49]

There was also a conspiracy theory spreading like wildfire. A *States-Item* column and an early WDSU editorial each introduced theories of everything being staged in advance. Art Burke planted the seed with his readers that the All-Stars came to New Orleans on a "freedom mission." He explained, "There is reason to believe that some of the Negro players might have been looking for trouble, and when they found a speck of it their mission was over."[50]

It was hard to find regret or even surprise over the bigotry the All-Stars encountered. The *Times-Picayune* even blamed the victims for not actively circumventing it. Apparently unaware of Dixon's skillful salesmanship, the official voice of the newspaper announced that the men should have expected that "they might encounter the very experiences they disliked unless they chose to avoid them."[51]

There was also a lot of finger-pointing. Many locals knew that the league had met racial problems elsewhere and wondered why those locales had not suffered like humiliation. The pool hall affair in Atlanta was brought up repeatedly, and Finney claimed it was "the club" of San Diego that had averted a boycott in Georgia. In reality, it was the intervention of city and state officials that made the difference in the much more isolated incident back East.[52]

Neither Mayor Schiro nor Governor McKeithen had taken such action, and none was immediately forthcoming. The mayor, still convalescing on Monday, released a statement that waffled between denying and excusing the city's need for greater racial progress. He professed New Orleans to be "a very cosmopolitan and tolerant city." He backed up his claim by saying, "Our experience thus far with integrated football, basketball, and even track meets has been exceptionally good," referring mainly to "experience" that was then less than a month old, extended no further than the Mid-Winter Sports calendar, and had encountered problems of its own, though these were far less publicized. He then flip-flopped and argued that the All-Stars should have both expected and accepted bigotry in his town. It was, he reminded them, still "a Southern city," in which "there are times when personal reaction is unpredictable."

Schiro was uncharacteristically hostile. "If these men," he said of the Black All-Stars, "would play football only in cities where everybody loved them, they would all be out of a job today." He added, "Almost all of them are educated, college men, who must be aware that you cannot change human nature overnight." Then, in what was likely his most reckless message as mayor, Schiro declared, "It seems to me the players who walked out should have rolled with the punch."[53]

Governor McKeithen likewise claimed that the AFL left without giving the city a fair chance. Speaking to the local chamber of commerce, McKeithen criticized the All-Stars for bolting "because a few taxis and nightclubs wouldn't let them in." He, too, dismissed the humiliation of segregation by adding that "there are some clubs down on Bourbon St. they won't even let our D.A. in." As he touted the state's "new day" of economic growth and good politics, McKeithen said he was proud of Louisiana's racial record. Following the Civil Rights Act, the avoidance of headline-making riots had been cause for celebration—and complacency. The governor noted that there were "no bodies dragged out of rivers, no murders on highways, no troops and no violence." McKeithen also labeled New Orleans the South's most racially progressive city, indicating no perceived need for change.[54]

Dave Dixon was far more politic than the politicians. He announced on Monday that he and his colleagues felt "no bitterness toward either Commissioner Foss or the owners of the league" and hoped to continue their "extremely warm and cordial relationships with these fine men." He also stated that he did not doubt "the sincerity of the feelings of the Negro players." Dixon was not buying the idea of premeditation. At worst, he thought, Gilchrist might have arrived "with a slight chip on his shoulder." And Dixon kept that thought to himself.

Still, his civic pride rivaled his business acumen, and he too was somewhat defensive, saying the boycott was an "unwarranted and unjust setback" to his beloved community. But Dixon affirmed his group's resolve. "To accept the actions of Sunday as a death warrant to our efforts is, in effect, to accept defeat of New Orleans," he announced, "which we will not do."[55]

On Monday night, Dixon was obligated to attend a New Orleans Recreation Department banquet for bantam football. He managed to smile most of the evening, but discussion of the AFL debacle was inevitable, especially with All-Star flanker Lance Alworth on the program as a guest speaker. Dixon repeatedly referred to his official statement. "It took me four hours to write," he told reporters, "and it said everything that could be said." Only one more sound bite was pulled from the promoter: "To say how long it will take the effect of what happened to wear off is hard to say at this time."[56]

|||||

Nationally, plenty of folks found it easy to predict the timeline. The *Los Angeles Times* speculated that "New Orleans now will be thrown back at least ten years in its efforts to land a major league football franchise." The *Washington Post and Times-Herald* said the boycott "appeared to end hopes by promoter Dave Dixon to put an AFL team in New Orleans"—ever.[57]

With many Patriots among the All-Stars, Boston media covered the walkout extensively. One *Boston Globe* writer quoted Dixon as saying "You can imagine what this will do to our chance of getting a pro franchise." The writer responded, "Yes, I can well imagine what it will do, and I think it's exactly what should have happened." He went on to inform Mayor Schiro that "the mayor of New Orleans, or any other city, ought to see to it that visitors don't get punched to begin with," and that although Schiro said human nature could not be changed *"overnight,"* that period had now "extended about 100 years."[58]

Another Beantown columnist lamented, "Pity of it all is that the game was awarded to New Orleans in the first place." He criticized the city's shady reputation for pleasure and stubborn aversion to progress, calling it "Good ol' fun-filled New Orleans, home of Antoine's, the Mardi Gras, all that good Bourbon Street jazz... and bigotry." Likewise, a *Boston Sunday Herald* writer pointed out that "apathy" continues indefinitely and "some prime mover or catalytic agent has to come along and start things." The piece concluded, "In the case of the megalopolis of New Orleans, a shock was needed."[59]

Not *all* external accounts sided with the athletes, however. A Midwest paper discussed the "unfortunate slur on New Orleans" and questioned why players were "touring these hot spots and booze joints" when they should be in training. The article even theorized a different conspiracy, which the entire league was in on, citing the logistical difficulty of relocating a game in just one week.[60]

Even several mainstream New York publications gave the Big Easy a pass. One called the transfer "hasty," and another described the grievances as "trivial." A Syracuse sportswriter cast doubt on a drastic reversion taking place in the ten days since the Sugar Bowl. A *New York Daily News* column faulted the Black All-Stars for condemning an entire town over "some slob cab driver" or "because some guy in some lousy gin mill insults you."[61]

Despite varying interpretations, the story was broadcast nationwide. Officials of the young American Football League knew they had to portray a firm, united stance. A year earlier, Commissioner Rozelle of the NFL had been named *Sports Illustrated*'s first nonathlete "Sportsman of the Year." The magazine cited "Rozelle's defense of the league's integrity" and his removal of the NFL's last remnants of segregation. The AFL certainly did not want the head of its league to earn a contrasting reputation. Thus, Commissioner Joe Foss defended the boycott, saying, "We have no recourse but to back the action of the players involved in the walkout because the players are all members of the AFL family." It was the only viable public relations move, and it worked. The AFL was praised for taking "the discomfiture and losses with complete acquiescence." League execs also knew they needed to distance themselves from any talk of expansion into New Orleans.⁶²

Behind closed doors in Houston's Shamrock Hotel, however, owners were far from being in full support of the walkout. Many had befriended Dixon over the years and felt awful watching his work go down the drain. No one approved of the Black players' mistreatment, but "immediately boycotting the game" was deemed "ill-advised." Even while they empathized with the injured All-Stars, it was hard for these businessmen to see how the walkout would resolve the root problem.⁶³

The headaches the walkout caused were much easier to identify. In addition to popularity and esteem, it was also costing the AFL a lot of money. ABC's TV contract stood, but Bud Adams predicted that Houston could produce only around twenty thousand fans—and only if the weather cooperated. Pregame calculations had the league breaking even, at best. Regardless, if the game's bottom line came out in the black, it would still be nowhere near the $67,500 New Orleans promoters had assured the league.

Likewise, white players were rumored to resent the smaller Houston gate lightening their pension fund, but the players association's words at the owners meeting displayed renewed unity. The report was originally expected to focus on divisive complaints by veterans over huge paydays for rookies like Joe Namath. Instead, player reps announced, "We came to a new understanding concerning the relations of men."⁶⁴

They also held league executives accountable to a degree and demanded proper investigation of future sites. To that end, the owners decided to keep All-Star games in franchised cities. Besides, after Judge Roy Hofheinz led a tour of the new Astrodome, Houston became the obvious choice for 1966.⁶⁵

|||||

Preparations in Houston were chaotic. Monday was completely lost as a practice day, and Tuesday did not shape up much better. For Gillman's group, late arrival of equipment from New Orleans delayed drills, and Ladd and Buchanan missed practice altogether because of an auto accident. The East team's jerseys were lost in transport, and Ernie Warlick and Elbert Dubenion did not make it down from Buffalo until Tuesday evening. Saban's two quarterbacks, Babe Parilli and Jack Kemp, lost practice time on offense when the coach realized that his roster was missing kickers. Flanker Gino Cappelletti, who handled the Pats placekicking, was the only East

All-Star who regularly booted the ball. Saban considered Kemp and Parilli "pretty good punters" and pulled them aside to work on that, and he assigned Gilchrist to handle kickoffs, as the fullback had done in the Canadian Football League.[66]

By Wednesday, logistical problems were ironed out, and coaches hoped for two-a-days in the little time remaining. But even when all the players were on the field, their heads were often elsewhere. Several copped attitudes, and coaches struggled to get information across. Most of the guys just wanted to "get the game behind them."[67]

When the All-Stars stepped onto the field at Jeppesen Stadium on January 16, however, there was something very right about it all. Over half a dozen players had haunting experiences of racial discrimination that would be exorcised that afternoon in a high school football stadium in East Texas.

Ernie Ladd, Sherman Plunkett, and Earl Faison had been with the Chargers when they played the Oilers there in November 1961. At that time, the stadium, property of the Houston Independent School District, was subject to the school board's segregation policies. Among the district's 22,000 seats, Black patrons could only sit in the four-dollar section behind the goal line. Although Bud Adams lobbied for integration, in 1961 only the 14,000 seats the Oilers provided were first-come, first-served.[68]

Local civil rights groups and the city's Black newspaper, the *Houston Informer*, pushed both fans and athletes to boycott sports at Jeppesen. They had success at the Meet of Champions in July 1961, when amateur track stars Ralph Boston and John Thomas refused to cross the picket line. In November, the paper asked the same of Ladd, Plunkett, Faison, and their six Black teammates.[69]

These men knew that Lloyd Wells, sports editor of the *Informer*, was calling them "every name in the book" and using emasculating invectives toward them. Wells especially singled out Ladd, with remarks like "Big Ernie Ladd, I see you." Ladd experienced great shame that autumn afternoon in 1961 and became convinced that Wells was right to berate him for playing where his "brothers and sisters" were restricted to the end zones. Now, in January 1965, he, Faison, and Plunkett were on that very field because they had taken a stand against segregation.[70]

Houston Antwine and Larry Garron also had been approached by CORE and the NAACP—back in 1962 in New Orleans. When the Patriots came down for DeFee's City Park exhibition, Black players were asked "to make an issue" of separate accommodations. Although they were prepared to support local demonstrations at the stadium, they refused to take the lead on a protest. And when no action materialized, they played.[71]

Before the All-Star game, players were guaranteed that things were different. When they arrived, however, the reality was painfully familiar. "Now we all stay in the same hotel, but nothing else has changed," Antwine said at the time of the walkout. Garron added, "Maybe we were not separated like before here, but we were still confined." So they refused to endure six days of second-class treatment in New Orleans. This time, they had "made an issue" and earned first-class treatment in Houston.[72]

When Jack Kemp entered Jeppesen for the All-Star tilt, the 1960 AFL Championship game was still fresh in his mind. He remembered his father sitting on the 45-yard line, while there was a roped-off section far downfield for the parents of his Black teammates. "My heart just went out to those guys," Kemp recalled. He knew they struggled with their compliance. Kemp struggled with it, too, but now he was part of a move no Chargers had been prepared to take four years earlier.[73]

The Denver Broncos' Willie Brown hoped to have the best performance of his young career in the relocated game precisely because of the city selected. He had been signed by the Oilers in 1963 but was cut before the regular season, despite what he considered a "fantastic" training camp. He understood that he was let go to give the team an even number of Black players. This practice was not exclusive to the Oilers or the AFL, having been established nearly two decades earlier with the NFL's Los Angeles Rams signing Woody Strode as a bunkmate for Kenny Washington. Still, signing a player to ensure segregated rooms was one thing; releasing him for that reason was something very different. Brown was proud of the action taken in New Orleans and felt "fortunate" it had landed him back in Houston as an All-Star.[74]

Brown also got his wish. He was voted the Most Valuable Player on defense in the postgame press box poll, after having a masterful day at cornerback, shutting down the East's receivers and logging an interception. But overall it was a messy game, especially for the East. Gillman's group racked up five touchdowns, and Saban's had as many missed field goals. The West's defense stopped runs for losses so often that the East netted only 7 yards on the ground. The entire afternoon was peppered with fumbles, and there were seven total turnovers on the day. Two even happened on the same play, when Butch Byrd intercepted John Hadl but then lateraled to keep the play alive and was picked off by Art Powell. The West won its fourth of four All-Star tilts and produced the most lopsided score yet, 38–14.[75]

Despite the local TV blackout, more than half of Jeppesen was empty that afternoon. On the other hand, Tulane Stadium was deserted, and the Big Easy box office was processing refunds rather than proceeds. In the speedily assembled All-Star program, Commissioner Foss included a note thanking Houston for hosting "on such short notice" and "in such major league fashion." A week earlier, New Orleans had anticipated going "major league," but now it looked more "bush" than ever.[76]

|||||

The first post-walkout *Louisiana Weekly* was issued on the day of the All-Star game. The newspaper's mailbox had been flooded with reactions to the boycott, which was also the subject of several columns and editorials as well as a long opinion piece by Norman Francis, an African American attorney rising through the administration of Xavier University. The paper's official statement expressed "regret" over losing the game but said the walkout would surely "bring some good to the city," perhaps more quickly than "many of the learned and sometimes meaningless discussions between the white power structure and the race relations experts." A running theme throughout the *Weekly* was that such civic leaders "have continued to bury their heads in the sand." One letter stated, "Our problems cannot be solved by ignoring them." Likewise, Francis declared, "We cannot be cosmopolitan by merely saying we are."[77]

The sports pages mourned the botched opportunity and pondered whether the city would "roll with the punch" if it ever got another shot at entering the pros. It would have to, Jim Hall argued, if New Orleans wanted to match the pace of "Miami, Atlanta, Houston, and other progressive Southern cities." One letter asked why locals repeatedly have to go to Houston to see pro sports. "Why did Joe Brown have to defend his championship in Texas?" it read, referring to the Ralph Dupas boxing scandal. "Is this because New Orleans is so liberal?"[78]

Slowly, white voices also started pointing out that civic leaders were fooling themselves about the city's racial climate. While still blaming the players, a few mainstream editors and columnists urged a more practical assessment. After describing the All-Stars as "militant," a WDSU editorial conceded, "It is, of course, questionable whether or not this city was truly 'prepared' for a week-long, integrated social gathering."[79]

Likewise, sportswriter Hap Glaudi called the players "mutinous" and questioned their "training" in the French Quarter's "late strip spots." Then he stated bluntly, "But let us be sincerely honest with ourselves. We weren't ready for complete integration necessary for the successful promotion of major professional sports." He asserted that Dixon and Schiro were victims of "costly optimism."[80]

An editor of the *Clarion Herald,* after saying the players were "apparently as emotionally undeveloped as the bigots who irked them," mocked claims from the mayor's office that New Orleans had made "extraordinary progress in race relations." He quipped, "Progress, yes. Extraordinary progress, no." He argued, "Through the years of racial strife in New Orleans, the civic, business, and government leaders sat on their hands."[81]

Phil Johnson, the popular editorialist for WWL-TV, cited the American Legion withdrawal and told viewers, "This is called learning the hard way." He did not absolve the players of all fault but suggested "perhaps New Orleans is to blame, also." Johnson reasoned, "If any good can come of this, perhaps it will be that this city must at last come face-to-face with facts." He noted that the city had been given an ultimatum. "Either we are going to compete in this world of ours—as other cities are competing oh, so successfully," he explained. "Or we close ourselves off from the rest of America and remain the petty, provincial capital of limited opportunity and dubious culture which some seem to enjoy."[82]

Most locals still shrugged off any accountability, but a spotlight had at least been shined on taxi drivers and club owners. The New Orleans Aviation Board, noting that the airport was clearly involved in interstate commerce, tried to get out ahead of the issue. The board passed a motion that "no cab driver who racially discriminates will be allowed to enter the airport for the purpose of doing business." It was stressed that this was no admission of wrongdoing on the airport's part but merely "reaffirmation" of policy. Even so, its effectiveness was questionable, and it did nothing to curb segregation of taxis elsewhere in the city. Actually, that practice was also "reaffirmed."[83]

The director of the taxicab bureau announced that white drivers refusing Black passengers were adhering to local code regulating white and "colored" permits. He said that accommodating both races was technically allowed since the Civil Rights Act but was "not required." "We encourage them not to," he added, claiming that the practice protected Black drivers from losing their African American clients.[84]

A similar "reaffirmation" of old practices occurred for local nightclubs. The city attorney announced that federal courts had not defined the "private club" exemption to the Civil Rights Act. Therefore, he said, the city could not prevent proprietors from operating segregated restaurants and bars.[85]

On the heels of such reports, Mayor Schiro received a series of pleas from some white locals urging the creation of a human relations committee, which they felt "would go a long way in restoring our tarnished image." They talked of past crises and losses and the threat of more to come. One proponent argued that the committee "would show prospective industries and tourists, and our own citizens, we know how to handle and to prevent such emergencies." Schiro took no action.[86]

The losses continued. By the end of January, plans for the first New Orleans International Jazz Festival were suspended. A massive concert series featuring musical greats like Louis Armstrong, Duke Ellington, and Count Basie had been arranged for May. After three years of preparations, sponsors announced that they "felt the festival could be better planned and staged if it was held at a later time." So New Orleans's first Jazz Fest remained, like much of the city's culture, in an arrested state of development.[87]

|||||

A week after the walkout, sportswriter David Moffit described Atlanta's Mayor Ivan Allen Jr. as being "too polite to chortle aloud," despite his city's clear competition with New Orleans for professional football. When goaded by Moffit about Atlanta benefiting from the Big Easy's loss, Allen merely offered, "I don't think this will hurt Atlanta's chances."[88]

In early 1965, Mayor Allen was personally pitching Atlanta to both pro football commissioners—until he thought to recruit the owner of the local WSB television station, Leonard Reinsch. Allen considered him "one of the best salesmen in the country" and knew that Reinsch's NBC affiliate would benefit from a local AFL club. Thereafter, the media mogul took over all the legwork in wooing the younger league.[89]

However, Hunt's bunch had backed off on expansion talk again as their 1965 spring meeting approached. Then, two days before AFL owners convened, Pete Rozelle announced he would advocate expanding the NFL with two new teams by 1967—maybe even fielding one in 1966. It was also clear that Atlanta topped his list. Joe Foss wasted no time in releasing his own statement that he would propose an AFL expansion by two teams for 1966 and two more by 1968. He also did little to conceal favoritism for Atlanta and Philadelphia.[90]

On June 7, when AFL execs assembled in New Jersey, their commissioner insisted that they should break trail into the most attractive city of the virgin Southeast. Foss anticipated receiving the half-dozen hands he needed, but in fact the owners unanimously voted to adopt Atlanta for 1966.[91]

Around 11:30 that night, Mayor Allen got a call from Reinsch, who crowed, "Ivan, I've got the contract and I'm coming over to your house." Allen thought the TV executive sounded like a child on Christmas morning. Reinsch had agreed to pay a record-setting $7.5 million for the franchise, and he showed up at midnight with documents in hand.

Allen, however, had news for the giddy businessman. First, the mayor asked a very important question: "Have you signed up the Stadium Authority?"

"They've got to come to me," Reinsch replied. "I've got the franchise and Atlanta's got to have it."[92]

For months Reinsch, with the stadium group's encouragement, had worked to bring the city a coveted pro football team. He saw no reason to worry about their approval once the deal was made. What he did not know was that the NFL commissioner had flown in earlier that day for appointments with city and stadium administrators the next morning.[93]

The Atlanta Stadium Authority's preference for the older league was no secret, but after their conference with Rozelle, they announced they would study the matter before signing any pro football tenant. In reality, this window was not designed for deliberation of the two leagues but rather for Rozelle to find a buyer and to garner votes from NFL owners. The battle between the leagues over the Deep South's first entry was happening just as Dixon envisioned, just not over New Orleans.

Mayor Allen soon received another call, this time from a wealthy insurance man and lifelong Atlantan named Rankin Smith. Governor Sanders had recommended Smith to Rozelle. "Do you have any objections to my bringing NFL football here?" Smith asked. Allen felt terrible for Reinsch, who had done all the heavy lifting, but the mayor also knew that if his administration chose the AFL, they would be "run out of town." So on June 30, 1965, the NFL announced that Atlanta would field the league's fifteenth team, in 1966.[94]

The same day, AFL execs found out that their second choice had also been poached. Philadelphia had drawn up plans for a $25 million downtown stadium complex, and Mayor James H. J. Tate denied sole tenancy to the NFL's Eagles. The club's owner sued, but the AFL was confident in its negotiations and continued interviewing potential buyers. Then, in late June, a committee appointed by a judge (and out of Tate's reach) granted an exclusive ten-year occupancy to the Eagles.[95]

On July 1, news was breaking of the previous day's fumbles and takeaways in pro football, and Dixon called his own press conference. As the AFL rallied from its losses, he had been contacted, and his bags were packed for a weekend with Lamar Hunt. With the battle for Atlanta fresh in his mind, Dixon did not slip away quietly. He tried to stir up a bidding war for his own town. He made a big announcement of the "authentic feeler" from the AFL and the "serious negotiation" his group was prepared to undertake. Naturally, Dixon was questioned about the walkout, now just over six months past. He called it a "closed issue" and declared, "We are too busy planning ahead to look back." He was also careful to mention that he had in no way lost interest in the NFL, where New Orleans would be "the obvious companion city choice for Atlanta."[96]

As Dixon met with Hunt and company, Pete Finney was entertaining readers with a fanciful scenario in which the city had a team in both leagues by the end of the weekend. Although he was writing tongue in cheek, he seriously urged locals to keep an open mind about the AFL. He argued that condemning the whole circuit for the actions of a few players was no different than what the All-Stars had done to New Orleans. With both leagues on the offensive, after all, anything seemed possible.[97]

By Monday, however, AFL officials had reached a preliminary agreement with Miami to establish the league's ninth franchise in the Orange Bowl stadium. They also announced that their expansion search for 1966 ended there. And the NFL did not call.

Dixon was heartbroken, again. After the walkout, Art Burke had written, "The AFL has slapped down the city of New Orleans for the last time." He was wrong. The on-again, off-again relationship between Dixon and the junior circuit went one more round. Then, on July 6, he announced, "We have withdrawn ourselves from consideration for an American Football League franchise."[98]

Sports Illustrated explained how an attorney and former politician, Joe Robbie, became the owner of a professional football club after only about six months of lobbying. It was a simple story. "Robbie got lucky," it began. "Atlanta, first in the hearts of the AFL expansion committee, was stolen away by the NFL, and New Orleans had a problem with the treatment of Negroes during the AFL All-Star game. So . . . Miami was voted in."[99]

CHAPTER 9
Unbeaten and Untied

For the first half of 1965, New Orleans simply stewed. Even Dixon neglected the franchise hunt, instead fostering his idea to create a new spring football league. The small number of locals treating the walkout as a wakeup call was nowhere near a critical mass, at least until Atlanta joined the NFL. Sure, it was the slightly later marriage between Miami and the American Football League that planted New Orleans firmly out in the cold, but a team in that circuit would have been a tough sell to locals anyway. After repeatedly outpacing Atlanta's attendance, Louisiana fans, much like *Sports Illustrated*, could find only one reason that the Falcons went first.[1]

Atlanta's entry alone might have simply stirred up additional anger, but the stick came with a carrot. The NFL's late June announcement of its fifteenth franchise was followed by news that the league would return to an even number of teams in 1967. This had the sound of a starter pistol. There would be another NFL expansion within a year and a half—*and* another New Orleans exhibition in a month and a half.

Before the All-Star debacle, Dixon had tentatively lined up a pair of late summer NFL games. However, the walkout also shook up the older league, which launched its own investigation. The NFL ultimately determined that "there was wrong on both sides," and it factored in its previous success with brief stopovers in New Orleans. So the National Football League kept the Crescent City on its calendar. Then, however, the schedule was shuffled to avoid baseball conflicts, nixing Dixon's plans for a second game, but he still had one contract, for the Baltimore Colts and St. Louis Cardinals at Tulane Stadium on August 14.[2]

For local sports fans—and for many proud New Orleanians who otherwise might not have cared about a preseason football game—this was a shot at redemption for, or perhaps contradiction of, the All-Stars' allegations.

Billboards all over town sported giant three-word ads: "Let's Go Pro!" It was unclear, however, whether hope for a franchise or anger over the walkout was a bigger promotional tool, and the more common slogan became "The Real Pros Are Coming." Advertisements were strange fusions of civil rights advocacy and mulish denial, reading, "Now is the time to show the real pros they are welcome in this city." The box office was plainly far busier than it would have been before the boycott.[3]

However, recent expansion had proved that a red carpet went a lot further than a full stadium. To this end, John McKeithen announced he would lend "aggressive cooperation" to New Orleans's quest for pro football. The governor told Dixon that Atlanta had beat the Big Easy into the big leagues because of the support of Georgia's political, civic, and business leaders, and McKeithen pledged to rally the necessary forces.[4]

By midmonth, McKeithen and Dixon were lunching in the governor's mansion with wealthy New Yorker David McConnell, heir to the Avon empire, who was eager to put down millions to own a pro club. Right away, a press conference was catered at Moran's Restaurant, a dinner at Antoine's engaged local businessmen, and air travel was arranged for an appointment with Pete Rozelle.[5]

McKeithen made several new commitments at that time. He did something on the state level that many Black and white New Orleanians had sought from their mayor for years: the governor established a biracial Louisiana Commission on Human Relations. He asked Black business, religious, and civic leaders from each congressional district to nominate African American members, rather than personally selecting what would be seen as a council of Uncle Toms. McKeithen wanted buy-in, not Band-Aids, seeking Black and white citizens whose "stature" could "quell any racial unrest by sheer weight of public opinion."[6]

Although it was not an official municipal committee, a biracial group of New Orleanians was also cleaning house in late July. Ten locals teamed up with Black attorneys A. P. Tureaud and A. M. Trudeau to file federal suit against the city's segregated taxicabs. One Black and four white residents charged denial of service because of race-based drivers' permits. Also on the suit were several Black cabbies, one of whom had been denied purchase of a white driver's business. On August 4, Judge Frank Ellis ruled, "Taxicabs in New Orleans should operate for the joint benefit of both white and Negro" and tossed out the 1957 licensing ordinance.[7]

Ellis then gave the utilities director two weeks to begin enforcement.

However, two integrated NFL teams were arriving in nine days, and by early August the citywide campaign for hospitality was far more than a ticket drive. While individual motivations differed, there was a common pressure mounting among locals, and the timing of the taxi suit was not accidental. On August 13, the day before the Colts and Cards faced off at Tulane, all drivers holding New Orleans taxi permits received orders to accept all passengers, "regardless of race."[8]

The mayor's office was also advocating both a hospitable welcome for the teams and a packed house for the tilt. Local papers printed Schiro's resolution to "show the world that we want and deserve an NFL franchise." He talked of pro sports as an integral part of the city's future. Whereas Schiro had previously placated locals clinging to the idea of the "traditional city," he now addressed the constraints of a "heritage-bound community." He insisted that by "awakening from the dormancy of laissez faire," the city could achieve "unparalleled prosperity."[9]

No Colts or Cardinals reported problems from the first half of their all-business, thirty-six-hour stopover, and the gates of Tulane Stadium opened on Saturday evening as planned. It was an especially hot night, and late afternoon rain turned the structure into a giant steel sauna. Still, fans packed in more and more tightly as kickoff approached. And when the Colts quarterback was introduced as Johnny Unitas, the thunderous applause Diliberto had anticipated in 1963 finally erupted, only much later and much louder than expected. By kickoff, attendance appeared to be near capacity.[10]

As Unitas jump-started his offense to a 16–0 first-half lead, Dixon went after big numbers of his own. The business manager of Tulane Athletics, Buddy de Monsabert, was cornered for a total on ticket sales. Having no way to tally it up on the spot, he said it seemed to be around 75,000. With that, New Orleans broke her earlier record for a nonleague crowd. Still, Dixon was not quite happy with the number, thinking it sounded like the guess it was. So he invented a figure of his own and took it upstairs. When fans were told over the PA system they were part of a record-setting turnout of 75,229, a raucous cheer erupted in the stands.[11]

Then the loudspeakers reported another number: only around forty thousand seats were occupied at the ribbon-cutting exhibition in Atlanta's $18 million future home of the Falcons. Fans went berserk. Tulane Stadium shook. For years, Atlanta had flip-flopped between companion and competitor. Now Atlanta was in pro football, and although New Orleanians did not have a team, they had a rival.

In the second half, even with Unitas on the Colts' bench and vendors out of cold drinks, fans were not going anywhere. The Cardinals notched a touchdown and field goal, and it remained a one-score game until late in the fourth quarter. The clock was down to three minutes before Baltimore chalked up its third touchdown and fans leaned back. At final whistle, a mass of proud New Orleanians left the stadium together, feeling they had scored a win that night.[12]

Local reporters could have written up most of the postgame exchanges with league officials beforehand. There was more gushing over attendance and several familiar but fruitless claims about how much support for the city existed within the NFL. Eventually, though, Cards owners Billy and Stormy Bidwill went off the old scripts and got a little more specific. After questioning how many free tickets were distributed and how early in the autumn the humidity drops, the Bidwills stated point-blank that the turnout would not be anything close to a determining factor. Billy disclosed that extensive market research was being conducted on every applicant city. He also said he could not imagine a decision before next May.

Stormy was even more forthcoming when Diliberto asked why Atlanta beat New Orleans into the league. Bidwill had two straight answers. "They went ahead and built a stadium without any iron-clad assurance of getting a team," he explained. "This showed the city had confidence in itself." He then addressed the elephant in the press box. "Atlanta worked out its race problems very well," Bidwill continued. "The Negro leaders in the community cooperated 100 percent with the mayor and the men who were seeking pro football," Stormy said matter-of-factly, "and vice versa."[13]

Diliberto typed up these conversations over the weekend, and the following week it appeared he had an extremely broad readership. First, Schiro made a bold announcement: "We now need or shall soon need a professional sports stadium in New Orleans," he told reporters. "We're not going to wait until we get a professional franchise before we get started on a stadium. We're starting now."[14]

Two days later, the Young Men's Business Club met in the grand ballroom of the Roosevelt Hotel. The topic was united, community-wide buy-in for local football. Reporters from all the city's papers were welcomed, including (for the first time) Jim Hall. Hall had noted that for the previous couple of months, since around the time the NFL moved into Atlanta, many doors long closed to him had been opened. On that Wednesday, he became part of a biracial think tank aimed at making New Orleans the great football town it claimed to be.[15]

They discussed at length the city's failure to support the Green Wave, which recently had taken on a newly unifying identity. "If you live in this city, this is your team," Coach O'Boyle proclaimed. Tulane's last local companion in college football, Dillard University, suspended its program that May, and Xavier had done so in 1960. Regardless of a fan's race or alma mater, the Greenies were the only Saturday show in town.[16]

"I'm ashamed to say that in this city of one million we have sold only 5,000 season tickets," O'Boyle moaned. At first it sounded like a hard sell, given that his team only won four games in his three years at the helm. However, Diliberto argued, lack of Tulane support bolstered skepticism over whether New Orleans would support a losing team, which any expansion club was expected to be. So one offshoot of the Let's Go Pro! campaign was a Let's Go, Tulane! drive to unite the city around its lone postprep football representative.[17]

Everyone in the ballroom knew about the NFL's market research and the importance of a good racial climate. Jim Hall, however, was arguably the most informed on the "nasty spots" that still needed cleaning, and he spoke openly on the subject. The fellowship and fraternity impressed him, and on the following Saturday he told his readers, "After last week, I believe we're on the 'right track.'"[18]

|||||

Just before noon on Friday, August 6, President Johnson arrived at the U.S. Capitol, where a large party of dignitaries was waiting: the vice president, congressional leaders, members of the cabinet, and several prominent civil rights leaders, including Roy Wilkins, James Farmer, John Lewis, and Dr. Martin Luther King Jr. Johnson's entourage then journeyed to the Rotunda. At a podium flanked by a statue and a giant bust of Abraham Lincoln, Johnson announced that within minutes he would sign the Voting Rights Act, eliminating all literacy, knowledge, and character tests long used in the South to deny African Americans a ballot.[19]

"Today is a triumph for freedom as huge as any victory that's ever been won on any battlefield," the president began. He spoke of the long history of Black men and women in America before declaring, "Today we strike away the last major shackle of those fierce and ancient bonds." Johnson spoke with great passion. "Through this act and its enforcement," he stressed, "an important instrument of freedom passes into the hands of millions."

He put much force behind his next statement. "But that instrument must be used." The president spoke to every African American, saying, "You must register. You must vote. You must learn, so your choices advance your interest and the interest of our beloved nation." He concluded that "the vote is the most powerful instrument ever devised by man for breaking down injustice and destroying the terrible walls which imprison men because they are different from other men."[20]

Following his address, Johnson moved to the small, seldom-used President's Room, just outside the Senate chamber. It was there, 104 years ago to the day, that Lincoln had signed a bill freeing slaves forced into the service of the Confederate Army. The air conditioner was no match for the congestion of onlookers as Johnson sat at a simple, green baize–covered desk beneath a giant, gilded chandelier and signed the Voting Rights Act of 1965.[21]

In New Orleans, the registrar of voters scrambled to prepare for compliance. There was no time to print new registration forms, so the old double-sided cards simply had large sections voided. On the front, four "character" questions regarding misdemeanors, common-law marriages, and "illegitimate" children would be disregarded. On the back, six multiple-choice "citizenship" questions and the Preamble excerpt testing literacy would also be ignored. With half a dozen of his twenty-two deputy registrars on long-scheduled vacations, Orleans Parish registrar A. P. Gallinghouse spent Tuesday giving his remaining staff a crash course in new procedures.[22]

Wednesday, August 11, was the office's first day of operating under the new legislation, and 243 citizens were registered, 201 of whom were Black. On Thursday, the number nearly doubled, with roughly six Black registrants for every white one. The same day, however, the Interdenominational Ministerial Alliance launched a massive registration drive. Reverends A. L. Davis and Milton Upton called on churches, labor unions, social clubs, and civic groups to ensure that all members were on the voter rolls and to use any available private car or group bus as a shuttle.[23]

Within a week, an early morning line at City Hall stretched beyond the ground-floor corridor and down the long driveway to the Civil Courts Building. Busloads of African Americans were chauffeured from every part of the city. By midday, around six hundred people were on site, and volunteers handed out sandwiches to those willing to wait hours in the August heat.

For nearly half the line, the wait would not end that day. Only 328 were registered before the doors closed. Civil rights leaders lodged complaints that the registrar was dragging his feet, requiring inordinate identification, and keeping his office understaffed. Telegrams went to the president, the governor, and the attorney general charging that Gallinghouse and his deputies were willfully hampering the registration of Black New Orleanians.

The fact that Gallinghouse filed a suit challenging the constitutionality of the Voting Rights Act did not give Black citizens much faith in the sincerity of his efforts. Still, he insisted that the decline in processing rates corresponded to an increase in illiterate registrants, who needed extra time and assistance. Gallinghouse also said he was hiring temporary workers and starting a night shift that could double productivity. He gave personal guarantees that all applications would be processed before October 6, when rolls closed for the November primaries.[24]

On September 1, numbers were telling. Nearly 5,500 Black New Orleanians were newly registered, putting the total number of African American voters over forty thousand, the highest such figure in the city's history. The ratio of Black to white registrants was now 14:1. This also was the first day since the Interdenominational Ministerial Alliance drive began that no one was turned away when Gallinghouse's office closed.[25]

By Thursday, September 9, the registrar's night shift was in effect, but at four o'clock that afternoon, doors were locked with no line outside. Over the previous twenty-four hours, ever-shifting Hurricane Betsy—at one point an almost certain threat to the Carolinas—again changed her trajectory. The eerily unpredictable storm's Mississippi-bound projections were realigned early Thursday to indicate that the Big Easy was directly in her path.[26]

The worst of the storm's impact came overnight, with most of Orleans Parish losing electricity and telephone service. In most parts of the city, residents emerged at sunrise to find uprooted trees, downed streetlights, and damaged roofs, but those in the Lower Ninth Ward instead woke in darkness as waters rushed into their homes and quickly rose as high as the structures' eaves. Levees had been breached, rapidly flooding thousands of houses in a three hundred–block area inhabited largely by poor African Americans. Not all were able to escape.

A ragtag fleet of boats went to work on Friday as National Guardsmen and private citizens rescued people stranded on rooftops or trapped in attics. Dead bodies were secured to trees or buildings for later recovery, and the search for survivors continued through the weekend. By Sunday, the coroner had received twenty-nine corpses, roughly half the city's ultimate death toll. Thousands of homeless people crowded into shelters, including newly appointed refuges like the first and second floors of City Hall. With time, waters subsided, additional provisions arrived, more permanent housing was arranged, and New Orleans was left with what the mayor termed "the greatest cleanup in the city's history." And Schiro would lead it.[27]

Running for reelection, with the primaries two months away, Schiro had every recovery effort scrutinized. Although the mayor and his leading opponent, popular city council president Jimmy Fitzmorris, agreed to a political moratorium where Betsy was concerned, this agreement did not extend to the press or public. Criticism and praise seemed to come in equal measure. Within the Black community, which was most affected by the hurricane and now included a historically high number of voters, opinions varied widely.

Many commended the mayor for his hands-on involvement, as he had personally toured hard-hit areas and visited shelters to verify proper conditions. Others condemned him for the city's lack of preparedness and his failure to adequately alert at-risk residents. Likewise, Schiro was acknowledged for fighting in Washington for the unprecedented "Betsy bill" that provided loan forgiveness to victims needing to rebuild. Just as powerful, however, was the widely accepted claim that levees were intentionally dynamited to spare the city's more affluent neighborhoods.[28]

Dramatic changes to New Orleans's political climate arose after Betsy, particularly as the national NAACP investigated local recovery efforts. The regional director, Clarence Laws, visited from Dallas and sat in on various agencies' progress reports. The lack of Black representation appalled him, especially since more African Americans than whites would be affected by the outcomes.

Laws confronted local NAACP leaders and argued for complete community involvement. He questioned whether the dearth of Black participation resulted from internal biases or the lethargy of Black locals. Either way, he charged, it was time for change. With big elections approaching and the huge upswing in voter registration, Laws challenged Black citizens to draw promises from political candidates and to become integrated into decision-making bodies. He asserted that Betsy had proven such involvement was not merely a matter of good citizenship but arguably one of life and death.[29]

|||||

"This increased registration has given the Negro a new dignity," Milton Upton announced at a late October rally. "He now feels that he can do something about his many legitimate grievances," the reverend rejoiced. "No candidate is going to toy with 50,000 votes to his own detriment." Roughly sixteen thousand Black names were added to the rolls before the primaries. In its last preelection issue, the *Louisiana Weekly* recalled that not long before, racial liberalism was "political suicide." Now, the paper observed, there are "those who will espouse the cause of liberalism realizing that it is 'political suicide' not to do so."[30]

All candidates were pressed on issues important to Black voters, and many promises were made. Candidates repeatedly mirrored their opponents when racial commitments were publicized. Both Schiro and Fitzmorris gave their word on nondiscriminatory hiring in city jobs, the establishment of an integrated commission on race, and reopening the city's pools.[31]

The African American community had unprecedented voting power but divided endorsements. Three Black voters' leagues backed Schiro, with the most surprising support coming from Reverends A. L. Davis and Avery Alexander. Schiro's Black backers argued that progress made should not be forfeited for an unknown newcomer. Schiro, after all, kept an open-door policy and welcomed negotiations with civil rights leaders. He had voluntarily removed racial designations from municipal buildings and had integrated hiring in several city departments.[32]

Supporters of Fitzmorris, like the Crescent City Independent Voters League and the *Louisiana Weekly*, argued that the mayor's previous term had provided ample opportunity to fulfill guarantees that were being made only now, under the heat of the election. On the other hand, the New Orleans Voters Association argued that this being Schiro's second—and final—campaign was his biggest selling point, reasoning that since he could not succeed himself again, he would have no fear of backlash for keeping commitments to the Black community. They also saw his support of Johnson, a rarity among Louisiana politicians, as a sign of courage.[33]

It was an extremely close race. Then, less than two weeks out, the mayor was hospitalized for an emergency appendectomy. A televised debate with Fitzmorris was ruled out by Schiro's doctors, even after his discharge from Mercy. While Fitzmorris campaigned, the mayor convalesced. The *States-Item* figured Schiro had "probably just about rested his case."[34]

However, on the night of Thursday, November 4, just before the Saturday election, Schiro held a press conference from his home. The sixty-one-year-old looked dapper seated in a rocking chair, wearing a pajama set and red smoking jacket. His engagement took the form of a fireside chat. His special guest was David Dixon.[35]

The pair disclosed months of planning for a $24 million, all-weather stadium. The rectangular structure would seat sixty thousand for football and use a revolutionary artificial turf. There would be a retractable roof, and sliding seats would allow configurations for a range of sports and events. They showed an elaborate drawing of the interior during a professional football game. The roof was peeled back, stands were full, and scoreboards had the Saints in the lead. There was even an instant replay being shown on the giant closed-circuit television screen, something Dixon was determined to include since missing a big LSU play at Tiger Stadium while getting Mary a soda.

Also in the Schiro home that night was Marvin Kratter, a land developer with extensive property in New Orleans East. Kratter confirmed he would donate a $2 million, one hundred–acre plot near the I-10 interchange at Paris Road. Furthermore, the mayor said, external investors had pledged half the money needed. He saw the remainder coming not from municipal funds but from debenture bonds, like those the Mid-Winter Sports Association had used to expand Tulane Stadium. The public was also reminded that the NFL would soon award its sixteenth franchise. Dixon claimed that commitment to a new sports arena would "put New Orleans in a commanding position."[36]

Forty-eight hours later, polling stations were closed. Schiro achieved a majority by just around five hundred votes, a number that many speculated was well within the total gained by his eleventh-hour stadium special. He did not receive the majority of the African American ballots, which were split 60/40, but his share was far greater than the five percent he had mustered four years earlier, when there was still a racial bloc.

Shortly thereafter, Schiro spoke about race and his reelection to the Press Club of New Orleans, saying that the decline in racial disturbances in recent years was "no accident." He explained, "This is the result of quiet, persistent work on the part of the mayor and a number of responsible men," but he also indicated an upcoming shift in his philosophy. Schiro stated that his second mayoral tenure would conclude his political activity and that he would run for no future political office. Echoing the New Orleans Voters Association's theory, he foreshadowed significant changes "for the better" during his final term, "because," he explained, "my hands are no longer tied."[37]

|||||

Just before the primaries, there was another important vote. More than seven years after Joe Dorsey's legal victory, the Louisiana Boxing Commission approved an interracial bout for persistent promoters "Leapin' Lou" Messina and Curley Gagliano. Jim Hall was ecstatic, cramming many columns with plugs for the event and believing that he could not oversell its significance. He and Mr. and Mrs. Joe Daly, who contributed heavily to Dorsey's donation-driven case, positioned themselves ringside.

The pairing of Eddie Perkins and Kenny Lane, however, reeked of a boxing *mismatch*. Both fighters had been wildly successful in the junior welterweight division, but Lane was five years older than Perkins and had not competed in twelve months. When Lane weighed in at Municipal Auditorium, he tipped the scales at 145.5 pounds. Entering the ring with a paunchy midsection and 2 to 1 odds against him, the elder fighter was dropped by a right cross to the jaw in the first minute. He got up, took his eight count, and lasted all twelve rounds, but it appeared that Perkins could have finished Lane off early. Instead, the twenty-eight-year-old African American toyed with his opponent, getting in potshots between boos from disenchanted fans.

Lane lost every round. Sitting in front of his dressing room mirror afterwards, he announced, "When you can't move anymore, you're a sitting duck and it's time to quit." The night was no less disappointing for the measly 3,811 ticket holders, or for Messina and Gagliano, who took a loss on the night.[38]

If any group could sympathize with a tragically underwhelming and underattended "first" it was the MWSA. However, in early November 1965, the Sugar Bowlers seemed to have the upper hand in wooing the nation's top two free agent teams, Nebraska and Alabama, for the second fully integrated New Orleans bowl. Moreover, that year's bidding war had been given an extra twist. For the first time, the Associated Press elected to hold its final ballot after the postseason, meaning that New Year's Day games could determine the national college championship.[39]

Third-ranked, unblemished Nebraska was also being courted for the unrestricted Orange Bowl and for the open spot in Dallas's game, but Sugar had a clear advantage over Cotton. The Cornhuskers had gone to Texas the previous year and fell to the likely repeating hosts, the number two, also unbeaten, Arkansas Razorbacks. It was assumed that the Cornhuskers preferred a change of both scenery and enemy. Besides, even if a rematch appealed, an upset in the Arkansas–Texas Tech finale could leave the Cornhuskers playing the Red Raiders, a formidable but far less glamorous opponent for impressing pollsters. The Orange Bowl stadium was also familiar turf, since Nebraska had rung in 1964 from Miami. A trip to New

Orleans would be their first Sugar experience and put them on a short list of teams playing in three different bowls in three years.[40]

Sugar's selling points did not stop there. As part of their giant new push to rebrand the game, scouts touted plans for weeklong entertainment. Unlike the year before, when Syracuse was warned away from training at Tulane, Sugar reps now promoted seven days of lavish treatment for all their guests. The MWSA was confident locals would support the classic, through both ticket sales and "some real Southern hospitality."[41]

Nebraska, unfortunately, was not so certain. After all the schmoozing and salesmanship, coach Bob Devaney announced he was accepting Orange's invitation. The last integrated team to move into the Crescent City for an extended stay had been the AFL All-Stars, and Devaney was frank about choosing South Florida to protect his Black players. In recent years, Orange Bowl officials had closed in on Sugar's reputation for vast entertainment. It was not yet clear, however, how close the Big Easy had come to matching Miami's racial harmony.[42]

Bear Bryant immediately committed his midranked SEC-leading squad to meet the Cornhuskers on January 1. Alabama's deference to Nebraska's choice gave the Crimson Tide its best chance in the championship race and gave Miami the hands-down best pairing. With that, Sugar was looking at a jumble of Southeastern options at the bottom of or just outside the top ten.[43]

However, there was only one ranked intersectional school up for grabs, so in the interest of ensuring national flavor, two MWSA reps flew to the Midwest to watch Missouri take on Oklahoma. Tigers quarterback Gary Lane rushed for three touchdowns and passed for a fourth to lead the home team to a 30–0 blowout, their first win against a visiting Sooner squad in twenty years. Afterwards, Dr. Fred Wolfe and Paul DeBlanc made their pitch to Missouri athletic director Don Faurot, who had coached the Tigers in the school's only previous Sugar Bowl. Faurot eagerly accepted, with hopes that this squad could atone for his 1942 team's 2–0 loss to Fordham.

Wolfe gushed with satisfaction. "It'll be wonderful to have a Big Eight team in New Orleans again," he crowed. It was announced that the team's vote was unanimous, and players told newsmen they were excited to play the postseason in New Orleans. Likewise, coach Dan Devine beamed and said he was proud of the invitation. However, he also let it slip to at least one sportswriter, "This was the only firm bid we had."[44]

The MWSA planned to nail down its SEC representative through a deal with Florida after its likely win over Tulane the same afternoon. The Gators had been ranked more weeks than not and would bring fresh faces in their first Sugar Bowl. So after Steve Spurrier and a string of backups coasted to a 51–13 victory over the Wave, an "unofficially official" agreement was made in the early afternoon. At nightfall, the handshake looked like quite a coup over Cotton, which by the end of the late games had seen both of its favorites lose. The Dallas group went into a frenzy to reignite talks with the Gators, who had sneaked into the number ten slot. But the Sugar agreement stood.[45]

On the following Saturday, Sugar Bowl president Theo Maumus walked into the Orange Bowl stadium with a sealed envelope for Gator head coach Ray Graves. Maumus, Corenswet, and Simons watched with delight as the team got off to a fast start in a fierce Sunshine State rivalry game. Leading on the scoreboard and in momentum at halftime, the 6–2 Florida squad was performing as expected against 4–4 Miami.

Then, in the second half, the Hurricanes found the weak spot they were looking for in the Gator defensive line. They more than doubled their rushing yards from the first two quarters and successfully implemented coach Charlie Tate's run scheme: "Shove it down their throats." Meanwhile, their defense held Florida's superstar quarterback to eight completed passes and 79 yards in twenty-two attempts, statistics Graves labeled "Spurrier's worst night of his career." By the end of the third, the game was tied at 13. A fourth-quarter field goal gave Miami the upset.[46]

Sugar reps faced an all too familiar unpleasant task. Their bid was not addressed to the coach being carried off the field of the Orange Bowl stadium, which—even more painfully—was the site of that year's hottest bowl, the game the MWSA lost out on because of racial problems back home. The Gator dressing room felt like a tomb. Coach Graves spoke to reporters through clenched teeth. When asked about the Sugar Bowl bid in the pocket of his brown sport coat, he half-mumbled that it was "still an honor." Likewise, Sugar Prexy Maumus stated that "you can't win 'em all."

Meanwhile, the Sugar Bowl was dealt another blow back home. In Baton Rouge, Tulane was playing its final football game as a member of the SEC. The perennially underdog Greenies had made some pretty cutting comments after the previous year's near upset of LSU. Although the Tigers' Coach McClendon told players not to retaliate through the press, the trash talk was bulletin board material. For the third time in eight years, LSU shut out Tulane with a familiar tally of 62–0. Afterwards, the Tigers admitted running up the score because of the previous year's chatter. Joe Labruzzo put it bluntly. "They are always saying how stupid we are," he said of the

Tulane squad. "Well, tonight we wanted to act stupid enough not to know when to quit."⁴⁷

After LSU's landslide victory, Cotton Bowlers happily handed McClendon an invitation to Dallas for a date with unbeaten Arkansas, causing another dip in Sugar's stock. Although both Florida and LSU had three losses, a team coming off a blowout victory was far more exciting than a squad licking wounds from an upset loss. Moreover, folks from the area were now more likely to follow the Tigers to Dallas for a game with championship implications than to stay for an arguably meaningless matchup between sixth-ranked Missouri and unranked Florida. Fans not road-tripping were at least expected to stay home and watch the Cotton Bowl on TV.⁴⁸

By bowl week, however, the MWSA's popularity was improving. The lure of endless entertainment—and warm weather—brought Mizzou down early, and the Sugar Bowlers delivered on their promises. From the moment the Tigers touched down to a jazz band reception, players, coaches, wives, and school officials were treated to nonstop amusements. The MWSA had authorized an increased fun budget, and it paid off. Player after player and coach after coach raved about how well they were treated.⁴⁹

Nevertheless, on New Year's Day, more than seventeen thousand seats were empty at Tulane Stadium. Even many loyal supporters in attendance held radios to their ears to follow Arkansas–LSU coverage from Dallas. Ticket holders who sat through three quarters of completely one-sided action and stayed for a fourth, however, witnessed one of the most exciting endings in Sugar Bowl history.

Late in the first half, Missouri had 14 points and the Gators had as many total yards. The Tigers ground game dominated time of possession, and when Florida did have the ball, Mizzou's wide tackle six suffocated Spurrier. Missouri held a 20–0 lead at the opening of the final quarter.⁵⁰

Then something clicked. The Florida offense, which had slept through forty-five minutes of competition, rebounded with such force that Spurrier broke three Sugar Bowl passing records, almost entirely in the fourth quarter. Scrambling away from charging linemen, he connected on six straight passes and led an 89-yard drive for the Gators' first touchdown of the day. A pass attempt for what would have been the classic's second two-point conversion fell incomplete, making the score 20–6. A Mizzou fumble on their next drive set up a Spurrier sneak into the end zone and another 6 points. After lining up for a PAT, Florida faked the kick and tried to make it a 6-point game. But halfback Jack Harper's pass was off target, and Florida lagged by 8.

After a tough Gator defensive stand, a Tigers punt put the ball in Spurrier's hands again, with little time remaining. The "blond bomber" orchestrated another 80-yard drive, this one capped by Charlie Casey's diving reception of a tipped pass at the goal line. Success on their third 2-point conversion attempt would tie the ballgame. Spurrier dropped back, fans held their breath, and an arching pass was broken up by a Mizzou defender in the back corner of the end zone.[51]

The Tigers left victorious, but the Gators' near completion of the greatest comeback in Sugar Bowl history made the 1966 classic one for the record books. Setting new marks for pass attempts, completions, and yards gained through the air, Spurrier became the first member of a losing Sugar Bowl team to receive the Miller-Digby trophy. As in recent years, postgame talk involved a lot of second-guessing. In the Big Easy, the game was heatedly debated. This time, however, the topic was Ray Graves's three decisions to go for 2 points and not the MWSA's choice of teams.[52]

Unfortunately, few other sports fans and media outlets were discussing the Sugar Bowl at all. Of the four big bowls, Sugar was the only one without an unbeaten team and without any bearing on the Associated Press poll. And, salting Sugar's wounds, the coveted Orange matchup determined the college champion. After a two-score victory over previously unbeaten Nebraska in Miami, the Crimson Tide was crowned the top team in the country.

Sports Illustrated's bowl preview edition had detailed the implications and intrigue of the upcoming Rose, Cotton, and Orange Bowl games. It also explained, "Sponsors of the Sugar Bowl, which once ranked second only to the Rose Bowl in importance, have of late grown accustomed to settling for leftovers." After the thrilling finish of the Missouri–Florida classic, however, the magazine published no such smear of the New Orleans affair. Actually, as it recounted all the New Year's Day action and excitement in college football, *Sports Illustrated* did not mention the 1966 Sugar Bowl at all.[53]

|||||

About a week later, that year's AFL All-Stars were flying to Houston, and three would have weather conditions reroute them into an unexpected overnight stop. Ernie Wright, Earl Faison, and Dave Grayson faced an extended layover in, of all places, New Orleans. They were promised an early morning flight and directed to the airport-adjacent Hilton Inn Motel.

Though they were leery, the temptation of an oyster dinner lured the three Black ballplayers into the city. They easily hailed an African American cabbie and asked for advice. Without hesitation, he headed toward Acme Oyster House in the French Quarter. To three guys with fresh scars and clear memories, hitting a tourist spot off Bourbon Street seemed unwise. As they debated, the driver realized why the group seemed familiar.

"Aw, I thought I recognized you guys," he said. "You're football players, right?" He tried to alleviate their confusion. "You don't know what you guys did last year," he stated bluntly. He explained that taxis had been completely integrated and long-standing segregation customs were abandoned throughout the city. He said New Orleanians wanted a pro team so badly they were yielding to the demands of modern American life.[54]

This was just the argument Dixon's group was making to the National Football League in its latest brochure. David Kleck's firm prepared a glossy, seventy-two-page, eleven-by-eighteen-inch book for the New Orleans Pro Football Club. By January 20, a copy was sent to every owner, GM, and head coach in the league, as well as to leading sportswriters in NFL cities. Six months of work had gone into the project, starting around the time Atlanta entered the pros.[55]

This massive volume differed from Dixon's earlier brochures even more in its content than in its size and glitz. It still raved about the city's tourist attractions, economy, and projected ticket sales, but there was a new overarching theme: change. Now, instead of spouting naive claims about a harmonious climate, the text spoke openly about the city's problematic past.

The first page read, "New Orleans today is a city of change, a city of change in a region of change, change so great and far-reaching in its implications that the imagination is burdened." One key difference was citywide buy-in and cooperation. In the latter half of 1965, the Pro Football Club had partnered with the governor, mayor, chamber of commerce, and local NAACP, as well as with numerous civic and business leaders of both races.

The brochure announced that New Orleans and Louisiana had "emerged from a doubtful past into a new era of political maturity and development." The area's leadership was said to be "writing a new and brilliant chapter in Southern history." It was celebrated that under McKeithen's guidance, "divergent elements of the state have worked in harmony," and Schiro's administration was dubbed "the builders of the new New Orleans." The piece also praised the city's "Negro leadership" for working alongside the mayor's team "to solve problems through peace and understanding."

Also included was a resolution passed by the local NAACP, giving full support to the city's NFL aspirations. It stated that the Pro Football Club's exhibitions had involved no discrimination and produced "nothing but benefits for the continued advancement of the citizens of this city." Admitting openly that "much progress remains to be made" on the local front, "as it remains in any city in America," the resolution professed confidence in the "reasonable leadership of outstanding men of both races."

The book was filled with slightly altered rewordings of the concept that New Orleans was in rapid transition. One of these reiterations asserted that the report would already be "outdated" when it left the printer. In early January, this claim became far more accurate than its authors could have expected. Local efforts picked up a lot of steam with the coming of the new year.[56]

On December 14, Ohio governor James Rhodes had held a luncheon for Cincinnati's civic and business leaders. His goal was to jump-start plans for a new stadium and give the Queen City an edge in its NFL franchise bid. To that end, he pulled out his secret weapon, surprise guest speaker Paul Brown.

Since being fired by Cleveland in 1963, Ohio's coaching icon had been out of football, and he was ready to get back to it. "I'm very interested in trying to get a team for Cincinnati," Brown stated. He revealed he had spoken with Rozelle and thought Cincy had "a good chance" at being the NFL's sixteenth club—*if* new facilities were erected in time.[57]

There was not a peep of opposition. The governor released a battle cry: "War has been declared by Cincinnati on any other city in the United States interested in a pro football team." From that moment, the dark horse candidate began moving ahead at an unbelievable clip. Rhodes immediately appointed a stadium steering committee, and multiple consulting firms were hired. City officials asked Atlanta's Arthur Montgomery for his old blueprints in hopes of saving months of planning. By New Year's Day, a competition had formed between different city, county, and private groups to finance the complex.[58]

Officials announced that there was "no doubt" Cincy would have its stadium by the start of the 1967 football season. This was a phenomenally ambitious—but necessary—timeline. The only alternative was the home of the Cincinnati Reds, Crosley Field. It was Major League Baseball's oldest and smallest park, seating only around thirty thousand, and was considered unacceptable even as an interim NFL site. A Labor Day opening would be miraculous, but they had help from Atlanta's masterminds, who pulled off their own miracle to meet the anticipated arrival of the Braves. Also like Atlanta, the Ohio contingent displayed confidence, guaranteeing the stadium without a promise from the NFL.

Back in Louisiana, sports-minded folks were taking notice of the Buckeye State's sudden upsurge in activity. Buddy Diliberto wavered on what he considered more impressive—and more threatening. He was in awe of both Ohio's momentum and the fact that its governor had "everyone working in harmony." Rhodes told local leaders, "It's my job to expedite this stadium drive," but he also reminded them of their responsibility. "All elected officials must work together," he demanded. "This is for Democrats and Republicans both."[59]

As New Orleanians were noticing, local efforts were disjointed. They were not split along party lines, just fractured. Mayor Schiro promised a lakefront complex financed by private donations and public debenture bonds. Governor McKeithen, who had a different location in mind, saw construction as possible only with state funds. Dixon dipped into both pools, appearing on TV with Schiro and flying to New York with McKeithen. A lot of new faces had been incorporated recently, including Black and white civic and business leaders, but there was no shared plan for everyone to rally behind.[60]

With publicity from Cincinnati reaching a critical volume, Governor McKeithen tried to quell concerns about the Big Easy being eclipsed, announcing that he was working diligently toward both a stadium and a franchise, just without the "flim-flam and bragging" of Governor Rhodes. McKeithen did, however, start making his own big guarantees. From Dallas, where he cheered LSU in the Cotton Bowl, he promised New Orleans "a new stadium—the best in the whole United States." Even then, however, he stressed that his plans had "nothing to do with" Schiro's proposal. Likewise, Schiro maintained that his deal with Kratter stood.[61]

News of northern progress accumulated like New Year's confetti and within two weeks Louisianans admitted they needed to work together. So, on January 10, Victor Schiro and David Dixon visited the governor in Baton Rouge. The main topics were, of course, pro football and a domed stadium, but the theme was "unity." They knew they needed to align behind a joint project, but Schiro took the concept to another level.

The mayor argued that, if handled properly, the drive for professional football could blur many old and deeply worn dividing lines within the state. He thought sports fever could transcend traditional divisions, referring not only to racial barriers but also to those between northern and southern parishes, urban and rural populations, and Catholic and Protestant groups. He hoped, too, that his city housing the state's pro team would abate long-held antipathy toward New Orleans on the part of the rest of Louisiana.[62]

Afterwards, the governor and mayor announced their merger and appointed steering committees to study all strategies. Invitations to a February 2 meeting were wired to an integrated group of more than sixty politicians, businessmen, and community leaders. McKeithen showed up ready to rally the troops.

"We're going to build this stadium, period," he announced, committing to the project regardless of where the NFL's next team was placed. "If they want to give the 16th franchise to Cincinnati and play the games in the sleet and snow," he barked, "let 'em." The governor trumpeted that once Louisianans had their unrivaled new facilities, the league would come to them. "All we ask is the cooperation and togetherness of all our citizens," he pushed.[63]

Following his rah-rah speech, the governor asked if anyone had reservations. The room was silent. Even the Sugar Bowlers were somewhat reluctantly on board, despite expectations that their classic would move into the new complex. After all the time, energy, money, and care the Mid-Winter Sports Association had invested in Tulane Stadium, they were devoted to their home turf, but they decided to back whatever stance Tulane took. Likewise, the university felt an indebtedness to the bowl group but was also quite interested in using the old stadium space for campus expansion, so Tulane defended the dome. Moreover, neither group wanted to be obstructionists on the project.

Even after the unanimous endorsement, McKeithen continued his salesmanship, saying that "if this state can't build a Dome Stadium then it deserves to have Houston, Atlanta, and Miami ahead of it in the field of big league sports." He then added one version of what became a personal tagline: "Will we just go out and sit by the banks of the Mississippi River and talk about our wonderful heritage and traditions and watch the rest of the world go by?"[64]

Within the week, Schiro and McKeithen appointed two integrated panels. Dillard University president Albert Dent was named to the finance body and Xavier administrator Norman Francis sat on the site committee. The groups were given fifteen days to present recommendations to the governor, who had no intention of letting momentum dip.[65]

As the Pelican State picked up its pace, its publicity also rose. *Sports Illustrated,* along with newspapers from San Francisco to New York, reported on

"Louisiana's new-horizons-minded governor" and New Orleans's elaborate designs for a first-of-its-kind, football-specific, domed stadium. One of Diliberto's readers raved over the positive public relations: "It has been a long time since we have been credited nationally with being 'revolutionary and ingenious' in anything." Diliberto replied in agreement, "How sweet it is."[66]

|||||

Victor Schiro was not waiting for the spring start of his second term before acting on its freedoms. He did not even wait for the new year to appoint a qualified African American to a government position. On December 27, 1965, A. M. Trudeau was sworn in as assistant city attorney, becoming the first Black man to hold such a position in New Orleans since Reconstruction. Also present was Trudeau's longtime mentor, A. P. Tureaud, counsel for the local NAACP. As Tureaud watched, his young protégé took the oath of an office that they had battled many times over civil rights.[67]

Also keeping their election season promises as 1966 bloomed were members of the Black community, who pledged active participation in city affairs. The new president of the local NAACP chapter, Horace Bynum, announced the new year's theme: "Total Community Involvement." He stated that under the Civil Rights Act of 1964 and the Voting Rights Act of 1965, it was Black citizens' "duty and responsibility to implement these laws with action." This naturally foreshadowed more events like the voter registration drive, but there were some more festive implications as well.[68]

In January and February, African American groups' Mardi Gras balls, receptions, and parties were held in formerly all-white hotels and clubs throughout the city. In recent years, civil rights groups had urged Blacks to boycott Carnival. It was argued that the money spent on costumes and decorations should be donated to their cause and that it was wrong to dance and parade when others were being jailed and beaten. In 1966, however, Blacks could consider it their duty to exercise freedom of movement and occupy shared spaces of revelry.[69]

Soon after Mardi Gras, there was another celebration spanning several days and involving numerous ceremonies. Albert Dent was honored for his twenty-five years as president of Dillard University and his vast contribution to the education of African Americans. Following an autographed photo from President Johnson came a presentation from Victor Schiro. The mayor handed Dent the keys to the city and a note saying, "Personally, I have been honored with your friendship and gratified at your unfailing cooperation in matters demanding our joint endeavors."[70]

Schiro continued fulfilling promises for his final term during the waning days of his first. In one month, he named eight Black civic leaders to city advisory posts. One appointment filled a vacancy on the housing committee. The other seven formed the mayor's new Pontchartrain Park board for the betterment of the expansive sports complex.[71]

Schiro's second tenure officially began on May 2, during a full day of ceremonies. That evening, all seven freshly installed council members addressed a packed banquet space at the Roosevelt Hotel. Councilman at-large Maurice "Moon" Landrieu stated that he believed every citizen of New Orleans deserved to share in the city's resources and "the good things of life." He expressed hope that the new administration would seek the "advice and counsel" of the community and make decisions benefiting all.

Councilman Walter F. Marcus Jr. argued that New Orleans could again be the "first city of the South" but needed to regain ground lost to Atlanta, Dallas, Houston, and Miami. However, he also said the community was beginning to realize what needed to be done. "This destiny can be ours," Marcus declared, "provided we have the courage and integrity to make it so."

John J. Petre, council president, announced, "Our city is in the midst of rapid economic growth and profound social change. To ignore either of these trends would be a denial of our responsibility." He noted the importance of listening to the "expanded electorate" and "new generation" in the city. "To the traditional political virtues of integrity, independence, and honesty," he preached, "we must add an awareness of change and a willingness to respond with a sense of responsibility to all the citizens of this city."

Before the program ended, Mayor Schiro addressed the crowd. "I am ready and able to make this as great a city as you would have it," he vowed. "Only if we work together can we accomplish our goals." He closed with a directive: "We must do whatever is necessary to ensure that New Orleans remains a city where all men can live and prosper in harmony and concord."[72]

|||||

Two weeks later, Moon Landrieu was on a private plane bound for the nation's capital. With him sat his dear friend and former law school classmate Norman Francis. Being the first integrated group in Loyola's law program and studying under courageous jurists like J. Skelly Wright, theirs had been, as Francis saw it, a class of revolutionaries for racial justice. That day, Landrieu and Francis were part of McKeithen's entourage pitching for an NFL franchise.[73]

While a Xavier administrator, Francis also served as counsel for the Congress of Racial Equity and worked to protect both the Freedom Riders from Alabama and students, such as Rudy Lombard, arrested for lunch counter sit-ins. He knew firsthand the local struggle, which would soon be discussed with the National Football League. The Stanford Research study on applicant cities had been delivered to the owners. "In six of the seven candidate areas," the document read, "consideration of racial relations in the United States would probably not be important; in New Orleans, it might be." The report recapped the AFL fiasco and stated, "There is, admittedly, still a hard core of segregationist business owners in the city, and people seeking to create racial incidents could do so."

However, the Stanford study also stated that "civic and business leaders in New Orleans have worked hard during the past year to remove any obstacles that might be sources of trouble in the future." Likewise, the text noted that many local interviewees "believe that an NFL team in New Orleans could be an agency of goodwill." McKeithen and his party hoped to drive these arguments home.[74]

Also on the flight were Dave Dixon and two colleagues from the Pro Football Club. Darwin Fenner of Tulane, hotelier Seymour Weiss, District Attorney Jim Garrison, and other representatives from the city council, chamber of commerce, and various state boards completed the passenger list. They would meet Schiro in Washington, and Louisiana congressmen were driving over in support.[75]

The plane belonged to John Mecom Sr., a wealthy oilman with holdings in both New Orleans and Houston. David McConnell had turned his attention westward when he heard rumors that San Diego's franchise was for sale. Around that time, Mecom and his son became the moneymen at McKeithen's meetings with Rozelle. Although a group was working to bring an NFL team into Houston's Astrodome, the Mecoms stayed clear of any war with the AFL's Oilers by backing the nearby Crescent City.

Loyalty to the Oilers created a delicate situation for Houstonians wanting to establish an NFL rival. The locals meeting with NFL execs in DC did not even release their names until they arrived. On the flip side, the colossal, state-of-the-art Astrodome had no pro football tenant. After the Oilers' great anticipation, Bud Adams found lease terms completely unacceptable and moved his club instead to Rice University's stadium. Consequently, putting a team on the AstroTurf was a huge temptation to both the NFL and the facility's operators.[76]

Houston was considered a top competitor, along with Cincinnati, and those towns fared well in the Stanford survey. Both cities had also already been showcased to the league by the time McKeithen's group arrived at the Shoreham Hotel. Houston's presentation predictably centered on "the wonders of the Astrodome," and Governor Rhodes was so efficient that he finished with two spare minutes and no need for questions.[77]

When McKeithen and Schiro rendezvoused, they only had about half an hour to finalize their presentation. It was understood that the delegation would stand in support but only the governor and mayor would speak. Scurrying to polish plans, McKeithen floated an idea to have Francis comment, but nothing more was said on the notion before the party filed into the conference room.

It was a massive space, with the owners and commissioner seated at a row of tables in the center. Louisiana's supporting cast lined up on one side, and the governor took center stage. As McKeithen preached the virtues of New Orleans in his heavy North Louisiana accent, Francis stood against the wall, thinking his governor could sell fire to the devil. McKeithen covered every pertinent topic with infectious confidence, addressing the racial climate directly and giving his word that the "law of the land" would be enforced and obeyed.[78]

Something must have distracted Francis, because suddenly Landrieu elbowed him and whispered that the governor had called his name, giving him however many seconds it took to walk to the microphone stand to figure out what the governor wanted. Then McKeithen asked Francis to tell the owners of the National Football League whether the city was prepared for a pro team.

Francis began by saying he was no official spokesman for his race but would share his personal beliefs. He also stated that, like any city, New Orleans had not solved all its racial problems. But he testified to the city's "new political climate," ushered in by "leaders who recognized that in trying to bring progress to the state one must look forward and not backwards." He spoke of "new days in the history of our city—ones which see us moving another step closer to the cosmopolitan atmosphere we should have reached long ago." He said Black citizens "expect to share in all of the operations of pro football," and he told the owners that "if the NFL came to New Orleans all of us would be bigger because of it."[79]

Back out in the halls, newsmen corralled Houston, Cincinnati, and New

Orleans reps into a group interview, and McKeithen quickly realized he could not let his guard down. The governor told reporters, "Louisiana State University has had fifty-six consecutive sellouts at home." He continued, "There's only one school in the country that draws more people for football games." A Cincinnati sportswriter asked what team outdrew LSU. "Ohio State," McKeithen replied. Dixon leaned over and said softly, "That man is from Ohio. That's just what he wanted you to say." The governor looked back at the columnist and sighed, "Touché."[80]

The next topic was stadium plans, and McKeithen again gave a forceful declaration, "If the National Football League gives us the word, we can move tomorrow." Judge Hofheinz, holding the keys to the Astrodome, countered, "We can go today."[81]

Then came the inevitable question about New Orleans's racial problems. McKeithen looked no further than DC for his answer. "Why just recently our Vice President Hubert H. Humphrey said that Louisiana was leading the way for all Southern states in solving the racial problem," he boasted. "Senator Ted Kennedy has said the same thing about the harmonious way we are handling things in our state," the governor continued, adding proudly, "I would say that those two men could be called liberals."[82]

|||||

As soon as they returned home, Landrieu and Schiro got back to fulfilling campaign promises. In his first month as councilman at-large, Landrieu introduced a resolution for equal hiring policies in all municipal agencies. The same week, the mayor named Dr. J. M. Epps the first African American to serve on the New Orleans Board of Health. It was the first of seven such appointments Schiro made that summer. A. P. Tureaud was tapped for a five-year term with the New Orleans Housing Authority. Reverends Davis and Upton joined the committee overseeing voter registration records. Norman Francis and Revius Ortique Jr. were named consultants for a new juvenile detention center. Civil rights attorney Nils Douglas was added to the traffic safety committee. And one of the city's first Black police officers, Carlton Pecot, was appointed to the city welfare board.[83]

One of Schiro's most popular pledges, however, was more difficult to execute than he had anticipated. After nearly four years of neglect, the city's swimming pools were unusable. Hurricane Betsy had damaged at least one, but all seventeen needed costly and time-consuming repairs. Engineers doubted that any could be functional for the summer of 1966. However, this promise was far too significant and symbolic to shirk. So funds were shuffled, work orders were rushed, and on June 13, the first day of the New Orleans Recreation Department's summer program, nine nonsegregated public pools opened in Orleans Parish.[84]

The rec department made another big change to that year's summer calendar: sports integration. After the 1963 federal decision on NORD-sponsored spaces and events, racial designations for parks and playgrounds were swiftly removed. The threat of violence on playing fields and basketball courts focused attention on the integration of NORD's grounds. When these fears subsided, though, so did supervision of NORD's compliance.

The recreation department continued to run two separate divisions. Many popular activities, like the Track Meet of Champions and the Babe Ruth Baseball League, remained closed to Black athletes. Some events stayed segregated through subtle "grandfathering" maneuvers while other practices were far more overt, testing the notion that no one was watching. Even the local soapbox derby, which had been canceled entirely in 1964 and 1965, was relaunched in 1966, again running opposite the skatemobile race for Black children.[85]

Too much had changed by then for that to stand, however. In May, African American community leaders aired their grievances to NORD. Outside, freedom songs were sung and placards read "End Jim Crow in Recreation" and "Try a New Game—Equality."[86]

When nothing came from the meeting, a federal contempt motion was filed against NORD officials. This case had A. P. Tureaud, counsel for the NAACP, facing the office of his young protégé, but in the form of another assistant city attorney, Ernest Salatich. Before the first hearing, an agreement was reached for the rec department to voluntarily comply with the original injunction. The case was dismissed, and NORD's summer program was opened on a single, integrated calendar. Skatemobile preliminaries were scheduled to begin in two weeks, however, and the soapboxes would roll less than a month later. Given all the prep time needed, the 1966 derbies again ran segregated.[87]

|||||

At noon on a Thursday in late June, a swank banquet room at Brennan's filled with newsmen. The Pro Football Club was throwing a luncheon to promote that summer's NFL exhibitions, the first of which featured the Minnesota Vikings' Tommy Mason, Tulane's last All-American. As Dixon's guest of honor, Mason said a few words, mostly assuring the crowd he would see playing time in town. After all, coach Norm Van Brocklin at least wanted to test the running back's recently repaired knee before the regular season.

Talk naturally turned to the franchise quest. When sportswriters were not badgering Mason, they flocked to John Mecom Jr. for any updates the handsome young moneyman might have. It was an afternoon of football junkies telling stories and making predictions. As per Dixon's design, it got newsmen excited enough to rally the support of their readers and viewers as well.

Jim Hall ate it up. He happily let the folks he referred to as his "13 faithful readers" know the only thing missing from the "'Boss' affair" was Jim Crow. "Every effort is now being made to eliminate any slip-up by the local group," he reported. "At long last, we are getting our heads together in a huddle," Hall rejoiced, ensuring fans that "the New Orleans Pro Football Club is going to have a united team."[88]

Hall and every other sportswriter in town hyped the August 6 exhibition and the Let's Go Pro! campaign. And around forty thousand fans bought in, paying increased prices, from $4.50 to $6.00, for entrance into sweltering Tulane Stadium. Unfortunately, the game was everything that gives exhibitions a bad rap.

Mason got a dozen carries but netted only 21 yards. Even Fran Tarkenton, despite some impressive scrambling, went 6 for 14 and a mere 40 yards before being subbed out early in the second half. The Lions offense was even more disappointing, putting up only 86 total yards on the night. The game ended in a tie, off two pairs of field goals. Especially after the starters were benched, the final twenty minutes were torturously slow, with the ball moving even less than the air. With nothing much to be excited about as they filed out, fans were even more aware of the heat and the horrid traffic around the on-campus stadium. The only silver lining was that the idea of a domed stadium was selling itself.[89]

After what Hall dubbed a "slow waltz" between the Vikings and Lions, it was anyone's guess what the turnout would be the next weekend for the Colts and Eagles. So the media's cheerleaders went back to work, drumming up excitement over Johnny U's return and reminding Frenchified fans of their ultimate goal: "Allons Pro!"[90]

On the next Saturday, despite week-old memories and early evening rain, the game drew as many as attended the previous week, plus a few thousand more. And fans were justly rewarded. In the first half, Unitas scored two touchdowns, both on passes of over 30 yards. He was 13 for 21 and picked up 209 yards in the air before Coach Shula gave the reins to Gary Cuozzo, who had his own 30- and 21-yard touchdown completions. Even so, the Eagles kept the game within two scores. The teams were still trading touchdowns late in the fourth, and fans stayed in their seats until the clock ran out. That night, folks left exhilarated. Many had not been bothered enough by the uptown traffic and parking to avoid dealing with those headaches again in the French Quarter.

Hours after the game Bourbon Street was hopping with happy fans, many on the lookout for players. The previous evening, the Colts had been treated to the posh dining room at Brennan's. When a wave of autograph seekers ambushed the players, however, an overlooked hazard of a French Quarter visit came to light. Some of the gridders were asked what they thought about putting a franchise in New Orleans, and one of the tackles revealed a big risk, with which his teammates concurred: "It would be great to have New Orleans in the league, although all this good food would probably create a weight problem for me."[91]

CHAPTER 10
Running Out the Clock

When Congressman Emanuel Celler called his antitrust committee to order on October 6, 1966, AFL and NFL brass were sitting side by side. Pete Rozelle held an eleven-page mimeographed statement, ready to give the session's first testimony. During opening discussions, however, the quorum buzzer sounded, and Chairman Celler gladly adjourned the meeting to the following Tuesday. That was a punch in the gut for Rozelle. Time was already running low. He hurriedly handed out copies of his address as representatives trooped to the House floor, but he would have to wait five days to give his official pitch to House Judiciary Subcommittee no. 5.[1]

The last time the NFL huddled in DC, at the Shoreham, in May, Rozelle had called an executive session and made one of the biggest announcements in league history. New York Giants owner Wellington Mara had signed a new placekicker. But it was not just any kicker. It was Pete Gogolak, whose contract with the AFL's Bills had just run out.

For the six years of the two circuits' coexistence, they had waged fierce and dirty battles over college draftees, often using the "babysitting" practice of stashing a recruit in a hotel while the other league attempted to sign him. Regardless, there had been an unwritten agreement that veterans were off-limits. No one broke that pact, until the Giants' Mr. Mara in 1966.

The other NFL execs were furious. Even Mara's dear friend Vince Lombardi seethed in disbelief at the end of the conference table. Carroll Rosenbloom, on the other hand, erupted. "Goddamnit, if you'd wanted a kicker, why didn't you just ask me? I'd have given you one," the Colts owner bellowed. They knew this could spark an all-out war, with the eagerly battle-planning commissioner Al Davis now at the enemy's helm. If that happened, they also knew, not all their clubs would survive.[2]

Competition for talent had already sent player contracts and bonuses through the roof. Most notably, Werblin's Jets lured Joe Namath away from the NFL with a record-setting $427,000 rookie contract and considerable fringe benefits. The presence of Broadway Joe as the face of Mara's crosstown rival was partly why the Giants' owner went after the flashy soccer-style kicker.³

Gogolak, even more than Namath, was the perfect player to bring the interleague rivalry to a head. Not only was his angled instep booting setting records and giving his team a curious new phenomenon to draw fans, but also he was consciously, although somewhat naively, testing the reality of the American dream. After being the second-highest AFL scorer his rookie season, he was offered a mere $2,500 raise, so he played out his option year with a 10 percent cut instead. After again being the league's number two scorer, in 1965, he turned down a doubled figure from the Bills and waited for the phone to ring.⁴

The Eastern European immigrant realized that no AFL team would conduct intraleague pilfering, but he never imagined that any such interleague deal existed. "I thought this is a free country, you put your goods out on the table, and you find out what they're worth," admitted Gogolak. "In every other profession, that's what happens," he discerned. "That's one reason we left communist Hungary to come to a country like this." As fate would have it, in May 1966, the Giants tripled his rookie salary and set off a mad scramble in both leagues.⁵

Reports of AFL retaliation arrived almost immediately, and before leaving the Shoreham, NFL owners decided on a merger. Secretive, unofficial, and fruitless discussions had already happened, with the NFL always holding a patient upper hand. Now, however, it was time to hammer out a deal.⁶

On June 8, the formation of a single professional football league was announced. Most importantly for the owners, there would be a common draft that January. A shared schedule and title were put off to 1970, but a world championship game was slated to cap the 1966 season. Most importantly for New Orleans, the NFL's plans to expand in 1967 were still a go—if the merger went through, that is. That was a big *if.* To finalize the deal, without the threat of endless suits, the leagues needed exemption from federal antitrust laws.⁷

Dave Dixon had predicted such a pickle in 1962, when he reached out to Hale Boggs. Still, when Dixon told Boggs that a "kind word from the very top" might one day be an effective prod for expansion, he could not have seen it going down quite like this. Not only had Boggs been reappointed House majority whip in 1965, but also Louisiana senator Russell Long, Earl's nephew, was elected to succeed Hubert Humphrey as Senate majority whip at the same time. The seed Dixon had planted more than four years earlier now had two powerful cultivators.[8]

Almost immediately after the merger handshake, Rozelle made himself comfortable in Washington. For months he lobbied congressmen for a bill sanctioning a common draft. In the beginning, he was quite successful. Several members of both the House and the Senate introduced such measures by mid-September. In the Senate, the Judiciary Committee unanimously approved the bill sponsored by Russell Long and Illinois's Everett Dirksen. A week later, it was cleared in a voice vote on the Senate floor. That was the easy part.[9]

The next hurdle was Celler's subcommittee. The chairman was openly opposed, but the bill still had plenty of supporters in the House, and even on Celler's panel. In the truncated meeting where Rozelle was to appear, New Jersey's Peter Rodino opined that "the bill promises exciting benefits for fans across the country and authorizes highly desirable expansion." He argued, "Millions will be disappointed if the championship game is not played."[10]

Rodino was right. It was a hugely popular bill, and Celler was cast as an obstructionist. It was believed that the New Yorker felt reluctant to grant exemptions after watching baseball's Dodgers and Giants make their cavalier moves to California. Likewise, the second-loudest opposition came from a Wisconsin representative who had just seen litigation fail to keep the Braves in Milwaukee. Moreover, Celler had coauthored the very bill from which the NFL and AFL were seeking immunity.

Celler said his committee would "plumb the depths" of the merger before approving anything. "Unfortunately, the Senate never held hearings on the bill it passed," he criticized. "I don't know what it does." He compared his position to "a blind man looking for a black cat in a dark room" and set hearings for as late as October 18.[11]

Congress was scheduled to adjourn on October 22. There was little chance the House would even act on the bill, and Rozelle said repeatedly that everything hinged on congressional approval. In fact, he stated, "Without the plan, contraction rather than expansion will be the ultimate consequence, as the developing economic conditions in professional football successively put more and more franchises into difficulty."[12]

Still, comparisons of player contracts and game receipts did not impress

Celler. "They are poor labor negotiators," he said of the leagues, "and are asking Congress to rescue them from their own ineptitude and folly."[13]

On October 11, Rozelle again appeared before Celler's committee. Early in his statement, he addressed the heart of the antitrust question. The merger clearly (further) curtailed competition for talent and limited players' bargaining power. Rozelle argued, however, that the merger actually protected players and the game itself. He explained that while it would end extravagant rookie contracts, the minimum salary would increase, as would pension and insurance figures. He claimed that pay discrepancies were divisive to a locker room and predicted that players earning outrageous sums "would lose the vital interest that has made the game great."

Rozelle claimed that the bill was "very limited," merely sanctioning the agreement to merge. Celler countered that such a measure "would be just as worthless as a wine cellar without a corkscrew." He believed approval would be a blank check for owners, making players vulnerable on issues like trades, releases, and strikes. The chairman argued that fans, too, could suffer if games were switched to "pay TV." Rozelle's vague, diplomatic answers, such as "We have no plans to do that," gave Celler little comfort. Excerpts from the Senate's report on the bill were read, only to have Celler declare, "That language is as broad as the barn door." He attempted to call Rozelle's bluff on a "limited scope" and asked for itemized exemptions. A Florida representative tried to quash this condition and pick up the pace, but as he argued such details could wait, the quorum buzzer sounded again.

"The House has gone in session. We have no permission to sit," Celler announced. "Mr. Rozelle, we will resume these hearings Thursday morning at ten o'clock."[14]

|||||

The October 13 session opened with the introduction of a special guest. "We have with us our distinguished member from Louisiana, and acting majority leader of the House," Celler announced. "Representative Boggs, we will be more than pleased to hear you."

Boggs thanked the committee for allowing him to appear at the top of the schedule, noting his urgent business on the floor that day but added, "I would say also, Mr. Chairman, that time is of the essence insofar as this proposed legislation is concerned." He began, "I come before the subcommittee today to plead a case that is very dear to me." Boggs explained that he had authored one version of the merger bill and did so because of pro football's link to "the growth of our communities." "We must spread this game to as many of our citizens as we can," he argued, saying that relieving the leagues of their present "burden" would expedite expansion, "which is something that all Americans are interested in today."

"There may be some defects about the proposed bill," Boggs conceded, "but, after all, Congress is a continuing body. We will be back here in January, and any difficulties that may be presented could be easily corrected." He closed by saying, "I am hopeful, Mr. Chairman, that you in your great wisdom will see the necessity for expeditious action on this legislation."[15]

As the hearing continued, however, it became clear that nothing would be expedited. The committee's counsel suggested a compromise in language, which the leagues' attorney deemed "so narrow as to be meaningless." Likewise, Celler remained adamant that he would not sign a free pass. When the session closed, the chairman said inquiry would resume the following week. He was effectively running out the clock. It seemed impossible for the bill to reach the House floor before Congress adjourned, meaning there would be no expansion for 1967.[16]

The next day, however, Senators Long and Dirksen made a cunning move. They attached the measure as a rider to the president's anti-inflation program. Dirksen explained that the football merger provided certain tax provisions for clubs and therefore could be bundled with Johnson's highly prioritized investment-credit bill. Long, floor manager for the tax package, made a speech in favor of the amendment, and it too passed in a voice vote.

It was an end run around Celler's subcommittee. Now all that was needed before the bill reached the House floor was negotiation of the different versions held by the House and Senate. Russell Long, chairman of the Finance Committee, would head the Senate representation, and Hale Boggs was among the House conferees.[17]

On October 17, while negotiators cut-and-pasted the tax measure, Rozelle paced the corridors. Inside the conference room, Celler pled his case yet again. When he emerged, he could not help but smile in defeat. "They caught me in bathing and sold my clothes," he reported.[18]

In essence, the final step in saving the NFL-AFL merger was approval on the floor of the House of Representatives. The bill would again go before the Senate, but there was little worry on that front. Then, of course, it would be on Johnson's desk, but LBJ's pet tax credit measure was assured his signature. So it all came down to the House session on October 20.[19]

That day, Boggs was about halfway up the Rotunda when Commissioner Rozelle stopped him. "I don't know how I can ever thank you enough for this," Rozelle remarked, anticipating favorable polling inside.

"What do you mean you don't know how to thank me?" Boggs fired back. He then voiced the yet unspoken assumption New Orleans would get the next NFL team.

"I'm going to do everything I can to make that happen," Rozelle responded.

Boggs turned around and continued walking toward the House chamber. "Well, we can always call off the vote while you—"

Before Boggs could get more than two steps away or any further into his threat, Rozelle grabbed him by the shoulder and looked him in the eyes. "It's a deal, Congressman. You'll get your franchise."[20]

Inside, the first motion was for a straight vote of the entire bill—before Celler could work to remove the football rider.

"Why the haste?" Celler asked in desperation.

Representative John Byrnes of Wisconsin offered a reply. He first made references to old legislation but then got to the meat of his answer. "Now this merger will let the Green Bay Packers become champions of the world," Byrnes crowed.

Both Boggs and Long flashed devilish grins as the measure went up for its final vote. It passed 161 to 76. The NFL and AFL got their merger, fans got their world championship game, and New Orleans got a promise of a pro football franchise.[21]

|||||

On the next Monday, Governor McKeithen received an early morning phone call from Pete Rozelle. It was a last-minute heads-up that a band of pro football executives would be dropping in on New Orleans—the next day. They were arriving from Cincinnati and leaving the following morning for Seattle. It was a final check of the last three cities in the running for a team.

Boggs and Long greasing the merger bill was well publicized, and the sports world assumed this gave New Orleans a boost. Still, the leagues were doing their due diligence. The merger eliminated Houston, but Cincinnati remained a fierce competitor. Seattle also had much to offer, including the University of Washington's iconic waterfront stadium.[22]

The blitz visit to the Big Easy was a whirlwind tour, which started at

Tulane Stadium. The expansion committee inspected the dressing rooms, grandstand, and playing field before squirreling away for an hour-long meeting with university execs about an interim lease until a new stadium could be built. From there, the group was whisked over to the Roosevelt for a grand reception and frenzied press conference. They were met by an integrated mass of political, civic, and business leaders. Albert Dent and Norman Francis were part of the city's official entourage, as were Jim Hall and C. C. Dejoie of the *Weekly*. Likewise, Louis Mason, proprietor of Mason's Motel, stood alongside Nathan J. King Jr. and Daniel Byrd of the local NAACP.

Reporters had a field day with Rozelle. Naturally, they tried to pin down when the franchise decision would be finalized. They also asked whether New Orleans was being considered as the site of the NFL-AFL championship game, which some were dubbing the "Super Bowl." One newsman even inquired whether Jimmy Taylor would re-up with Green Bay or be free to sign with the Saints.[23]

Rozelle soon took off for Washington, but he left an executive assistant behind. Buddy Young had an assignment not applicable to the Seattle leg. The commissioner wanted the African American former pro halfback to do one more assessment of the Crescent City's racial climate. Local promoters took Young to the best restaurants, bars, and nightclubs. But he also did some snooping on his own, talking to members of the Black community and visiting an old friend from the Texans. There was not a single problem to report.[24]

Then, toward the end of Young's stay, Dixon invited him to Antoine's. As the six-foot-three Dixon and five-foot-four Young walked to the center of the dining room, the former gridder likely felt more conscious of their heights than their races, being acutely aware of what he called "size discrimination." The men enjoyed a slow, relaxed meal, which was repeatedly interrupted by Dixon's many friends coming over to chat.[25]

At one point, Dixon glanced over Young's right shoulder and found a pair of eyes staring intently back. He recognized the fellow, whom his mother had once described as an obstinate racist. Dixon felt he could see the man's eyes glazing over with rage and started to get nervous. When the guy stood up and walked toward their table, Dixon went into a full-blown panic. He imagined headlines in the *New York Times* describing the scene that was about to erupt. He could again feel all his franchise efforts going up in smoke.

The man bypassed Dixon completely and raised one arm in the halfback's direction. "You're Buddy Young, aren't you?" the guy asked, as he reached for a handshake, introducing himself as a University of Illinois alum. As the two former Fighting Illini recounted old rivalry games against Michigan, Dixon realized the glazed eyes came from too many martinis. Once the other gentleman staggered back across the room, Dixon explained his poorly veiled anxiety attack. Young found the rundown hysterical and told his host to lighten up. He said he had already reached his verdict, which local papers proudly quoted: "New Orleans with a franchise will do well for everyone."[26]

|||||

On All Saints Day 1966, Pete Rozelle held a packed press conference at New Orleans's Pontchartrain Hotel. While media latecomers scavenged for a few square feet to crouch with their cameras and notepads, Senator Long remarked, "I think I have some idea what Mr. Rozelle is going to say here today." He elicited a few chuckles by adding, "Matter of fact, I'd be very embarrassed if he said anything different."[27]

When David Dixon was spotted, organizers rushed over to say seats in the very front were reserved for him and his wife, prompting a curious response. "I want to sit in the back row," he insisted. Folks who saw him ushered out of the spotlight were appalled. Many who missed it were left whispering to each other, "Where's Dixon?"[28]

He was certainly not afraid of cameras or attention, but he wanted Boggs and Long to get the credit that day. In one week, Boggs was up for reelection. Although he often said, "I work to bring people together—not to divide them," some such work split voters in his district. Dixon knew the congressman's numbers were down since his rousing speech in favor of the Voting Rights Act. While it had earned him support from his Black constituency (and a standing ovation in the House), it cost him approval from more reactionary members of his base. Dixon hoped football could make up for some of that. So when the crowd quieted, Hale Boggs, Russell Long, and John McKeithen were behind the podium. Victor Schiro was engaged elsewhere, but Moon Landrieu stood in his stead behind the jungle of microphones.[29]

"Halloween brings all sorts of surprises, and I have one for you today," the commissioner began, before telling everyone exactly what they expected to hear. "Professional football has voted a franchise to the state of Louisiana and the city of New Orleans..." Whatever Rozelle tried to say next was drowned out by raucous and lingering cheers.[30]

The commissioner then recapped how the NFL had landed in the Big

Easy. He described Dixon being an "onlooker" at the Baltimore suit and then "hounding" league meetings for the next half decade. Rozelle commented, "I think that the great civic interest he's shown should certainly be recognized here today," prompting a hearty salute from the stage and an ovation from the crowd. "Of course, there were Sen. Long and Rep. Boggs, who, fortunately, knew and loved football," Rozelle continued, granting that to say they had a "major role" would "probably be understating it." "On the other hand . . ." the commissioner emphasized, "the city won the franchise on its merits."[31]

There was just one more catch. Rozelle was clear that the franchise was contingent on a suitable, *permanent* home field, and university officials were equally clear it would not be Tulane Stadium. One big reason for the hastily scheduled announcement was to rally support behind the following Tuesday's statewide vote on constitutional amendment number 10, the stadium legislation. McKeithen and Dixon had been stumping for the measure. Their task was to convince northern Louisianans they were not buying New Orleans a new playhouse out of pocket. Plans were to finance the dome by raising hotel taxes in Orleans and Jefferson Parishes. McKeithen stressed that no teacher, highway, or policeman would lose a penny to the stadium. Rather, all of Louisiana would benefit from increased state revenue.[32]

The week before the election, McKeithen and Dixon had a lot of help. Newsmen across the state churned out columns arguing that the vote would signal either a statewide sports renaissance or contentment with the "bush league." One writer called a nay vote "a vote against progress and a slap in the face for Louisiana." Moon Landrieu told voters that the area had "lost too many opportunities in its history to lose another." Dixon even retained the services of Jimmy Taylor, who appeared in TV spots plugging the dome.[33]

Senator Long gave a curious endorsement. Arguing the state needed "first-class" status, he said, "That is what Amendment No. 10 proposes. I hope every citizen of Louisiana votes for it." To enable this, he recommended that if lines were long and slowly moving at the polls, folks should mark amendments 1 and 10 and leave the rest blank.[34]

The only nonstadium measure Long prioritized, amendment 1, would allow a governor to run for two consecutive terms. The state's law against back-to-back stints was a relic, heavily debated over the previous decade. In fact, Uncle Earl had schemed to sidestep it by resigning just before the end of his third term so he could be reelected without succeeding himself. The present governor's overwhelming popularity and momentum was convincing proof that the regulation had outlived its usefulness. During his two years in office, McKeithen had introduced vast new industries, improved the economy, and quelled racial unrest across the state. And efforts to bring pro football to Louisiana certainly had not hurt his reputation. His mission was progress, and McKeithen said a favorable vote would be proof "that the people of Louisiana did not want to turn back, that they want to go forward."[35]

Amendments 1 and 10, along with Boggs's run for reelection, were the biggest items on the ballot. Each, in some way, tested the area's progressiveness and unity. In the end, each was a landslide victory.[36]

| | | | |

Now New Orleans needed the league to choose an owner. The Mecoms were assumed to have the inside track. Even Dixon expected NFL execs to rubber-stamp John Jr. into their inner circle and accepted an early invitation to be chairman of the younger Mecom's board.

As it turned out, many prominent locals entered the race, including several candidates Dixon believed would be better suited for the role. On the list were entrepreneur Edgar Stern Jr., a founder of WDSU, and attorney Harry Kelleher, who teamed up with moneyman Herman Lay of Texas. Oil tycoon William Helis, Dave's Paris confidant, wanted a second shot at ownership, and another oilman and financier, Louis Roussel, had Senator Long in his corner. A quick show of hands would not settle the issue.[37]

Headway was expected to be made at the NFL's late November meeting. However, the first two days of talks did not even settle the league's realignment into four 4-team divisions. There were many factors to weigh, such as weather, travel, and baseball conflicts, but the real key was preserving rivalries. No team wanted separation from its chief foe. Logic put one fledgling franchise in each conference, but Falcons owner Rankin Smith urged rethinking even that, given that Atlanta and New Orleans were already "natural" rivals.[38]

Schedules and the Super Bowl were next on the agenda, so the mystery of New Orleans's ownership remained, even after the conference. Then, on December 7, candidates were summoned to the Royal Orleans hotel for more interviews. Harry Kelleher and Herman Lay arrived just before eleven that morning. Edgar Stern and associates nestled in by the afternoon. Mecom passed time down the block at Antoine's. And reporters endured hours of waiting on hard benches near the hotel check-in desk. There was no sign of the NFL.

Around 5:00 p.m., Bert Rose, Rozelle's right-hand man, walked into the lobby and explained that mechanical trouble at one airport had caused a missed connection at the next. There was still time for one interrogation, so Rose led his ensemble to Stern's fourth floor suite for an hour and a half of questioning.[39]

Meanwhile, the sixth candidate was having his own trouble getting to New Orleans. Jack Sanders, an ex-Marine who played guard in pro football both before and after losing part of his left arm in Iwo Jima, was trying to get back from Casablanca. Sanders, now running a local steel corporation, was on a trade mission to Africa with the U.S. Department of Commerce. He received approval to return early but found himself stuck clearing customs in Paris, about to miss the last transatlantic flight. So he offered a "pretty French gal" a bottle of Chanel No. 5 perfume to hold the plane, which she did.[40]

The next morning, the remaining applicants were set to rotate through the committee's wringer of ownership criteria, such as business acumen and financial responsibility. A commitment to the community was also high on the list. The league insisted on a singular majority stockholder, but for out-of-towners, they encouraged the inclusion of locals as minority investors.[41]

One such option existed in Kelleher's group, which was up first. The battle-tested reform leader had the fiscal backing of the chairman of Pepsi and Frito-Lay, who had recently funded new offices for the New Orleans Boy Scouts.

Next came Louis Roussel, a former New Orleans streetcar conductor who had secured his fortune through investments in oil leases. The policies of his National American Bank were unique for the area. Many "old money" financiers thought New Orleans was growing too fast, but Roussel funded ventures others feared and had contributed heavily to the recent building boom, including the erection of the city's first true skyscraper.[42]

Around midday, the committee met with Jack Sanders, the only applicant with an insider's knowledge of pro football. The war veteran's ties and investment in the community were well established, and the U.S. Secretary of Commerce officially sanctioned his business expertise.[43]

Then entered John Mecom Jr., the twenty-seven-year-old heir to his father's oil industry, whose young legacy involved mostly a lust for race cars and thoroughbreds. He did not have the others' thick dossier, but he had David Dixon, whose opinion mattered to the NFL. Dixon stood by his endorsement of Mecom, despite esteem for other applicants and misgivings about his candidate's youthful inexperience. Still, there were rumored reservations about the Texan not being "local" enough, so that afternoon Mecom announced that four additional stockholders had been enlisted from Dixon's Pro Football Club, including Edward Poitevent and Robert Monsted.

About an hour later, NFL officials packed their suitcases and rushed off to interview Bill Helis while en route to the airport. The tall, charismatic Mecom returned to the lobby and chatted with tired but eager reporters. He briefly recapped the interview and released his new list of five coinvestors, but he also said tellingly, "The possibility exists that this will not be the complete group."[44]

Within a week, Dixon's cohorts recruited thirteen other members. Two additions, Joe David and Charles Rosen, rounded out the group of friends who had long supported Dixon's dream. From there, they diversified, and businessmen were incorporated from areas outside Orleans Parish, including Baton Rouge, New Iberia, and Denham Springs. They even signed trumpeter Al Hirt, who was already working on a special rendition of "When the Saints Go Marching In" to charm guys like Jimmy Taylor and Billy Cannon back home.[45]

Also invited aboard were two other gentlemen who had helped Dixon's group along the way. Mecom's entourage reached out to the *Weekly*'s C. C. Dejoie, and Dixon paid a personal visit to Norman Francis. Even before Francis's appearance with McKeithen in Washington or his service on the dome committee, Francis and Dixon had chatted about the enterprise. Now Dixon asked for his friend's official buy-in. Both Dejoie and Francis agreed, and if Mecom's group was chosen, these two men would become the first Black owners in pro football history.[46]

On the morning of December 14, Mecom and Poitevent entered Rozelle's New York office, carrying Dixon's continued blessing and an expanded membership list. The trio wrapped everything up by the evening. After a telephone polling, the owners' decision was said to be unanimous, and a press conference was convened for the big reveal: John Mecom Jr. would own New Orleans's NFL club. As soon as the final flashbulb popped, Mecom rushed away, trying to get to his wife before the stork did, and the media put their spins on the NFL's latest news. Local reporters were rapturous and proud, but elsewhere skeptics spilled plenty of ink.[47]

"That New Orleans, a laggard in the past, stands for progress regarding racial matters seemed to be the point," one national paper said of the inclusion of Dejoie and Francis. It then added cynically, "It was quick progress, too," pointing out only two years had passed since the city was deemed too intolerant to host an All-Star game.[48]

Likewise, the apparent quid pro quo between the NFL commissioner and Louisiana congressmen did not instill much faith in New Orleans's qualifications. Another newsman called the ordeal "a neat job" in an article titled, "You Scratch My Back, I'll Scratch Yours." He sympathized with other cities vying for franchises but asked, "What had their congressmen done in an hour of need?"[49]

New York Times sportswriter William Wallace, however, had kept his finger on the pulse of New Orleans since the walkout, and he took a different view. "The admission of New Orleans may be remembered as the way the NFL eased a political indebtedness," he told readers, "but that would be unfair." He countered, "This city has been made ready for pro football."[50]

| | | | |

Coach Bob Devaney now believed New Orleans was ready for bowl teams, too. Sam Corenswet admitted that Sugar's landing of Nebraska for 1967 "wasn't the best kept secret in the world." He had been in Lincoln so much, he said, "I think I could legally vote." Bringing along entertainment films of thoroughly pampered players, he made a successful, if not exactly stealth, sales pitch.[51]

Both Alabama and Nebraska were undefeated and untied, ranking third and fourth, respectively, and the nation's top two teams were not bowling. Notre Dame maintained a no-invitation policy, and the Big Ten's no-repeat rule excluded Michigan State. So the previous year's Orange Bowl contestants were again the highest-ranked eligibles. Moreover, in mid-November, it was undecided whether final polls would be held before or after bowl games, meaning a Huskers–Tide rematch could have championship implications. Consequently, Bryant told Devaney, "We'd like to get together with you folks some place." By November 19, it was clear that would be New Orleans.[52]

Even aside from bid expectations, that was a big weekend for local fans. A sellout crowd was expected for Tulane's game against LSU. The Let's Go, Tulane! campaign, plugged in the *Times-Picayune* and *Louisiana Weekly* alike, was getting a lot of help from first-year head coach Jim Pittman's rapid revamping of the Wave in its first season as an independent. They were 5–3–1 and on the Sun Bowl's list of prospects. Locals also eagerly awaited coverage of Notre Dame and Michigan State's meeting. At least one of the nation's top two teams would leave with a blemished record, likely affecting the rankings of the Sugar squads and the championship implications of their rematch.[53]

Saturday's outcomes were a mixed bag. LSU, favored only by 5, came away with a two-score victory over the Greenies. Nebraska's and Alabama's wins were capped off by eagerly accepted bids from Sugar Bowlers, who hoped they were bringing in their first pair of unbeaten and untied teams since 1952. The matchup of the Irish and Spartans, expected to reduce the count of the undefeated, resulted in a 10–10 tie. Rankings went unaltered, but the draw gave the spotless records of Alabama and Nebraska new significance.

Sugar's ticket sales were frenzied. Both universities fielded thousands of requests before their allotments arrived, and by Thanksgiving, local outlets only had a few upper-end zone seats left. The classic's paid attendance record was 81,141, set by LSU–Ole Miss in 1960, the last Sugar Bowl before the school integration crisis. By early December it was clear that 1967 would bring a new all-time high.[54]

Then, in what was becoming a tradition for the Sugar Bowlers, one of their teams lost its last game. Nebraska was inched out by Oklahoma in a one-point heartbreaker. Sugar stock dipped even further when the wire services set their final polls for the end of the regular season. Still, even if New Orleans's game could not name the national champions, it might showcase them. For that to happen, though, Alabama would need to perform well enough against Auburn on December 3 to be vaulted two spots. And the past week's season finale for the first-place Fighting Irish—a 51-point shutout of Rose Bowl–bound Southern California—would be hard to outshine.[55]

Bryant, however, was already miffed that his team's perfect season was not ranked higher. "I just wish the players and I knew what the people who vote wanted," the coach groaned to reporters. "If they want it, we'll try triple reverses, forward laterals, laterals forward, dipsy-doodles, doodles-dipsy or even run quarterback sneaks with third and nine."[56]

Whatever the judges wanted was clearly more than a 32–0 taming of the Tigers. In the final tallies, the top three were unchanged. Then the National Football Foundation decided on its award for the best college team and elected Notre Dame and Michigan State to share the MacArthur prize. Again, the only team with a flawless record was overlooked.

"I hope they're bothered about it," Bear Bryant said of his team. "I hope they're bothered a great deal about it. If we've got it, we can prove it." They were going into the Sugar Bowl hungry to prove they were America's best.[57]

There also was one national title not yet assigned. The Football Writers Association of America always assigned its Grantland Rice Award after the postseason. Both *Sports Illustrated* and Bear Bryant argued that a persuasive Sugar Bowl showing could make the Tide's case for the last unassigned "champion" label. As the country's top sports magazine pointed out, until there was an NCAA playoff, the "championship smorgasbord" would legitimize varying shares of the number one spot. Besides, winning the last vote could cast doubt on the others. So, in that sense, in 1967 New Orleans had the only bowl with championship implications.[58]

The Tide was admittedly on a mission, but the Cornhuskers had their own agenda: revenge. They were out to prove the previous Orange Bowl a fluke. Both squads came in a week early to train, tour New Orleans, and offer trash talk to local media. And while sportswriters lined their columns, local businesses lined their coffers. The week after Christmas, the French Quarter was filled with early-arriving visitors wearing varying shades of red and spending a lot of green.[59]

Game day, as reporters scrambled for typewriter territory in the press box, Bob Roesler looked out at nearly 83,000 fans packing into Tulane Stadium and started to worry. From all reports, the new arena would have a much smaller capacity, as the pros preferred. He thought, "Where would they all go if our new domed stadium is built to seat a mere 65,000?" It was a good fear to have, however, considering the past two Sugar Bowl crowds would have been quite comfortable in such a space.[60]

The rain Devaney had prayed for ended just before kickoff, and the MWSA's trusty tarpaulin kept the field in pretty good condition. Only a small patch near the north end zone looked much like a handicap for the lighter, faster Bama squad. In fact, after only one snap the Huskers coach realized he should have asked for stronger showers.[61]

Alabama's first play was exactly what Devaney had told his defense to expect, and they still could not contain it. From the Tide's 28, running back Les Kelley took a fake handoff straight into the line while Kenny "Snake" Stabler dropped back and launched an aerial to Ray Perkins well past midfield. The speedy Perkins got free, made the catch, and cruised to the Nebraska 27 before he was brought to the turf. Five minutes were not off the clock before Kelley dove into the end zone and invited former Crimson kicker Tim Davis's kid brother Steve out for a PAT.

Bama's D forced a punt, and the Tide's next possession covered 71 yards in four plays, including another 40-plus-yard completion from Stabler to Perkins and a 9-yard slither around left end to the goal by Snake himself. Bama's lead was 14 halfway through the first period. That was before a fumble recovery by Alabama set up a 30-yard Davis field goal.

Bear Bryant was using every combination in his playbook. He put thirty-five different white jerseys on the field in the first quarter alone. Bama was not playing to just win but to embarrass the early pollsters. Their third touchdown came after Bryant, up by 17, went for it on fourth-and-1 in easy field goal range. Nebraska, on the other hand, got into Alabama territory only once in the first half, just a minute before it expired. Even then, they turned the ball over on downs. While Cornhuskers licked their wounds in the locker room, the Tide marching band wrote out the 24–0 score centerfield.[62]

When the second half opened up, so did Nebraska's air game. However, this led to two interceptions by the Tide's Bobby Johns in the third quarter. The first was redressed by the Huskers defense, which forced a punt. The second led to more fruitful kicking, and Bama's Davis put up another 3 from the 30.

Not until early in the fourth did Nebraska's passing game click. After reaching the red zone for the first time, they finished the drive with a 15-yard pass under the uprights, which were then split to put 7 up for the underdogs.

Alabama, who had shut out their last four regular-season opponents, quickly sought redemption. Stabler marched his crew to the Nebraska 45 but wasted no more time. He took the snap, shook a few defenders, and sailed a pass to his favorite target on the 30. Perkins pulled in the ball, broke free from one Nebraskan, juked clear of a second, and outran two others into the end zone.

As the final period ticked away, the game got wild, with each team trying to go out in dramatic fashion. The Bama secondary picked off two more desperate Nebraska heaves, but the Cornhuskers also stole the ball themselves, once in the air and once on the ground. The chaos came to a close when Alabama tackle Dick Cole landed on a loose ball, which the Tide carried—along with their coach—off the field.[63]

That year, Sugar was the only bowl to get a full recap in *Sports Illustrated*. It was, as the article explained, "the only resemblance to a contest of importance." While the other games got a sentence or two, the Sugar Bowl was detailed as "a clinic" on "what a top team is supposed to look like." According to this issue, New Orleans's classic had gone from "leftovers" to a title audition, and the Alabama squad had proven itself.[64]

Beating a hefty, talented Big Eight team 34–7 was still not enough, however, to give Alabama any official claim to championship, as the Football Writers Association presented the Grantland Rice Award to Notre Dame. Yet it voided neither the debate over Alabama's deservedness nor the magnitude of the first fully integrated, intersectional, sold-out Sugar Bowl.[65]

CHAPTER 11
Open Field

In early January 1967, Edward Poitevent filed a charter for "New Orleans Saints Inc.," tucking away the name for safekeeping. But the franchise was not yet branded. Although most locals latched onto Dixon's "Saints" label, there were some grumbling it was "sacrilegious" or "irreverent," and the young John Mecom feared a shaky start right out of the tunnel. So one night at a local restaurant, when Dixon spotted someone who could help, he threw an arm back to block the person's passage. Dixon then jumped up to beg his pardon and to ask an opinion from Archbishop Philip Hannan.

"Oh, I think 'Saints' is a wonderful name for our team," Hannan replied, single-handedly settling the issue. But before leaving, he added, "Besides, I have this terrible premonition that we might need all the help we can get."[1]

By the end of the month, Mecom announced two other big decisions. First, Tom Fears was named the Saints' first head coach. Fears was an All-American at UCLA and an All-Pro receiver with the Los Angeles Rams before becoming a branch on Vince Lombardi's coaching tree. He had spent the previous season in another first-year franchise, molding the offense of the Atlanta Falcons.

Mecom also revealed that he was not hiring a general manager. He would largely fill that role himself, as part of a three-man executive committee. The plan was to bring in two veterans of the Cowboys front office, Bedford Wynne and Larry Karl, to help develop the club from the ground up.[2]

On Ash Wednesday, Tom Fears realized he still needed to see his first Mardi Gras. He had been preparing for the stockpiling draft, watching film and studying rosters nonstop. On Thursday morning, Fears joined Mecom's "Committee of Three" on the thirty-eighth floor of New York's Waldorf Astoria. They were handed 154 player names ripe for picking. Except for the fledgling Falcons, each club put eleven veterans in a grab bag, and the Saints brain trust was on the clock. Much of the next twenty-four hours involved staring at player names on chalkboards and repositioning puzzle pieces.[3]

Naturally, they took big risks. In a group considered castoffs, even the best players carried red flags of medical histories or advancing age. The most sensational selection was the Golden Boy himself, Paul Hornung, whose injuries made him a long shot from the outset. Likewise, tackle Charlie Bradshaw would have to be coaxed out of plans to retire.

On the flip side, one unexpected quarterback had not even been evaluated, but he also could not be passed up. Gary Wood had filled in ably for the Giants' injured Earl Morrall the prior season, and he reminded Fears of Fran Tarkenton, who sadly was not available despite having "resigned" from the Vikings earlier in the week. New Orleans also grabbed the 49ers' third-string signal caller, Billy Kilmer, who was renowned for both his arm and his legs but had fallen in the depth chart while benched by a car accident.[4]

This did not end the Saints' quarterback search, however. As soon as the list of retreads was handed to Rozelle, Saints execs started digging through free agents and thinking about trades, and an extraordinary opportunity appeared.

Carroll Rosenbloom had just consented to Gary Cuozzo's request to leave Unitas's shadow. The backup had impressed in his few opportunities to sub. In fact, in 1965 he threw five touchdown passes in a 41–21 win over Van Brocklin's Vikings. "Maybe on another team a day like that would move you up to No. 1," Cuozzo thought. "But with Johnny Unitas at quarterback, you just go back to the bench as soon as he gets well." And the legend planned to play as long as possible. So in a move that Cuozzo considered "fine and generous," the Colts owner gave his second-stringer a shot at getting off the sideline in his prime. Of course, he did not exactly give the player away, but Fears felt "No matter what you pay for a quarterback the quality of Cuozzo, it's cheap."[5]

A couple of weeks after signing with the Saints, Cuozzo was part of New Orleans's St. Joseph's Day parade. He essentially filled in for Vince Lombardi, who was being honored by the local Italian American Society but canceled his appearance due to "business commitments." It was probably for the best. The new Saints quarterback was celebrated. Lombardi would have been bombarded with questions about his most coveted free agent, Jimmy Taylor.[6]

Louisianans, happy to see antitrust exemptions approved for pro football, were getting a lesson on free agency in the hermetically sealed NFL. Or rather, as Bob Roesler explained, they were learning that "the term 'free agent' doesn't mean a thing in the National Football League." Taylor played out his option year with the Packers in 1966, after seeing rookie price tags but not having his salary adjusted accordingly. Per league rules, however, any club wanting to sign Taylor would have to give the Packers "adequate compensation." A free agent could only relocate to a team able to meet both his demands and those of his former employer. Roesler's readers were realizing that "a chap like Jimmy Taylor" in the NFL was "no freer to peddle his muscles than a Russian youth is to paint 'Communism is for the birds' on the walls of the Kremlin."[7]

Regardless, New Orleanians were gaga over pro football. Season tickets went on sale on March 8, but fans lined up the night before, camping in front of the Saints offices at 944 St. Charles Avenue. When doors opened at 9:00 a.m., a line curved around Lee Circle, down a block of Howard Avenue, and onto Camp Street. Despite the magnitude of Tulane Stadium, which worried the pros, the Saints sold around twenty thousand season ticket books in the first nine hours. This was a third more than the Cowboys, with comparably sized Cotton Bowl Stadium, had sold for all of 1966.[8]

Another attendance concern was also quelled at that time. There had long been doubts about locals supporting both the Green Wave and a pro team. But in addition to the town's infectious football fever and Coach Pittman's phenomenal first year, Tulane now even had a service academy team, Air Force, back on its home schedule. The Greenies had already doubled their previous year's season ticket sales when Saints books went on the market.[9]

A week later, Mecom's management group was back on the clock, this time for the first combined NFL/AFL college draft. As part of their generous expansion package, they would have the biggest haul, thirty-five draftees. Their number one overall pick had gone to Baltimore in the Cuozzo exchange, but they had one first-round selection remaining.

Fears went in with an eye toward offensive linemen, but the crew's strategy was to take the top talent on the board. Their first pick was Les Kelley, Alabama's star fullback from the previous Sugar Bowl. Next, they took Bo Burris, who quarterbacked the University of Houston but whom Fears pegged as a safety or flanker. Late in the second round, Fears believed he had snagged "the second fastest man in football, after the Cowboys' Bob Hayes." The six-foot-one, 190-pound John Gilliam was said to run the hundred in 9.5 seconds and to clear 40 yards, wearing full pads, in 4.5 seconds. His new coach was salivating over the roles Gilliam could fill, including halfback, flanker, defensive back, and kick returner.[10]

After seventeen rounds, the Saints brass felt good about the talent they had tapped. Next, Fears would assemble his coaching staff and work on positional weaknesses through trades. Meanwhile, Mecom would oversee assembly of the other pieces of his young franchise. He and his GM committee had a lot of personnel vacancies to fill. From the film library in Los Angeles to the ticket window on Lee Circle, the eager Texan—or "nouveau Cajun," as a local paper called him—had his hands on each brick while the club was built.[11]

|||||

For the former singer/songwriter/disc jockey Morton Downey Jr., as for Mecom, the birth of a baby girl came with a New Orleans pro sports team. Just months after pro football moved into the Crescent City, the upstart American Basketball Association followed suit. In the league's April 2 draft, Downey's New Orleans Buccaneers used the second overall pick on the six-foot-four All-American guard Jim Jones out of Grambling. For another All-American, Ron Widby, they could wait until the fifth round. Since the Saints had drafted the six-foot-five forward as a punter, the other basketball clubs left the two-sport athlete on the board for New Orleans.[12]

A week later, Major League Baseball was back at Kirsch-Rooney Stadium for a pair of exhibitions between the Cleveland Indians and the Cincinnati Reds. It was the first professional baseball in New Orleans since 1960, just before school integration, but already guesswork churned about how quickly the city could get its own team. Locals envisioned a full sports renaissance. There were even rumblings about housing an entry in the new National Professional Soccer League.[13]

On Friday, June 9, at 9:00 a.m., more than three hundred men gathered on Tulane's baseball diamond, but not for the nation's pastime. The Saints were holding open tryouts. Coach Fears shouted through his megaphone, John Mecom observed from the sidelines, and curious locals passed judgment. There were several sprained ankles and at least one pulled hamstring as men of a vast range of sizes and ages attempted drills in sprinting, agility, ball handling, and rope running. By the end of the blazing hot day, Fears's horde of "prospects" and "suspects" was whittled down to forty-five invitees to the next day's session. Ultimately, eleven walk-ons joined the first training camp in San Diego on July 1.[14]

Mecom and Fears took more than a hundred hopefuls to the campus of California Western University. With the task being, as Fears said, "to start from scratch," everyone was fighting for a role, rookies and retreads alike.

Thirty cuts were expected the first week. But as hands-on as Mecom liked to be, he missed part of it. He had important business in Baton Rouge.[15]

Mecom rushed through sheets of rain up the steps of the Louisiana Capitol and into the governor's office. There, waiting in a pair of alligator shoes, was Jimmy Taylor. McKeithen used every ounce of sway he had to ensure that Taylor would finish his career in his home state. So it was appropriate that right there on the governor's desk the former Packer signed with the New Orleans Saints. The trio then entered a nearby conference room and cameras started flashing. McKeithen approached the rostrum and glanced back.[16]

"Which one of you gentlemen should I introduce first?" the governor asked.

"Jim Taylor. He's making more than I am now," Mecom quipped.

The deal, months in the making, was huge. Both Taylor and Mecom spent time at the podium but neither discussed the contract. What *was* public knowledge, however, was that Mecom had promised Lombardi, among other things, the Saints' first selection in next year's draft.[17]

When Taylor checked in to the dorms in San Diego, he found a familiar face from the Packer backfield. His roommate was Paul Hornung—briefly. The Golden Boy's career as a Saint ended before training camp did, as tests on his neck indicated that one more jarring injury could be his last. Fears was asked in a press conference if the superstar could be kept as a kicker. That reporter clearly had just arrived on the scene of what was a notoriously brutal training camp. "Even our kickers hit," Fears replied.[18]

Fears was reducing his squad to nearly a third its size, and toughness was an easy indicator. "We haven't got time for the guys who don't want to hit," he was heard saying, as castoffs packed their bags. He was under the gun to find the right players in time for them to learn each other and his system.[19]

Three weeks into camp, however, Fears was given new help. Mecom hired Bert Rose as the Saints' first full-time general manager. Rose, who had filled that role for the Vikings' first four years, was given authority to develop the Saints according to his vision. Wynne and Karl were out, but Mecom said he would remain actively involved. He did, however, see the need to centralize decision-making.[20]

It was easy to criticize aspects of how Mecom assembled the club, such as trading first-round picks for a relatively untested quarterback and a thirty-one-year-old fullback. However, it was not just football gurus making assessments. The whole nation was curious about how New Orleans would handle her cunningly begotten team.[21]

There was speculation from the outset about whether the city had truly righted its racial climate and whether African Americans would be justly included in team operations. There was also plenty of skepticism about the green, twenty-seven-year-old oil heir's ability to run a sports franchise. He had a lot to prove. In some ways, that might have made him the best choice for New Orleans. In attempting to find and sign the best person for each position, both on and off the field, Mecom emerged as a textbook equal opportunity employer. From the college draft to open tryouts, a quarter of the signees were African American, and that ratio stayed steady through cuts and trades. Far from a quota system, Mecom's strategy even resisted the governor's urging to bring home as many Louisiana boys as possible.[22]

There was a similar racial ratio within the scouting department. Sizing up talent from the fifteen-state South Central area was Al Tabor, a forty-one-year-old African American with a decade and a half of coaching experience in the college ranks. Unlike the first Black pro football scouts, such as Houston's Lloyd Wells, who were hired to study players from Black universities, Tabor was assigned one of five sections of the country. Likewise, another longtime veteran of his profession, Jim Hall, was cherry-picked for the Saints public relations department, based on his twenty years in sports journalism.[23]

For an equipment manager, the Saints crew followed the course of their coaching hire and snagged Atlanta's number two man in that role, African American Charlie Shepherd. For Shepherd's understudy, they plucked a local park supervisor and youth sports coach, Wallace Brown. The Black Dillard alum quickly sold the team on his work ethic, and it did not hurt morale that Brown was rarely without a smile.[24]

The team had been integrated from the very beginning and at the very top, when Dejoie and Francis joined the ownership group. This inclusion extended all the way down to the volunteer cheerleading squad, which invited any high school junior or senior—male or female, Black or white—to perform two cheers at tryouts. This trend did not go unnoticed.

Mecom proved himself a pioneer, at the very least in the eyes of Atlanta's One Hundred Percent Wrong Club. This prestigious group of African American sportsmen hosted an annual awards program to recognize athletes, coaches, and contributors from across the country. Their Pioneer Award originally honored Branch Rickey, for his daring work integrating professional baseball. In 1966, the title went to John Mecom Jr.[25]

These Atlantans believed that Mecom had "pioneered in depth in the area of not only being a good sportsman but in giving every individual the same sporting chance to be recognized on merit and merit alone." They acknowledged that New Orleans "has not always had reason to be proud of its record in race relations" but that the Saints owner had advanced "the quest of human dignity for every man." Mecom was said to have, like Branch Rickey, "a record of achievement in sports promotion" that was "equaled by his record in the promotion of human relations."[26]

|||||

One week into their California training camp, the Saints had their first joint scrimmage of league veterans and fresh draftees. That evening, there was another unprecedented meeting of rookies and vets back home. At 6:30 p.m., around one hundred eleven- to fifteen-year-old boys raced down the Wisner overpass in the local soapbox derby. Among them were African American adolescents with the names of Black-owned businesses painted on their cars. Experience prevailed, and Schiro presented the first-place award to the previous year's runner-up. Two Black first-timers, however, were handed trophies by their sponsors and smiled from their driver's seats for a photograph printed in the *Louisiana Weekly*.[27]

|||||

"Fretful" was how Bert Rose felt, late in the preseason. They were winning too much. Rose and Fears both knew an expansion franchise took a long time to steady, but heady hopes were fostered as the team set a record for inaugural exhibition wins. Rose worried that "folks in New Orleans might have come to expect too much right away" and preached, "There's no shortcut to success in the NFL."[28]

Coach Fears was likewise trying to quell premature celebrations. "Don't think we're going to have a .500 season or anything like that," he told reporters at training camp. "I'm not being pessimistic," he explained. "I'm just being a realist."[29]

John Mecom was hoping for sunnier forecasts on the California sidelines. "How many games you figure we can win?" he asked bystanders.

"Three or four," one replied. "Five if you're lucky."

Sports Illustrated's Tex Maule thought that was generous, but he watched the owner's face drop a little at the response. Then, as Jimmy Taylor schooled rookies with his choppy legwork, Mecom perked up and said,

"Maybe we'll do better than that. You never can tell." Slightly amused, Maule warned Mecom that he would have a stressful season if he expected more than a few ticks in the win column.[30]

There was no stopping the fervor, though. After dropping the opener to the Rams, the Saints won their next four exhibitions. Most New Orleanians had not even seen their team in action. The first five games were on the road, so it was mostly just locals watching Sunday morning replays on WWL-TV who witnessed any of it.[31]

It really did not matter. In early September, New Orleanians knew that their Saints were winning and were finally coming home. When the team was scheduled to arrive, around a thousand rooters gathered at the airport to greet the flight. They had to wait, however. A JetProp had veered off the tarmac and nose-planted into soft ground with part of its tail blocking the runway. The Saints' plane circled for half an hour while the mangled aircraft was towed. Still, fans waited patiently for their gridders to emerge, like a band of mail-order brides first exposed to smitten suitors.[32]

The next day was Labor Day, but the Saints box office was open. When the doors were unlocked, a mob was already waiting. Reserving seats proved a popular way to spend the day off. On-site tickets were quickly depleted, and the manager made a mad dash to the vault for more.

The Saints' first drills at their David Drive camp were light, as several players were banged up. Jimmy Taylor had been sidelined by a broken cheekbone and injured eye during week four against San Francisco, and the number two fullback, Les Kelley, had hurt his knee in the same game. Both were working out Monday, though, and hopeful of making an appearance against Atlanta that weekend. The third fullback in the depth chart, Tulane's Gordon Rush, was out for the season after a 49ers hit landed the kicking specialist turned runner on the operating table.[33]

Fears not only had to move halfbacks to fullback but also had to find subs at placekicker. Rush was out, and the only man left holding a tee, Charlie Durkee, had a pulled groin. If one of the two still-competing punters could not learn the job quickly enough, Taylor was on deck for field goals. Fears figured the fullback was reliable from at least 35 yards. As for kickoffs, the coach thought about getting inventive and punting them instead. "Who knows," he reasoned. "We might uncover something and stay with it."[34]

Such was the first Saints training camp. This was what Fears was working with to assemble the team's roster and playbook. Still, locals were expecting a powerhouse, especially against the Falcons.

It *was* just a preseason game, and the two teams were not in the same division—not even the same conference. Still, it was the first meeting of the Atlanta Falcons and the New Orleans Saints, a rivalry that had existed before either team and that went both ways. The Falcons front office told the squad to "tighten their chin straps Saturday night."[35]

Nearly seventy thousand fans turned out at Tulane, and got there early. As players limbered up, the six-foot-three, two hundred–pound owner roamed the field. Shagging a few footballs, Mecom could have been mistaken for a tight end if not for his sweater and dress slacks. Al Hirt tried to teach fans some chants, calling, "Way down yonder in New Orleans..." and expecting them to respond, "The Saints go marching in!" Before long, though, it was clear Hirt was a better bandleader than cheerleader, and it became the announcer's job to evoke a crowd response.[36]

As Mel Leavitt introduced the players, many of them (veterans and rookies alike) had never heard such a welcoming. Each was given a thunderous reception, but it seemed that Gary Cuozzo was the most beloved Saint—until Leavitt began, "From Louisiana..." Before he could get out Jimmy Taylor's full name, fans drowned out the PA system.[37]

On the opening kickoff, Walter "Flea" Roberts danced and dodged from his own goal line to the midfield stripe before being brought down. It was a spectacular first play for the hometown crowd, but a pair of penalty flags nullified the gain and, apparently, the momentum. The Saints did not get that far downfield again in the first twenty minutes. The Falcons, however, put together a nine-play, 72-yard touchdown drive, between Saints punts.

In the second period, the Saints defense allowed a 54-yard run up the middle and a 6-yard rushing touchdown, both by Junior Coffey. However, it took a little shuffling for folks in the booth to identify the back. Before the game, someone had broken into the visitors' locker room and stolen several Atlanta jerseys. Nine Falcons, including Coffey, quarterback Steve Sloan, and reigning Rookie of the Year Tommy Nobis wore borrowed numbers that night. Numbers on the scoreboard, however, were unmistakable. Atlanta was up 14–0 with New Orleans trapped on their own side of the 50.

Then, late in the second, a 29-yard completion by Cuozzo and a spot foul by Atlanta's defense landed the Saints in the red zone. On third-and-9, Cuozzo dropped back to pass.[38]

Cuozzo had entered the trade looking like the next Johnny U. However, the preseason revealed little about mechanics learned from the master. It seemed to show how protective Baltimore's offensive line had been—or perhaps how green the Saints line was. Either way, Cuozzo's inability to maneuver a collapsing pocket moved Bill Kilmer into the likely starting role because of his quick release and scrambling feet. They might be ducks, but Kilmer's passes got out of his hands and to his receivers.[39]

Once again, Cuozzo was tackled for a double-digit loss. So on came punter Ron Widby to try his hand—or rather, his foot—at placekicking. The field goal attempt was no good.

The Saints had one more possession before halftime. With less than two minutes, Cuozzo enjoyed something he had sorely missed since leaving Baltimore: pass protection. From the Saints 23, the quarterback set his feet and sailed a perfect spiral 23 yards to one of his biggest targets, six-foot-four Kent Kramer. Kramer was hit immediately, but the 235-pound tight end shook his defender and took off. With two Falcons nipping at his heels, he scorched Atlanta territory. Ken Reaves lunged for Kramer's ankles at the 7 but the Saint entered the Promised Land standing up. This time Widby found the space between the uprights, and at intermission it was 14–7.

The halftime program alone was worth the price of admission. One of the Saints' biggest off-season signings was Tommy Walker, former entertainment director for Disneyland and producer of the pregame and halftime shows for the inaugural Super Bowl. Even for this preseason match, Walker and Hirt put on quite a show.

Stadium lighting was cut and a spotlight shined on the northeast end zone, where the stockholding trumpeter played "When the Saints Go Marching In," accompanied by flambeaux-wielding dancers. Then, at the south end of the stadium, a giant fireworks display created an outline of Hirt and his horn in the sky. After a couple more well-known jazz numbers, a second pyrotechnics show spelled "SAINTS" and formed the team's trademark fleur-de-lis. Meanwhile, in the Saints locker room, Coach Fears was pulling out some fire of his own as he "chewed up" his squad a little. Except for one big play, New Orleans had looked like a new team in the sense that they clearly had not played together long.[40]

When they returned to the field, though, the Saints looked like a new team in the sense that they were little like the one from the first half. Kilmer subbed in at quarterback, racked up yardage with one short pass after another, and threw for three touchdowns. Moreover, one was set up by a 20-yard toss to none other than Jimmy Taylor, and another was capped by the same hometown hero's PAT. For locals, that was lagniappe.

The Saints kept the Falcons out of scoring range for the final two periods (with the help of two takeaways), and when coach Norb Hecker subbed in his backup quarterback in the fourth, the birds started going backwards altogether. Finally, the recently hobbled Gary Wood came on as signal caller for the Saints, moving the ball and his ankle cautiously downfield until time expired, with the home team up 27–14.[41]

After the game, fans so aggressively swarmed players that Fears worried they needed an underground tunnel to get guys to their lockers. Once the squad escaped, locals spilled out of the stadium thinking that the long wait for a franchise was mitigated by their instant powerhouse. From corner bars to high-rise boardrooms, the team was the talk of the town. On Monday, the Saints even appeared in an advice column on parenting: "The way to diaper the baby is not the baseball diamond pitch. That went out with the Pelicans. Now it's the Saints. You fold your diaper into a football field (twice as long as it is across). Then get behind your team's goal..."[42]

With the first regular season game five days out, Tuesday's *States-Item* bore the headline "New Orleans Awaits Greatest Day in Long Sports History." That afternoon, the Saints strode through the ballroom of the Jung Hotel at a welcoming luncheon sponsored by the chamber of commerce. Coach Fears spoke for the club, saying they were all "moved emotionally" by their reception, and Councilman Landrieu responded on behalf of the city. He proclaimed with conviction, "The Saints are responsible for a new birth in the spirit of New Orleans."[43]

|||||

On Sunday, David Dixon and his family set up base camp at his mother's house on Palmer Avenue before strolling to Tulane Stadium. Along the way, folks waved and called out to them. "Great work, Dave!" one group shouted. "Oh, nothing to it," he hollered back in jest. Dixon now let the praise wash over him.[44]

Half an hour before kickoff, programs were sold out. "This is going to be a souvenir for my grandchildren," one buyer remarked, "our first game in the NFL." Fans scurried to their seats for the pregame show. The Dixons found familiar faces in their usual Tulane and Sugar Bowl spots. Norman Francis and his wife settled into the seats he had purchased near midfield, about halfway up the lower deck, but he got binoculars out to keep an eye on his children sitting in a section farther up. And sportswriters in the press box were joined by a big VIP, commissioner Pete Rozelle.[45]

Al Hirt's bandstand sat behind the bench, at the 50-yard line, for a few hours of intermittent jazz tunes and the occasional "Charge!" prompt. Mecom again warmed up with the players, and the official mascot, a seventy-five-pound St. Bernard named Gumbo, strutted around the field with his handler.

Archbishop Hannan delivered the invocation, praying, "Give in full measure the virtue of modesty to the victors and to the defeated, the virtues of hope and patience." As Hannan left the field, Schiro jogged up to praise the fine words, adding, "But we're going to win."[46]

Next, the all–African American Xavier University choir performed "America the Beautiful" and "The Star-Spangled Banner" from midfield. Afterwards, hundreds of doves of peace were released from the floor of Tulane Stadium.

At 1:30 p.m. on September 17, 1967, the Los Angeles Rams kicked off to the New Orleans Saints. Just 6 yards outside his own end zone, John Gilliam fielded the ball. A wedge started off in front of him. He saw his window, a tiny hole on the 20, dead center between the hash marks, and even his blockers were shocked by how quickly he zipped through.[47]

Mary Dixon jumped up and chimed, "He's gone!" Dave looked down skeptically at the half-dozen Rams still in front of Gilliam, but even the returner's shoelaces evaded diving defenders. He made one final juke to his right on the Saints 30 and from there it was a clean sprint. The rookie took the opening kickoff 94 yards to put the Saints ahead by a touchdown fifteen seconds into their NFL debut. The response of 80,879 stomping and hollering ticket holders sparked legends of cracks forming in the stadium's foundation and dishes vibrating off tables in nearby homes.[48]

Dave Dixon's mind flashed to other big moments he had witnessed on that field, back in Tulane's glory days, watching games with his father as a child. There was something so undeniably powerful about the game of football. Tears filled his eyes. Mary put her arms around her husband as the stadium shook and roared, and said, "Well, sweetheart, we did it."[49]

Nearby, Moon Landrieu also took in the enormity of it all, and he too thought back to an earlier day of sports in New Orleans. He pictured old Pelican Stadium, the all-white baseball teams, and the segregated fans. Around him were tens of thousands of Black and white New Orleanians, all intermingled, and all cheering wildly for an African American football player whose home turf was Tulane Stadium. Not that long ago such a thing was "unheard of," he thought.[50]

Following Durkee's PAT, it took a while for either offense to get rolling. When one did, it belonged to the Rams. Behind quarterback Roman Gabriel's arm and the legs of fullback Dick Bass, they rolled to the Saints 2. Fears's defense tightened up, though, and on fourth-and-goal coach George Allen sent out his placekicker. The chip shot was true, and Los Angeles had its first points.

Following swapped punts, the Rams again got within single-digit distance of the Saints end zone. Two incomplete passes later, L.A. lined up on third-and-goal. At that point, however, the crowd noise grew so loud that it forced Gabriel to call a time-out, and when he finally got the play off, he was dropped for a 7-yard loss. The stadium became even more raucous as the Rams settled for another short field goal that kept the Saints in the lead by 1.

Moreover, the home team answered immediately. Durkee hit a 44-yard 3-pointer, making it 10–6 with only a few minutes left before intermission. With time ticking away, the Rams found themselves at third-and-25 on their 30. It looked like a good time to start the concessions rush. Then Gabriel connected with Bernie Casey on a 48-yard pass to the New Orleans 22. The pair followed it up with a 20-yard completion on the next play. With one spare second, Gabriel rolled out to his left, faced a wall of defenders, and quickly cut back through the middle and over the goal line for a touchdown. The ensuing kick gave L.A. a 3-point lead.[51]

Hometown fans blinked at the scoreboard as players jogged off, but entertainers soon took the field for another of Walker's elaborate halftime shows, flaunting a distinct New Orleans vibe. First, African American women from the Jolly Bunch Social and Pleasure Club danced in brightly colored ruffles to the music of the twelve-member Eureka Brass Band, one of the oldest in the city. Next, Hirt's ensemble played another jazzy rendering of "When the Saints Go Marching In." They then began "Up, Up, and Away" while hundreds of helium balloons were released. But the biggest part of the segment was a big flop. In what many feared was a bad omen, the giant red-and-white-striped hot air balloon set to launch from the center of the field barely cleared the turf before it split, deflated, and collapsed, requiring that it be wrestled cumbersomely out of the stadium instead of soaring away.[52]

Once the field was cleared, a quick takeaway and some penalty yardage got the Saints in the red zone. Although from there the Rams' defensive line, the famed Fearsome Foursome, started pushing them backwards, Durkee's 26-yard boot made it a whole new ballgame with nearly two full quarters remaining.

Unfortunately, New Orleans's next big play was a fumbled fourth-down snap in their end zone. Punter Tom McNeill scooped up the ball and tried to advance it with his legs instead of his toes but only made it to the 17, which was not enough for a first down. From that distance, it only took two rushing plays for Los Angeles to punch in another touchdown, and it was 20–13 Rams.

By then, the defense that had kept the Saints in the game was wilting in the eighty-degree sunshine. The final period opened with another Rams touchdown, this one off a 15-yard aerial, and Los Angeles went up 27–13. It nearly became a three-score game on the next Rams drive, but Dave Whitsell redirected a field goal attempt.

As for the Saints' offense, each of their next three possessions ended in either a lost fumble or an interception. Their last turnover occurred with 1:10 on the clock, which the Rams mercifully ran out.[53]

As Archbishop Hannan had asked, the defeated left more hopeful than downhearted. Fans were heard saying things like "This team is a darn good team" and "We'll get 'em next week." The Rams game, however, was a good representation of how the 1967 season took shape. The Saints looked surprisingly strong at the outset but were weary when it really mattered.[54]

They had training camp a full two weeks longer than any other team, and it had been an exceptionally tough one. This was partly because of Fears's style but also just the nature of an expansion team. With an empty depth chart, veterans, rookies, and walk-ons all battled for a spot; no one let up. When starters were named, Fears needed to see as much as possible in unfriendly scrimmages. The Saints did very little subbing in exhibitions and always played to win. After the long, six-game preseason, they were 5–1. But when it was time to start playing for keeps, Fears's guys were worn out and banged up. Lest fans forget, they also were still just a first-year team.[55]

New Orleans hosted the Redskins the next weekend. Seventy-five thousand fans showed up to see the Saints fall 30–10. Washington's first-round pick, Ray McDonald, had more rushing yards and touchdowns than the entire Saints team, whose first-round running back was on the bench nursing a preseason knee injury.[56]

Still, a week later, two thousand additional ticket holders cranked the turnstiles to watch Cleveland clobber New Orleans 42–7. The threat of the Browns power sweep kept the rush off Frank Ryan and his two sprained ankles, giving him all day to throw his three touchdowns. The Saints, on the other hand, went through as many quarterbacks, none of whom could get the ball off quickly enough. The home team's only score was a 2-yard carry by Taylor, his first touchdown in black and gold.[57]

From there, they had three road games, and lost them all. They fell to the

Giants by a mere pair of field goals and trailed the Cowboys by only 4 points at final whistle. San Francisco bested them by two touchdowns, but it was still nothing like the last beatings they had taken at home.[58]

On October 29, the winless Saints were back in Tulane Stadium to take on the Pittsburgh Steelers. Attendance was just shy of seventy thousand. The Saints had a 10–0 halftime lead and were still up by a field goal with less than two minutes to go. But they were beaten by another team's rookie running back when Don Shy's 33-yard scamper gave the Steelers a 4-point advantage. Cuozzo and Taylor got their offense to Pittsburgh's 24 with ten seconds left, but two would-be game-saving passes into the end zone were incomplete and drained the clock.[59]

"The darlings of the Grapefruit League" were 0–7, and the 4–3 Eagles were headed to New Orleans. Not even sixty thousand seats were filled for the November 5 tilt. The tens of thousands of locals not braving another heartbreak would have to be told: the Saints won. It was a game filled with heroics. For starters, Walt Roberts returned the opening kickoff for a touchdown, Gilliam style. Next, Roberts scooped up a Taylor fumble and carried it for 28 yards and another touchdown. Flea then secured a 49-yard pass from Cuozzo for his third end zone celebration of the day. Whitsell traveled about the same distance on a pick-six off Norm Snead, and that was only one of the defense's interceptions. The other, by Dave Simmons, occurred on the Saints 3-yard line to preserve New Orleans's 7-point lead.[60]

That did it. Football fever had swept through the city long ago. Now, however, New Orleanians were fully indoctrinated in the Any Given Sunday mentality. The next weekend, when Tom Landry, Don Meredith, and the Dallas Cowboys entered Tulane Stadium, a complete sellout crowd surrounded the Saints home turf. Contrite fans were prepared to prove their devotion. They were plenty supportive for three quarters, answering Hirt's prompts for cheers and emitting the occasional well-timed hecklings and hisses at referees.

Then, with the Saints down by 14 in the final period, Cuozzo passed to Gilliam just outside the end zone. Running step for step with the receiver, defender Cornell Green got his hands on the ball first. As momentum carried the players a few steps forward, Gilliam knocked the ball loose and simply let it bounce, but the play was not blown dead. Cornerback Mel Renfro snatched the pigskin and returned it 26 yards. The refs ruled it a Green fumble and the Cowboys' ball. On top of that, some late hitting tacked on another 15.

After a single completion to Dan Reeves chewed up nearly half the field, the Saints were defending their goal from 13 yards out. Then it started. When Meredith tried to get his guys lined up, the roar from the stands was so deafening that a time-out was his only option. The fans' realization of their effectiveness only egged them on, and officials stopped play for around ten minutes, waiting for the crowd to quiet. Regardless, when the Cowboys lined up again, no one could hear the count, the snap was fumbled, and Meredith landed on it to save the drive. After two more futile attempts at an offensive play, Landry sent out his kicker, who put the final score at 27–10.[61]

The crowd's involvement and volume were unprecedented. The football world was a bit stunned. One Dallas sportswriter was even calling on Rozelle to reprimand the Crescent City. With a three-score victory, however, Cowboys players and coaches were not overly concerned. Actually, the night's leading rusher was rather impressed. Don Perkins commented, with some bewilderment, "In other cities when the home team is hopelessly behind late in the game the fans get on the home boys." Then he laughed and said, "But here they got on us."[62]

Likewise, Mecom fielded questions from beat reporters on the appropriateness of this phenomenon, and he defended his faithful flock, saying, "I think it's great that our fans are that way." Unable to hold back a smirk, he added, "I'll bet the Cowboys wish they'd had this many fans who cared their first year."[63]

|||||

Back on All Saints Day 1966, when Rozelle announced New Orleans's entry, there had been a letter of resignation on Victor Schiro's desk. A twenty-year member of the city planning commission was stepping down to protest Albert Dent's appointment to the agency. The detractor told Schiro, "I am not surprised that you appointed a Negro," and accused the mayor of forfeiting "'Southern Traditions' for political expedience." Schiro consented to both the resignation and the self-sorting of the city's progressive new front office.[64]

While John Mecom had been seeking the best candidates for his club, city administrators also continued equalizing opportunities. That summer, two prominent Black lawyers were appointed to new posts. Robert Collins was one of a pair of assistant city attorney hires, and Benjamin Johnson was sworn in as an assistant district attorney. Norman Francis also was busy in the warm months, with the city again soliciting his service. The motion to name Francis to the Civil Service Commission had listed all seven city council members as authors.[65]

Toward the end of the summer, there were suddenly twenty-eight municipal positions to fill at once. New Orleans was finally creating a human relations commission. Moon Landrieu's motion gave the mayor a nudge to meet this promise, but Schiro backed it, and in late September the city had a permanent, fully staffed board tasked to "inquire into, discourage, and seek to prevent discriminatory practices against any individual because of race, color, creed, religion, national origin, or ancestry."[66]

That fall, it was up to voters to fill a few job openings, and Orleans Parish pioneered another racial first. Dutch Morial was elected as a state representative, the first African American to hold such an office since Reconstruction. With the endorsement of all the city's major newspapers, he achieved a majority in the primaries and unseated the incumbent with no need for a runoff.[67]

In another historic November vote, John McKeithen became the first twentieth-century Louisiana governor elected to consecutive terms. Around two thousand McKeithen supporters packed the Jung Hotel's ballroom for a hundred-dollar-a-plate appreciation dinner later that month. Many of McKeithen's African American advocates were there that night, including Reverends A. L. Davis and Avery Alexander, who years before had suspected the governor of inaction and lip service. They had been converted.

After several toasts and speeches, the tall, forty-nine-year-old governor approached the podium, looking particularly stately in the latest double-breasted suit. He hailed the state's coming-of-age. "Louisiana is no longer a biological specimen in a bottle," he celebrated. He spoke of the need to abandon the notion of the "good old days," saying, "The celebrated past is a romantic graveyard of wishful thinking." Then he elicited a standing ovation by proclaiming, "Never again must we allow ourselves to be torn apart, compartmentalized away from each other, transformed into a sad species that looked with suspicion upon those who differed from us or whose color or politics or religion was not our own."[68]

|||||

After a renewed sellout crowd atoned for its lack of faith through a *makeup* game, the Saints went back on the road for a rematch with the Eagles, who got revenge in a 48–21 rout at Franklin Field. Fears's crew then returned for their last home game of the season, bringing a 1–9 record with them.[69]

Early that week, Fears termed the upcoming match the "Cellar Bowl." They were facing the 1–8–1 Atlanta Falcons to, in all likelihood, determine who would occupy the league's cellar at season's end. By Friday afternoon, tickets were gone. Attendance was an absolute-capacity, standing-room-only 83,437, meaning a couple thousand fans paid to stand up for three hours or so to watch their one-win team take on another one-win team.[70]

It was a wild game. There was not a single punt in the opening two periods. Both teams got in the red zone early only to find a stiffened enemy defense. Atlanta's first scoring threat ended in a stolen fumble. When the Saints got stifled within spitting distance of 6 points, however, they eked out 3 from Durkee and a first-quarter lead.

However, the next seven drives all ended in either a fumble, a touchdown, or a field goal attempt. All the fumbles were from New Orleans; all the touchdowns belonged to the birds. With less than five minutes to go in the first half, the Saints were down 21–3.

Then halfback Don McCall returned a post-touchdown Falcon kick to midfield and sparked his sleepy offense. Cuozzo went back to the air, hitting Jimmy Taylor once and tight end Ray Poage twice. They were in the red zone at the two-minute warning. When Cuozzo targeted Kent Kramer under the goalposts for 7 yards, it resulted in as many points and cut their halftime deficit to 11.

The third quarter started with a bang. Fears subbed Kilmer for Cuozzo, and in four plays his offense marched to the Falcons 22. On the next snap, Kilmer handed off to halfback Randy Schultz on a trap play. The blocking was perfect. He zipped through the hole, zigzagged around a few would-be tacklers, and slipped into the end zone. The score became 21–17 in little more than three minutes.

Both teams ended their next several possessions with either a placekicker or a punter. Durkee missed one field goal attempt but made up for it with a true 32-yarder. The Falcons quickly answered those 3 points, and late in the fourth quarter the Saints were again down by 4.

After Atlanta's kickoff, Kilmer's offense had 97 yards to go in under five minutes. A handoff to Ernie Wheelwright was shut down just a few steps from scrimmage, but a personal foul pushed the Saints to their 20. A single pass over the middle to Gilliam got him 35 yards and into Atlanta territory. Next, Kilmer overthrew Flea but made amends with an 18-yard connection to Poage. Then Tom Barrington ran up the middle for 14 on a draw. His next run, however, was only three steps. And on second down, Schultz was tackled for a 5-yard loss. On third, Kilmer's toss to Danny Abramowicz was incomplete.

With that, it was fourth-and-14 on the Falcons 17-yard line with 1:12 on the clock. Kilmer took the snap, dropped back, and again spotted Abramowicz in the end zone. Kilmer got the pass off before he was touched, but cornerback Ken Reaves intercepted it behind the goal line, killing New Orleans's comeback. Or so it seemed.

A yellow flag went up. A different defensive back was called for pass interference, and the ball was spotted at the 7-yard line. It was first-and-goal. Kilmer handed off to Wheelwright, but he was stopped for no gain. There were fifty-eight seconds remaining.

The crowd was electrifying. Kilmer thought he "could feel something going right through" his body as the fans screamed. The ball was snapped, and in an exchange between 49er alums, Kilmer rifled to Kramer, who had just broken free of a Falcon safety. The pass was complete in the end zone. The stadium boomed as a true point-after provided a field goal–sized cushion. The Saints were forty-three seconds away from their second win of the regular season and their second defeat of the Atlanta Falcons.

Atlanta's kickoff returner got them to their own 31, and Randy Johnson got under center. Long pass plays were being called, starting with a completed 15-yarder to Junior Coffey. They were already knocking on the door of Saints territory. Johnson again dropped back as his receivers took off downfield, but linebacker Jackie Burkett and tackle Lou Cordileone broke through the Atlanta line, gained on the retreating quarterback, and brought him down on his own 33.

There were two seconds on the game clock. Johnson lined up in shotgun formation. At the snap, he faded back to the 25 and launched a 50-yard pass to a wide-open Jerry Simmons. There was no one between the receiver and the goal. Simmons got both hands on the ball—just not at the same time. He bobbled it from left to right, and it fell to the turf incomplete. It was 3:49 p.m. on November 26, 1967. Jim Hall would write it up as the happiest moment in the lives of those tens of thousands of New Orleanians, all of whom were on their feet, even if they had genuine seats.[71]

|||||

The New Orleans Buccaneers were scheduled to tip off with the New Jersey Americans less than a half hour later, at 4:15, next door at Loyola Field House. The Bucs general manager was giving Saints ticket holders half-priced admission and advertised the hardwood tilt as a good way to wait out postgame traffic. He even promised that the teams would not jump center until football fans had time to walk over, if necessary. That vow was about to be tested.

No one was going anywhere; another GM had won out. Bert Rose had put a request in the local papers for fans to stick around for a special closing ceremony. So back on the field came Rose, Fears, and Mecom. Each thanked the crowd for faithful and spirited support during a shaky inaugural season. Then the squad returned and the players were introduced one by one, gesturing their gratitude as every last member of the team was given another thunderous ovation.[72]

|||||

It was twelve years to the day since the Sugar Bowlers' long-distance call between New Orleans and Atlanta set up the Crescent City's first integrated game. That football classic had been one of the earliest instances of the Big Easy bending to the demands of the nation's reckoning with civil rights, and it seemed to occur with the ease and calmness expected of a place known to be lazy, dispassionate, and proud of it. But that well-earned reputation as slow-moving and unexcitable became a double-edged sword when locals proved equally uninspired to combat the reactionary forces that soon overran the city.

When the civil rights movement swept Louisiana, little was more out of sync with the Big Easy's branding than change. Even as race riots and violence blacklisted the town, progress was kept behind closed doors, in the interest of public approval, at least until the action of fifty-eight Black and white AFL All-Stars made it clear that inch-wise, piecemeal, behind-the-scenes advancement did not befit a big league city. As a result, for the first time New Orleanians had a popular cause and a common goal to rally behind en masse and out in the open. Suddenly, conservatism was obstructionism and a socially perilous stance.

Moreover, locals found a way to be, as Schiro proposed, both the traditional city and the city of change. A locale long renowned for enchanting stagnation found itself advertising its shiny new modernity, and civic identity was in flux. The pro club was immediately folded into the city's defining features of Mardi Gras, jazz, and red beans and rice, and locals' absolute fanaticism over the franchise was a common denominator breaching barriers of race, generation, or politics. Perhaps most powerfully, since an enemy's enemy is a friend, the existence of common (external) rivals gave a new complexion to the dichotomy of *"us* versus *them.*"[73]

Many times over the previous dozen years it had seemed that racial division would prevent New Orleans from having any place in national football, on any level. But the city came together, largely around and for the game. Despite the home finale against the Falcons coming down to a 13-yard double-team sack and fingertips on a juggled pass, the most impactful contact that afternoon was in the standing-room-only crowd of Black and white football fans hovering elbow to elbow with weary bodies and teary eyes, united in a shared devotion to *their* team.

A lot happened for the city to get to that point, and more than a few key players had been beaten up along the way. That was in the past now. Before the integrated teammates and ticket holders left Tulane Stadium on that warm, late November afternoon, everyone joined in a chorus of "Auld Lang Syne."[74]

NOTES

INTRODUCTION:
Motion Prior to the Snap

1. *New Orleans States*, December 24, 1954; *Times-Picayune*, December 9 and 26, 1954; *Sun* (Baltimore, MD), December 7, 1954; Stephen H. Norwood, "The Sugar Bowl: Manhood, Race, and Southern Womanhood in New Orleans, 1935–1965," in *New Orleans Sports: Playing Hard in the Big Easy*, ed. Thomas Aiello (Fayetteville: University of Arkansas Press, 2019), 165.

2. Marty Mulé, *Sugar Bowl: The First Fifty Years* (Birmingham, AL: Oxmoor House, 1983), 89–94, 101; *Times-Picayune*, November 26, 1953; *New Orleans States*, December 27, 1954; *New Orleans Item*, November 26, 1953, January 3, 1954; *Los Angeles Times*, November 27, 1953.

3. Charles H. Martin, "Integrating New Year's Day: The Racial Politics of College Bowl Games in the American South," *Journal of Sports History* 24, no. 3 (Fall 1997): 360–370; Norwood, "Sugar Bowl," 153, 168–169; Mulé, *Sugar Bowl*, 101; Fred Digby, "Growth of the Sugar Bowl Classic," series 4.6, Sugar Bowl Collection (SBC), Historic New Orleans Collection.

4. *Times-Picayune*, December 26, 1954; Norwood, "Sugar Bowl," 165; Mulé, *Sugar Bowl*, 96.

5. *Times-Picayune*, December 22 and 24, 1954; Lane Demas, *Integrating the Gridiron: Black Civil Rights and American College Football* (New Brunswick, NJ: Rutgers University Press, 2010), 86.

6. *Times-Picayune*, December 22 and 24, 1954; *Louisiana Weekly*, December 8, 1955; C. Martin, "Integrating New Year's Day," 369.

7. *Time*, November 24, 1947; Adam Fairclough, *Race and Democracy: The Civil Rights Struggle in Louisiana, 1915–1972* (Athens: University of Georgia Press, 2008), 9–10; Edward F. Haas, *DeLesseps S. Morrison and the Image of Reform: New Orleans Politics, 1946–1961* (Baton Rouge: Louisiana State University Press, 1974), 36–37, 252–253.

8. *Times-Picayune*, December 30, 1955, October 24, 2002; Demas, *Integrating the Gridiron*, 84; *Washington Post and Times-Herald*, July 30, 1956; *Christian Science Monitor*, January 3, 1949.

9. *Washington Post and Times-Herald*, December 24, 1954; *Times-Picayune*, December 24, 1954; *Louisiana Weekly*, January 1, 1955.

10. 1955 Sugar Bowl program, series 4.1.1, folder 5, SBC.

11. *Louisiana Weekly*, January 8, 1955.

12. *Louisiana Weekly*, January 8, 1955.

CHAPTER 1
The Concession Stands

1. Mid-Winter Sports Association (MWSA) minutes, November 3, 1955, series 1.1, folder 7, SBC; *New Orleans Item*, November 13, 1955; *New York Times*, November 8, 1955.

2. *Times-Picayune*, November 13, 1955; *New York Times*, January 15, 1953; *Washington Post and Times-Herald*, November 6 and 13, 1955.

3. MWSA minutes, November 18 and 21, 1955, series 1.1, folder 7, SBC; *Times-Picayune*, November 22, 1955; *Washington Post and Times-Herald*, November 20, 1955; *Pittsburgh Courier*, November 19, 1955; *New York Times*, November 20, 1955.

4. *Times-Picayune*, November 20 and 22, 1955; *New Orleans Item*, November 22, 1955; *Pittsburgh Post-Gazette*, January 2, 1956; Mulé, *Sugar Bowl*, 101.

5. MWSA minutes, November 21, 1955; *New Orleans Item*, November 22, 1955.

6. *Times-Picayune*, November 23, 1955; *New Orleans States*, November 22, 1955; *New Orleans Item*, November 22, 1955.

7. *Pittsburgh Courier*, December 3 and 10, 1955; *New York Times*, November 23, 1955; Demas, *Integrating the Gridiron*, 86.

8. 1955 Sugar Bowl Vertical File, Georgia Institute of Technology Archives (GITA); Demas, *Integrating the Gridiron*, 84, 86; *Pittsburgh Post-Gazette*, January 2, 1956; *Times-Picayune*, December 30, 1955; 1954 Sugar Bowl program, series 4.1.1, folder 5, SBC, 21.

9. Charles Glueck, interview by Mark Cave, October 25, 2007, Sugar Bowl Memories (SBM) Oral History Project, Historic New Orleans Collection; *New Orleans Item*, November 22, 1955.

10. MWSA minutes, November 21 and 25, 1955, series 1.1, folder 7, SBC; *New Orleans Item*, November 22, 1955; *Times-Picayune*, November 25, 1955.

11. MWSA minutes, November 26, 1955, series 1.1, folder 7, SBC; *New Orleans States*, November 22, 1955; *Times-Picayune*, November 27, 1955; *Technique* (Georgia Tech), December 2, 1955, GITA; 1955 Sugar Bowl Vertical File.

12. 1955 Sugar Bowl Vertical File; *Chicago Daily Tribune*, November 27, 1955; MWSA minutes, November 26, 1955.

13. *Louisiana Weekly*, December 3, 1955; Bobby Grier, interview by Mark Cave, June 18–24, 2014, SBM; Bobby Dodd and Jack Wilkinson, *Dodd's Luck: Life and Legend of a Hall of Fame Quarterback and Coach* (Savannah, GA: Gold Coast), 183–184; 1955 Sugar Bowl Vertical File; Charles H. Martin, "Racial Change and 'Big-Time' Football in Georgia: The Age of Segregation, 1892-1957," *Georgia Historical Quarterly* 80, no. 3 (Fall 1996): 552; *Atlanta Daily World*, December 3, 1955; Demas, *Integrating the Gridiron*, 80–83.

14. *Washington Post and Times-Herald*, December 3, 1955.

15. *Technique*, December 6, 1955; John Sayle Watterson, *College Football: History, Spectacle, Controversy* (Baltimore: Johns Hopkins University Press, 2000); "Student Riots, Sugar Bowl," digital portal, GITA.

16. Wade Mitchell, interview by author, March 10, 2014; report by Pinkerton's National Detective Agency, December 7, 1955, box 10, folder 23, George C. Griffin Papers, GITA; Carl Vereen, interview by author, March 10, 2014.

17. 1955 Sugar Bowl Vertical File; *Technique*, December 6, 1955; Demas, *Integrating the*

Gridiron, 72, 87; *Plain Dealer* (Kansas City, KS), December 9, 1955; *Los Angeles Times*, December 4, 1955; *Pittsburgh Courier*, December 10, 1955; Mitchell interview; Dodd and Wilkinson, *Dodd's Luck*, 185.

18. Riot investigation documents, box 10, folder 23, George C. Griffin Papers, GITA; 1955 Sugar Bowl Vertical File.

19. *Atlanta Constitution*, December 6, 1955; 1955 Sugar Bowl Vertical File.

20. 1955 Sugar Bowl Vertical File; C. Martin, "Racial Change," 553; *Los Angeles Times*, December 4, 1955; Dodd and Wilkinson, *Dodd's Luck*, 187.

21. *New York Times*, December 4, 1955; *Atlanta Constitution*, December 6, 1955; 1955 Sugar Bowl Vertical File.

22. 1955 Sugar Bowl Vertical File; Demas, *Integrating the Gridiron*, 88, 93; Dodd and Wilkinson, *Dodd's Luck*, 188.

23. *Pittsburgh Courier*, December 10, 1955; *Louisiana Weekly*, December 17, 1955; Grier interview; Demas, *Integrating the Gridiron*, 80; *Atlanta Constitution*, January 5, 1956.

24. *Pittsburgh Courier*, December 3 and 10, 1955.

25. *Pittsburgh Courier*, December 10, 1955.

26. 1955 Sugar Bowl Vertical File; *Times-Picayune*, December 27 and 28, 1955; *Louisiana Weekly*, December 31, January 7, 1955.

27. 1955 Sugar Bowl Vertical File; *Times-Picayune*, December 28, 29, and 30, 1955; 1956 Sugar Bowl program, series 4.1.1, folder 7, SBC.

28. *Atlanta Constitution*, January 2, 1956; 1955 Sugar Bowl Vertical File; *Times-Picayune*, December 31, 1955.

29. Grier interview; Demas, *Integrating the Gridiron*, 82; *Sports Illustrated*, October 21, 1957; Vereen interview; *New Orleans States*, November 22, 1955; Mitchell interview; Allen Ecker interview by author, March 10, 2014; 1955 Sugar Bowl Vertical File; *Atlanta Journal*, December 31, 1955.

30. 1955 Sugar Bowl Vertical File; *Atlanta Journal*, December 31, 1955; Dodd and Wilkinson, *Dodd's Luck*, 189; Vereen interview; Ecker interview; Mitchell interview; *Sports Illustrated*, January 9, 1956; Glueck interview.

31. *Atlanta Journal*, December 29, 1955, January 1, 1956; 1955 Sugar Bowl Vertical File; *Times-Picayune*, December 28 and 31, 1955, January 2, 1956; Dodd and Wilkinson, *Dodd's Luck*, 189.

32. 1956 Sugar Bowl program; Mulé, *Sugar Bowl*, 14, 41–45; C. Martin, "Integrating New Year's Day," 361–362; Demas, *Integrating the Gridiron*, 85.

33. *Times-Picayune*, December 30 and 31, 1955; 1955 Sugar Bowl Vertical File; *Atlanta Journal*, December 31, 1955; 1956 Sugar Bowl game tape, series 3.1, folder 22, SBC.

34. 1956 Sugar Bowl game tape; Dodd and Wilkinson, *Dodd's Luck*, 189–190; Mulé, *Sugar Bowl*, 102–103; Sam Corenswet Jr., interview by Mark Cave, July 26, 2007, SBM; *Pittsburgh Post-Gazette*, January 3, 1956.

35. *Times-Picayune*, January 4, 1956.

36. 1956 Sugar Bowl game tape; *Atlanta Constitution*, January 4, 1956; *Times-Picayune*, January 4, 1956; Mulé, *Sugar Bowl*, 103–104; 1955 Sugar Bowl Vertical File.

37. *Times-Picayune*, December 30, 1955, January 3, 1956; Dodd and Wilkinson, *Dodd's Luck*, 182, 190; *Atlanta Constitution*, January 4, 1956.

38. *Times-Picayune,* January 3, 1956.

39. "1956 Bobby Grier in Locker Room," series 2.3.2, folder 30, SBC; *Los Angeles Times,* January 3, 1956; *Times-Picayune,* January 3, 1956.

40. 1956 Sugar Bowl game tape; 1955 Sugar Bowl Vertical File.

41. *Louisiana Weekly,* January 7 and 21, 1956; *New Journal and Guide* (Norfolk, VA), January 14, 1956; Glueck interview; *Times-Picayune,* January 3, 1956; 1955 Sugar Bowl Vertical File; 1956 Sugar Bowl game tape.

42. 1956 Sugar Bowl official red bound photo album, series 2.3.1, folder 10, SBC; Samuel Zurich, interview by Mark Cave, October 2, 2008, SBM; *Atlanta Constitution,* January 5, 1956; *Los Angeles Times,* January 3, 1956.

43. Mitchell interview; Vereen interview; Ecker interview; *Times-Picayune,* January 3, 1956; Grier interview; *New York Times,* January 1, 2006.

44. *Atlanta Daily World,* January 8, 1956; Bill Nunn Jr. to Tom Dent, January 23, 1956, box 1, folder 14, Dent Family Papers addendum, Amistad Research Center (ARC); *New Journal and Guide,* January 7, 1956.

45. Demas, *Integrating the Gridiron,* 77–78; Grier interview.

46. *Atlanta Daily World,* January 4 and 8, 1956; *Atlanta Constitution,* January 5, 1956.

47. MWSA minutes, November 25, 1955, January 5, 1956, series 1.1, folder 7, SBC; *Louisiana Weekly,* December 24, 1955, January 14, 1956.

48. Paul DeBlanc member file, series 1.7, folder 10, SBC; MWSA minutes, March 1, 1956, series 1.1, folder 7, SBC; *Louisiana Weekly,* February 4, 1956.

49. MWSA minutes, June 7, 1956, series 1.1, folder 7, SBC.

50. Demas, *Integrating the Gridiron,* 83–84; Stephen A. Berrey, *The Jim Crow Routine: Everyday Performances of Race, Civil Rights, and Segregation in Mississippi* (Chapel Hill: University of North Carolina Press, 2015), 142–143; Fairclough, *Race and Democracy,* 170, 205; *Louisiana Weekly,* June 9, 1956.

51. *Times-Picayune,* June 15, 1956.

52. *Times-Picayune,* April 24, July 3 and 17, 1956; *Dallas Morning News,* June 21, 1956.

53. *Times-Picayune,* June 15 and 16, July 6, 1956; *Dallas Morning News,* June 21, 1956.

54. *Times-Picayune,* February 4 and 7, April 8, 1956; *Louisiana Weekly,* February 11 and 25, March 10, 1956; *Dallas Morning News,* April 9, 1956.

55. *Times-Picayune,* July 6, 1956.

56. *Times-Picayune,* July 6 and 16, 1956.

57. *Louisiana Weekly,* January 21 and 28, February 25, May 19, June 16, 1956.

58. *Louisiana Weekly,* April 2, July 2, 1955, February 18, 1956; *Times-Picayune,* February 8, July 15, 1956.

59. MWSA minutes, July 12, 1956, series 1.1, folder 7, SBC.

60. MWSA minutes, July 13, 1956, series 1.1, folder 7, SBC; *Times-Picayune,* July 15, 1956.

61. *Times-Picayune,* July 15 and 16, 1956.

62. MWSA minutes, June 7, 1956; *Times-Picayune,* July 15, 1956.

63. *Times-Picayune,* July 15, 1956; 1965 Sugar Bowl program, series 4.1.1, folder 11, SBC.

64. *Times-Picayune,* July 15, 1956.

65. *Times-Picayune,* June 17, July 15 and 17, 1956.

CHAPTER 2
A Long Return

1. *Times-Picayune,* June 9, 12, and 23, 1956; Fairclough, *Race and Democracy,* 170, 185, 205; *Louisiana Weekly,* June 9, 1956.

2. *Times-Picayune,* June 9, 12, and 17, 1956; *Louisiana Weekly,* June 9, 1956.

3. *Times-Picayune,* November 8, 1955, January 26, June 12 and 22, 1956; Ellis P. Laborde to Board of Commissioners, February 19, 1956, board minutes archives, City Park Improvement Association (CPIA), New Orleans.

4. Ellis P. Laborde to Board of Commissioners, January 15 and 16, 1955, CPIA; City Park minutes, September 30, 1953, January 16, 1955, January 15, 1956, CPIA; Ellis P. Laborde to Julian Parker, January 19, 1955, CPIA; *New Orleans States,* January 12, 1955; *Times-Picayune,* August 10 and 30, November 28, 1956; *Louisiana Weekly,* July 30, August 18, October 15, 1955.

5. City Park minutes, April 23, May 28, June 25 and 27, 1955, CPIA; Laborde to Parker, January 19, 1955; Ellis P. Laborde to Board of Commissioners, March 18, April 23, 1956, CPIA; *Times-Picayune,* May 24, June 5, 7, 9, and 12, November 8, 1956.

6. Demas, *Integrating the Gridiron,* 83–84, 92; *New York Times,* December 25, 1955; *Atlanta Daily World,* December 25, 1955; *Pittsburgh Courier,* December 31, 1955, January 7, 1956.

7. *New York Times,* December 24, 1955; Scott E. Buchanan, *"Some of the People Who Ate My Barbecue Didn't Vote for Me": The Life of Georgia Governor Marvin Griffin* (Nashville: Vanderbilt University Press, 2011), 3, 9, 137–138, 157, 168; *Atlanta Daily World,* November 29, December 16 and 23, 1955; *Sun,* December 23, 1955.

8. Haas, *DeLesseps S. Morrison,* 252.

9. Fairclough, *Race and Democracy,* 170, 185, 196, 205; *Times-Picayune,* January 31, May 18, June 9, 1956.

10. *Times-Picayune,* February 16, May 18, 1956; *Atlanta Daily World,* February 23, 1957; *Wall Street Journal,* March 18, 1958.

11. *New Orleans Item,* July 3 and 17, 1956; *Times-Picayune,* June 17, 1956.

12. *New Orleans Item,* July 17, 1956; *Louisiana Weekly,* July 21, December 22, 1956, November 16, 1957; *Times-Picayune,* July 30, 1956; *New Orleans States,* July 13 and 28, 1956.

13. Fairclough, *Race and Democracy,* 206.

14. *Louisiana Weekly,* June 23, July 21 and 28, December 8, 1956, September 21, 1957; *Times-Picayune,* August 23, 1956.

15. *New Orleans States,* August 26, 1954, November 22, 1955, July 13 and 20, 1956; *New Orleans Item,* January 23, 1953, June 19 and 22, 1956, July 11, 12, 18, 19, 22, 24, and 27, 1956.

16. *Times-Picayune,* January 3, February 8, 1956.

17. *Times-Picayune,* July 5 and 15, August 21, 1956; *New Orleans States,* December 11, 1952.

18. *Times-Picayune,* July 18, August 10, 1956; *Louisiana Weekly,* August 4 and 18, 1956; Arnold Rampersad, *Jackie Robinson: A Biography* (New York: Knopf, 1997), 296–297; *Chicago Daily Tribune,* June 8, 1954.

19. *New Orleans Item,* June 17, July 18 and 30, 1956; *Atlanta Daily World,* August 19, 1956; *Louisiana Weekly,* November 27, 1954, March 16, 1957; *Crusader* (Rockford, IL), October 19, 1956.

20. *New Orleans Item,* July 25 and 30, 1956; *Louisiana Weekly,* August 4, 1956; *Washington Post and Times-Herald,* July 25, 1956; *Pittsburgh Courier,* July 28, 1956.

21. *Washington Post and Times-Herald,* July 30, 1956.

22. MWSA minutes, August 5, 1954, August 16, 1956, series 1.1, folder 7, SBC; *Chicago Daily Tribune,* August 5, 1956.

23. *Dallas Morning News,* July 26, 1956; *New Orleans Item,* July 23, 1956; *Afro-American* (Baltimore), August 4, 1956; MWSA minutes, August 16, 1956.

24. MWSA minutes, July 26, 1956, series 1.1, folder 7, SBC.

25. MWSA minutes, July 31, 1956, series 1.1, folder 7, SBC.

26. MWSA minutes, August 16, 1956.

27. *Dallas Morning News,* September 30, 1956; *Washington Post and Times-Herald,* July 30, 1956; *New Orleans States,* July 7 and 20, 1956; *Times-Picayune,* August 21 and 30, 1956.

28. *New Orleans States,* July 7, 1956; *Times-Picayune,* August 24, 1956.

29. MWSA minutes, August 16, 1956; Michael L. Kurtz and Morgan Peoples, *Earl K. Long: The Saga of Uncle Earl and Louisiana Politics* (Baton Rouge: Louisiana State University Press, 1990), 35.

30. MWSA minutes, August 16 and 27, 1956, series 1.1, folder 7, SBC; *Times-Picayune,* August 24 and 30, 1956; Fairclough, *Race and Democracy,* 206; *New Orleans Item,* July 17 and 27, 1956.

31. MWSA minutes, August 27 and 28, 1956, series 1.1, folder 7, SBC; Mulé, *Sugar Bowl,* 16; *Times-Picayune,* August 29, 1956; *New York Times,* September 1, 1956; *New Orleans States,* August 23, 1956.

32. MWSA minutes, August 27 and 28, 1956; Kurtz and Peoples, *Earl K. Long,* 54, 89, 126.

33. MWSA minutes, August 27 and 28, 1956; *Times-Picayune,* August 28, 1956.

34. *New York Times,* September 1, 1956; *Times-Picayune,* August 29 and 31, 1956.

35. *Times-Picayune,* May 17, August 24 and 30, 1956.

36. MWSA minutes, August 27, September 6, 1956, series 1.1, folder 7, SBC; *Times-Picayune,* August 31, September 1, 1956; *Louisiana Weekly,* September 8, 1956.

37. *Washington Post and Times-Herald,* September 1, 1956.

38. *New York Times,* September 1, 1956; *Louisiana Weekly,* March 14, 1964.

39. *Times-Picayune,* September 1, 1956; *Louisiana Weekly,* September 8, 1956.

40. J. Mark Souther, *New Orleans on Parade: Tourism and the Transformation of the Crescent City* (Baton Rouge: Louisiana State University Press, 2006), 79; *New Orleans Item,* July 8 and 18, 1956; *New Orleans States,* June 23, 1956; *Times-Picayune,* July 22, 1956.

41. *Times-Picayune,* October 7, 10, 12, and 18, 1956; *Atlanta Constitution,* March 27, 1898.

42. *Times-Picayune,* October 24, 2002; Clarence L. Mohr and Joseph E. Gordon, *Tulane: The Emergence of a Modern University, 1945–1980* (Baton Rouge: Louisiana State University Press, 2001), 28–29.

43. *Times-Picayune,* February 5, June 10, September 2 and 13, October 7, 10, 11, and 13, 1956.

44. *Times-Picayune,* October 11, 13, and 14, 1956; *New York Times,* November 21, 1955.

45. *Washington Post and Times-Herald,* October 14, 1956; *Times-Picayune,* October 14, 1956.

46. *Washington Post and Times-Herald,* October 14, 1956; *Times-Picayune,* October 14, 1956.

47. "Sugar Bowl Belongs to Nation," Sugar Bowl histories, 1965, series 4.3.1, folder 2, SBC.

48. *New Orleans Item,* July 8, 1956.

49. 1955 Sugar Bowl sponsorship program, series 1.4, folder 6, SBC; *Dallas Morning News,* September 30, 1956; *Washington Post and Times-Herald,* July 30, 1956.

50. MWSA minutes, September 6, October 4 and 8, 1956, series 1.1, folder 7, SBC.

51. Mulé, *Sugar Bowl,* 105; *Times-Picayune,* December 3, 1956; *New York Times,* November 26, December 5, 1956; *Los Angeles Times,* November 26, 1956; *Afro-American,* December 29, 1956.

52. Mulé, *Sugar Bowl,* 105; *New York Times,* December 3, 1956; *Los Angeles Times,* December 2, 1956.

53. Mulé, *Sugar Bowl,* 105; *New York Times,* December 2, 1956; *Los Angeles Times,* November 26, 1956; *New Orleans States,* November 12, 1956; *Times-Picayune,* December 3, 1956; *Washington Post and Times-Herald,* December 30, 1956.

54. MWSA minutes, October 8, December 6, 1956, series 1.1, folder 7, SBC; *Times-Picayune,* December 7, 1956; *Afro-American,* December 29, 1956; *New Orleans States,* January 1, 1957; *Washington Post and Times-Herald,* December 23, 1956.

55. *Dallas Morning News,* January 1, 1957; *Times-Picayune,* December 5 and 28, 1956; *New Orleans States,* December 27 and 31, 1956; *New Orleans Item,* January 2, 1957.

56. 1957 Sugar Bowl game tape, series 3.1, folder 23, SBC; *Times-Picayune,* December 28, 1956, January 2, 1957; *Dallas Morning News,* January 2, 1957; *New Orleans States,* January 2, 1957; Mulé, *Sugar Bowl,* 106–107; *Los Angeles Times,* January 2, 1957.

57. *Times-Picayune,* January 2, 1957; *New Orleans States,* January 2, 1957; *Tulane Hullabaloo,* December 14, 1956; MWSA minutes, January 17, February 14, 1957, series 1.1, folder 7, SBC.

58. Chamber of Commerce bulletin, September 13, 1957, series 1.4, folder 4, SBC; *New Orleans Item,* September 18, 1957; MWSA minutes, October 3, November 7, 1957, series 1.1, folder 7, SBC; *Washington Post and Times-Herald,* December 23, 1956; *Times-Picayune,* December 7, 1956; *Daily Boston Globe,* November 20, 1957.

59. *Arkansas State Press,* November 9, 1956; *Times-Picayune,* September 1, 5, and 6, 1957; *Daily Boston Globe,* September 5, 1957.

60. *New York Times,* September 1, 1957; *Times-Picayune,* September 5, 1957; *Louisiana Weekly,* September 7, 1957.

61. *Louisiana Weekly,* September 14 and 21, 1957; *Afro-American,* September 21, 1957.

62. *Louisiana Weekly,* September 7 and 21, 1957.

63. *New York Times,* September 17, 1957; Mohr and Gordon, *Tulane,* 162–163; *Times-Picayune,* September 17, 1957.

64. *Times-Picayune,* September 17, 1957; *Washington Post and Times-Herald,* September 17, 1957.

65. *Times-Picayune,* July 5, 1956, November 13, 17, and 18, 1957; *Atlanta Daily World,* November 17, 1957; *Washington Post and Times-Herald,* November 17, 1957.

66. *Times-Picayune,* November 17, 1957.

67. *New York Amsterdam News,* September 21, 1957; *Louisiana Weekly,* December 14, 1957.

68. *Louisiana Weekly,* June 11, 1955, January 26, March 9, October 3, 1957; *Times-Picayune,* August 10, 1956.

69. *Louisiana Weekly,* May 11, June 1, November 9, 1957.

70. *Louisiana Weekly,* May 11, June 1, November 9, 1957; *Times-Picayune,* May 6, 1952, March 21, May 16 and 29, 1957; *Arkansas State Press,* May 24, 1957.

71. *Times-Picayune,* November 22, 1957, February 14, March 29, December 22, 1958; R. M. Salvant to Board of Commissioners, December 1957, CPIA; *Louisiana Weekly,* October 25, November 1, 1958; *Plain Dealer,* October 31, 1958; City Park minutes, October 26, December 21, 1958, CPIA; Claude W. Duke, Louis B. Porterie, and Leon F. Davison to City Park Legal Committee, December 10, 1958, CPIA.

72. *Louisiana Weekly,* January 10, 1959.

73. *Louisiana Weekly,* January 10 and 17, 1959; *Times-Picayune,* December 23, 1958; City Park minutes, January 18, February 15, 1959, CPIA; City Park Improvement Association to South Louisiana Citizens Council, March 16, 1959, CPIA; Ellis P. Laborde to Board of Commissioners, January 18, February 15, 1959, CPIA; *Cleveland Call and Post,* January 17, 1959.

74. City Park minutes, April 27, 1959, CPIA.

75. *Louisiana Weekly,* May 25, 1957.

76. *Afro-American,* April 6, 1957; *Times-Picayune,* March 12 and 29, April 3 and 9, 1957.

77. *New Orleans States,* May 1, August 27, 1957; *Times-Picayune,* December 13, 1960; *Los Angeles Tribune,* April 11, November 14, 1958; *Dallas Morning News,* August 30, 1957; *Jet,* January 5, 1961; *Afro-American,* August 31, 1957; *Cleveland Call and Post,* December 6, 1958; *Pittsburgh Courier,* December 24, 1960.

78. *Cleveland Call and Post,* December 6, 1958; *Los Angeles Tribune,* November 14, 1958.

79. *Louisiana Weekly,* January 11 and 18, December 5, 1958; *Times-Picayune,* November 29, 1958.

80. Mulé, *Sugar Bowl,* 111–112; *Dallas Morning News,* November 29 and 30, December 3, 1958; *Times-Picayune,* November 27 and 29, December 1, 1958, May 26 and 27, 1959; Richard B. McCaughan, *Socks on a Rooster: Louisiana's Earl K. Long* (Baton Rouge, LA: Claitor's Book Store, 1967), 170–181.

81. Kurtz and Peoples, *Earl K. Long,* 205–206; *Times-Picayune,* May 26, 1959.

82. Kurtz and Peoples, *Earl K. Long,* 205–206; *Times-Picayune,* May 26, 1959; McCaughan, *Socks on a Rooster,* 167–168.

83. *Times-Picayune,* May 25, 1959.

84. *Times-Picayune,* May 25, 1959.

85. *Times-Picayune,* May 26 and 28, 1959; McCaughan, *Socks on a Rooster,* 170–181; Kurtz and Peoples, *Earl K. Long,* 212–216.

86. *Times-Picayune,* May 25, 26, and 27, 1959; Kurtz and Peoples, *Earl K. Long,* 216.

87. *Times-Picayune,* May 27, 1959; Kurtz and Peoples, *Earl K. Long,* 207–208.

88. Kurtz and Peoples, *Earl K. Long,* 211–218; McCaughan, *Socks on a Rooster,* 168–181; *Times-Picayune,* May 28, 1959.

89. Kurtz and Peoples, *Earl K. Long,* 211–218; *Louisiana Weekly,* June 13, 1959; *Dallas Morning News,* May 26, 1959; *Times-Picayune,* November 29, 1958, May 26, 1959.

CHAPTER 3
Three and Out

1. City Park minutes, March 20, 1960, CPIA; *Louisiana Weekly,* April 11, 1959; *Times-Picayune,* March 16 and 21, 1960.

2. *Times-Picayune,* May 26 and 27, 1959, March 16, 1960; *Louisiana Weekly,* May 30, 1959.

3. *Dallas Morning News,* November 29, 1958; MWSA minutes, March 5, 1959, series 1.1, folder 7, SBC.

4. *Times-Picayune,* May 26, 1959; *Louisiana Weekly,* May 30, 1959.

5. *Louisiana Weekly,* May 30, June 6, 1959.

6. *Times-Picayune,* May 26, 1959, March 6, 1960; *Louisiana Weekly,* May 30, December 19, 1959, February 14, April 23, 1960; *Dallas Morning News,* May 26, 1959.

7. City Park minutes, April 27, June 22, 1959, CPIA; Ellis P. Laborde to Board of Commissioners, March 15, December 20, 1959, February 21, 1960, CPIA; *Louisiana Weekly,* October 3, November 28, 1959.

8. *Louisiana Weekly,* April 16, May 7 and 14, 1955, June 1, 1957, September 19, 1959; *Times-Picayune,* March 6, April 24, May 31, 1959, March 16 and 21, 1960.

9. *Times-Picayune,* March 21, 22, and 23, 1960; *Louisiana Weekly,* July 13, November 9, 1957, March 26, 1960; City Park minutes, October 20, November 17, 1957, CPIA; *New Orleans States-Item,* March 16, 1960.

10. Haas, *DeLesseps S. Morrison,* 73, 239–243; *Louisiana Weekly,* April 16, 1955, July 13, November 9, 1957, February 15, 1958; City Park minutes, July 9, 1957, CPIA; *New Orleans States-Item,* March 16, 1960; *Times-Picayune,* March 23 and 31, April 2 and 3, 1960.

11. *Times-Picayune,* April 3, 1960.

12. *Times-Picayune,* March 31, 1957, March 23, 1958, March 22, 1959, April 10, 11, and 12, 1960; *Louisiana Weekly,* October 27, 1956, March 16, 1957, April 16, 1960; *New Orleans Item,* June 17, 1956; *Crusader,* October 19, 1956.

13. *Times-Picayune,* March 29 and 31, April 6, 7, and 10, 1960; *Los Angeles Sentinel,* April 7, 1960; *Louisiana Weekly,* April 9, 1960; *Daily Boston Globe,* April 9, 1960.

14. Ellis P. Laborde to Board of Commissioners, April 25, 1960, CPIA; *Times-Picayune,* April 10, 11, and 12, 1960; *Louisiana Weekly,* April 16, 1960.

15. *Times-Picayune,* April 30, 1960.

16. Laborde to Board of Commissioners, April 25, 1960; City Park minutes, April 25, 1960, CPIA; *Times-Picayune,* January 17, February 11, March 22, May 5, June 20, July 24, August 11, 1960.

17. Michael MacCambridge, *America's Game: The Epic Story of How Pro Football Captured a Nation* (New York: Anchor Books, 2004), 116–118; *Washington Post and Times-Herald,* January 18, 1960; *Los Angeles Times,* December 15, 1959, March 16, 1960; *Sports Illustrated,* February 8, 1960.

18. *Times-Picayune,* July 7, 1960.

19. *Times-Picayune,* May 5, June 16, July 24, September 4, 1960; MacCambridge, *America's Game,* 75, 96, 116–117; *Louisiana Weekly,* August 13, 1960.

20. MacCambridge, *America's Game,* 75, 96, 116–117; *Times-Picayune,* April 12, May 5, July 24, August 7 and 13, 1960.

21. *Times-Picayune,* August 7, 12, and 13, 1960; *Chicago Daily Tribune,* December 14, 1959; David Maraniss, *When Pride Still Mattered: A Life of Vince Lombardi* (New York: Simon & Schuster, 1999), 230; *Louisiana Weekly,* August 13, 1960.

22. *Louisiana Weekly,* August 13 and 20, 1960; *Times-Picayune,* May 5, July 24, August 7, 13, 14, 15, and 16, 1960; *Chicago Daily Tribune,* August 14, 1960; *New York Times,* August 14, 1960; *Los Angeles Times,* August 14, 1960; City Park minutes, October 16, 1960, CPIA.

23. David Dixon to Joseph Merrick Jones, August 5, 1959, folder 612, David F. Dixon Papers (DFD), Historic New Orleans Collection; MacCambridge, *America's Game*, 116–125.

24. Dixon to Jones, August 5, 1959; Mohr and Gordon, *Tulane*, 182, 263; David Dixon's handwritten notes, undated, folder 623, DFD; David Dixon to Joseph Merrick Jones, November 14, 1961, folder 612, DFD; David Dixon to Robert Monsted, November 30, 1961, folder 613, DFD.

25. Dixon to Jones, August 5, 1959; Michael S. Martin, "New Orleans Becomes a Big League City," in *New Orleans Sports: Playing Hard in the Big Easy*, ed. Thomas Aiello (Fayetteville: University of Arkansas Press, 2019), 111.

26. Dixon to Jones, November 14, 1961.

27. *Washington Post and Times-Herald*, August 18, 1960; *Chicago Daily Tribune*, August 18, 1960; *New York Times*, August 18, 1960; *Los Angeles Times*, August 18, 1960.

28. *Louisiana Weekly*, July 25, 1959, May 14 and 21, July 9, 1960; Fairclough, *Race and Democracy*, 234–238; *Times-Picayune*, August 20, 1960; *Philadelphia Tribune*, August 20, 1960; *New York Times*, August 18, 1960.

29. Fairclough, *Race and Democracy*, 231–232; Kurtz and Peoples, *Earl K. Long*, 119–121, 244–246; Haas, *DeLesseps S. Morrison*, 247–248; *Louisiana Weekly*, December 26, 1959.

30. *Chicago Daily Tribune*, August 18 and 20, 1960; *New York Times*, August 18, 1960; *Times-Picayune*, August 20, 1960; *Dallas Morning News*, August 20, 1960; *Chicago Daily Defender*, August 22, 1960; *Louisiana Weekly*, August 27, 1960.

31. *Times-Picayune*, August 27 and 28, 1960; *New York Times*, August 27, 1960; Fairclough, *Race and Democracy*, 238.

32. Fairclough, *Race and Democracy*, 234–239; *Louisiana Weekly*, October 15, November 5, 1960; *Times-Picayune*, August 28, 29, 30, and 31, 1960.

33. Fairclough, *Race and Democracy*, 242–244, 252; *Louisiana Weekly*, November 12 and 19, 1960; *Times-Picayune*, November 8, 11, 13 and 15, 1960; Haas, *DeLesseps S. Morrison*, 263–271.

34. *Times-Picayune*, November 15, 1960; *New York Times*, November 15, 1960; *Boston Globe*, November 15, 1960; Fairclough, *Race and Democracy*, 242–244.

35. Ruby Bridges, guest lecture, Brigham Young University, November 19, 2015; *Times-Picayune*, November 15 and 16, 1960; *New York Times*, November 15, 1960; Fairclough, *Race and Democracy*, 242–244.

36. *Washington Post and Times-Herald*, November 15 and 16, 1960; *Times-Picayune*, November 15 and 16, 1960; *Boston Globe*, November 15, 1960.

37. *Louisiana Weekly*, April 23 and 30, 1960; *Times-Picayune*, April 25, November 16, 1960; Fairclough, *Race and Democracy*, 252.

38. *Times-Picayune*, November 16, 1960.

39. *Washington Post and Times-Herald*, November 17, 1960; *Chicago Daily Defender*, November 17, 1960; *Los Angeles Times*, November 17, 1960.

40. *Times-Picayune*, November 17, 1960; *Chicago Daily Tribune*, November 17, 1960; *Chicago Daily Defender*, November 17, 1960; *Washington Post and Times-Herald*, November 17, 1960; *Los Angeles Times*, November 17, 1960; *Time*, November 28, 1960.

41. *Times-Picayune*, November 18 and 19, 1960; Fairclough, *Race and Democracy*, 248–249.

42. *Chicago Defender*, December 10, 1960; *Time*, December 12, 1960; *Atlanta Daily World*, December 4, 1960; *Boston Globe*, December 6 and 7, 1960; *Washington Post and Times-Herald*, December 2, 20, and 22, 1960; Fairclough, *Race and Democracy*, 248–249; *New Journal and*

Guide, December 3 and 17, 1960; *Chicago Daily Defender,* December 7, 1960; Shannon Frystak, *Our Minds on Freedom: Women and the Struggle for Black Equality in Louisiana, 1924–1967* (Baton Rouge: Louisiana State University Press, 2009), 86, 94.

43. *Washington Post and Times-Herald,* December 22, 1960; *Time,* December 12, 1960; John Steinbeck, *Travels with Charley: In Search of America* (New York: Viking, 1962), 189, 193–195; *New Journal and Guide,* December 10, 1960; Fairclough, *Race and Democracy,* 244–248; *Guardian* (London), November 18, 1960; Souther, *New Orleans on Parade,* 82.

44. MWSA minutes, November 3, December 3, 1960, series 1.1, folder 8, SBC; Mulé, *Sugar Bowl,* 116, 120; *Times-Picayune,* October 29, 1959; Edna Engert personnel file, series 1.7, folder 18, SBC; Marty Mulé, *Game Changers: The Rousing Legacy of Louisiana Sports* (Lafayette: University of Louisiana at Lafayette Press, 2013), 36–38.

45. MWSA minutes, January 5, 1961, series 1.1, folder 8, SBC; *Times-Picayune,* December 17, 1960, January 2, 1961; MWSA minutes, January 5, 1956.

46. Mulé, *Sugar Bowl,* 120; MWSA minutes, January 5, 1961; 1961 Sugar Bowl program, series 4.1.1, folder 9, SBC; Souther, *New Orleans on Parade,* 82.

47. *Wall Street Journal,* February 14, 1961; Souther, *New Orleans on Parade,* 82; *Pittsburgh Courier,* December 17, 1960; *New York Times,* November 28, 1960; Mulé, *Sugar Bowl,* 3–11; 1965 Sugar Bowl program.

48. *Guardian,* November 18, 1960; *Los Angeles Times,* December 11, 1960; *New York Times,* November 28, 1960.

49. *Washington Post and Times-Herald,* December 20 and 22, 1960; *Louisiana Weekly,* September 17 and 24, 1960; *Times-Picayune,* September 10 and 13, 1960; Fairclough, *Race and Democracy,* 252.

50. *Washington Post and Times-Herald,* December 20, 1960; *Louisiana Weekly,* March 4, 1961; *Pittsburgh Courier,* February 18, 1961; Fairclough, *Race and Democracy,* 252.

51. Haas, *DeLesseps S. Morrison,* 262, 273–274; Fairclough, *Race and Democracy,* 239, 251–253; *Wall Street Journal,* February 14, 1961; *Los Angeles Times,* December 11, 1960; *New York Times,* November 28, 1960; Frystak, *Our Minds on Freedom,* 99–100.

52. Fairclough, *Race and Democracy,* 254; *Times-Picayune,* June 23, November 6, 1960.

53. *Los Angeles Times,* September 6, December 11, 1960; *Louisiana Weekly,* April 16, May 20, 1961; *Atlanta Daily World,* September 7, 1961; *Chicago Daily Tribune,* September 7, 1960; *Afro-American,* September 16, 1961.

54. *Louisiana Weekly,* May 20, August 5, 1961; *New York Times,* September 3, 1961; *Los Angeles Times,* September 7, 1961; *Atlanta Daily World,* May 18, 1961; *Afro-American,* September 2, 1961.

55. *Louisiana Weekly,* January 21, March 18, April 16, 1961; *Chicago Defender,* April 15, 1961; *Cleveland Call and Post,* September 2, 1961.

56. *Louisiana Weekly,* May 13, 1961; *Chicago Defender,* April 15, 1961.

57. *Cleveland Call and Post,* September 9, 1961; *Afro-American,* September 16, 1961.

58. *Los Angeles Times,* September 7, 1961; *Louisiana Weekly,* September 16, 1961; *Chicago Daily Defender,* September 7, 1961; *Atlanta Daily World,* September 7, 1961.

59. *Times-Picayune,* August 6, 13, and 31, 1961; *Dallas Morning News,* September 8, 1961; Fairclough, *Race and Democracy,* 254.

60. *Times-Picayune,* September 5, 1961.

61. *Times-Picayune,* September 5, 1961.

62. *Chicago Daily Defender,* September 11, 1961; *Times-Picayune,* September 8, 1961; Fairclough, *Race and Democracy,* 254; *New York Times,* September 8, 1961; *Dallas Morning News,* September 8, 1961.

63. *Times-Picayune,* November 15, 1960, September 5 and 9, 1961; Fairclough, *Race and Democracy,* 255.

64. City Park minutes, June 27, 1960, March 19, 1964, CPIA; *Philadelphia Tribune,* August 12, 1961; *Chicago Daily Tribune,* September 10, 1961; *New York Times,* August 26, September 2, 1961; *Los Angeles Times,* August 20, 1961.

65. *New Orleans Item,* December 14, 1933; *Dallas Morning News,* December 21, 1933.

CHAPTER 4
A Naked Bootleg

1. David Dixon to Robert Monsted, November 11, 1961, folder 611, DFD; Dixon to Jones, November 14, 1961; series of letters, November 1961, folders 610–614, DFD.

2. *Kingfish* (Metairie, LA), January 2002; David Dixon to Robert Monsted, undated, ca. November 1961, folder 610, DFD.

3. Dixon to Jones, November 14, 1961.

4. Corenswet interview; David Dixon, interview by Mark Cave, April 24, 2009, New Orleans Life Story Project (NOLS), Historic New Orleans Collection; *Times-Picayune/States-Item,* August 6, 1986; David Dixon to Lester Lautenschlaeger, November 14, 1961, folder 612, DFD.

5. Dixon to Lautenschlaeger, November 14, 1961; Dixon to Jones, November 14, 1961; series of letters, November 1961, folders 610–614, DFD.

6. *Sports Illustrated,* January 6, 1964; *Louisiana Weekly,* August 26, 1961; David Dixon to Pete Rozelle, November 10, 1961, folder 611, DFD.

7. Dixon to Monsted, undated, ca. November 1961, November 30, 1961; David Dixon to Robert Monsted, undated, ca. November 14, 1961, folder 612, DFD.

8. Dixon to Monsted, undated, ca. November 14, 1961.

9. Dixon to Lautenschlaeger, November 14, 1961; Dixon to Monsted, undated, ca. November 1961; David Dixon to Robert Monsted, December 17, 1961, folder 614, DFD; David Dixon to Robert Monsted, November 30, 1961, folder 613, DFD.

10. *Times-Picayune,* November 27, December 21, 1961, August 7, 1988; Dixon to Monsted, November 30, 1961; Dixon to Monsted, December 17, 1961; David Dixon to Robert Monsted, January 10, 1962, folder 633, DFD.

11. Dixon to Monsted, undated, ca. November 1961; Dixon to Monsted, December 17, 1961.

12. Dixon to Monsted, January 10, 1962; Dixon to Monsted, November 30, 1961.

13. David Dixon to Robert Monsted, undated, after December 21, 1961, folder 615, DFD; David Dixon's handwritten notes, December 22, 1961, folder 618, DFD; Dixon to Rozelle, November 10, 1961.

14. David Dixon to Pete Rozelle, December 24, 1961, folder 619, DFD; David Dixon to Hale Boggs, January 19, 1962, folder 644, DFD; Dixon to Monsted, undated, ca. November 14, 1961.

15. *Times-Picayune,* December 31, 1961; MWSA minutes, March 2, 1961, series 1.1, folder 8, SBC.

16. MWSA minutes, March 2 and 9, April 6, 1961, series 1.1, folder 8, SBC; *Times-Picayune*, December 14, 1958.

17. MWSA minutes, March 2, December 1961, series 1.1, folder 8, SBC; *Times-Picayune*, December 17 and 28, 1961.

18. Mulé, *Sugar Bowl*, 124; *Times-Picayune*, October 2, 1960, November 19, 1963; Demas, *Integrating the Gridiron*, 57; MWSA minutes, November 9, 1961, series 1.1, folder 8, SBC; *Dallas Morning News*, November 7 and 14, 1961.

19. MWSA minutes, January 5, February 23, October 5, 1961, series 1.1, folder 8, SBC; 1965 Sugar Bowl program; *Louisiana Weekly*, November 25, 1961; *Times-Picayune*, November 30, 1959, December 29, 1961; *Dallas Morning News*, November 16, 1961.

20. MWSA minutes, June 1, August 15, 1961, series 1.1, folder 8, SBC.

21. Mulé, *Sugar Bowl*, 124–125; *Louisiana Weekly*, November 25, 1961; *Times-Picayune*, November 6, 1961; *Dallas Morning News*, November 7 and 14, 1961; MWSA minutes, November 9, 1961.

22. Mulé, *Sugar Bowl*, 124; *Dallas Morning News*, November 16, 1961; MWSA minutes, November 9, 1961.

23. MWSA minutes, November 9, 1961.

24. *Dallas Morning News*, November 16, 18, and 26, 1961; *New York Times*, November 26, 1961.

25. Mulé, *Sugar Bowl*, 124–125; *Times-Picayune*, November 20 and 29, 1961; *New York Times*, November 29, 1961; *Los Angeles Times*, December 25, 1934; MWSA minutes, February 11, 1960, January 25, 1962, series 1.1, folder 8, SBC; *Dallas Morning News*, November 22, 1961; *Washington Post and Times-Herald*, December 6, 1961.

26. *Times-Picayune*, November 29, December 3, 27, and 29, 1961; Mulé, *Sugar Bowl*, 125; *Boston Globe*, December 3, 1961; MWSA minutes, November 30, December 1961, series 1.1, folder 8, SBC.

27. MWSA minutes, December 1961.

28. David Dixon to Pete Rozelle, undated, folder 620, DFD; David Dixon to Robert Monsted, January 1, 1962, folder 628, DFD; David Dixon's NFL brochure draft, folder 621, DFD.

29. Dixon's NFL brochure draft; draft of "type letter" for brochure, folder 617, DFD; "Suggested Revisions to National Football League Brochure," February 4, 1962, folder 657, DFD.

30. Dixon's NFL brochure draft; David Dixon to Robert Monsted, January 9, 1962, folder 632, DFD; Dixon to Monsted, January 10, 1962.

31. Dixon to Monsted, January 10, 1962; David Dixon to Robert Monsted, January 18, 1962, folder 640, DFD.

32. Dixon interview, April 24, 2009; Dixon to Poitevent, January 13, 1962; David Dixon to Robert Monsted, January 8, 1962, folder 631, DFD.

33. Dixon to Poitevent, January 13, 1962; Dixon to Monsted, January 8, 1962.

34. Dixon to Poitevent, January 13, 1962.

35. David Dixon to Robert Monsted, January 16, 1962, folder 637, DFD; David Dixon to Bill Helis, January 16, 1962, folder 638, DFD.

36. Dixon to Monsted, January 16, 1962; David Dixon to Joseph Merrick Jones, January 18, 1962, folder 640, DFD; David Dixon to Pete Rozelle, January 18, 1962, folder 641, DFD; David Dixon to Pete Rozelle, January 27, 1962, folder 647, DFD; David Dixon to Pete Rozelle,

January 30, 1962, folder 651, DFD; David Dixon to Pete Rozelle, February 5, 1962, folder 654, DFD; David Dixon to Pete Rozelle, February 4, 1962, folder 658, DFD; Dixon to Monsted, January 18, 1962.

37. David Dixon to Robert Monsted and Edward Poitevent, February 3, 1962, folder 655, DFD; series of letters, dated January–February 1962, folder 655, DFD.

38. Dixon to Monsted, January 1, 1962; David Dixon to Robert Monsted, January 29, 1962, folder 650, DFD; Dixon's NFL brochure draft.

39. Joseph M. Jones to David Dixon, January 30, 1962, folder 655, DFD; Dixon to Jones, January 18, 1962.

40. David Dixon to Robert Monsted, January 11, 1962, folder 634, DFD; Dixon to Helis, January 16, 1962; David Dixon, handwritten note, January 27, 1962, folder 648, DFD; David Dixon to Robert Monsted and Leo Nomellini, February 4, 1962, folder 657, DFD.

41. Dixon to Monsted and Nomellini, February 4, 1962; David Dixon, handwritten note, February 4, 1962, folder 658, DFD; David Dixon to Robert Monsted, February 7, 1962, folder 660, DFD.

42. Edward Poitevent to David Dixon, February 6, 1962, folder 659, DFD.

43. Dixon to Monsted, February 7, 1962; David Dixon to Pete Rozelle, February 19, 1962, folder 661, DFD; Pete Rozelle to David Dixon, February 1, 1962, folder 654, DFD; *Dallas Morning News,* May 22, 1962; Dixon to Monsted and Nomellini, February 4, 1962.

44. David Dixon to Robert Monsted, undated, folder 652, DFD.

45. David Dixon to Robert Monsted, February 1962, folder 653, DFD; David Dixon to Pete Rozelle, March 2, 1962, folder 663, DFD.

46. Series of letters to NFL executives, March 6, 1962, folders 608, 664–670, DFD; *Times-Picayune,* January 2, March 6, 1962; Dixon to Rozelle, March 2, 1962.

47. David Dixon to Edward Poitevent, February 3, 1962, folder 656, DFD.

48. *Chicago Daily Tribune,* January 11, 1962; Dixon to Boggs, January 19, 1962; Dixon interview, April 24, 2009; *New York Times,* May 20, 1981.

49. Dixon to Boggs, January 19, 1962; Dixon to Poitevent, February 3, 1962.

50. David Dixon to K. S. Adams Jr., February 1962, folder 655, DFD; Dixon to Monsted, January 18, 1962; David Dixon's personal notes, January 25, 1962, folder 646, DFD; Dixon to Boggs, January 19, 1962; Dixon to Monsted, January 8, 1962.

51. David Dixon to Lester Lautenschlaeger, March 8, 1962, folder 671, DFD; David Dixon to Lester Lautenschlaeger, March 10, 1962, folder 672, DFD; David Dixon to Robert Monsted, January 6, 1962, folder 630, DFD; David Dixon to Joseph M. Jones, January 2, 1962, folder 629, DFD; Dixon to Monsted, January 18, 1962; Rozelle to Dixon, February 1, 1962.

52. *Atlanta Daily World,* January 30, 1962; Poitevent to Dixon, February 6, 1962; *Dallas Morning News,* January 20, August 24, 1962; *Times-Picayune,* January 29, August 14, 1962; City Park minutes, January 21, 1962, CPIA.

53. Dixon to Adams, February 1962.

54. *Times-Picayune,* January 29, March 17, 1962; City Park minutes, February 18, 1962, CPIA; *Atlanta Daily World,* January 30, 1962; Poitevent to Dixon, February 6, 1962.

55. David Dixon to Lamar Hunt, March 18, 1962, folder 673, DFD; David Dixon to K. S. Adams Jr., March 21, 1962, folder 674, DFD; David Dixon to K. S. Adams Jr., March 23, 1962, folder 676, DFD.

56. *Times-Picayune,* June 20 and 23, 1962; Dixon to Adams, March 21, 1962; *New York Times,* June 27, 1962; *Boston Globe,* June 24, 1962; Dixon to Hunt, March 18, 1962; Dixon to Adams, March 23, 1962.

57. David Dixon to Lester Lautenschlaeger, March 22, 1962, folder 675, DFD.

58. "Introduction" reports, folder 677, DFD.

59. "Introduction" reports, folder 677, DFD; Dixon to Lautenschlaeger, March 10, 1962.

60. "Introduction" reports, folder 677, DFD.

61. David Dixon to Edward Poitevent, June 11, 1962, folder 678, DFD; Dixon to Adams, March 23, 1962.

62. *Dallas Morning News,* May 22, June 3, 1962; *Times-Picayune,* June 10, 1962.

63. *Washington Post and Times-Herald,* May 24, 1962; Dixon to Monsted, January 9, 1962.

64. Dave Dixon, *The Saints, the Superdome, and the Scandal: An Insider's Perspective* (Gretna, LA: Pelican, 2008), 31; Dixon to Poitevent, June 11, 1962.

65. Sanborn Map Company, *Digital Sanborn Maps (Black and White): Louisiana, 1867–1970* (ProQuest Information and Learning, 2001); *Times-Picayune,* June 2, 1940; City Park minutes, June 18, 1962, CPIA.

66. *Times-Picayune,* June 5 and 20, 1962; *Boston Globe,* June 24, 1962.

67. *Times-Picayune,* May 18, June 8, 1962.

68. *Times-Picayune,* May 18, 1962.

69. *Boston Globe,* June 24, 1962; *New York Times,* June 27, 1962; *Times-Picayune,* May 18, June 5 and 10, 1962; *Dallas Morning News,* June 3, 1962.

70. Michael MacCambridge, *Lamar Hunt: A Life in Sports* (Kansas City, MO: Andrews McMeel, 2012), 132; *Times-Picayune,* June 27, 1962; AFL Executive Committee meeting minutes, June 25–27, 1962, AFL minutes, Ralph Wilson Jr. Research and Preservation Center (RPC), Canton, OH; *Dallas Morning News,* June 3, 1962.

71. *Atlanta Daily World,* January 30, June 20, 1962; AFL meeting minutes, June 25–27, 1962.

72. AFL meeting minutes, June 25–27, 1962.

73. *New York Times,* June 27, 1962; *Boston Globe,* June 26, 1962.

74. *Dallas Morning News,* May 30, June 3 and 19, 1962; *Times-Picayune,* June 20, 1962; *Christian Science Monitor,* June 21, 1962; *Afro-American,* June 30, September 1, 1962; *Louisiana Weekly,* July 7, 1962.

75. *Afro-American,* September 1, 1962; AFL meeting minutes, June 25–27, 1962.

76. *Atlanta Daily World,* July 10 and 11, August 14, 1962; *Dallas Morning News,* August 23, 1962.

77. *Pittsburgh Courier,* March 31, June 2, 1962; *Louisiana Weekly,* June 2 and 16, July 7, 1962; *New Journal and Guide,* June 16, 1962; *Atlanta Daily World,* January 30, June 12, August 14, 1962.

78. *Dallas Morning News,* August 3, 5, 12, 18, and 23, 1962; *Atlanta Daily World,* July 10, August 14, 1962.

79. *Dallas Morning News,* August 11 and 18, 1962; *Atlanta Daily World,* July 11, August 14, 1962.

80. *New York Times,* August 13, 1962; *Atlanta Daily World,* August 14, 1962.

81. *Times-Picayune,* August 14, 1962; *Chicago Daily Defender,* June 13, 1962.

82. *Times-Picayune,* August 5, 14, and 18, 1962.

83. "Approach #1" document, folder 626, DFD; Lamar Hunt to David Dixon, July 16, 1962, folder 478, DFD; David Dixon to Pro Football Club associates, folder 680, DFD; *Atlanta Daily World,* June 24, 1962.

84. Dixon, *Saints,* 43; "New Orleans Saints 1963" pencils, folder 475, DFD; *Times-Picayune,* August 9, 2010; Dixon interview, April 24, 2009; David Dixon, interview by Mark Cave, May 5, 2009, NOLS.

85. *Times-Picayune,* August 18, 19, and 20, 1962.

86. *Times-Picayune,* August 19, 22, 26, and 27, 1962; *Dallas Morning News,* August 24, 25, and 27, 1962.

87. *Louisiana Weekly,* August 18 and 25, 1962; *Afro-American,* September 8, 1962.

88. *Louisiana Weekly,* August 25, 1962.

89. *Louisiana Weekly,* September 1, 1962; *Dallas Morning News,* August 27, 1962.

90. *Dallas Morning News,* September 3, 1962; *Washington Post and Times-Herald,* September 3, 1962; *Afro-American,* September 1, 1962.

91. *Afro-American,* September 1 and 8, 1962.

92. *Afro-American,* September 8, 1962.

93. *Afro-American,* September 8, 1962.

94. *Times-Picayune,* October 2, 1962.

95. *Times-Picayune,* August 26, October 2, 1962; MacCambridge, *Lamar Hunt,* xviii–xx.

96. *Times-Picayune,* November 3, 1962.

CHAPTER 5
Crossing Routes

1. *Dallas Morning News,* November 21, 22, and 26, 1962; *Times-Picayune,* November 3 and 20, 1962.

2. *Dallas Morning News,* November 22 and 26, 1962; *Times-Picayune,* November 20, 21, and 22, 1962.

3. *Dallas Morning News,* November 26, 1962; *Times-Picayune,* November 29, 1962.

4. Commissioner Joe Foss to AFL owners and general managers, November 28, 1962, AFL memos, RPC; *Boston Globe,* March 16, 1963; *Dallas Morning News,* November 22 and 26, 1962; *Washington Post and Times-Herald,* December 11, 1962; *Times-Picayune,* November 29, 1962.

5. *Times-Picayune,* November 28 and 29, 1962.

6. Dixon interview, April 24, 2009; MacCambridge, *Lamar Hunt,* 125–126, 132–133; Dixon, *Saints,* 54.

7. MacCambridge, *Lamar Hunt,* 132–133; David Dixon to Pro Football Club, July 30, 1962.

8. David Dixon to Pro Football Club, July 30, 1962; *Washington Post and Times-Herald,* August 5, 1962; *New Orleans States-Item,* August 4, 1962.

9. MacCambridge, *Lamar Hunt,* 132–133.

10. MacCambridge, *Lamar Hunt,* 126–127; *Times-Picayune,* November 29, 1962; *Dallas Morning News,* March 17, 1962; Dixon, *Saints,* 54–55; Dixon interview, April 24, 2009; *New York Times,* June 27, 1962.

11. MacCambridge, *Lamar Hunt,* 127–133.

12. MacCambridge, *Lamar Hunt,* 131–133.

13. Dixon interview, April 24, 2009.

14. Dixon interview, April 24, 2009.

15. Mohr and Gordon, *Tulane,* 143–145, 152, 193–195, 199–201.

16. Fairclough, *Race and Democracy,* 262–263; Mohr and Gordon, *Tulane,* 205–206, 213–214; Kim Lacy Rogers, *Righteous Lives: Narratives of the New Orleans Civil Rights Movement* (New York: New York University Press, 1993), 97–99.

17. Mohr and Gordon, *Tulane,* 214–216, 230.

18. Fairclough, *Race and Democracy,* 262–263; Mohr and Gordon, *Tulane,* 215, 227, 233–234; *Louisiana Weekly,* December 15, 1962.

19. *Times-Picayune,* January 29, 1963; *Dallas Morning News,* February 9, 1963; Mohr and Gordon, *Tulane,* 235.

20. Dixon, *Saints,* 46; Dixon interview, April 24, 2009.

21. Dixon, *Saints,* 45–47.

22. Dixon, *Saints,* 45–47; Dixon interview, April 24, 2009.

23. Dixon, *Saints,* 39.

24. Dixon interview, April 24, 2009.

25. Dixon interview, April 24, 2009; Dixon, *Saints,* 39, 43, 46–47; Souther, *New Orleans on Parade,* 88.

26. *Times-Picayune,* March 31, 1963.

27. *Louisiana Weekly,* April 27, 1963; *Times-Picayune,* May 19, 1963.

28. *Times-Picayune,* May 19, 1963.

29. *Louisiana Weekly,* February 10, 1962; Souther, *New Orleans on Parade,* 85.

30. *Times-Picayune,* April 23, May 21, 24, and 26, 1963; Souther, *New Orleans on Parade,* 89–90; *Louisiana Weekly,* April 27, May 24, 1963.

31. Souther, *New Orleans on Parade,* 90; *Times-Picayune,* May 21 and 26, 1963.

32. Dixon, *Saints,* 51–52.

33. *Louisiana Weekly,* January 13, July 21, 1962; Wiltz W. Wagner to Horace Bynum, April 13, 1962, box 61, folder 8, Ernest "Dutch" Morial Papers, ARC; *Times-Picayune,* January 9, 1962.

34. Robert Carter to Dutch Morial, July 13, 1962, folder 73, NAACP New Orleans Branch Collection, Earl K. Long Library, University of New Orleans; *Louisiana Weekly,* July 21, 1962.

35. *Louisiana Weekly,* June 29, 1963.

36. *Times-Picayune,* July 2, 1963.

37. *Louisiana Weekly,* July 13 and 20, August 3, 1963.

38. *Louisiana Weekly,* August 3, 1963; *Times-Picayune,* July 23, 1963.

39. *Times-Picayune,* August 6, 1963; Dixon, *Saints,* 42, 52.

40. *Times-Picayune,* June 27, 1963; *Louisiana Weekly,* May 25, June 22, 1963.

41. *Times-Picayune,* June 27, 1963; *Louisiana Weekly,* July 20 and 27, 1963.

42. *Louisiana Weekly,* April 28, 1962, May 11, 1963; *Times-Picayune,* June 27, 1963; *Atlanta Daily World,* March 19, 1964.

43. *Louisiana Weekly,* July 6 and 20, 1963; *Times-Picayune,* July 8, 1963; *Dallas Morning News,* August 3, 1963.

44. *Times-Picayune,* August 2, 1963.

45. "National Football League: A Booming Industry," WDSU TV and Radio editorial, May 4, 1963, folder 479, DFD.

46. Editorial transcripts, folder Spr-51, Victor H. Schiro Records (VHS), City Archives, New Orleans Public Library; Victor Schiro to David Dixon, June 26, 1963, folder Spr-51, VHS; *Times-Picayune,* September 6 and 7, 1963.

47. Souther, *New Orleans on Parade,* 90–91; *Times-Picayune,* July 11, 1963; *Call and Post* (Cleveland, OH), September 21, 1963; *New York Times,* September 11, 1963; Edward F. Haas, *Mayor Victor H. Schiro: New Orleans in Transition, 1961–1970* (Jackson: University Press of Mississippi, 2014), 171–190; *Louisiana Weekly,* September 14, 1963.

48. *Louisiana Weekly,* April 13 and 27, May 11, June 22, July 13 and 27, 1963; 1957 Sugar Bowl game tape; Souther, *New Orleans on Parade,* 88; Dixon interview, April 24, 2009.

49. David Dixon to Robert Monsted, undated, ca. November 1961; *Times-Picayune,* May 8, 1963.

50. *Louisiana Weekly,* April 13 and 27, May 11, June 22, July 13, August 10, 1963.

51. Dixon interview, April 24, 2009; MWSA minutes, September 12, 1963, series 1.1, folder 10, SBC; Dixon, *Saints,* 48, 51; *Louisiana Weekly,* August 10 and 31, 1963.

52. Dixon interview, April 24, 2009; Dixon, *Saints,* 48; *Louisiana Weekly,* August 31, 1963.

53. *Times-Picayune,* July 19, August 18 and 30, September 1, 1963; *Louisiana Weekly,* April 6, 1963.

54. *Louisiana Weekly,* August 24, September 7, 1963; *Times-Picayune,* August 15, September 7 and 8, 1963.

55. *Times-Picayune,* September 8, 1963.

56. *Times-Picayune,* September 8, 1963; *Dallas Morning News,* September 8, 1963.

57. *Times-Picayune,* September 8, 1963; Dixon interview, April 24, 2009; MWSA minutes, October 5, 1961.

58. Dixon interview, April 24, 2009; Dixon, *Saints,* 49.

59. Dixon interview, April 24, 2009; Dixon, *Saints,* 49.

60. *Dallas Morning News,* September 8, 1963; *Times-Picayune,* September 7 and 8, 1963.

61. *Times-Picayune,* September 7, 1963.

62. *Times-Picayune,* September 7 and 8, 1963.

63. *Times-Picayune,* September 8, 1963.

64. *Louisiana Weekly,* September 14, 1963.

65. MWSA minutes, September 12, 1963, January 16, 1964, series 1.1, folder 10, SBC; *Times-Picayune,* September 22, 1963.

66. *Sports Illustrated,* December 2, 1963; *Dallas Morning News,* November 26, 1963; *New York Times,* November 23, 1963; *Times-Picayune,* November 22, 1963.

67. *Pittsburgh Courier,* December 28, 1963; Mulé, *Sugar Bowl,* 132; *Times-Picayune,* November 22, 1963.

68. *Times-Picayune,* November 22, 1963; *Washington Post and Times-Herald,* November 23, 1963; *New York Times,* November 23, 1963; Mulé, *Sugar Bowl,* 132–133.

69. *Times-Picayune,* December 1, 1963; *Washington Post and Times-Herald,* December 3, 1963.

70. *Times-Picayune,* November 22, December 2, 1963; *Washington Post and Times-Herald,* November 19, 23, and 27, December 2 and 3, 1963; *Los Angeles Times,* December 11, 1963; *Dallas*

Morning News, November 26, 1963; *Beaver County (PA) Times,* December 26, 2006; *New York Times,* November 25, December 8, 1963.

71. Keith Dunnavant, *The Missing Ring* (New York: Thomas Dunne, 2006), 40–42; *Times-Picayune,* December 10, 1963; *Dallas Morning News,* January 2, 1964.

72. Clifford H. Kern, interview by Mark Cave, November 12, 2007, SBM; MWSA minutes, October 5, 1961, May 8, 1962, series 1.1, folder 8, SBC; Clifford Kern, audiotape, series 5, box 1, SBC.

73. Kern, audiotape; Corenswet interview; *Times-Picayune,* December 31, 1963, January 1, 1964; *New York Times,* January 1, 1964; *Boston Globe,* January 1, 1964; MWSA minutes, January 16, 1964.

74. Corenswet interview; *Dallas Morning News,* January 2, 1964; *Times-Picayune,* January 2, 1964; Kern, audiotape; Kern interview; Mulé, *Sugar Bowl,* 133–134.

75. Kern, audiotape; Kern interview; *Times-Picayune,* January 2, 1964.

76. 1964 Sugar Bowl game tape, series 3.1, folder 33, SBC; Glueck interview; Mulé, *Sugar Bowl,* 133–134; *Louisiana Weekly,* December 7, 1963.

77. *Times-Picayune,* January 2, 1964; Kern, audiotape; Kern interview.

78. Mulé, *Sugar Bowl,* 132–134.

79. *Washington Post and Times-Herald,* January 2, 1964; 1964 Sugar Bowl game tape; *Times-Picayune,* January 2, 1964.

80. *Times-Picayune,* January 2, 1964; 1964 Sugar Bowl game tape.

81. 1964 Sugar Bowl game tape; *Times-Picayune,* January 2, 1964; *Pittsburgh Courier,* January 11, 1964.

82. *Dallas Morning News,* January 2, 1964; *Times-Picayune,* January 2, 1964; *States-Item,* January 2, 1964.

83. *Times-Picayune,* January 2, 1964; Mulé, *Sugar Bowl,* 136.

84. *Pittsburgh Courier,* January 11, 1964.

CHAPTER 6
Check Downs

1. Rogers, *Righteous Lives,* 67–69; *Louisiana Weekly,* April 16, May 7, 1960, August 4–10, 2014.

2. *Louisiana Weekly,* September 17 and 24, 1960; Rogers, *Righteous Lives,* 69–70; *Times-Picayune,* September 13, 1960; Fairclough, *Race and Democracy,* 252; *Chicago Defender,* December 10, 1960.

3. Rogers, *Righteous Lives,* 67–70, 119; Donald E. Devore, *Defying Jim Crow: African American Community Development and the Struggle for Racial Equality in New Orleans, 1900–1960* (Baton Rouge: Louisiana State University Press, 2015), 218–219; Frystak, *Our Minds on Freedom,* 113–114.

4. Rogers, *Righteous Lives,* 67–70; *Louisiana Weekly,* September 17 and 24, 1960; Devore, *Defying Jim Crow,* 219–220; Frystak, *Our Minds on Freedom,* 119–120.

5. Rogers, *Righteous Lives,* 74–75, 85–89.

6. Souther, *New Orleans on Parade,* 85; Rogers, *Righteous Lives,* 74–75, 85–91; *Louisiana Weekly,* September 15, 1962, July 27, 1963.

7. Rogers, *Righteous Lives,* 90; *Louisiana Weekly,* May 11, 1963.

8. *Louisiana Weekly,* August 3 and 10, September 7 and 14, 1963.

9. Rogers, *Righteous Lives*, 91; *Louisiana Weekly*, August 17 and 24, September 21, 1963.

10. Rogers, *Righteous Lives*, 91–92; *Louisiana Weekly*, October 5, 1963.

11. *Louisiana Weekly*, October 5, November 9 and 23, 1963.

12. *Louisiana Weekly*, February 29, 1964; *Chicago Defender*, October 14, 1961; *New Journal and Guide*, February 4, 1961.

13. *Louisiana Weekly*, February 29, March 14, 1964.

14. *Times-Picayune*, February 20, 23, 26, 1964.

15. *Louisiana Weekly*, May 16, 1964.

16. *Louisiana Weekly*, February 15, May 2, 1964; *Dallas Morning News*, February 12, 1964; *Times-Picayune*, February 13, 1964; "As New Orleans Recovers, Will the Dew Drop Inn Swing Again?," NPR *Morning Edition*, August 24, 2015.

17. *Louisiana Weekly*, January 18, June 6, 1964.

18. *Times-Picayune*, July 4, 1964; *New York Times*, July 3, 1964; Haas, *Mayor Victor H. Schiro*, 176–177.

19. *Times-Picayune*, July 4, 1964; *Louisiana Weekly*, July 11, 1964.

20. *Times-Picayune*, July 3 and 4, 1964.

21. *Times-Picayune*, July 7, 1964; *Louisiana Weekly*, July 11, 1964.

22. *Times-Picayune*, July 7, 1964; Haas, *Mayor Victor H. Schiro*, 178–179; Souther, *New Orleans on Parade*, 91; *Chicago Daily Defender*, July 6, 1964.

23. *Times-Picayune*, July 7 and 31, 1964; *Louisiana Weekly*, July 11, September 19, 1964; Souther, *New Orleans on Parade*, 91–92.

24. *Times-Picayune*, July 3, 1964.

25. Haas, *Mayor Victor H. Schiro*, 179–182.

26. Rogers, *Righteous Lives*, 109; *Louisiana Weekly*, November 21, 1964; Souther, *New Orleans on Parade*, 91; *Chicago Daily Defender*, July 6, 1964.

27. *Louisiana Weekly*, June 22, 1963, March 7, July 11 and 18, 1964; *Atlanta Daily World*, March 19, 1964; *Times-Picayune*, July 19 and 31, 1960, June 11, July 19, 1961, July 10, August 7, 1962, July 8, 1963, August 16, 1964.

28. AFL Executive Committee meeting minutes, May 21–22, 1964, AFL minutes, RPC; *Times-Picayune*, February 23, May 22 and 24, July 2 and 13, 1964; *Los Angeles Times*, January 8, 1962; *New York Times*, January 14, 1963, January 20, 1964; *Sports Illustrated*, October 7, 1963; *Dallas Morning News*, November 15, 1963; newspaper clippings, folder 681, DFD.

29. Newspaper clippings, folder 681, DFD; *Times-Picayune*, June 5, 1963, July 2, 1964; Sports Committee outline, September 6, 1963, folder Spr-51, VHS.

30. *Times-Picayune*, February 23, July 17, 1964; newspaper clippings, folder 681, DFD.

31. Dixon, *Saints*, 58–59; *New Orleans Advocate*, February 10, 2018.

32. Dixon, *Saints*, 59–60.

33. Dixon, *Saints*, 60; *Times-Picayune*, August 8 and 10, 1964.

34. *Times-Picayune*, August 9, 10, and 21, 1964; *New Orleans States-Item*, August 12, 1964.

35. *Christian Science Monitor*, July 29, 1964; *Los Angeles Times*, July 25, 1964; *Boston Globe*, July 25, 1964.

36. *New Orleans States-Item*, July 25, 1964; *Times-Picayune*, July 25, 1964; *Christian Science Monitor*, July 29, 1964; *Washington Post and Times-Herald*, July 30, 1964.

37. *Times-Picayune*, August 10, 1964.

38. *Times-Picayune*, August 10 and 11, 1964; newspaper clippings, folder 681, DFD.

39. *Times-Picayune*, August 18, 1964; *New York Times*, June 28, 1964; *Evening Star* (Washington, DC), June 4, 1964; Ivan Allen Jr. and Paul Hemphill, *Mayor: Notes on the Sixties* (New York: Simon and Schuster, 1971), 152–160.

40. *Atlanta Daily World*, April 14, 1964; *Louisiana Weekly*, January 18, 1964.

41. *Louisiana Weekly*, July 18, 1964; *Times-Picayune*, August 10, 15, and 18, 1964; Matt Winkeljohn, *Tales from the Atlanta Falcons Sideline* (New York: Sports Publishing, 2012), 7–13.

42. *Times-Picayune*, August 24 and 31, 1964.

43. *New Orleans States-Item*, August 12, 1964; *Times-Picayune*, August 8, 9, and 10, September 4, 1964; *Sports Illustrated*, September 7, 1964; *Dallas Morning News*, August 8, 1964.

44. *Dallas Morning News*, August 6 and 8, 1964; *Boston Globe*, August 16, 1964; *Chicago Tribune*, August 23, 1964.

45. *Chicago Tribune*, August 29 and 30, 1964; *Times-Picayune*, June 25, September 4, 1964.

46. *Times-Picayune*, August 30 and 31, 1964; *Chicago Tribune*, August 30, 1964; *Dallas Morning News*, August 30, 1964.

47. *Times-Picayune*, August 31, September 3, 1964; *Dallas Morning News*, August 30, 1964.

48. *Times-Picayune*, August 31, 1964.

49. *Times-Picayune*, August 30, 1963, August 31, 1964.

50. *Times-Picayune*, May 18, 1962, August 30, 1963.

51. *Times-Picayune*, August 31, 1964.

52. *Los Angeles Sentinel*, September 10, 1964; *Raleigh Register* (Beckley, WV), September 9, 1964.

53. *Los Angeles Sentinel*, September 10, 1964.

54. *Times-Picayune*, August 24, September 5, 1964; Knights of the Charley Horse banquet program, folder 687, DFD; newspaper clippings, folder 681, DFD; Mayor's Sports Advisory Committee master list, August 19, 1965, folder Spr-51, VHS; Dixon interview, May 5, 2009.

55. *Times-Picayune*, September 9, 1964.

56. *Times-Picayune*, September 5, 1964; *Sports Illustrated*, September 7, 1964; Mohr and Gordon, *Tulane*, 163–180.

57. *Times-Picayune*, September 5 and 7, 1964; newspaper clippings, folder 681, DFD; Dixon interview, May 5, 2009; Dixon, *Saints*, 49.

58. *Times-Picayune*, September 7, 1964.

59. *Times-Picayune*, September 7, 1964.

60. *Sports Illustrated*, September 7, 1964; *Times-Picayune*, April 10, September 5, 1964, January 5, 1965.

61. Milt Woodard to AFL executives, November 17, 1964, AFL memos, RPC; newspaper clippings, folders 681, 687, DFD; *Times-Picayune*, April 10, August 18, 1964; Joe Foss to AFL Executive Committee, March 16, 1964, AFL memos, RPC; AFL Executive Committee meeting minutes, May 21–22, 1964, AFL minutes, RPC.

62. *Sports Illustrated*, September 7, 1964; newspaper clippings, folders 681, 687, DFD; *New Orleans States-Item*, September 16, 1964.

63. *Times-Picayune*, July 11 and 18, 1964.

CHAPTER 7
Stutter Step

1. *Times-Picayune,* October 29, 1964; MWSA minutes, November 5, 1964, series 1.1, folder 10, SBC.

2. MWSA minutes, January 16, April 2, June 11, September 3, 1964, series 1.1, folder 10, SBC; *Times-Picayune,* March 12, October 29, November 22, 1964; Dwayne D. Cox and William J. Morrison, *The University of Louisville* (Lexington: University Press of Kentucky, 2000), 128; *Sports Illustrated,* January 9, 1967.

3. MWSA minutes, September 3, 1964; *Times-Picayune,* December 27, 1964, January 7, 1965; 1965 Sugar Bowl game tape, series 3.1, folder 34, SBC.

4. *Times-Picayune,* December 27, 1964; MWSA minutes, June 11, October 18, 1964, series 1.1, folders 8 and 10, SBC.

5. *Times-Picayune,* December 20, 21, and 27, 1964; MWSA minutes, October 18, 1964; *Louisiana Weekly,* December 26, 1964.

6. Mulé, *Sugar Bowl,* 138; *Times-Picayune,* October 29, November 14, 16, and 23, 1964; MWSA minutes, November 5, 1964; *Dallas Morning News,* November 14, 1964; *Washington Post and Times-Herald,* November 10, 1964.

7. MWSA minutes, December 19, 1964, series 1.1, folder 10, SBC; *Times-Picayune,* November 12, 14, and 23, 1964; Mulé, *Sugar Bowl,* 138; *Washington Post and Times-Herald,* November 10, 1964; *Los Angeles Times,* January 25, 1964.

8. Mulé, *Sugar Bowl,* 138; *Times-Picayune,* November 12, 1964; *Los Angeles Sentinel,* December 3, 1964.

9. *Times-Picayune,* November 14, 15, and 16, 1964; *Washington Post and Times-Herald,* November 18, 1964.

10. *Times-Picayune,* November 21 and 22, 1964; Mulé, *Sugar Bowl,* 138; *Los Angeles Times,* November 22, 1964; MWSA minutes, December 2, 1965, series 1.1, folder 10, SBC.

11. Mulé, *Sugar Bowl,* 138; *Times-Picayune,* November 22, 1964.

12. *Times-Picayune,* November 17 and 22, 1964.

13. *Times-Picayune,* November 22, 1964.

14. *New York Times,* November 25, 1964; *Washington Post and Times-Herald,* November 24, 1964; *Times-Picayune,* November 12, 1964; *Los Angeles Times,* November 22, 1964.

15. *Times-Picayune,* November 23, 1964.

16. *Times-Picayune,* November 23 and 27, 1964.

17. *Times-Picayune,* October 4, 1964; *New York Times,* December 6, 1964; *Washington Post and Times-Herald,* January 1, 1965; *Dallas Morning News,* January 1, 1965.

18. *Washington Post and Times-Herald,* January 1, 1965; *Dallas Morning News,* January 1, 1965; MWSA minutes, March 12, December 7 and 17, 1964, series 1.1, folder 10, SBC.

19. MWSA minutes, December 7, 1964; *Dallas Morning News,* December 27, 1964; *Los Angeles Times,* December 1, 1964; *Times-Picayune,* December 27, 1964; Mulé, *Sugar Bowl,* 140.

20. *Times-Picayune,* December 20, 1964.

21. *Times-Picayune,* December 21, 1964.

22. *Clarion Herald,* January 14, 1965; *Louisiana Weekly,* March 7, 1964; *Times-Picayune,* December 3, 1964.

23. *Times-Picayune,* December 26, 30, and 31, 1964; Glueck interview.

24. *Times-Picayune,* December 31, 1960, December 27, 1961, December 29, 1962, December 27 and 31, 1964.

25. MWSA minutes, January 21, 1965, series 1.1, folder 10, SBC; Mulé, *Sugar Bowl,* 140–141; *Dallas Morning News,* January 2, 1965; *Pittsburgh Courier,* December 19, 1964; *Los Angeles Tribune,* December 26, 1958; *Louisiana Weekly,* December 21, 1957, December 20, 1958, January 7, 1961, December 26, 1964, January 2, 1965.

26. *Louisiana Weekly,* January 9, 1965; 1965 Sugar Bowl program.

27. *Washington Post and Times-Herald,* December 13 and 30, 1964; *Dallas Morning News,* January 1, 1965; *Times-Picayune,* December 22 and 27, 1964, January 1, 1965.

28. *Times-Picayune,* January 2, 1965; *Washington Post and Times-Herald,* January 2, 1965; *Dallas Morning News,* January 2, 1965.

29. 1965 Sugar Bowl game tape; *Washington Post and Times-Herald,* January 2, 1965; Mulé, *Sugar Bowl,* 140–141.

30. 1965 Sugar Bowl game tape; *Times-Picayune,* December 30, 1964, January 2, 1965; Mulé, *Sugar Bowl,* 140–142.

31. 1965 Sugar Bowl game tape; *Times-Picayune,* December 27 and 30, 1964, January 1 and 2, 1965; Mulé, *Sugar Bowl,* 140–142; *Washington Post and Times-Herald,* January 2, 1965.

32. *Times-Picayune,* January 2, 3, and 4, 1965; 1965 Sugar Bowl game tape.

33. *Times-Picayune,* November 19, 1964, January 2 and 3, 1965.

34. *Louisiana Weekly,* January 9, 1965; MWSA minutes, February 11, 1960, June 1, 1961.

35. *Louisiana Weekly,* January 9, 1965.

36. *Louisiana Weekly,* January 9, 1965; Mulé, *Sugar Bowl,* 142; William P. Tolley to Theo Maumus, January 5, 1965, Sugar Bowl histories, series 4.3.1, folder 2, SBC.

37. *Jet,* January 28, 1965; J. Mark Souther, "Into the Big League: Conventions, Football, and the Color Line in New Orleans," *Journal of Urban History* 29, no. 6 (September 2003), 712; *Louisiana Weekly,* January 9, 1965.

38. *Jet,* January 28, 1965; *Louisiana Weekly,* January 9, 1965.

39. *Louisiana Weekly,* January 9, 1965.

40. *Times-Picayune,* January 10, 1965; *New Orleans States-Item,* January 6, 8, and 11, 1965.

41. "National Football League: A Booming Industry"; "Resolution of Appreciation," August 11, 1964, folder 486, DFD; *Times-Picayune,* January 6, 1965.

42. *Times-Picayune,* October 20, December 3 and 16, 1964; *New Orleans States-Item,* November 13, 1964, January 13, 1965.

43. *New York Times,* January 20, 1964; *Washington Post and Times-Herald,* January 12, 1965; *Hartford Courant,* January 13, 1965; *Times-Picayune,* December 30, 1964; *Dallas Morning News,* January 14, 1965.

44. *New Orleans States-Item,* January 11, 1965; *Times-Picayune,* November 26, 1964, January 5 and 10, 1965.

45. *Times-Picayune,* January 6, 1965; Jeff Miller, *Going Long: The Wild 10-Year Saga of the Renegade American Football League in the Words of Those Who Lived It* (Chicago: Contemporary Books, 2003), 155; Milt Woodard to All-Star players, December 15, 1964, AFL memos, RPC; Woodard to AFL, November 17, 1964; *New Orleans States-Item,* July 31, 1964.

CHAPTER 8
Busted Coverage

1. *Santa Cruz Sentinel,* January 28, 1965; newspaper clippings, folder 687, DFD; Miller, *Going Long,* 159.

2. Newspaper clippings, folder 687, DFD.

3. *New Orleans Advocate,* January 12, 2015; Alan Levy, interview by Theresa Moore, June 22, 2010, "Third and Long: The History of African-Americans in Pro Football 1946–1989," T-Time Productions, 2011.

4. *New Orleans Advocate,* January 12, 2015; Bobby Bell, interview by Theresa Moore, October 6, 2010, "Third and Long: The History of African-Americans in Pro Football 1946–1989," T-Time Productions, 2011.

5. Bell interview; Bobby Bell, correspondence with the author, February 2018.

6. Abner Haynes, interview by Theresa Moore, undated transcript, "Third and Long: The History of African-Americans in Pro Football 1946–1989," T-Time Productions, 2011.

7. Willie Brown, interview by Theresa Moore, July 19, 2010, "Third and Long: The History of African-Americans in Pro Football 1946–1989," T-Time Productions, 2011; Milt Woodard to All-Star players, December 15, 1967, AFL memos, RPC.

8. *Santa Cruz Sentinel,* January 28, 1965; *Boston Globe,* January 11, 1965; *Oneonta Star,* January 14, 1965.

9. *New Orleans States-Item,* January 11, 1965; newspaper clippings, folder 687, DFD.

10. *Santa Cruz Sentinel,* January 28, 1965; newspaper clippings, folder 687, DFD.

11. Miller, *Going Long,* 156; *Los Angeles Times,* January 12, 1965.

12. Miller, *Going Long,* 156.

13. *Times-Picayune,* January 11, 1965; *Boston Globe,* January 11, 1965.

14. *Times-Picayune,* January 11, 1965; Todd Tobias, "Dick Westmoreland—November 23, 1998," *Tales from the American Football League,* http://talesfromtheamericanfootballleague.com/afl-interviews.

15. *New Orleans Advocate,* January 12, 2015.

16. Alan H. Levy, *Tackling Jim Crow: Racial Segregation in Professional Football* (Jefferson, NC: McFarland and Company, 2003), 141–142; *Louisiana Weekly,* January 2, 1965; Harry Edwards, interview by Theresa Moore, July 15, 2010, "Third and Long: The History of African-Americans in Pro Football 1946–1989," T-Time Productions, 2011; Levy interview.

17. Westmoreland interview; *Times-Picayune,* January 11, 1965.

18. Miller, *Going Long,* 157.

19. Westmoreland interview.

20. Miller, *Going Long,* 157.

21. Newspaper clippings, folder 687, DFD; Levy, *Tackling Jim Crow,* 141–144; *Times-Picayune,* January 11, 1965.

22. *Santa Cruz Sentinel,* January 28, 1965.

23. Newspaper clippings, folder 687, DFD; Larry Felser, *The Birth of the New NFL: How the 1966 NFL/AFL Merger Transformed Pro Football* (Guilford, CT: Lyons Press, 2008), 100; *New Orleans Advocate,* January 12, 2015.

24. Milt Woodard to All-Star players, December 15, 1964, AFL memos, RPC; *Santa Cruz Sentinel,* January 28, 1965.

25. Miller, *Going Long,* 157–158.

26. *Sports Illustrated,* January 18, 1965.

27. *Sports Illustrated,* January 18, 1965; Bell interview.

28. *Sports Illustrated,* January 18, 1965.

29. *Santa Cruz Sentinel,* January 28, 1965.

30. *Times-Picayune,* January 11, 1965.

31. *Times-Picayune,* January 11, 1965.

32. *Times-Picayune,* January 12 and 13, 1965; Rogers, *Righteous Lives,* 74–75; *New Orleans Advocate,* January 12, 2015; newspaper clippings, folder 687, DFD.

33. *Times-Picayune,* January 11, 1965.

34. *Times-Picayune,* January 11, 1965; Miller, *Going Long,* 159; Levy, *Tackling Jim Crow,* 141–144.

35. McCambridge, *America's Game,* 250; *Times-Picayune,* January 12, 1965; Haas, *Mayor Victor H. Schiro,* 183–185; *Louisiana Weekly,* January 16, 1965; Miller, *Going Long,* 159; *Jet,* January 28, 1965.

36. *Times-Picayune,* January 11, 1965.

37. Levy, *Tackling Jim Crow,* 144; *New Orleans Advocate,* January 12, 2015.

38. *Santa Cruz Sentinel,* January 28, 1965; Miller, *Going Long,* 159.

39. *New Orleans Advocate,* January 12, 2015.

40. *Times-Picayune,* January 11, 1965.

41. *Times-Picayune,* January 11, 1965.

42. *Jet,* January 28, 1965; *Boston Globe,* January 12, 1965; *Times-Picayune,* January 11, 1965; *Washington Post and Times-Herald,* January 11, 1965; *New York Times,* January 11, 1965.

43. *Sports Illustrated,* January 18, 1965; *New Orleans States-Item,* January 7, 1965.

44. Haynes interview; Todd Tobias, "Keith Lincoln—December 9, 1998," *Tales from the American Football League,* http://talesfromtheamericanfootballleague.com/afl-interviews; Miller, *Going Long,* 158–159; *Boston Traveler,* January 11, 1965.

45. Miller, *Going Long,* 160; *Times-Picayune,* January 12, 1965; *Chicago Daily Defender,* January 12, 1965; *Jet,* January 28, 1965.

46. *Times-Picayune,* January 12, 1965; Miller, *Going Long,* 160; *Boston Traveler,* January 11, 1965; Brown interview; Felser, *Birth of the New NFL,* 100–101.

47. *Times-Picayune,* January 13, 1965.

48. *New Orleans States-Item,* January 11, 1965; *Times-Picayune,* January 13, 1965.

49. Newspaper clippings, folder 700, DFD; *New Orleans States-Item,* January 11 and 13, 1965.

50. "Dave Dixon's Sports Revival," WDSU TV and Radio editorial, January 15, 1965, folder 687, DFD; Haas, *Mayor Victor H. Schiro,* 185; newspaper clippings, folder 687, DFD.

51. *Times-Picayune,* January 13, 1965.

52. "Dave Dixon's Sports Revival" editorial; *New Orleans States-Item,* January 11, 1965.

53. Haas, *Mayor Victor H. Schiro,* 185; *Times-Picayune,* January 12, 1965.

54. *Times-Picayune,* January 12, 1965.

55. *Times-Picayune,* January 12, 1965; Miller, *Going Long,* 160.

56. *Times-Picayune,* January 12, 1965; *States-Item,* January 12, 1965; newspaper clippings, folder 710, DFD.

57. *Los Angeles Times,* January 12, 1965; *Washington Post and Times-Herald,* January 12, 1965.

58. *Boston Globe,* January 18, 1965.

59. *Times-Picayune,* January 14, 1965; *Boston Sunday Herald,* January 17, 1965.

60. Newspaper clippings, folder 687, DFD; *St. Louis Globe-Democrat,* January 13, 1965.

61. *Post-Standard* (Syracuse, NY), January 12, 1965; Felser, *Birth of the New NFL,* 101; *New Orleans Advocate,* January 12, 2015.

62. *Sports Illustrated,* January 6, 1964; *Times-Picayune,* January 11, 1965; *Boston Sunday Herald,* January 17, 1965; *Louisiana Weekly,* January 23, 1965; *New Orleans States-Item,* January 12, 1965.

63. *New York Journal American,* January 12, 1965; AFL meeting minutes, January 13–16, 1965, AFL minutes, RPC.

64. AFL meeting minutes, January 13–16, 1965; newspaper clippings, folder 690, DFD; *Hartford Courant,* January 10 and 13, 1965; *Times-Picayune,* January 11, 13, and 15, 1965.

65. AFL meeting minutes, January 13–16, 1965.

66. *New Orleans States-Item,* January 12 and 13, 1965; Brian Marshall, "The Pro Football Career of Cookie Gilchrist," *Coffin Corner* 24, no. 2 (2000); *New York Times,* January 13, 1965.

67. *New York Times,* January 13, 1965; Miller, *Going Long,* 160.

68. *Chicago Daily Defender,* November 29, 1961; *Dallas Morning News,* December 22, 2012; AFL meeting minutes, January 8–10, 1962, AFL minutes, RPC; Charles K. Ross, *Outside the Lines: African Americans and the Integration of the National Football League* (New York: New York University Press, 1999), 144–146.

69. *New Journal and Guide,* June 17, 1961; *Dallas Morning News,* December 22, 2012; *Chicago Daily Defender,* November 29, 1961.

70. Miller, *Going Long,* 153–154; *Los Angeles Sentinel,* November 30, 1961.

71. *Boston Globe,* January 11, 1965; *Louisiana Weekly,* August 25, 1962.

72. *Jet,* January 28, 1965; *Boston Globe,* January 11, 1965.

73. Miller, *Going Long,* 153–154; *Washington Post and Times-Herald,* January 1, 1961.

74. Brown interview; Willie Brown biography, Pro Football Hall of Fame (HOF), Canton, Ohio; Ross, *Outside the Lines,* 144–146; Theresa Moore, dir., *Third and Long,* episode 1 (T-Time Productions, 2011), DVD.

75. *Times-Picayune,* January 17 and 18, 1965; *Chicago Tribune,* January 17, 1965; *Washington Post and Times-Herald,* December 31, 1964.

76. Newspaper clippings, folder 690, DFD; *Times-Picayune,* January 13 and 17, 1965; 1965 AFL All-Star Game program, HOF.

77. *Louisiana Weekly,* January 16, 23, and 30, 1965; Norman C. Francis, interview by author, June 23, 2016.

78. *Louisiana Weekly,* January 16 and 30, February 6, 1965.

79. "Dave Dixon's Sports Revival" editorial.

80. Haas, *Mayor Victor H. Schiro,* 186; *Clarion Herald,* January 14, 1965.

81. *Clarion Herald,* January 14, 1965.

82. *Louisiana Weekly*, January 16, 1965; newspaper clippings, folder 687, DFD.

83. *Times-Picayune*, January 14, 1965; *New Orleans States-Item*, January 13, 1965.

84. *New York Times*, January 12, 1965; *Times-Picayune*, January 12, 1965.

85. *New Orleans States-Item*, January 15, 1965.

86. Souther, *New Orleans on Parade*, 95–96; *Times-Picayune*, January 15, 1965.

87. Souther, *New Orleans on Parade*, 119–120; *Times-Picayune*, December 27, 1964, January 9 and 14, 1965; *Louisiana Weekly*, January 30, 1965.

88. *New Journal and Guide*, January 16, 1965.

89. Allen and Hemphill, *Mayor*, 105, 158–164.

90. *New York Times*, June 6, 1965; *Washington Post and Times-Herald*, June 7, 1965.

91. AFL Executive Committee meeting minutes, June 7–8, 1965, AFL minutes, RPC; *Los Angeles Times*, June 8, 1965.

92. Allen and Hemphill, *Mayor*, 158–164.

93. Allen and Hemphill, *Mayor*, 158–164; *Los Angeles Times*, June 8, 1965.

94. *New York Times*, June 9, 1965; *Los Angeles Times*, June 8, 1965; Allen and Hemphill, *Mayor*, 158–164; *Times-Picayune*, July 1, 1965.

95. *Washington Post and Times-Herald*, June 23, July 1, 1965; *Los Angeles Times*, July 3, 1965.

96. *Times-Picayune*, July 1 and 2, 1965.

97. *New Orleans States-Item*, July 1 and 7, 1965.

98. *Washington Post and Times-Herald*, July 3 and 6, 1965; *New Orleans States-Item*, January 13, 1965.

99. *Sports Illustrated*, August 8, 1966.

CHAPTER 9
Unbeaten and Untied

1. Newspaper clippings, folder 714, DFD; *Washington Post and Times-Herald*, June 22, 1965.

2. *Washington Post and Times-Herald*, June 24, 1965; *Times-Picayune*, January 31, 1965; *News American* (Baltimore), August 15, 1965; *Louisiana Weekly*, May 15, 1965.

3. Stanford Research Institute, "An Evaluation of Seven Candidate Areas for the 16th National Football League Franchise," February 1966, AFL archives, RPC, 186–187; *News American*, August 15, 1965.

4. *Times-Picayune*, June 29, July 14, 1965.

5. *Times-Picayune*, July 9, 12, 13, and 14, 1965.

6. *Louisiana Weekly*, July 31, August 7, 1965.

7. *Louisiana Weekly*, July 24, August 14, 1965; *Times-Picayune*, July 14, August 5, 1965.

8. *Times-Picayune*, August 14, 1965.

9. *Times-Picayune*, August 14, 1965.

10. *Louisiana Weekly*, August 21, 1965; *New Orleans States-Item*, August 17, 1965; *Times-Picayune*, August 15 and 16, 1965.

11. Dixon interview, April 24, 2009; *Times-Picayune*, August 15 and 16, 1965; Dixon, *Saints*, 60.

12. *Times-Picayune,* August 15 and 16, 1965; *New Orleans States-Item,* August 16 and 17, 1965.

13. *Times-Picayune,* August 13 and 15, 1965.

14. *New Orleans States-Item,* August 16, 1965; *Times-Picayune,* August 17, 1965; press release, June 4, 1963, and news release, August 16, 1965, folder Spr-51, VHS; Haas, *Mayor Victor H. Schiro,* 252–253.

15. *Louisiana Weekly,* August 21, 1965; *Times-Picayune,* August 19, 1965.

16. *Times-Picayune,* August 19, 1965; *Louisiana Weekly,* May 15, 1965.

17. *Times-Picayune,* August 19, 1965.

18. *Louisiana Weekly,* August 21, 1965.

19. *New York Times,* August 7, 1965; *Dallas Morning News,* August 8, 1965; *Times-Picayune,* August 10 and 11, 1965.

20. "Voting Rights Act of 1965 Speech and Bill Signing," *American History TV,* C-SPAN, video, https://www.c-span.org/video/?326896-1/voting-rights-act-1965-speech-bill-signing; *Dallas Morning News,* August 7, 1965.

21. *New York Times,* August 7, 1965; *Dallas Morning News,* August 7 and 8, 1965.

22. *Times-Picayune,* August 11, 12, and 26, 1965.

23. *Times-Picayune,* August 12 and 13, 1965; Haas, *Mayor Victor H. Schiro,* 250–251.

24. *Times-Picayune,* August 11, 12, 13, 14, 17, 19, and 26, 1965; Haas, *Mayor Victor H. Schiro,* 250–251; *Louisiana Weekly,* August 21, 1965.

25. *Times-Picayune,* September 2, 1965; *Louisiana Weekly,* September 11, 1965.

26. *Times-Picayune,* September 10, 1965; Haas, *Mayor Victor H. Schiro,* 226–234; *Dallas Morning News,* September 4, 1965.

27. *Dallas Morning News,* September 11 and 12, 1965; *Times-Picayune,* September 11 and 12, 1965; Haas, *Mayor Victor H. Schiro,* 226–230; *Advocate* (Baton Rouge, LA), September 13, 2015; *Los Angeles Times,* September 16, 1965.

28. Haas, *Mayor Victor H. Schiro,* 225–245; *Times-Picayune,* September 11 and 12, 1965; *Los Angeles Times,* September 16, 1965; *Advocate,* September 13, 2015.

29. Haas, *Mayor Victor H. Schiro,* 242; *Louisiana Weekly,* October 23, 1965.

30. *Louisiana Weekly,* October 30, 1965, January 1, 1966.

31. *Louisiana Weekly,* October 23, November 6 and 27, 1965.

32. *Louisiana Weekly,* September 11, October 16 and 23, 1965; Haas, *Mayor Victor H. Schiro,* 256–259.

33. *Louisiana Weekly,* October 9, 16, and 23, November 6, 1965; Haas, *Mayor Victor H. Schiro,* 256–259.

34. Haas, *Mayor Victor H. Schiro,* 260–261.

35. Haas, *Mayor Victor H. Schiro,* 262; Dixon, *Saints,* 87–88.

36. *Times-Picayune,* November 5, 1965; *Louisiana Weekly,* November 13, 1965; Haas, *Mayor Victor H. Schiro,* 262–264; Dixon, *Saints,* 83–88, 91.

37. *Louisiana Weekly,* November 20, 1965; Haas, *Mayor Victor H. Schiro,* 262–264; newspaper clippings, folder 714, DFD; Dixon, *Saints,* 87–88; *Times-Picayune,* November 16, 1965.

38. *Louisiana Weekly,* October 16, 23, and 30, November 6, 1965; *Times-Picayune,* October 23 and 26, 1965.

39. Mulé, *Sugar Bowl,* 144–145; Dunnavant, *Missing Ring,* 97.

40. *Dallas Morning News,* November 15, 1965; MWSA minutes, February 11, April 1, May 13, 1965, series 1.1, folder 10, SBC; Mulé, *Sugar Bowl,* 144–145; *Times-Picayune,* November 2, 4, and 8, 1965.

41. *Times-Picayune,* November 7, 14, and 18, 1965; MWSA minutes, April 1, December 2, 1965, February 10, 1966, series 1.1, folder 10, SBC.

42. *Times-Picayune,* November 2, 7, and 11, 1965; Mulé, *Sugar Bowl,* 144–145; newspaper clippings, folder 714, DFD.

43. Mulé, *Sugar Bowl,* 144–145; Dunnavant, *Missing Ring,* 97; *Washington Post and Times-Herald,* November 11 and 24, 1965; *Boston Globe,* November 16, 1965; *Times-Picayune,* November 10, 1965; *Dallas Morning News,* November 16, 1965.

44. *Times-Picayune,* November 12 and 14, 1965.

45. *Washington Post and Times-Herald,* November 15, 1965; Mulé, *Sugar Bowl,* 144–145; *Times-Picayune,* November 15 and 17, 1965; *Dallas Morning News,* November 15, 1965.

46. *Times-Picayune,* November 20, 21, and 22, 1965.

47. *Times-Picayune,* November 21 and 22, 1965; MWSA minutes, December 2, 1965.

48. *Times-Picayune,* November 21 and 22, 1965; *Boston Globe,* January 1, 1966; Mulé, *Sugar Bowl,* 148.

49. MWSA minutes, December 2, 1965, February 10, 1966, series 1.1, folder 10, SBC; *Times-Picayune,* November 18 and 29, 1965, January 3, 1966.

50. *Louisiana Weekly,* January 8, 1966; *Dallas Morning News,* January 2, 1966; *Times-Picayune,* January 2, 1966; *New York Times,* January 2, 1966; Mulé, *Sugar Bowl,* 144–148.

51. *Dallas Morning News,* January 2, 1966; *New York Times,* January 2, 1966; Mulé, *Sugar Bowl,* 144–148; 1966 Sugar Bowl game tape, series 3.1, folder 35, SBC.

52. *Dallas Morning News,* January 2, 1966; *Times-Picayune,* January 2 and 3, 1966.

53. Mulé, *Sugar Bowl,* 148; newspaper clippings, folder 714, DFD; *Boston Globe,* January 1, 1966; *Sports Illustrated,* January 3 and 10, 1966.

54. Todd Tobias, "Ernie Wright—November 13, 1998" and "Ernie Wright—January 13, 2003," *Tales from the American Football League,* http://talesfromtheamericanfootballleague.com/afl-interviews; *New Journal and Guide,* January 15, 1966.

55. *Times-Picayune,* January 29, 1966.

56. David M. Kleck and New Orleans Pro Football Club, *New Orleans, Strategic City of the Gulf South: A Pictorial–Statistical Presentation to the National Football League* (S.I.: s.n, 1965).

57. *Washington Post and Times-Herald,* December 15, 1965; *Chicago Tribune,* December 15, 1965.

58. *Wall Street Journal,* December 30, 1965; *Times-Picayune,* December 28, 1965, January 10, 1966; *Chicago Tribune,* December 23, 1965; *Louisiana Weekly,* January 8, 1966.

59. *Washington Post and Times-Herald,* January 10, 1963, December 15, 1965; *Chicago Tribune,* December 15 and 23, 1965; *Times-Picayune,* December 28, 1965, January 10, 11, 12, and 18, 1966; *Wall Street Journal,* December 30, 1965; *Louisiana Weekly,* January 8, 1966.

60. *Louisiana Weekly,* January 29, 1966; newspaper clippings, folder 714, DFD; *Times-Picayune,* November 5, December 28, 1965, January 12 and 13, 1966; Haas, *Mayor Victor H. Schiro,* 300–302; Kleck and New Orleans Pro Football Club, *New Orleans.*

61. *Times-Picayune,* December 30, 1965, January 13, 1966; Haas, *Mayor Victor H. Schiro,* 300–302.

62. *Times-Picayune*, January 13 and 14, 1966; Haas, *Mayor Victor H. Schiro*, 300–302.

63. *Times-Picayune*, January 14, 18, and 28, February 1 and 3, 1966; Haas, *Mayor Victor H. Schiro*, 302.

64. *Times-Picayune*, February 3, November 7, 1966; MWSA minutes, January 20, February 10, 1966, series 1.1, folder 10, SBC.

65. *Louisiana Weekly*, February 12, 1966.

66. *Sports Illustrated*, February 21, 1966; *New York Times*, January 16, 1966; *Times-Picayune*, January 24 and 31, 1966.

67. *Louisiana Weekly*, January 1, 1966; *Times-Picayune*, June 20 and 27, 1963, December 28, 1965; Haas, *Mayor Victor H. Schiro*, 265–266; *Louisiana Weekly*, July 6, 1963; Francis interview; Rachel Lorraine Emmanuel, *A More Noble Cause: A. P. Tureaud and the Struggle for Civil Rights in Louisiana* (Baton Rouge: Louisiana State University Press, 2011), 56, 124.

68. *Louisiana Weekly*, January 1, 1966.

69. *Louisiana Weekly*, February 8 and 15, 1958, February 18, 1961, October 12, 1963, March 5, 1966.

70. *Times-Picayune*, March 17, 18, and 21, 1966; Haas, *Mayor Victor H. Schiro*, 265–266.

71. *Louisiana Weekly*, March 5, April 9, 1966; Haas, *Mayor Victor H. Schiro*, 265–266.

72. *Times-Picayune*, May 3, 1966.

73. Francis interview; *Times-Picayune*, May 19, 1966.

74. Francis interview; Stanford Research Institute, "An Evaluation."

75. *Times-Picayune*, May 18 and 19, 1966; *Louisiana Weekly*, May 28, 1966; *New Orleans States-Item*, May 19, 1966.

76. *Times-Picayune*, March 15, April 24, 1966; *Washington Post and Times-Herald*, May 14, 1966; *New York Times*, August 16, 1965; *Los Angeles Times*, June 6, 1965.

77. *Sports Illustrated*, February 28, 1966; *Washington Post and Times-Herald*, May 19, 1966; *Times-Picayune*, May 18, 1966.

78. Francis interview; *Louisiana Weekly*, May 28, 1966.

79. Francis interview; *Louisiana Weekly*, May 28, 1966.

80. *Post and Time Star* (Cincinnati), May 19, 1966.

81. *Evening Star*, May 19, 1966.

82. *Times-Picayune*, May 19, 1966.

83. *Louisiana Weekly*, June 4, August 13, 1966; *Times-Picayune*, May 13 and 31, 1966; Haas, *Mayor Victor H. Schiro*, 266; *Dallas Morning News*, February 13, 1966.

84. *Louisiana Weekly*, November 27, 1965, March 5, June 11, 1966; *Times-Picayune*, July 21, 1966.

85. *Louisiana Weekly*, March 7, 1964, May 14, June 4, 1966; *Atlanta Daily World*, March 19, 1964; *Times-Picayune*, June 12, 13, and 14, 1966.

86. *Louisiana Weekly*, May 14, 1966.

87. *Times-Picayune*, May 13 and 26, June 12 and 14, 1966; *Louisiana Weekly*, June 4, 1966, July 29, 1967.

88. *Louisiana Weekly*, April 23, July 9, 1966; *Times-Picayune*, July 1, 1966.

89. *Louisiana Weekly*, July 23, August 6, 13, and 20, 1966; *Times-Picayune*, August 3, 4, 5, 6, 7, 8, and 15, 1966.

90. *Louisiana Weekly,* August 13, 1966; *Times-Picayune,* August 10, 11, 12, 13, and 15, 1966.

91. *Louisiana Weekly,* August 20, 1966; *Times-Picayune,* August 14 and 15, 1966.

CHAPTER 10
Running Out the Clock

1. *New York Times,* October 7, 1966; *Washington Post and Times-Herald,* October 7, 1966; *Chicago Tribune,* October 7, 1966; *Professional Football League Merger: Hearings on S. 3817 Before the Antitrust Subcommittee of the House Committee on the Judiciary, 89th Cong., 2d Sess. 37 (1966).*

2. MacCambridge, *America's Game,* 220–223; Miller, *Going Long,* 163–175, 191, 197–200; *Times-Picayune,* June 9, 1966.

3. Felser, *Birth of the New NFL,* 54; Alex Marvez, "Joe Namath Almost a Cardinal?," *Fox Sports,* April 23, 2015, https://www.foxsports.com/stories/nfl/joe-namath-almost-a-cardinal-50-years-later-the-nfl-afl-draft-wars-that-birthed-a-league; Miller, *Going Long,* 172, 189; *Times-Picayune,* June 9, 1966; *Sports Illustrated,* May 31, September 13, 1965.

4. MacCambridge, *America's Game,* 221; "Why Do Pro Kickers Opt for Soccer Style?," *Scientific American,* November 8, 2010, https://www.scientificamerican.com/article/football-why-do-pro-kickers-use-soccer; Felser, *Birth of the New NFL,* 51; Doug Williams, "How European Soccer-Style Kickers Started A Revolution 50 Years Ago," ABC News, October 12, 2016, https://abcnews.go.com/Sports/european-soccer-style-kickers-started-revolution-50-years/story?id=42756874; Miller, *Going Long,* 197.

5. Miller, *Going Long,* 197–201.

6. Miller, *Going Long,* 189–205; MacCambridge, *America's Game,* 216–228.

7. *Times-Picayune,* June 9, 1966; MacCambridge, *America's Game,* 227–228; *Washington Post and Times-Herald,* October 7, 1966; *Chicago Tribune,* October 7, 1966.

8. Dixon to Boggs, January 19, 1962; Dixon to Poitevent, February 3, 1962; *Louisiana Weekly,* January 16, 1965; *Times-Picayune,* January 5, 1965.

9. *Washington Post and Times-Herald,* September 9, 23, and 27, October 7, 1966; *Chicago Daily Defender,* September 15 and 27, 1966; *Professional Football League Merger hearings.*

10. *Washington Post and Times-Herald,* October 7, 1966.

11. *Washington Post and Times-Herald,* October 7, 1966; Jerold J. Duquette, *Regulating the National Pastime* (Westport, CT: Praeger, 1999), 52; *New York Times,* October 14, 1966; *Chicago Tribune,* October 7, 14, and 21, 1966; M. Martin, "New Orleans Becomes a Big League City," 114.

12. *Washington Post and Times-Herald,* October 7 and 15, 1966; *Professional Football League Merger hearings.*

13. *New York Times,* October 21, 1966; *Washington Post and Times-Herald,* October 7, 1966.

14. *Professional Football League Merger hearings.*

15. *Professional Football League Merger hearings.*

16. *Boston Globe,* October 14, 1966; *New York Times,* October 14, 1966.

17. *New York Times,* October 15 and 21, 1966; *Washington Post and Times-Herald,* October 15, 1966; *Chicago Tribune,* October 18 and 21, 1966.

18. *Chicago Tribune,* October 18, 1966.

19. *New York Times,* October 21, 1966; *Chicago Tribune,* October 18 and 22, 1966.

20. MacCambridge, *America's Game,* 229; Dixon interview, April 24, 2009; Dixon, *Saints,* 69–70; Peter Finney Jr., "The Story of New Orleans Being Awarded the Saints," *New Orleans Saints,* November 1, 2016, http://www.NewOrleansSaints.com/news/the-story-of-new-orleans-being-awarded-the-saints-17995409.

21. *Chicago Tribune,* October 21, 1966; *Boston Globe,* October 21, 1966.

22. *Times-Picayune,* October 26, 1966; *Louisiana Weekly,* October 29, 1966; *New York Times,* October 21, 1966; *Chicago Tribune,* October 21, 1966; *New Orleans States-Item,* June 9, 1966.

23. *Times-Picayune,* October 26, 1966; *Louisiana Weekly,* November 5, 1966; Devore, *Defying Jim Crow,* 202–204.

24. *Times-Picayune,* October 26, 1966; Edwards interview; Dixon interview, April 24, 2009.

25. Dixon interview, April 24, 2009; *New York Times,* September 20, 1983.

26. Dixon interview, April 24, 2009; Dixon, *Saints,* 61–63; *Times-Picayune,* October 26, 1966.

27. *Times-Picayune,* November 2, 1966.

28. *Times-Picayune,* November 2, 1966; David Dixon interview, April 24, 2009; Dixon, *Saints,* 71.

29. Dixon interview, April 24, 2009; Dixon, *Saints,* 71–73; *Louisiana Weekly,* November 5 and 19, 1966; United States House of Representatives, "Majority Whip Hale Boggs' Support of the Voting Rights Act of 1965," History, Art & Archives, https://history.house.gov/historicalhighlight/detail/36267; *Afro-American,* July 17, 1965; Cokie Roberts, "The Voting Rights Act of 1965," interview, June 23, 2009, History, Art & Archives, https://history.house.gov/oral-history/events/civil-rights/vra65; *Times-Picayune,* November 2, 1966.

30. *Chicago Tribune,* November 2, 1966; *Times-Picayune,* November 2, 1966.

31. *Times-Picayune,* November 2, 1966.

32. *Times-Picayune,* November 2, 1966; *Cincinnati Enquirer,* November 2, 1966; *Louisiana Weekly,* October 1, November 5, 1966; Dixon interview, May 5, 2009.

33. *Times-Picayune,* November 1, 6, and 7, 1966; *Louisiana Weekly,* November 5, 1966; Dixon interview, May 5, 2009.

34. *Times-Picayune,* November 3, 1966.

35. *Times-Picayune,* October 9 and 13, November 3 and 9, 1966; *Louisiana Weekly,* October 29, November 19, 1966; Kurtz and Peoples, *Earl K. Long,* 204.

36. *Louisiana Weekly,* November 12 and 19, 1966; *Times-Picayune,* November 9, 1966; Dixon interview, May 5, 2009.

37. Dixon, *Saints,* 77–78; *Times-Picayune,* November 3, December 16, 1966; Dixon interviews, April 24 and May 5, 2009; *Aspen Times,* October 14, 2008.

38. *Times-Picayune,* November 19, 29, and 30, 1966.

39. *Times-Picayune,* December 2, 3, and 8, 1966.

40. *Times-Picayune,* November 3, December 9 and 17, 1966; *Christian Science Monitor,* September 13, 1945.

41. *Times-Picayune,* November 18, December 9, 1966; Dixon, *Saints,* 76; *Dallas Morning News,* December 16, 1966.

42. *Times-Picayune,* November 3 and 18, 1966; Haas, *Mayor Victor H. Schiro,* 86, 167, 177–178, 204, 284.

43. *Times-Picayune,* November 3, December 8, 9, and 17, 1966.

44. *Washington Post and Times-Herald,* December 16, 1966; *New York Times,* December 16, 1966; Dixon interview, April 24, 2009; Dixon interview, May 5, 2009; Dixon, *Saints,* 75–80; *Times-Picayune,* December 9 and 16, 1966; *Dallas Morning News,* December 16, 1966.

45. *Times-Picayune,* December 16, 17, and 18, 1966; "NFL New Orleans Ownership," New Orleans History file, RPC.

46. Francis interview; *Los Angeles Sentinel,* December 22, 1966; Haas, *Mayor Victor H. Schiro,* 305; *New York Times,* December 18, 1966.

47. *Times-Picayune,* December 16 and 17, 1966.

48. *New York Times,* December 18, 1966.

49. *Milwaukee Journal,* November 2, 1966.

50. *New York Times,* November 2, 1966.

51. *Times-Picayune,* November 21 and 22, 1966; MWSA minutes, December 8, 1966, series 1.1, folder 10, SBC.

52. *Sports Illustrated,* January 2, 1967; *Times-Picayune,* November 22, 1966; Mulé, *Sugar Bowl,* 148; *Dallas Morning News,* November 22, 1966.

53. *Times-Picayune,* November 4, 8, 14, 18, 21, and 23, 1966; *Louisiana Weekly,* September 17, 1966.

54. *Times-Picayune,* November 14, 21, 22, and 23, 1966; *Dallas Morning News,* November 22, 1966.

55. Mulé, *Sugar Bowl,* 148; *Times-Picayune,* November 27, 28, and 30, December 3, 1966; *Dallas Morning News,* November 24, 1966.

56. *Times-Picayune,* November 28, 1966.

57. *Times-Picayune,* November 28, 1966; *Dallas Morning News,* November 29, December 4, 1966; *Chicago Tribune,* January 1, 1967; Dunnavant, *Missing Ring,* 258.

58. *Sports Illustrated,* January 2 and 9, 1967; Dunnavant, *Missing Ring,* 256–258.

59. Dunnavant, *Missing Ring,* 256–258; *Chicago Tribune,* January 1, 1967; *Times-Picayune,* November 22, December 14, 27, and 28, 1966.

60. *Times-Picayune,* November 15, 1966, January 3, 1967.

61. *Times-Picayune,* January 3, 1967; *Dallas Morning News,* January 3, 1967; Mulé, *Sugar Bowl,* 149.

62. *Chicago Tribune,* January 2 and 3, 1967; Mulé, *Sugar Bowl,* 149–152.

63. *Chicago Tribune,* January 3, 1967; Mulé, *Sugar Bowl,* 149–152; *Times-Picayune,* November 28, 1966, January 3, 1967.

64. *Sports Illustrated,* January 9, 1967.

65. Dunnavant, *Missing Ring,* 268.

CHAPTER 11
Open Field

1. Dixon, *Saints,* 73–74; *Times-Picayune,* January 6, 14, and 15, 1967; John Mecom Jr., interview by Mark Cave, August 16, 2012, NOLS.

2. *Times-Picayune,* January 11 and 28, July 21, 1967; *Dallas Morning News,* January 28, 1967; *Sports Illustrated,* December 9, 1968.

3. *Sports Illustrated*, August 14, 1967; *New York Times*, February 11, 1967; *Washington Post and Times-Herald*, February 9, 1967; *Chicago Daily Defender*, February 7, 1967; *Dallas Morning News*, February 9, 1967; *Times-Picayune*, February 7 and 11, 1967.

4. *Times-Picayune*, February 11, 1967; *Chicago Tribune*, February 11, 1967; *Washington Post and Times-Herald*, February 11, 1967; *New York Times*, February 11, 1967.

5. *Sports Illustrated*, August 14, 1967; *Times-Picayune*, March 18, 1967; *Dallas Morning News*, March 7, 1967.

6. *Times-Picayune*, March 7, 14, 18, and 19, 1967.

7. *Sports Illustrated*, August 14, 1967; *Times-Picayune*, May 24, July 9, 1967.

8. *Times-Picayune*, March 8 and 9, 1967.

9. *Times-Picayune*, March 9, April 19, 1967; *Louisiana Weekly*, August 26, 1967.

10. *Times-Picayune*, March 14, 15, 16, and 17, 1967; *Chicago Daily Defender*, March 9, 1967; *Dallas Morning News*, March 10, 1967.

11. *Times-Picayune*, March 9, 14, and 17, July 9, 1967.

12. *Times-Picayune*, April 12, 1966, January 20, 25, and 29, February 3, March 16, April 3, 1967; *Louisiana Weekly*, April 8, 1967.

13. *Times-Picayune*, November 2, 1966, April 2, 1967; *Louisiana Weekly*, November 5, 1966, March 25, April 8, 1967; *Los Angeles Times*, February 23, 1967.

14. *Louisiana Weekly*, June 17 and 24, 1967; *Times-Picayune*, May 18, June 9, 10, 11, 14, and 15, 1967.

15. *Times-Picayune*, June 24, July 1, 1967; *Sports Illustrated*, August 14, 1967.

16. *Times-Picayune*, July 7, 1967; *Dallas Morning News*, July 7, 1967; Jimmy Taylor, conversation with the author, December 2, 2017.

17. *Times-Picayune*, July 7, 1967.

18. *Sports Illustrated*, August 14, 1967; *Times-Picayune*, July 29, 1967.

19. *Sports Illustrated*, August 14, 1967.

20. *Times-Picayune*, July 15 and 21, August 16, 1967; *Sports Illustrated*, December 9, 1968.

21. *Times-Picayune*, June 24, July 8, 1967; *Los Angeles Sentinel*, December 22, 1966; *New York Times*, December 18, 1966; *Louisiana Weekly*, June 4, 1966.

22. *Atlanta Daily World*, January 30, 1968; *Call and Post*, September 23, 1967; *Times-Picayune*, February 11, March 16, September 12, 1967; *Louisiana Weekly*, May 13, 1967; *Dallas Morning News*, July 7, 1967.

23. *Times-Picayune*, March 21, 1967; MacCambridge, *America's Game*, 196; *Louisiana Weekly*, December 10, 1966, August 5, 1967; *Los Angeles Sentinel*, August 10, 1967.

24. *Times-Picayune*, November 19, 1967, September 10, 1968; *New Pittsburgh Courier*, August 12, 1967.

25. *Louisiana Weekly*, July 22 and 29, 1967, January 20 and 27, February 3, 1968.

26. *Atlanta Daily World*, January 30, 1968.

27. *Times-Picayune*, July 11, 1967; *Louisiana Weekly*, July 29, 1967.

28. *Sporting News*, December 23, 1967; *Times-Picayune*, July 21, September 10, 1967; *Sports Illustrated*, August 14, 1967.

29. Jeff Duncan, "Arrival of Saints Heralded 'Sea Change' for City of New Orleans in 1960s," NOLA.com, June 1, 2016.

30. *Sports Illustrated*, August 14, 1967.

31. *Times-Picayune,* July 30, August 6 and 13, 1967; *Louisiana Weekly,* August 12, September 9, 1967; *Dallas Morning News,* August 13 and 20, 1967.

32. *Times-Picayune,* September 4 and 5, 1967; Duncan, "Arrival of Saints."

33. *Times-Picayune,* August 28 and 29, September 5 and 8, 1967.

34. *Times-Picayune,* September 2, 4, and 5, 1967.

35. Duncan, "Arrival of Saints"; *Times-Picayune,* September 6, 1967.

36. *Sports Illustrated,* August 14, 1967; *Times-Picayune,* September 10, 1967.

37. *Times-Picayune,* September 10, 1967; newspaper clippings, New Orleans History file, RPC.

38. *Times-Picayune,* September 10, 1967; *Louisiana Weekly,* September 16, 1967.

39. George Becnel, *When the Saints Came Marching In* (Bloomington, IN: AuthorHouse, 2009), 21, 34; *Times-Picayune,* September 5, 1967; *Los Angeles Times,* September 18, 1967.

40. *Times-Picayune,* September 10 and 11, 1967.

41. *Times-Picayune,* September 5, 10, and 11, 1967; *Louisiana Weekly,* September 16, 1967; *Dallas Morning News,* August 20, 1967.

42. *Times-Picayune,* September 9, 11, and 13, 1967.

43. *Times-Picayune,* September 13, 1967; Duncan, "Arrival of Saints."

44. Dixon interview, April 24, 2009.

45. *Times-Picayune,* September 18, 1967; Dixon interview, April 24, 2009; Francis interview; Becnel, *When the Saints,* 35.

46. *New York Times,* September 18, 1967; *Times-Picayune,* September 18, 1967.

47. *Times-Picayune,* September 18, 1967; Becnel, *When the Saints,* 35–36; "Saints Legends Profile: John Gilliam," video, NewOrleansSaints.com/video/saints-legends-profile-john-gilliam-17654933.

48. Dixon interview, April 24, 2009; Dixon, *Saints,* 81; "Saints Legends Profile"; *Los Angeles Times,* September 18, 1967; *Times-Picayune,* September 18, 1967; newspaper clippings, New Orleans History file, RPC.

49. Dixon, *Saints,* 80–81; Dixon interview, April 24, 2009.

50. Duncan, "Arrival of Saints."

51. *Times-Picayune,* September 18, 1967; Becnel, *When the Saints,* 35–36; *Los Angeles Times,* September 18, 1967; *Dallas Morning News,* September 18, 1967.

52. *Times-Picayune,* September 18, 1967; *New York Times,* September 18, 1967; Duncan, "Arrival of Saints."

53. *Times-Picayune,* September 11 and 18, 1967; Becnel, *When the Saints,* 35–36; *Los Angeles Times,* September 18, 1967; *Dallas Morning News,* September 18, 1967.

54. *Times-Picayune,* September 18 and 19, 1967.

55. *Times-Picayune,* September 10 and 11, 1967; Becnel, *When the Saints,* 26, 33; *Sports Illustrated,* August 14, 1967.

56. *Dallas Morning News,* September 25, 1967; *Times-Picayune,* September 25, 1967; Becnel, *When the Saints,* 37–38.

57. *Dallas Morning News,* October 2, 1967; *Times-Picayune,* October 2, 1967; Becnel, *When the Saints,* 38–39.

58. *Dallas Morning News,* October 9, 16, and 23, 1967.

59. *Dallas Morning News,* October 30, 1967; Becnel, *When the Saints,* 43–44.

60. Becnel, *When the Saints*, 44–46; *Sporting News*, December 23, 1967; *Times-Picayune*, November 6, 1967; *Dallas Morning News*, November 6, 1967.

61. *Dallas Morning News*, November 13, 1967; *Times-Picayune*, November 13, 1967; Becnel, *When the Saints*, 46–47; *Sporting News*, December 23, 1967.

62. *Times-Picayune*, November 13, 1967; *Dallas Morning News*, November 13, 1967; *Washington Post and Times-Herald*, November 13, 1967; *New York Times*, November 13, 1967.

63. *Dallas Morning News*, November 13, 1967.

64. *Louisiana Weekly*, November 5, 1966; *Times-Picayune*, November 1 and 9, 1966.

65. *Louisiana Weekly*, June 3 and 10, August 5, 1967; *Times-Picayune*, May 25 and 28, June 6, 1967.

66. *Times-Picayune*, July 28, August 15, September 8 and 22, 1967; *Louisiana Weekly*, August 19, September 30, 1967.

67. *Louisiana Weekly*, May 22, 1965, November 11 and 18, 1967; Haas, *Mayor Victor H. Schiro*, 268–269; *Times-Picayune*, November 6, 1967.

68. *Times-Picayune*, November 4, 6, and 7, 1967; *Louisiana Weekly*, November 11, 1967.

69. *Philadelphia Tribune*, November 18, 1967; Becnel, *When the Saints*, 47.

70. *Times-Picayune*, November 27, 1967; *Sporting News*, December 23, 1967; *Los Angeles Herald-Examiner*, November 29, 1967.

71. *Times-Picayune*, November 26 and 27, 1967; *Louisiana Weekly*, December 2, 1967; Becnel, *When the Saints*, 47–48.

72. *Times-Picayune*, November 25, 26, and 27, 1967; *Louisiana Weekly*, December 2, 1967; *Sporting News*, December 23, 1967.

73. *Louisiana Weekly*, November 12, 1966; Elizabeth Booksh Burns, "When the Saints Went Marching In: Social Identity in the World Champion New Orleans Saints Football Team and Its Impact on Their Host City," in *New Orleans Sports: Playing Hard in the Big Easy*, ed. Thomas Aiello (Fayetteville: University of Arkansas Press, 2019), 242, 244, 554.

74. *Times-Picayune*, November 27, 1967; *Louisiana Weekly*, December 2, 1967; *Sporting News*, December 23, 1967.

BIBLIOGRAPHY

Manuscript Collections

Amistad Research Center, Tulane University, New Orleans, LA
    Dent Family Papers
    Ernest "Dutch" Morial Papers
City Archives, New Orleans Public Library, New Orleans, LA
    Victor H. Schiro Records
City Park Improvement Association, City Park, New Orleans, LA
    Board Minutes Archives
Earl K. Long Library, University of New Orleans, New Orleans, LA
    NAACP Collection
Georgia Institute of Technology Archives, Atlanta, GA
    1955 Sugar Bowl Vertical File
    Digital Portal
    George C. Griffin Papers
The Historic New Orleans Collection, New Orleans, LA
    David F. Dixon Papers
    New Orleans Life Story Project
    Sugar Bowl Collection
    Sugar Bowl Memories Project
Manuscript Division, Library of Congress, Washington, DC
    Jack Kemp Papers
Pro Football Hall of Fame, Canton, OH
Ralph Wilson Jr. Research and Preservation Center, Canton, OH
United States House of Representatives, Washington, DC
    History, Art & Archives (website)

Interviews

Bell, Bobby. Correspondence with author, February 2018.
Bell, Bobby. Interview by Theresa Moore, October 6, 2010. "Third and Long: The

History of African-Americans in Pro Football 1946–1989," T-Time Productions, 2011.

Bodenheimer, Henry. Interview by Mark Cave, October 30, 2007. Sugar Bowl Memories Oral History Project, Historic New Orleans Collection.

Bridges, Ruby. Guest lecture, Brigham Young University, November 19, 2015.

Brown, Willie. Interview by Theresa Moore, July 19, 2010. "Third and Long: The History of African-Americans in Pro Football 1946–1989," T-Time Productions, 2011.

Corenswet, Sam, Jr. Interview by Mark Cave, July 26, 2007. Sugar Bowl Memories Oral History Project, Historic New Orleans Collection.

Dixon, David. Interviews by Mark Cave, April 24 and May 5, 2009. Sugar Bowl Memories Oral History Project, Historic New Orleans Collection.

Ecker, Allen. Interview by author, March 10, 2014.

Edwards, Harry. Interview by Theresa Moore, July 15, 2010. "Third and Long: The History of African-Americans in Pro Football 1946–1989," T-Time Productions, 2011.

Francis, Norman C. Interview by author, June 23, 2016.

Glueck, Charles. Interview by Mark Cave, October 25, 2007. Sugar Bowl Memories Oral History Project, Historic New Orleans Collection.

Grier, Bobby. Interview by Mark Cave, June 18–24, 2014. Sugar Bowl Memories Oral History Project, Historic New Orleans Collection.

Haynes, Abner. Interview by Theresa Moore, transcript undated. "Third and Long: The History of African-Americans in Pro Football 1946–1989," T-Time Productions, 2011.

Kern, Clifford H. Interview by Mark Cave, November 12, 2007. Sugar Bowl Memories Oral History Project, Historic New Orleans Collection.

Levy, Alan. Interview by Theresa Moore, June 22, 2010. "Third and Long: The History of African-Americans in Pro Football 1946–1989," T-Time Productions, 2011.

Lincoln, Keith. Interview by Todd Tobias, December 9, 1998. *Tales from the American Football League,* http://talesfromtheamericanfootballleague.com/afl-interviews.

Mecom, John, Jr. Interview by Mark Cave, August 16, 2012. Sugar Bowl Memories Oral History Project, Historic New Orleans Collection.

Mitchell, Wade. Interview by author, March 10, 2014.

Mix, Ron. Interview by Theresa Moore, July 15, 2010. "Third and Long: The History of African-Americans in Pro Football 1946–1989," T-Time Productions, 2011.

Taylor, Jimmy. Conversation with author, December 2, 2017.

Vereen, Carl. Interview by author, March 10, 2014.

Westmoreland, Dick. Interview by Todd Tobias, November 23, 1998. *Tales from the*

American Football League, http://talesfromtheamericanfootballleague.com/afl-interviews.

Wright, Ernie. Interviews by Todd Tobias, November 13, 1998, and January 13, 2003. *Tales from the American Football League,* http://talesfromtheamericanfootballleague.com/afl-interviews.

Zurich, Samuel. Interview by Mark Cave, October 2, 2008. Sugar Bowl Memories Oral History Project, Historic New Orleans Collection.

Newspapers and Magazines

Advocate (Baton Rouge, LA) (2015)
Afro-American (Baltimore, MD) (1956–1965)
Arkansas State Press (1956–1957)
Aspen Times (2008)
Atlanta Constitution (1898–1956)
Atlanta Daily World (1955–1968)
Atlanta Journal (1955)
Beaver County (PA) Times (2006)
Boston Globe (1960–1966)
Boston Sunday Herald (1965)
Boston Traveler (1965)
Call and Post (Cleveland, OH) (1963–1967)
Chicago Daily Defender (1960–1967)
Chicago Daily Tribune (1954–1962)
Christian Science Monitor (1945–1964)
Cincinnati Enquirer (1966)
Clarion Herald (New Orleans, LA) (1965)
Cleveland Call and Post (1958–1961)
Crusader (Rockford, IL) (1956)
Daily Boston Globe (1957–1960)
Dallas Morning News (1933–2012)
Evening Star (Washington, DC) (1964–1966)
Guardian (London) (1960)
Hartford Courant (1965)
Jet (1961–1965)
Kingfish (Metairie, LA) (2002)
Los Angeles Herald-Examiner (1967)
Los Angeles Sentinel (1960–1967)
Los Angeles Times (1934–1967)
Los Angeles Tribune (1958)
Louisiana Weekly (1954–2014)

Milwaukee Journal (1966)
New Journal and Guide (Norfolk, VA) (1956–1966)
New Orleans Advocate (2015–2018)
New Orleans Item (1933–1957)
New Orleans States (1952–1957)
New Orleans States-Item (1960–1966)
News American (Baltimore, MD) (1965)
New York Amsterdam News (1957)
New York Journal American (1965)
New York Times (1953–2006)
Oneonta (NY) Star (1965)
Philadelphia Tribune (1960–1967)
Pittsburgh Courier (1955–1967)
Pittsburgh Post-Gazette (1956)
Plain Dealer (Kansas City, KS) (1955–1958)
Post and Time Star (Cincinnati, OH) (1966)
Post-Standard (Syracuse, NY) (1965)
Raleigh Register (Beckley, WV) (1964)
Sporting News (1967)
Sports Illustrated (1956–1968)
St. Louis Globe-Democrat (1965)
Sun (Baltimore, MD) (1954–1955)
Technique (Georgia Tech) (1955)
Time (1947–1960)
Times-Picayune (New Orleans, LA) (1952–2010)
Tulane Hullabaloo (1956)
Wall Street Journal (1958–1965)
Washington Post and Times-Herald (1954–1967)

Secondary Sources

Allen, Ivan, Jr., and Paul Hemphill. *Mayor: Notes on the Sixties*. New York: Simon and Schuster, 1971.

Becnel, George. *When the Saints Came Marching In*. Bloomington, IN: AuthorHouse, 2009.

Berry, Stephen A. *The Jim Crow Routine: Everyday Performances of Race, Civil Rights, and Segregation in Mississippi*. Chapel Hill: University of North Carolina Press, 2015.

Buchanan, Scott E. *"Some of the People Who Ate My Barbecue Didn't Vote for Me": The Life of Georgia Governor Marvin Griffin*. Nashville: Vanderbilt University Press, 2011.

Burns, Elizabeth Booksh. "When the Saints Went Marching In: Social Identity in the World Champion New Orleans Saints Football Team and Its impact on Their Host City." In *New Orleans Sports: Playing Hard in the Big Easy*, ed. Thomas Aiello, 241–256. Fayetteville: University of Arkansas Press, 2019.

Cox, Dwayne D., and William J. Morrison. *The University of Louisville*. Lexington: University Press of Kentucky, 2000.

Demas, Lane. *Integrating the Gridiron: Black Civil Rights and American College Football*. New Brunswick, NJ: Rutgers University Press, 2010.

DeVore, Donald E. *Defying Jim Crow: African American Community Development and the Struggle for Racial Equality in New Orleans, 1900–1960*. Baton Rouge: Louisiana State University Press, 2015.

Dixon, Dave. *The Saints, the Superdome, and the Scandal: An Insider's Perspective*. Gretna, LA: Pelican, 2008.

Dodd, Bobby, and Jack Wilkinson. *Dodd's Luck: Life and Legend of a Hall of Fame Quarterback and Coach*. Savannah, GA: Gold Coast, 1987.

Dunnavant, Keith. *The Missing Ring*. New York: Thomas Dunne, 2006.

Duquette, Jerold J. *Regulating the National Pastime*. Westport, CT: Praeger, 1999.

Emmanuel, Rachel Lorraine. *A More Noble Cause: A. P. Tureaud and the Struggle for Civil Rights in Louisiana*. Baton Rouge: Louisiana State University Press, 2011.

Fairclough, Adam. *Race and Democracy: The Civil Rights Struggle in Louisiana, 1915–1972*. Athens: University of Georgia Press, 2008.

Felser, Larry. *The Birth of the New NFL: How the 1966 NFL/AFL Merger Transformed Pro Football*. Guilford, CT: Lyons Press, 2008.

Frystak, Shannon. *Our Minds on Freedom: Women and the Struggle for Black Equality in Louisiana, 1924–1967*. Baton Rouge: Louisiana State University Press, 2009.

Haas, Edward F. *DeLesseps S. Morrison and the Image of Reform: New Orleans Politics, 1946–1961*. Baton Rouge: Louisiana State University Press, 1974.

———. *Mayor Victor H. Schiro: New Orleans in Transition, 1961–1970*. Jackson: University Press of Mississippi, 2014.

Kleck, David M., and New Orleans Pro Football Club. *New Orleans, Strategic City of the Gulf South: A Pictorial-Statistical Presentation to the National Football League*. S.l.: s.n, 1965.

Kurtz, Michael L., and Morgan Peoples. *Earl K. Long: The Saga of Uncle Earl and Louisiana Politics*. Baton Rouge: Louisiana State University Press, 1990.

Levy, Alan H. *Tackling Jim Crow: Racial Segregation in Professional Football*. Jefferson, NC: McFarland and Company, 2003.

MacCambridge, Michael. *America's Game: The Epic Story of How Pro Football Captured a Nation*. New York: Anchor Books, 2004.

———. *Lamar Hunt: A Life in Sports*. Kansas City, MO: Andrews McMeel, 2012.

Maraniss, David. *When Pride Still Mattered: A Life of Vince Lombardi*. New York: Simon & Schuster, 1999.

Marshall, Brian. "The Pro Football Career of Cookie Gilchrist." *Coffin Corner* 24, no. 2 (2002).

Martin, Charles H. *Benching Jim Crow: The Rise and Fall of the Color Line in Southern College Sports, 1890–1980*. Urbana: University of Illinois Press, 2010.

———. "Integrating New Year's Day: The Racial Politics of College Bowl Games in the American South." *Journal of Sports History* 24, no. 3 (Fall 1997): 358–377.

———. "Racial Change and 'Big-Time' Football in Georgia: The Age of Segregation, 1892–1957." *Georgia Historical Quarterly* 80, no. 3 (Fall 1996): 532–562.

Martin, Michael S. "New Orleans Becomes a Big League City: The NFL-AFL Merger and the Creation of the New Orleans Saints." In *New Orleans Sports: Playing Hard in the Big Easy*, ed. Thomas Aiello, 109–122. Fayetteville: University of Arkansas Press, 2019.

McCaughan, Richard B. *Socks on a Rooster: Louisiana's Earl K. Long*. Baton Rouge, LA: Claitor's Book Store, 1967.

Miller, Jeff. *Going Long: The Wild 10-Year Saga of the Renegade American Football League in the Words of Those Who Lived It*. Chicago: Contemporary Books, 2003.

Mohr, Clarence L., and Joseph E. Gordon. *Tulane: The Emergence of a Modern University, 1945–1980*. Baton Rouge: Louisiana State University Press, 2001.

Moore, Theresa, dir. *Third and Long*. T-Time Productions, 2011. DVD.

Mulé, Marty. *Game Changers: The Rousing Legacy of Louisiana Sports*. Lafayette: University of Louisiana at Lafayette Press, 2013.

———. *Sugar Bowl: The First Fifty Years*. Birmingham, AL: Oxmoor House, 1983.

Norwood, Stephen H. "The Sugar Bowl: Manhood, Race, and Southern Womanhood in New Orleans, 1935–1965." In *New Orleans Sports: Playing Hard in the Big Easy*, ed. Thomas Aiello, 151–176. Fayetteville: University of Arkansas Press, 2019.

Rampersad, Arnold. *Jackie Robinson: A Biography*. New York: Knopf, 1997.

Rogers, Kim Lacy. *Righteous Lives: Narratives of the New Orleans Civil Rights Movement*. New York: New York University Press, 1993.

Ross, Charles K. *Outside the Lines: African Americans and the Integration of the National Football League*. New York: New York University Press, 1999.

Sanborn Map Company. *Digital Sanborn Maps (Black and White): Louisiana, 1867–1970*. ProQuest Information and Learning, 2001.

Souther, J. Mark. "Into the Big League: Conventions, Football, and the Color Line in New Orleans. *Journal of Urban History* 29, no. 6 (September 2003): 694–725.

———. *New Orleans on Parade: Tourism and the Transformation of the Crescent City*. Baton Rouge: Louisiana State University Press, 2006.

Steinbeck, John. *Travels with Charley: In Search of America.* New York: Viking, 1962.
Watterson, John Sayle. *College Football: History, Spectacle, Controversy.* Baltimore: Johns Hopkins University Press, 2000.
Winkeljohn, Matt. *Tales from the Atlanta Falcons Sideline.* New York: Sports Publishing, 2012.

Websites

abcnews.go.com
C-Span.org
FOXSports.com
NewOrleansSaints.com
NOLA.com
NPR.org
ScientificAmerican.com
TalesfromtheAmericanFootballLeague.com

INDEX

Act 579 of 1956. See sports segregation law
Adams, Bud, 89, 185–186; and All-Star game, 119, 156; and Dixon, 54, 77, 78, 79, 119; on New Orleans, 77, 86, 87, 88, 90, 119; and segregation, 88, 157
Afro-American, 82–83, 88–89
Air Force football, 34, 40, 210
Alabama, University of, 131; and 1962 postseason, 70, 71–72; and 1964 postseason, 107, 108, 110–111; and 1966 postseason, 174, 175; and 1967 postseason, 203, 204–207
Alexander, Avery: 118; and demonstrations, 112, 113, 114; and McKeithen, 116, 224; and Schiro, 172
Allen, Ivan, Jr., 83, 121, 122, 126, 161–162
All-Star walkout: announcement of, 150–151; causes of, 142–146; deliberation of, 145–148, 149–150, 151; and game relocation, 151–152, 156–159; league response to, 151, 155–156; local reactions to, 152–154, 159–161, 164–165, 179, 185, 227 (*see also* Let's Go Pro! campaign); national reactions to, 154–156, 175; outlook preceding, 120, 127–128, 139–141; Sugar Bowl impacted by, 175–178
Alworth, Lance, 154
American Basketball Association, 211, 226
American Broadcasting Company (ABC), 28–29, 34, 38, 156
American Football League (AFL): 1962 expansion efforts of, 77, 78, 80, 81–83, 86–87, 88–89; 1965 expansion efforts of, 127, 161–163; and *Afro-American*, 82–83, 88–89; development of, 54, 66, 79, 127–128; exhibitions of, 77, 82, 83–86, 87, 157–158; NFL sued by, 75, 77, 79–80; segregation within, 87–89, 157–158; and team relocations, 90–93, 95, 185. *See also* All-Star walkout; draft, pro football; merger, pro football
American Legion, 96–98, 101, 151, 160
Angelle, Robert, 31, 45
antitrust laws, 75, 76, 191–196, 209–210
Antoine's, 109, 155, 165, 197, 200
Antwine, Houston, 143, 151, 157–158
Arkansas, University of, 71, 72, 131, 174, 177
Army football, 18, 27, 34, 38–40
arrests, 99, 116, 145; of civil rights workers, 61, 113, 114, 115, 185; during school integration, 57, 59, 61
Associated Press polls, 174, 175, 178, 203, 204–205, 206
Astrodome, 156, 185–186, 187
Atkins, Asa H., 23
Atlanta: and 1956 Sugar Bowl, 7–11, 24; and AFL, 77, 78, 82–84, 89, 125–126, 161–162; and Braves, 122, 128, 181; business desegregation in, 62, 83, 98, 122; as companion to New Orleans, 78, 81, 122, 163; compared to New Orleans, 11, 24, 41, 64, 97, 123, 141, 159, 182, 184; as competitor to New Orleans, 81, 161, 164, 166, 200, 216; fandom in, 82, 83–84, 123, 166; franchise efforts in, 82, 121–123, 161–162, 165, 167; and NFL, 84, 121–123, 127, 161–162, 167 (*see also* Atlanta Falcons); pool hall incident in, 125–126, 148, 153; pools in,

Atlanta, *(continued)*
  100; pro exhibitions in, 83–84, 122–123,
  125–126, 166; school desegregation in,
  61–62; sports desegregation in, 24–25,
  41, 61–62, 82, 83, 115, 167; stadia in, 82,
  83–84, 121, 122, 166, 167, 180–181
Atlanta Falcons, 208; establishment of,
  161–162, 163, 164; and Saints, 166, 200,
  215–218, 224–226

Baltimore Colts: and Cuozzo, 209, 210,
  216–217; exhibitions of, 96, 103, 104–105,
  164, 166–167, 189–190
bars. *See* nightclub segregation
Bartle, H. Roe "The Chief," 92–93
baseball, 54; minor league, 18, 30, 49, 50, 218,
  219; in youth sports, 100, 188. *See also*
  Major League Baseball
basketball: Loyola's integration of, 27, 48–49,
  75; professional, 211, 226; recreational,
  100, 188. *See also under* Mid-Winter
  Sports Association (MWSA)
Baxter, Al, 139
Baylor University, 35, 36–38
Bell, Bobby, 142–143, 146
Bidwill, Bill, 121, 167
Bidwill, Charles "Stormy," 121–122, 167
block seating: de facto, 65, 73, 102; enforced,
  87–89
Boggs, Hale: and football, 76–77, 192–193,
  194–195, 196, 199; reelection of, 198, 200
Boston, Ralph, 157
Boston Patriots, 84–85, 86, 87, 154, 157–158
Boston Red Sox, 47, 49, 50, 65
boxing: integration of, 19, 173–174; segregation of, 42–43, 48, 159; seating for, 99,
  115–116
boycotts (sports), 26, 38–39, 102–103; and
  boxing 99, 115; and Jeppesen Stadium,
  157; of Pelicans, 49; by segregationists,
  39, 50, 136; and Sugar Bowl, 7, 11, 27, 106,
  109, 135. *See also* All-Star walkout
Brennan's, 118, 188, 190

Bridges, Ruby, 57
Brown v. Board of Education (1954), 25, 94
Brown, Joe, 43, 159
Brown, Paul, 180
Brown, Wallace, 213
Brown, Willie, 143, 152, 158
Bryant, Bear, 175; and 1962 postseason, 70,
  71; and 1964 postseason, 107, 108, 110–
  111; and 1967 postseason, 203, 204–206
Buchanan, Buck, 143, 152, 156
Buffalo Bills, 84, 149, 191, 192
Buncom, Frank, 145
Burke, Art, 152, 163
Bynum, Horace, 183
Byrnes, John, 196

Cannon, Billy, 85, 86, 90, 140, 202
Castle, Oretha, 112–113, 114, 116
Celler, Emanuel, 191, 193–196
chamber of commerce, 63, 140, 153, 179, 185,
  218
cheerleaders (Saints), 213
cheerleaders (segregationist), 59, 61, 63, 112
Chicago Bears, 84, 96, 103, 104, 123–124
Christenberry, Herbert W., 97, 101
Cincinnati, 180–181, 182, 186–187, 196
Ciolino, Jack, 51, 52, 53, 55, 64
Citizens' Committee, 113–114, 116
Citizens' Council. *See* White Citizens'
  Council
city council, 50, 114, 184, 185, 223
City Hall (building), 30, 58, 114, 115, 169, 170
City Park, 23; desegregation of, 41–42, 49,
  50–51; and Major League Baseball,
  47–48, 49, 50–51, 65; and Pelicans, 47,
  49, 50; pools in, 42, 100; and pro football
  exhibitions, 51, 77, 85; and pro football
  franchise, 54, 79, 80, 82, 93
Civil Rights Act of 1964: and Atlanta, 122;
  and New Orleans, 117, 135, 139, 154,
  160–161, 183
Clarion Herald, 160
Cleveland Browns, 180, 221

Cleveland Indians, 47, 51, 65, 211
community involvement (campaign), 171–172, 183
Congress (U.S.), 76, 191, 193–196
Congress of Racial Equality (CORE): and AFL, 157; and boxing, 115; and Civil Rights Act, 118; and direct action, 112–114, 115, 185; and hotels, 97, 116, 157. *See also* Citizens' Committee
Consumers' League, 99, 112, 113. *See also* Citizens' Committee
Corenswet, Sam, 14, 20, 70, 72, 176, 203
Cotton Bowl: and race, 2, 38, 69–70; and tie-ups, 1, 29, 34; vying for teams, 35, 107–108, 174, 176, 177
court rulings: and boxing, 42–43, 44, 48, 115–116; on hotels, 97; on parks, 17–18, 23, 24, 41, 49; and pro football, 75, 79–80; and racial identity, 42–43; on recreation, 17–18, 24, 41, 100–101, 188; on schools, 17, 55–56; on seating, 49, 98–100; and sports segregation, 42, 43, 44, 48; on taxis, 165–166; and Tulane, 94–95
Crescent City Independent Voters League, 172
Cuozzo, Gary, 190, 209, 210, 216–217, 222, 225
Curley's Gym, 19
Curry, Butch, 11, 111

Dallas: compared to New Orleans, 54, 64, 97, 184; desegregation in, 24, 61–62, 88, 98
Dallas Cowboys: development of, 51, 66, 75, 80, 91, 121; exhibitions of, 96, 103–104, 124; and Saints, 210, 222–223
Dallas Texans: games of, 83–84, 90–91; relocation of, 91–93, 95, 101
Daniels, Clem, 142–143, 144–145, 147, 148, 149, 150
David, Joseph, 20, 105, 202
Davis, A. L., 114–115, 116, 169, 172, 187, 224
Davis, Jimmie, 55–56
Davis, Tim, 110, 111, 205

DeBlanc, Paul: and bowl bids, 5, 6, 38, 175; on sports segregation, 17, 20–21, 25, 28, 29–30, 31, 69
DeBlieux, J. D., 18, 19
Dee, Bob, 151
DeFee, Jack: and accommodations, 87–88, 125, 157; and baseball, 47, 49, 50, 64; and football, 51, 53, 77, 80, 84–85
Dejoie, C. C., 102, 197, 202, 213
Dent, Albert, 16, 182, 183, 197, 223
Detroit Lions, 52, 95, 103–104, 189
Devaney, Bob, 175, 203, 205
Devenport, Ed, 52, 105, 120
Dew Drop Inn, 116, 143–144
Digby, Fred, 3, 6, 17, 28, 35
Diliberto, Buddy: on AFL franchise efforts, 81, 128; and All-Star walkout, 148–149, 150, 151; and Atlanta, 121–122, 123, 167; on NFL franchise efforts, 123, 124, 125, 167, 168, 181, 183; on segregation, 81, 125, 131, 167; and Sugar Bowl, 110, 111, 129, 131, 132, 133, 137
Dillard University, 16, 23, 40–41, 94, 168, 183
direct action, 112–115. *See also specific tactics, such as* sit-ins
Dirksen, Everett, 193, 195
Dixon, David: 1961 NFL pitch of, 66–69, 72–76; 1966 NFL pitch of, 179–180; and AFL formation, 53–54, 66; and AFL-NFL lawsuit, 75–76, 77; and All-Star arrangements, 119–120, 140–141, 148; and All-Star walkout, 149–151, 154, 156, 160; on antitrust laws, 76–77, 192–193; and Atlanta, 122–123, 163; and City Park, 77, 79, 80, 82; and domed stadium, 127, 172–173, 181, 199; on early AFL expansion, 78–81, 82, 85, 86–87, 88; and exhibition attendance drive, 120–121, 123–125, 127; and integration of Tulane Stadium, 95–96, 98, 100, 102–103; and Jones, 54, 66, 67, 73, 74, 96; and Lautenschlaeger, 66, 78, 93; and Let's Go Pro! campaign, 164–165, 166, 172–173, 181, 185, 189; and

Dixon, *(continued)*
  NAACP, 98–99, 100, 179–180; and NFL doubleheader, 95–96, 102–104; and pro expansion duel, 141, 162, 163; and Saints franchise, 85, 198–199, 200, 201–202, 208, 218–219; and Schiro, 101, 120, 172–173, 181; and school integration, 55, 65, 66, 76; seeking Raiders franchise, 90, 91; seeking Texans franchise, 91–93; on segregated seating, 65–66, 72, 73, 74, 82; and Young, 197–198
Dixon, Mary, 67, 74–75, 96, 102, 219
Dodd, Bobby, 7–8, 10, 12–13, 14, 15, 16
domed stadium, 127, 189, 205; and Let's Go Pro! campaign, 181–183; and Schiro, 167, 173; vote on, 199, 200
Dorsey, Joe, 42, 43, 173, 174
draft, pro football, 191; combined AFL/NFL, 192, 193, 210–211; stockpiling, 78, 85, 208–209
Dubenion, Elbert, 156
Dufour, Pie, 111
Dupas, Ralph, 42–43, 159
Duplantier, Cro, 72–73

Elie, Lolis, 113
Ellis, Don, 14, 15
Ellis, Frank Burton, 95, 96, 165
Elloie, Pearlie Hardin, 94
employment, Black, 116; demonstrations for, 61, 112, 114–115; municipal, 114, 172, 183, 184, 187, 223–224; negotiations for, 113, 114; and Saints, 213–214

Faison, Earl, 125–126, 157; in New Orleans, 142–143, 145, 146, 147–148, 149, 178–179
Fears, Tom: building roster, 208–209, 210–211, 211–212, 215, 221; coaching style of, 212, 217, 221; on fans, 214, 218, 227
Fenner, Darwin, 113, 185
Finney, Pete, 141, 163; on All-Star walkout, 152, 153; and Syracuse, 131, 132, 133
Fitzmorris, Jimmy, 171, 172
Florida, University of, 133, 175–176, 177–178

Fontainebleau Motor Hotel, 87, 142, 145, 146, 148, 151
Ford, William Clay, 95, 96
Ford Foundation, 94, 95
Foss, Joe, 80, 90–91, 140; and *Afro-American*, 88; and All-Star game, 119, 151, 154, 155, 159; on expansion, 161–162
Fourteenth Amendment, 43, 94, 97
Francis, Norman: on All-Star walkout, 159; career of, 159, 185; municipal appointments of, 187, 223; and NFL franchise campaign, 182, 184–185, 186, 197; and Saints, 202–203, 213, 218
Fulton, James, 38–39

Gagliano, Curley, 174
Gallinghouse, A. P., 169–170
Garrett, John, 22, 25, 44–45; and school integration, 56, 58; on sports, 46, 48
Garron, Larry, 86, 143, 151, 157–158
Georgia Tech, 1, 26, 71, 131; and 1956 Sugar Bowl, 7–11, 12–16
Giarrusso, Joseph, 42, 63
Gibbs, Lawrence, 25, 28, 30
Gilchrist, Cookie, 157; in New Orleans, 142, 143, 144, 146; reputation of, 142, 150, 154; and walkout decision, 148, 149, 150
Gilliam, John, 210, 219, 222, 225
Gillman, Sid, 126, 146–147, 148–149, 156–157
Glaudi, Hap, 6–7, 26, 34, 159–160
Gleason, E. D., 25
Gogolak, Pete, 191, 192
golf, 17, 22, 24, 41, 100–101
Grayson, Dave, 144–145, 178–179
Greater Atlanta Athletic Association, 82, 83, 84
Green Bay Packers, 196; and Jimmy Taylor, 197, 210, 212; and New Orleans, 51–53, 64, 120–121, 123–124
Gremillion, Jack, 56
Grenrood, Bernie, 3
Grier, Bobby, 6, 7, 8–11, 12–14, 15–16, 27
Griffin, Marvin, 8–11, 24, 25, 30–31
Guillory, Barbara Marie, 94

Halas, George, 76, 96, 104, 124, 126, 127
Hall, Jim, 99, 100, 105, 159, 174; on block seating, 87, 88, 102, 103; and Let's Go Pro! campaign, 167–168, 189, 197; and Saints, 213, 226; on Sugar Bowl, 135, 138
Hamilton, Tom, 5, 6
Hannan, Philip, 208, 219, 221
Hartsfield, William, 24, 62, 83
Haynes, Abner, 83, 143, 148, 150
Hebert, F. Edward, 39, 88
Helis, William, 67, 68, 73, 200, 202
Hickey, Theodore M., 18
high school sports, 23, 40–41, 42, 49, 50
Hill, Winston, 150
Hilton Inn Motel, 102, 120, 178
Hirt, Al, 144, 152; and Saints, 202, 216, 217, 219, 220, 222
Hofheinz, Roy, 156, 187
Holmes, Alfred, 24
Holmes, Oliver, 24
Holt, Ben, 44–45
Hornung, Paul, 53, 123, 124, 209, 212
hotel segregation, 83, 122; and AFL, 87, 143, 157–158; and American Legion, 98; and Civil Rights Act, 117, 183; and CORE, 116; and Dixon, 68, 72, 75, 82, 102, 120; enforced by choice, 97, 98, 101; enforced by law, 75, 97; publicity on, 75, 88–89; and Sugar Bowl, 6, 11, 16, 135; terminated by choice, 101
Houston, 185–187, 196; and AFL All-Stars, 151–152, 156–159, 178; compared to New Orleans, 141, 159, 182, 184; and desegregation, 41, 61, 88, 100, 157–158; as substitute for New Orleans, 43, 49, 98, 151, 159
Houston Informer, 157
Houston Oilers, 77, 84–86, 157, 158, 185
human relations commission: for Louisiana, 165; for New Orleans, 161, 172, 224
Hunt, Lamar, 80, 90, 119; and *Afro-American,* 83, 88; and Dixon, 54, 78, 79, 85, 86–87, 163; and expansion, 85, 86–87, 88, 89, 161, 163; and team relocation, 91–93, 95

Hunter, Billy, 138–139
Hurricane Betsy, 170–171, 187

Interdenominational Ministerial Alliance, 169, 170
Irwin, Emmett, 20, 30–31

Jack, Wellborn, 31, 45
Jazz Fest, 161
Jeppesen Stadium, 152, 157–159
Johnson, Lyndon, 117, 168–169, 183, 195
Johnson, Phil, 160
Joint Legislative Committee on Segregation (JLCS), 18, 22–23, 25, 44, 46
Jones, Joseph Merrick, 54, 66, 67, 73, 74, 96
Jung Hotel, 101, 116, 126, 138, 218, 224

Kansas City, 81–82, 92–93, 95, 98, 101
Keefe, Bill, 39–40, 41, 42, 52; on sports segregation, 26–27; on Sugar Bowl, 6, 14, 26
Kelleher, Harry, 113, 149, 200, 201
Keller, Rosa, 94
Kelley, Les, 205, 210, 215, 221
Kemp, Jack, 142, 144, 146, 151, 156–157, 158
Kennedy, John F., 62, 107–108
Kern, Cliff, 108–109
Kilmer, Billy, 209, 217, 225, 226
Kleck, David, 96–97, 102, 150, 179
Kratter, Marvin, 173, 181

Laborde, Ellis, 23
Lacy, Sam, 83, 88–89
Ladd, Ernie, 125, 156, 157; in New Orleans, 144–146, 148, 149, 150
Landrieu, Maurice "Moon": as councilman at-large, 184, 187, 198, 218, 224; and pro football, 184–185, 186, 198, 199, 218, 219
Lane, Kenny, 174
Lautenschlaeger, Lester, 66, 67, 77, 78, 93
Laws, Clarence, 171
Let's Go Pro! campaign: beginning of, 164–168; development of, 179–180, 181–183, 184–185, 186–187, 188–190, 197; and election, 199–200

Lewis, Theron, 130
Lincoln, Keith, 125, 151
Liska, Alvin, 117
Liston, Sonny, 99, 100, 115, 116
Little, Floyd, 131, 136, 137, 138–139
Loew's Theatre, 115
Lombard, Rudy, 112–113, 185
Lombardi, Vince, 52, 120–121, 123, 191, 209, 212
Long, Earl K., 44, 96, 199; Black supporters of, 19, 44, 46; and Black voting rights, 44–46; and MWSA, 20, 29–30, 31, 96; on segregation laws, 19, 20, 21, 22, 25–26, 96; and state legislature, 21, 22, 44–46
Long, Russell, 193, 195, 196, 198, 199, 200
Los Angeles Rams, 158, 215, 219, 220–221
Louisiana legislature, 24; and Long, 22, 29–30, 44–46; and Morial, 224; on parks, 22–23; and school desegregation, 56, 57, 58; and sports segregation, 17–19, 20–21, 25, 27, 29–31; and voting rights, 44–46
Louisiana State University (LSU), 187; and Cotton Bowl, 177, 181; and segregation, 18–19, 25, 27; and Sugar Bowl, 43, 60, 69–71, 131–133, 136–139; and Tulane, 7, 132–133, 176–177, 203–204
Louisiana Weekly, 99, 118, 197, 203, 214; on All-Star walkout, 159; on pro exhibitions, 87–88, 102, 103; on sports segregation law, 26; on Sugar Bowl, 3–4, 139; on voting, 172. *See also* Hall, Jim
Lowry, Frank, 14, 15
Loyola Field House, 17, 48–49, 108–109, 226
Loyola University, 25, 27, 48–49, 184

Major League Baseball, 81–82, 213; franchise moves in, 122, 129, 193; in New Orleans, 27, 47–48, 50–51, 64, 211
Mara, Wellington, 191, 192
Marcus, Walter F., Jr., 184
Mardi Gras, 57, 60, 155, 183, 227
marshals, federal, 55, 56–57
Martinez, Harry, 6, 26

Mason's Motel, 87, 197
Maule, Tex, 214–215
Maumus, Theo, 129, 176
Mays, Jerry, 151
McCane, Bill, 82, 83–84
McDonogh 19 Elementary, 57, 59, 64
McKeithen, John: on All-Star walkout, 153–154; and civil rights leaders, 116, 165, 179, 224; and domed stadium, 181, 182, 199; on Louisiana's image, 116, 154, 182, 187; and NFL franchise campaign, 165, 179, 181, 182, 185–187, 196; on progress, 182, 187, 200, 224; and racial unrest, 116, 154, 165, 179, 187, 200; and Saints, 198, 199, 212
Mecom, John, Jr.: building Saints, 208, 210, 211–214; and NFL franchise campaign, 185, 189; and Pioneer Award, 213–214; and Saints ownership, 200, 201–203; and Saints season, 214–215, 216, 219, 223, 227
Mecom, John, Sr., 185
merger, pro football, 79, 128, 192–196
Messina, Lou, 174
Miami: and AFL, 54, 77, 163, 164; compared to New Orleans, 41, 141, 159, 175, 182, 184; desegregation in, 24, 41, 61, 115; as substitute for New Orleans, 98, 106, 151
Michelosen, John, 5, 12, 15, 34
Michoud, 63, 73
Mid-Winter Sports Association (MWSA): and basketball, 17, 20, 27, 28, 108–109, 129–130; and boxing, 48; and conference tie-ups, 1–2; on domed stadium, 182; fighting segregation law, 17, 20–21, 28–31, 48; on initial integration, 3, 6, 7, 16, 17; and public relations, 17, 21, 28, 134; regatta of, 69; on reintegration, 17, 48, 69, 105–106, 129–130; track events of, 106, 130. *See also* Sugar Bowl
Milwaukee Braves, 122, 128, 193
Minnesota Vikings, 51, 66, 75, 121, 189, 212
Mississippi, University of, 7, 26, 130; and

1955 postseason, 1, 2, 3; and 1960 postseason, 60, 204; and 1964 postseason, 106–107, 110–111; as Sugar Bowl crutch, 69–70, 106, 111

Missouri, University of, 175, 177–178

Mitchell, Clarence, 2

Mitchell, Wade, 9, 13, 14

Mix, Ron, 147–148, 151

Monsted, Robert, 65, 67, 68, 73, 74–75, 202

Montgomery, Arthur, 121, 180–181

Morial, Ernest "Dutch," 99, 100, 113–114, 118, 150, 224

Morrison, Chep, 25, 55; and civil rights groups, 57, 61, 112; and Dixon, 54, 67, 68, 72; and school desegregation, 56, 60–61, 112; and sports, 30, 34, 49–50, 54

Municipal Auditorium, 57, 99–100, 115–116, 174

Namath, Joe, 108, 110, 156, 192

Nance, Jim, 131, 136, 137, 138–139

NASA, 63–64

National Association for the Advancement of Colored People (NAACP), 24, 26, 56, 97, 118; changing tactics of, 112–114; and community involvement, 171, 183; and football, 2, 38, 39, 157, 179–180, 197; and Municipal Auditorium, 57, 98–99; and recreation, 100–101, 188. *See also* Citizens' Committee

National Broadcasting Company (NBC), 20, 29, 38, 70, 72, 161

National Football League (NFL): and Atlanta, 84, 121–123, 161, 162; and Cincinnati, 180–181, 186–187, 196; Dixon's pitches to, 66–67, 68–69, 72, 73–74, 163, 179–180; and doubleheader in New Orleans, 95–96, 103–105; on expansion, 52, 121, 127, 161, 162, 164, 167; and Houston, 185–187, 196; market research of, 167, 168, 185, 186; owners' meetings of, 68, 72, 80, 185–187; and Saints franchise, 196–198, 198–199, 200–203; and segregation, 66, 89, 155, 158; and single exhibitions in New Orleans, 52–53, 120–121, 126–127, 166–167, 188–189, 189–190; sued by AFL, 75, 77, 79–80. *See also* draft, pro football; merger, pro football

Navy football: and bowl games, 1, 2, 3, 35, 107–108; and Tulane, 18, 27, 32–34, 39

Nebraska, University of, 107, 129, 131; and 1966 postseason, 174–175, 178; and 1967 postseason, 203, 204, 205–207

negotiations (civil rights), 62, 112–114, 173, 179, 227

Nelson, John P., 94–95

New Orleans Buccaneers, 211, 226

New Orleans Item, 6–7, 26, 34, 64

New Orleans Pelicans, 47, 49, 50, 218, 219

New Orleans Pro Football Club, 79, 80, 185, 202; and All-Stars, 140, 148, 149, 154; and integration, 100, 102, 105, 148, 180, 189; NFL brochure of, 179–180; and pro exhibitions, 95, 102, 127, 189–190

New Orleans Professional Sports Inc., 51, 52, 53, 77, 85. *See also* DeFee, Jack

New Orleans Recreation Department (NORD), 100–101, 119, 154, 187–188, 214

New Orleans Saints: attendance for, 216, 219, 221, 222, 225; cynicism regarding, 202–203, 212–213; drafts by, 208–209, 210–211; establishment of, 196, 198–200; and Falcons, 216–218, 224–226; management of, 208, 211, 212–214; naming of, 85, 208; ownership of, 200–203; pageantry of, 217, 219, 220; preseason of, 214–218, 221; and race, 213–214, 219, 227–228; regular season of, 218–223, 224–226; and ticket sales, 210, 215, 225; trades by, 209, 210, 212; training camp of, 211–212, 214–215; tryouts for, 211

New Orleans States, 6–7, 26

New Orleans States-Item, 140, 152, 172, 218. *See also names of specific reporters*

New Orleans Voters Association, 172, 173

New York Giants (football), 191, 192, 222

nightclub segregation, 116, 117, 119, 144–145, 160–161, 197

Oakland Raiders, 83–84, 90–91
O'Boyle, Tommy, 126, 132, 168
Oelkers, Johnny, 130
One Hundred Percent Wrong Club, 213–214
Orange Bowl, 1, 176, 178; and race, 2, 106, 175; vying for teams, 107, 174–175
Orleans Parish School Board, 55–57, 58
Ortique, Revius, Jr., 113, 187

Paluck, John, 5, 7
Pania, Frank, 116, 144
Parilli, Babe, 86, 151, 156, 157
parks, public, 17–18, 22–24, 41, 50, 100–101, 188. *See also* City Park
Pelican Stadium, 25, 27, 41, 42, 49, 219
Perkins, Eddie, 174
petitions (civil rights): to athletes, 115; to politicians, 20, 38–39, 116; to sports administrators, 2, 23, 82
Petre, John J., 184
Philadelphia, 161, 162–163
Philadelphia Eagles, 66; and AFL expansion, 162–163; exhibitions of, 52, 189–190; and Saints, 222, 224
picketing: by integrationists, 9, 61, 87, 112–115, 157, 188; by segregationists, 58, 63, 136
Pioneer Award, 213–214
Pittsburgh, University of: and 1956 Sugar Bowl, 5–8, 10–16, 26; racial policy of, 27, 106, 107–108
Pittsburgh Courier, 11, 27, 111
Pittsburgh Steelers, 51, 52–53, 84, 87, 222
Plunkett, Sherman, 145, 157
Poché, Irwin, 34; on integration, 17, 20, 28, 29, 31, 48; and pageantry, 106, 130
Poitevent, Edward, 73, 76, 80, 95; and Saints, 202, 208; and segregation laws, 74, 75, 81
police, 9–10, 16, 42, 117, 140, 187; and civil rights workers, 61, 112, 114, 118; and

school integration, 56–57, 58–59, 60–61, 62, 63
Pontchartrain Park, 41, 184
pools, public, 17–18, 22, 100; in New Orleans, 42, 100, 119, 172, 187–188
Povich, Shirley, 27
Powell, Art, 143–144, 146, 147, 158
pupil placement plans, 56
Pye, Brad, 126

Rainach, William, 55; and Long, 44–46; and school segregation, 58; and sports segregation, 18, 25, 31, 32, 42, 46, 48
"redemptive suffering," 113, 114
Reinsch, Leonard, 161–162
restaurant segregation, 62, 81, 83, 122; and All-Stars, 143, 146, 149; in City Hall, 114, 115; and Civil Rights Act, 117, 118, 160–161; Louisiana law on, 75; and lunch counters, 113, 185; and NFL franchise campaign, 188–189, 190, 197–198; and Sugar Bowl, 12, 106
Rhodes, James, 180, 181, 186
Rickey, Branch, 213, 214
rioting: in Atlanta, 9–10; in New Orleans, 58–59, 60, 227
Rittiner, Lloyd, 57
Roberts, Walter "Flea," 216, 222, 225
Robinson, Jackie, 16, 27
Rodino, Peter, 193
Roesler, Bob, 50, 51, 89, 152, 205, 209–210
Roosevelt Hotel, 117; fully desegregated, 167, 197; and segregation, 97, 116, 118, 135, 138, 143
Rose, Bert, 201, 212, 214, 227
Rose Bowl: reputation of, 3, 27, 38, 71, 178; team selections for, 1–2, 35, 71, 107, 204
Rosen, Charles, 66, 67, 202
Rosenbloom, Carroll, 191, 209
Roussel, Louis, 200, 201
Royal Orleans Hotel, 101, 200
Rozelle, Pete: and Atlanta, 121, 127, 161, 162; and Congress, 191, 193–194, 195, 196;

Dixon's pitches to, 66–67, 68–69, 72, 74, 75–76, 78; and expansion, 127, 161, 162, 180; and New Orleans exhibitions, 123, 124, 126, 127; and Saints, 196, 197, 198–199, 202, 218; and segregation, 66, 155

Saban, Lou, 146, 148, 156, 157, 158
Saenger Theatre, 115
sailing, 69
San Diego Chargers, 90, 91, 185; and Atlanta pool hall, 125–126, 153; and Jeppesen Stadium, 157, 158
Sanders, Carl, 122–123, 126, 162
Sanders, Jack, 201
Schiro, Victor: and All-Star walkout, 149, 153, 155, 160; on Civil Rights Act, 117; and civil rights leaders, 114, 172, 179, 183; on hotels, 98; and human relations commission, 161, 224; and Hurricane Betsy, 171; and NFL franchise campaign, 126, 166, 167, 172–173, 181–182, 185, 186; on progress, 63, 166, 173, 184, 227; reelection of, 171, 172–173; and Saints, 198, 219; second term of, 183, 184, 187–188, 223; on sports, 101, 116, 120, 140
school desegregation, 17, 22, 61–62; in New Orleans, 55–59, 60–61, 63–64
Schramm, Tex, 96, 105, 124–125, 127
"selective buying," 112, 113, 115
Shaw, Billy, 143, 146
Shepherd, Charlie, 213
Sheraton-Charles Hotel, 101, 135, 138
Simons, Claude "Monk," 5, 48, 70–71, 131, 176
sit-ins, 62, 113, 115, 185
skatemobile race, 101, 188
Smith, Jerome, 112–113
Smith, Rankin, 162, 200
soapbox derby, 100–101, 119, 188, 214
Sports Illustrated: on Bobby Dodd, 12; on New Orleans, 106, 163, 182–183; on Pete Rozelle, 155; on Sugar Bowl, 106, 178, 205, 206

sports segregation law (Act 579 of 1956): commencement of, 32, 34; passing of, 17–21; reactions to, 25–27, 28–29, 38, 96; repeal (partial) of, 42, 43–44, 46, 47–49, 74, 75, 82; repeal (full) of, 98–100; sports association (MWSA) challenge to, 29–31
Spurrier, Steve, 133, 176, 177–178
St. Charles Hotel, 16, 135
St. Louis Cardinals (football), 68, 121–122, 123, 164, 166–167
stand-ins, 115
Steadman, Jack, 92–93
Stebbins, Richard, 130
Stern, Edgar, Jr., 200–201
Stratton, Mike, 144, 146
Sugar Bowl: after All-Star walkout, 174–178; after Let's Go Pro! campaign, 203–207; initial integration of, 3, 5–11, 11–16, 26; reintegration of, 129, 130–133, 134–138, 138–139; struggling after segregation law, 106–108, 109–111; struggling under segregation law, 43–44, 48, 59–60, 69–71; threatened by segregation law, 20, 21, 27, 29–31, 34–36; thriving under segregation law, 36–39, 71–72. *See also* Mid-Winter Sports Association (MWSA)
Sullivan, Billy, 86
Super Bowl, 192, 193, 196, 197, 200, 217
Syracuse University, 35, 107, 131–133, 134–139, 175

Tabor, Al, 213
taxis: desegregation of, 62, 165–166, 179; segregation of, 138–139, 142–144, 145, 146, 160
Taylor, Jimmy: and Dixon, 199; fandom for, 52, 197, 202, 209, 216; as Packer, 52, 53; as Saint, 214, 215, 216, 217, 221, 222, 225; trade for, 210, 212
Tennessee, University of, 13, 35, 36–38
tennis, 41
Tessier, George, 30–31, 45
"testing" integration, 49, 118

Thomas, Charles, 2
Thomas, John, 157
Time, 2, 12, 59
Times-Picayune, 98, 118, 203; on All-Star walkout, 152, 153; on Sugar Bowl integration, 135. *See also names of specific reporters*
tourism, 82, 98, 139, 161; and school integration, 60, 63; and Sugar Bowl, 16, 17, 70, 72, 205
track, 101, 106, 130, 153, 157, 188
Trudeau, A. M., 165, 183
Tulane football: deemphasis of, 32, 36, 132; and LSU, 7, 132–133, 176–177; and pro football, 54, 210; and SEC, 3, 176; and segregation, 18, 27, 32, 38–39, 40, 210; and service academies, 33, 35, 40; support for, 3, 32, 168, 203, 210
Tulane Stadium: expansion of, 21, 173, 182; full integration of, 96, 98–100, 102–103, 105; partial integration of, 3, 7, 11, 18, 32, 49; pro use of, debated, 54, 66, 73, 77, 78–79, 82, 93; pro use of, granted, 95–96, 197, 199
Tulane University: on domed stadium, 182; integration of, 94–95; as Sugar Bowl host, 11–12, 134, 175
Tureaud, A. P., 26, 100, 165, 183, 187, 188

Unitas, Johnny, 96, 105, 166, 189–190, 209
Upton, Milton, 169, 171–172, 187

Vainisi, Jack, 52, 53
Van Leer, Blake, 8, 10
voter registration, 44–46, 168–170, 171–172, 183, 187
Voting Rights Act of 1965, 168–169, 170, 183, 198

Walker, Tommy, 217, 220
walkout. *See* All-Star walkout
Wallace, William, 203
Walton, Joe, 5, 7, 13
Ward, Arch, 34
Warlick, Ernie, 142, 144, 146, 150, 156
Washington Redskins, 66, 221
Weiss, Seymour, 97, 117, 135, 185
Wells, Lloyd, 157, 213
Wells, Ruthie, 115
West, E. Gordon, 97
West Virginia University, 1, 5, 6, 132
Westmoreland, Dick, 144–146
Wheelwright, Ernie, 225, 226
"When the Saints Go Marching In," 85, 202, 217, 220
White Citizens' Council, 18, 24, 99; and school integration, 57, 58, 59; and sports, 7, 19, 20, 25, 50, 87, 88; and voting rights, 44
William Frantz Elementary School, 57, 59, 63, 64
Wisconsin, University of, 18–19, 27
Wisdom, Betty, 61
Wisdom, John Minor, 97, 99, 100, 101
Wismer, Harry, 84–85, 87, 88, 90, 91, 126
Wright, Ernie, 125, 178–179
Wright, J. Skelly, 41, 49, 55, 56, 95, 184

Xavier University, 23, 40–41, 159, 168, 185, 219

Young, Buddy, 197–198
Young Men's Business Club, 167

www.ingramcontent.com/pod-product-compliance
Lightning Source LLC
Chambersburg PA
CBHW030527230426
43665CB00010B/792